Dr Uzi Rabi (Ph.D., Tel Aviv University) is the Chair of the Department of Middle Eastern and African History, head of the University Institute for Diplomacy and Regional Cooperation, a Senior Research Fellow at the Center for Iranian Studies and Vice Director of the S. Daniel Abraham Center for International and Regional Studies at Tel Aviv University. Among his numerous books is *The Emergence of States in Tribal Societies: Oman under Sa'id Bin Taymur, 1932–1970* (2006) and he was editor of *Iran's Time* (2008, in Hebrew).

LIBRARY OF INTERNATIONAL RELATIONS

Series ISBN: 978 1 84885 240 2

See www.ibtauris.com/LIR for a full list of titles

INTERNATIONAL INTERVENTION IN LOCAL CONFLICTS

Crisis Management and Conflict Resolution Since the Cold War

EDITED BY

UZI RABI

TAURIS ACADEMIC STUDIES
an imprint of
I.B. Tauris Publishers
LONDON • NEW YORK

Published in 2010 by Tauris Academic Studies,
An imprint of I.B.Tauris & Co Ltd
6 Salem Road, London W2 4BU
175 Fifth Avenue, New York NY 10010
www.ibtauris.com

Distributed in the United States and Canada
Exclusively by Palgrave Macmillan
175 Fifth Avenue, New York NY 10010

Library of International Relations 48

ISBN: 978 1 84885 318 8

A full CIP record for this book is available from the British Library
A full CIP record for this book is available from the Library of Congress

Library of Congress catalog card: available

Printed and bound in India by Thomson Press (India)
Camera-ready copy edited and supplied by Oxford Publishing Services, Oxford

Contents

PART IV   THE TANGLED WEB OF REGIONAL CONFLICT

PART V   CONCLUDING CHAPTER

Acronyms and Abbreviations

ACBAR	Agency Coordinating Body for Afghan Relief
ADF	Arab Deterrent Force
AFL-CIO	American Federation of Labor and Congress of Industrial Organizations
AFP	Agence France-Presse
AIPAC	American Israel Public Affairs Committee
ANA	Afghan National Army
ANDS	Afghan National Development Strategy
AP	Associated Press
APNI	Alliance Party of Northern Ireland
AU	Africa Union
AWACS	Airborne Warning and Control System
BAM	Border Assistance Mission
B-H	Bosnia and Herzegovina
BLDP	Buddhist Liberal Democratic Party
BNL	Banca Nazionale del Lavoro
CBRN	chemical, biological, radiological and nuclear weapons
CCRP	Command and Control Research Program
CDC	community development council
CENTCOM	United States Central Command
CESP	Common European Security and Defence Policy
CFDP	Common Foreign and Defence Policy
CFSP	Common Foreign and Security Policy
CIA	Central Intelligence Agency
COM	Council of Ministries
CPP	Cambodian People's Party
CSCE	Commission on Security and Cooperation in Europe
DK	Khmer Rouge
DRC	Democratic Republic of the Congo
DUP	Democratic Unionist Party

EC	European Community
ECMI	European Centre for Minority Issues
ECOWAS	Economic Community of West African States
EMP	European Mediterranean Partnership
ENP	European Neighbourhood Policy
ENPI	European Neighbourhood and Partnership Instrument
ESDI	European Security and Defence Identity
ESDP	European Security and Defence Policy
ESS	European Security Strategy
EUCOPPS	European Union Coordinating Office for Palestinian Police Support
EUFOR	European Forces in Bosnia and Herzegovina
EULEX	European Union Rule of Law Mission in Kosovo
EUMM	European Union Monitoring Mission
EUPM	EU Police Mission
EUPT	European Union planning team
EUSR	EU Special Representative
FLN	*Front de Libération nationale* (National Liberation Front)
FUNCINPEC	National United Front for an Independent, Neutral, Peaceful, and Cooperative Cambodia
GDP	gross domestic product
GFA	Good Friday Agreement
GOP	Grand Old Party (Republican Party)
HOA	Heads of Agreement
HR	High Representative
IAEA	International Atomic Energy Agency
ICC	International Criminal Court
ICFY	International Conference on Former Yugoslavia
ICG	International Crisis Group
ICISS	International Commission on Intervention and State Sovereignty
ICRC	International Committee of the Red Cross
ICTY	International Criminal Tribunal for the former Yugoslavia
IDF	Israel Defense Forces
IRA	Irish Republican Army

ISAF	International Security Assistance Force
IRA	Irish Republican Army
JNA	*Jugoslovenska Narodna Armija* (Yugoslav People's Army)
KFOR	Kosovo Force
KPCP	Kampuchean People's Revolutionary Party
MEAS	Middle East Action Strategy
MEDA	Mediterranean Economic Development Area
MNF	Multinational Force
NATO	North Atlantic Treaty Organization
NDI	National Democratic Institute
NGO	non-governmental organization
NIE	National Intelligence Estimate
NIWC	Northern Ireland Women's Coalition
NSC	White House National Security Council
OHR	Office of the High Representative
OSCE	Organization for Security and Co-operation in Europe
PA	Palestinian Authority
PfP	Partnership for Peace
PIC	Peace Implementation Council
PLO	Palestine Liberation Organization
PRC	People's Republic of China
PRT	provincial reconstruction team
PSC	Political and Security Committee
PUP	Progressive Unionist Party
PSC	Political and Security Committee
PSP	Progressive Socialist Party
R2P	Responsibility to Protect
RIP	Regional Indicative Programme
RRM	Rapid Reaction Mechanism
RSP	Regional Skills Partnership
SANA	Syrian Arab News Agency
SCR	Security Council Resolution
SDLP	Social Democratic and Labour Party
SFOR	Stabilisation Force
SG/HR	Secretary General/High Representative
SHAPE	Supreme Headquarters Allied Powers Europe

SLA	South Lebanon Army
SNA	Somali National Alliance
SNF	Somali National Front
SNM	Somali National Movement
SPM	Somali Patriotic Movement
SOC	State of Cambodia
SRSG	Special Representative of the Secretary General
SSDF	Somali Salvation Democratic Front
STV	single transferable vote
TEU	Treaty on European Union
TNC	Transitional National Council
UAE	United Arab Emirates
UDA	Ulster Defence Association
UKUP	United Kingdom Unionist Party
UNAMA	United Nations Assistance Mission in Afghanistan
UNAMIR	United Nations Assistance Mission for Rwanda
UNDI	United Nations Documents Index
UNHCR	United Nations High Commissioner for Refugees
UNIFIL	United Nations Interim Force in Lebanon
UNITAF	Unified Task Force
UNMIK	United Nations Mission in Kosovo
UNO	United Nations Organization
UNOSOM	United Nations Operation in Somalia
UNPROFOR	United Nations Protection Force
UNSC	United Nations Security Council
UNTAC	United Nations Transitional Administration in Cambodia
UNTAET	United Nations Transitional Administration in East Timor
USC	United Somali Congress
UUP	Ulster Unionist Party
WEU	Western European Union
WFP	World Food Programme

Acknowledgements

This endeavour could not have been successful without the aid and financial support of three centres at Tel Aviv University, the S. Daniel Abraham Center for International and Regional Studies, the Tami Steinmetz Center for Peace Research, and the Moshe Dayan Center for Middle Eastern and African Studies. I would like to express my sincere gratitude to the heads of the centres respectively, Professor Raanan Rein, Professor Mordechai Tamarkin and Professor Eyal Zisser, for their encouragement and moral support. I would also like to express my thanks and gratitude to Talma Kinarti, Yael Karny-Alon, and Ilana Greenberg, for the indispensable administrative assistance that they provided during the production of this volume. I would like to extend a special thank you to Dr Bruce Maddy-Weitzman of the Moshe Dayan Center for his good advice and intellectual support. I would also like to thank my research assistant, Chelsi Mueller, for her devotion to the project and essential editorial assistance. I wish to express appreciation to Joanna Godfrey at I.B.Tauris for recognizing the potential of the project, and for all her patient correspondence and editorial guidance. I would also like to thank Maria Marsh who ably took over the project and guided it to completion. To Jason and Selina Cohen of Oxford Publishing Services, I would like to express my gratitude for a job well done. Last but not least I am deeply grateful to all the contributors whose assiduous efforts, expertise and collegiality have allowed this project to come to fruition.

Preface

The contributors to this volume examine the impact of international intervention on the resolution of local conflicts as well as the roles of local actors in determining their course. The idea for the book arose out of an international conference at Tel Aviv University in Summer 2008 organized under the auspices of the S. Daniel Abraham Center for International and Regional Studies, the Tami Steinmetz Center for Peace Research, and the Moshe Dayan Center for Middle Eastern and African History. Entitled 'The Global and the Local: The Impact of International Intervention on the Resolution of Local Conflicts', the conference brought together an international array of distinguished scholars to assess the impact of international intervention on the resolution of local conflicts. The driving logic behind the conference was to concentrate on the conflict in the Middle East, but also to deal comparatively with other cases such as Cambodia, Somalia, Ireland and Yugoslavia.

Most of the 13 studies in this volume deal with international involvement in conflict resolution after the Cold War, but several pieces also straddle the Cold War in that they provide comparative analyses of the American and European experiences in the Middle East both prior to and after the disintegration of the Soviet Union.

The transition from the Cold War to the post-Cold War era and its implications for local conflicts is the focus of Janice Gross Stein's introductory chapter, 'From Bipolar to Unipolar Order: System Structure and Conflict Resolution'. It suggests a theoretical framework for understanding how the structure of the international system has shaped the practices of conflict resolution both during the Cold War and in the subsequent period of American hegemony.

The next section of the volume takes stock of the record of international involvement in resolving local conflict in a broad range of contexts. Chen Kertcher compares the UN's intervention in Cambodia and Somalia; James Gow discusses the efforts of international institutions to prevent the break-up of Yugoslavia; Stephan Wolff and Annemarie Peen Rodt present a detailed analysis of the European Union's management of ethnic conflicts in the western Balkans; and Adrian Guelke compares the roles played by the British and Irish governments in the peace process in Northern Ireland.

The volume then shifts attention to the American and European involvement in Middle East conflicts. To understand better the often conflicting nature of a nation's intervention in regional conflicts, it is necessary to be aware that there is an ongoing intersection between the international arena and the internal bureaucratic rivalries within each outside actor.

The United States has been the most relevant actor in conflict resolution processes in the Middle East. Robert David Johnson's essay provides a picture of how internal bureaucratic and institutional rivalries have affected America's involvement in the Middle East. In that vein, Robert J. Lieber analyses how the George W. Bush administration's policy was applied to Middle Eastern realities and how local responses affected it.

The European Union – representing the amorphic but nonetheless substantive collective political will of the continent – is becoming increasingly involved in local processes of conflict resolution. This can be seen in Georg Simonis's analysis of the EU's collective efforts, alongside those of the United States, to resolve the Israeli–Palestinian conflict. Furthermore, individual European states have become directly involved in conflict resolution processes in the Middle East, as seen in Jean-Pierre Filiu's analysis of France's historic efforts under François Mitterrand and Jacques Chirac to resolve the intractable conflict in Lebanon.

Finally, the role of regional actors and local actors in determining the course of conflicts in the Middle East deserves due attention. When it comes to vital and domestically contested issues, local decision makers often face contradictory pressures from their domestic constituencies and international patrons. Taken together – the intervention of the Western powers, the influence of state and non-state actors, and the constraints on local decision makers arising from domestic conditions – coalesce into a 'tangled web' of regional conflict. Therefore it is incumbent on us to ask – how do the local elements affect the international efforts to resolve conflicts?

The final section of this volume takes into account the complex ways in which domestic political considerations and regional factors affect international efforts to resolve and mediate conflicts in the Middle East. Uzi Rabi and Brandon Friedman's chapter describes the changing nature of the Middle East as a result of the deeply entrenched divisions in the Persian Gulf between the Arab states and Iran. Eyal Zisser's chapter shows how the Arab-Iranian 'Cold War' has coloured international efforts to resolve the Lebanese conflict by providing a lucid picture of how local Islamist forces in Lebanon, backed by their Iranian and Syrian patrons, brought the Lebanese government to a grinding halt, flying in the face of Western governments' attempts to fashion a different domestic and regional order. The Arab-Iranian competition has also coloured the Arab-Israeli peace process. Joseph Kostiner and Chelsi Mueller examine how two local state actors, Egypt and Saudi Arabia, have used the Arab–Israeli conflict to try to bolster their regional position *vis-à-vis* Iran. Finally, Marvin Weinbaum offers insight into the repercussions of international intervention on local Afghani actors, particularly how alternative local and international visions of what a reconstituted, post-Taliban state should actually look like might colour the state-building process.

Rajan Menon concludes the volume by raising serious questions about the ability of the international community to mount an effective response to civil conflicts, seeing its record of impotence in the face of the horrible atrocities that have occurred just in the last four decades. He weighs the successes and failures of multilateral peacekeeping operations in places like Kosovo, Bosnia and Darfur and concludes that the failures greatly outweigh the successes. In his thought provoking piece, Menon describes the source of failure of the collective action to stop large-scale violence and offers a much needed assessment of what the 'international community' is and what it is not.

Uzi Rabi

PART I

THEORETICAL FRAMEWORK

1

From Bipolar to Unipolar Order: System Structure and Conflict Resolution

Janice Gross Stein

The structure of the international system has an enabling and a constraining impact on the resolution of international conflict. Rules and practices develop informally among those who lead the system and these practices are refracted through the system. In the nineteenth century, for example, it was the 'concert' of the great powers that shaped the informal rules of conflict resolution to their own advantage. The great powers of Europe competed for territory and empire in far-flung parts of the world and resolved conflict among themselves with little attention to the interests of the peoples they controlled. These practices of conflict resolution among European imperial powers shaped the modern Middle East. The borders of many of the states that configure the Middle East today are the consequence of these practices of conflict resolution, practices that engendered much of the conflict that wracks the Middle East today.

During the cold war, the conflict between the two superpowers shaped the governance of the system and the practices of conflict resolution. In the first global system of nuclear powers, the superpowers competed but expected that they could resolve conflicts before they escalated to a nuclear confrontation. After the Cuban missile crisis, the United States and the Soviet Union were less inclined to confront one another directly, but did so indirectly through the allies they supported in their global competition.

Not all members of the international community shared the emphasis on the avoidance of war that the two nuclear powers had learnt. At times, their smaller allies considered the use of force an optimal instrument to achieve their goals against regional adversaries. Equally dangerous, when smaller allies wanted crucial military, political, or economic resources from the superpowers to help them manage their own conflict, they deliberately sought to create and exploit crisis between the superpowers to focus attention on their regional conflicts. Under these circumstances, superpowers could misjudge their allies, underestimate the differences in interests and priorities, and overestimate their capacity to 'manage' their friends.

In part because smaller allies at times sought not to avoid war but to provoke conflict, conflict resolution proved difficult even when the superpowers were highly motivated. Effective communication and control between superpower and ally was necessary but insufficient. Leaders in Washington and Moscow not only had to control their own military forces and bureaucracies as they communicated with each other, but they also had simultaneously to persuade their allies to refrain from a use of force and to compromise their fundamental objectives. They struggled not only to manage an adversary who shared their aversion to war but, equally important, to restrain an ally that considered the use of force an acceptable if not preferred instrument of conflict management. The tacit norm that impelled a superpower to restrain its victorious regional ally did not work automatically; rather, it was often activated by a credible threat of intervention by the defending superpower. The tacit rules of conflict management and resolution were not a stable, reliable, basis for enabling superpowers to back their regional client states without being drawn into war with each other. Conflict resolution was difficult in a tightly configured bipolar international system.

It was the transition from the bipolar system to the unipolar system that saw the sharpest changes in the incidence of violent conflict, the type of violent conflict, and the success and practices of conflict resolution. The 15 years of the 'unipolar moment' – from 1990 to 2005 – marked a qualitative change in the trajectory of violence and its resolution. I look first at the trends in conflict, then at the trends in conflict resolution, and then at changing practices. I return finally to an analysis of the likely implications of evolving multipolarity or 'nonpolarity' for the rules and practices of conflict resolution.

The 'Unipolar Moment' and the Trajectory of Conflict

Three important trends in the trajectory of violent conflict merit special attention.[1] These three trends highlight changes in the patterns of conflict resolution and in the practices of conflict resolution.

First, there is a sharp decline in armed conflict involving a state, the traditional pattern of violent conflict throughout most of the twentieth century. The decade after the cold war was violent. The number of new conflicts in the 1990s was double that of the 1980s, but as the data show, an even greater number of conflicts ended than began during that decade. By 2003, there were 40 per cent fewer state-based conflicts being waged than in 1992.

The trend line of these kinds of conflicts, however, is not unambiguous. From 2002 to 2005, there was a decline in the number of armed conflicts (from 66 to 56), but most of that continuing decline has come in sub-Saharan Africa. In four other regions of the world, however, the number of armed conflicts increased between 2002 and 2005 and central and south Asia is now the most conflict-affected region. Armed conflict is, however, claiming fewer casualties (down from 22,736 to 14,085).

Second, there has been a dramatic decline (90 per cent) in genocides and politicides since the end of the cold war. In 2005, there was only one ongoing genocide (in Darfur), whereas in 1989 there had been ten.

Third, at the same time as traditional, high-intensity armed conflict involving a state declined by more than 40 per cent from 1992 to 2005, campaigns of organized violence against civilians have increased by 56 per cent since 1989. Most are concentrated in sub-Saharan Africa. In the 17 years between 1989 and 2005, non-state armed groups instigated more violent campaigns against civilians than did governments. The significant drop in armed conflict with at least one state as a participant took place despite the fact that 'structural' factors associated with heightened risks of armed conflict – poverty, low growth, economic shocks and lack of state capacity – have changed little or worsened. The decline is associated with a major increase in international support for efforts to end wars.[2]

How Wars End

The 'unipolar moment' has seen a startling increase in conflict resolution. It is the increase in conflict resolution that explains the aggregate reduction in conflict. The number of new conflicts in the 1990s was double that of the 1980s, fuelling the perception that the post-cold war decade was uniquely dangerous. But an even greater number of wars ended than began during that decade. By 2003, there were 40 per cent fewer state-based conflicts being waged than in 1992.

During the cold war years, more wars started than ended each decade, which drove the number of conflicts steadily upwards for 40 years. Over the past 15 years, the number of global conflicts has been driven down again because more wars ended than started.

Changes in Practices

What do we know about the way conflicts ended? An unprecedented 35 per cent of all conflicts ended in some form of negotiated settlement. For the first time, more wars (42) ended by negotiated settlement than by military victory (23). This trend is accelerating: between 2000 and 2005, 17 conflicts ended in negotiated settlements and just 4 ended in victory. This is a reversal of a century-long pattern. However, this pattern is not as encouraging as it seems.

Wars that end in negotiated settlements last three times longer than those that end in victories and are nearly twice as likely to restart again within five years. And negotiated settlements are three times more prone to failures than are victories. Negotiated settlements are associated with longer wars and a greater risk of reoccurrence.

In the 1990s, negotiated settlements became much more unstable. During that decade, 43 per cent of all conflicts that ended in negotiated settlements started again within five years, compared with just 9 per cent of conflicts that ended in victories. The average failure rate for peace settlements in the cold war had been just 13 per cent.[3]

Some types of conflict appear more difficult to resolve than others. While most conflicts have been fought over control of territory, most peace settlements have been negotiated in conflicts fought over who should control the government.[4] Territorial conflicts, therefore, are much more resistant to resolution.

Provisions associated with the successful settlement of territorial conflicts are quite different from those that successfully end conflicts fought over control of the state. After 1989, to settle territorial conflicts, governments were willing to agree to greater autonomy, cultural freedoms and regional development. But while provisions for referenda on the future status of the disputed territory were common, only one (Kosovo) resulted in succession. Peace agreements that follow wars over control of a government have very different terms. They usually focus on the creation of a transitional government, elections and the demobilization of militias.

We also know something about how conflicts ended. Peacemaking efforts by the United Nations increased significantly between 1990 and 1999, along with similar increases by regional organizations, individual governments and non-governmental organizations.[5] The United Nations' increased commitment to conflict resolution is directly attributable to the change in system structure. Throughout the cold war, a veto exercised by one or other of the superpowers disabled the Security Council. Freed of that constraint in 1990, the United Nations dramatically increased its engagement in conflict resolution.

Regionalization has become an especially important focus of conflict resolution.[6] As the UN increased its activity, so too did regional organizations. Since 1990, regional organizations have conducted ten peace operations designed to resolve conflict in Africa.[7] Within Europe, NATO and the EU have led peace operations. Moreover, of the nine UN operations created since 1999, all but one – the 'classical' operation between Ethiopia and Eritrea – were closely affiliated with regional organizations or regional powers. Since the end of the cold war, the UN has moved from becoming the primary actor to providing legitimacy for others.[8] Outside military and economic interventions, on the other hand, increased the duration and hostility levels and made the termination of civil conflicts less likely.[9]

Conflict termination that ends in neither victory nor a peace agreement, where the fighting simply dies down, has the highest probability of failure. Critics argue, therefore, that it is preferable to 'give war a chance' and pursue a stable military solution.[10] But ending a conflict through victory is not a choice when neither party can defeat the other.[11]

As a result of the increase in conflict resolution, the twenty-first century begins with fewer conflicts, but many of these are stalemated.[12] The average length of ongoing civil wars, for example, has increased from two years in 1946 to 15 years in 1999 – suggesting that civil wars were becoming more intractable.[13] This picture, however, may be overly pessimistic. Some long-lasting conflicts have been resolved – Aceh (Indonesia), Nepal, Angola and Liberia – but others – Sierra Leone, Israel/Palestine, the Democratic Republic of the Congo, and Colombia – continue unabated. Yet, of the conflicts that are ongoing today, 71 per cent have lasted fewer than ten years; that does not support a pattern of deeply intractable conflicts. Of course, the Israel–Palestine conflict – a state-based conflict between Israel and Palestine as well as a civil conflict among Palestinians – is the longest enduring conflict that remains unresolved.

Changes in Norms

The change in practices – more engagement by the United Nations to promote negotiated settlements and greater regional engagement in conflict resolution – has been accompanied by a profound normative change in the conceptualization of sovereignty. The normative change is best reflected in the doctrine of 'the responsibility to protect', officially adopted by the United Nations General Assembly in 2005.

Sovereignty as responsibility

The secretary general drew on the United Nations' bitter failure in Rwanda to engage directly with the meaning of sovereignty when security no longer means only state security but human security. In his analysis of the growing crises of the internally displaced, Francis Deng pioneered a concept of sovereignty not only as right but also as responsibility.[14] The International Commission on Intervention and State Sovereignty (ICISS), an independent panel Canada created that worked closely with the secretary general, extended the concept of sovereignty as responsibility.[15] The commission noted the gap in the mandate of international institutions to deal with governments that turned against their own citizens, engaged in widespread and systematic abuse, and created mass human suffering.

International institutions, the commissioners observed, have no mandate to intervene to stop this kind of suffering. The 'responsibility to protect', the report argued, was an emerging principle of customary international law supported both by a range of legal sources and by state practices.[16]

The secretary-general appointed a panel to review threats and challenges and to identify necessary changes. In its report, the panel insisted that all signatories to the UN charter not only accept their obligations to fellow members, as the conventional understanding of collective security suggests, but also take responsibility to protect their citizens.[17] Sovereignty is contingent, then, as much on internal as on external behaviour. This concept of sovereignty changes the foundation of the post-Westphalian order that had governed states for the last three and a half centuries. Sovereignty is no longer defined exclusively as international and domestic autonomy and could no longer be invoked to shield a government's failure to protect its own citizens from the interference of others. On the contrary, states are obligated to come to the assistance of citizens who are being systematically harmed or abused by their own government.

The panel was careful to specify the kinds of actions that obligated member states to exercise their responsibility to protect the citizens of other states. Genocide and other large-scale killing, ethnic cleansing and serious violations of international humanitarian law are at the highest end of the conflict spectrum and involve the most severe abuses of human rights. Here the panel joins human rights to global security and extends the meaning of security beyond states to individuals, groups and citizens.

The secretary general affirmed all these conceptual changes and more.[18] He explicitly asked the heads of government attending the special sixtieth anniversary session of the General Assembly to affirm 'the right of the Security Council to use military force, including preventively, to preserve international peace and security, including in cases of genocide, ethnic cleansing, and other such crimes against humanity.'

This change to the meaning of sovereignty was highly controversial. Many people in the developing world with memories of their colonial histories saw this language as a thinly veiled disguise of a new imperialism, an imperialism wrapped in international law to justify the forcible intervention by the North against the South. Only hard and persistent work by the secretary general and like-minded states allayed some of these fears. In September 2005, the concept of the 'responsibility to protect' was incorporated into the outcome document that the General Assembly subsequently adopted and the Security Council affirmed the following year.[19] The passage of these resolutions constitutes the most sweeping changes to normative concepts of sovereignty in modern times and extends the protection of international humanitarian law inside states. From the introduction of the concept by ICISS to its codification by the General Assembly and Security Council took only a matter of five years.

What has been codified, however, remains a matter of some dispute. The various defining documents differ significantly on the critical issue of whose responsibility it is to take collective action. The outcome document, which has more standing than its predecessors, uses language that suggests a voluntary rather than a mandatory commitment.[20] Nor, on the other hand, is it clear that Security Council authorization is a fundamental pre-requisite of action.[21] What the United Nations did was codify a norm, rather than create a positive duty, a mandatory obligation, under law. All the documents remain silent on the fundamental question of how to deal with violations of the responsibility to protect.

The practice, moreover, has fallen short of the weak normative standard. It was the shameful failure of the Security Council to act during the genocide in Rwanda and its deadlock during the ethnic cleansing in the Balkans that led to the creation of the ICISS and to the articulation of the norm of responsibility to protect. Yet, when large-scale killings of civilians and the displacement of millions of people occurred in Darfur, it took the Security Council almost eighteen months to pass a resolution condemning the killings. At no point has the Security Council threatened to use military force, after the fact, to enforce the responsibility to protect. So, although norms may have changed, the Security Council through acts of omission stands in violation of the changes to norms it has promulgated. Practices of conflict management and resolution do not reflect the change in norms. The gap is very wide.

The changes in practices and the evolution of a norm of 'responsibility to protect' occurred during the 'unipolar moment' of undisputed American hegemony. The end of the cold war unleashed the United Nations to ramp up its activities in conflict termination and, at the same time, opened up the possibility of enforcement actions under Chapter VII of the Charter. Much of this activity became possible because the veto no longer paralysed the Security Council. This enhanced activity, along with more active engagement by regional organizations and 'coalitions of the willing' help to explain the much higher incidence of conflict resolution in the last decade.

What Kind of 'Moment' are We In?

A Bloodied Giant

The first decade of the twenty-first century appears to be ending on a very different note. The last decade was rife with optimism. American power as a maker and enforcer of rules was unchallenged, globalization was acceler-ating, and optimists predicted that an 'electronic herd' of investors would create disincentives for conflict. In a globalizing world functioning within the architecture of American power, countries would be punished for fighting and conflicts would be ghettoized rather than globalized.[22]

An intense debate on the end of unipolarity, the end of US dominance and the shape of the international system that is evolving, has replaced the triumphal claims of American exceptionalism. There is little consensus on what lies ahead, but broad agreement that the USA no longer stands astride the globe unchallenged and unchallengeable. Some predict a new, unstable and fragmented phase of global politics – 'nonpolarity' – in which power diffuses beyond states to networks that operate transnationally and violence rises as the rules change.[23] Others argue that a multipolar system is already in place.[24] The challenges to the global order grow out of deepening economic globalization, new technologies and a governance system that lags badly behind the emergent order and global challenges. There are deep disconnects in this period of transition.

It seems inconceivable that the 'unipolar moment' could last only a decade. At the turn of the century, US military dominance was unquestioned and its economy the most technologically innovative and productive in the world. It led the post-industrial revolution and was a magnet for the most talented, the 'best and the brightest' from around the world.

Then the sobering second thoughts came. The attacks on New York and Washington visibly demonstrated the vulnerability of even the strongest to a handful of people thousands of miles away. Far more damaging has been the unending war in Iraq, the Taliban insurgency in Afghanistan, the resurgence of al-Qaeda in the tribal areas of Afghanistan and Pakistan, and the strain on the military forces of the United States. The giant Gulliver seems to be tied up by the Lilliputians, bound and unable to move.

The enormous advantage that the United States continues to enjoy in sophisticated weapons confers little benefit in street-to-street fighting in Sadr City. The 'revolution in military affairs', which promised so much, has delivered far less; the vision of a small, highly sophisticated military that could deter through its capacity to punish offshore is just that, a vision rather than a reality. The crisis in global financial markets, which began in the United States when American banks securitized mortgages and flourished on greed, has only heightened the perception that the United States may be a giant, but it is a bloodied and weakened giant.

The 'Rise of the Rest'

Compounding the difficulties facing the United States is 'the rise of the rest'.[25] Fareed Zakaria argues that we are now in the midst of the third great tectonic power shift of the last 500 years. The first was the rise of the West, which inaugurated the modern era – science, technology, commerce, capitalism, the industrial revolution, post-industrial revolution and then the digital revolution. The second was the rise of the United States in the twentieth century. We are now at the beginning of the third revolution, the rise of 'the rest': China, India, an increasingly united Europe and a revived Russia.

It is not only America's decline but the rise of the others that suggests that the short-lived unipolar moment is over and that an evolution towards a tripolar system is already under way. China, the European Union, and the United States will compete for markets and influence. Economic globalization is deepening, creating at one and the same time, deep interdependence and the rise of new economic powers.

Economic analyses project that by 2020 China will be a first-rate military and economic power, and that the European Union will have a larger economy than the United States.[26] Both China and India could triple their economic output in the next decade and it is conceivable, some argue, that China could overtake the United States as the world's largest economy by 2030. China today exports more in a single day than it exported in all of 1978. 'Asia is shaping the world's destiny – and exposing the flaws of the grand narrative of Western civilization in the process,' argues Parag Khanna.[27] 'Because of the East, the West is no longer master of its own fate.'

Yet, even as the new powers rise, they are increasingly dependent on one another in a globalizing economy. China depends on US consumers to buy its exports and the United States depends on China to buy and hold its dollars. It is China and other Asian powers that are increasingly financing growth in the United States and it is American consumers who are financing development in China. The United States currently relies on infusions of cash from China, from the Gulf states and from the sovereign wealth funds of Malaysia and Singapore to finance its global reach.

In this tripolar competition for wealth and influence, the 'second world' is increasingly important.[28] It is in the second world that the three great powers will compete for influence, resources and markets. Brazil, Russia, India, Venezuela and the oil-rich countries – including Canada – will benefit from a very long cycle of a demand for oil and natural resources in a market with tightening supply.

For the last 40 years there have been cyclical predictions of a world transformed, the decline of the USA, of imperial overreach, and a new global order. Japan did not, however, displace the United States and it was the Soviet Union and not America that unexpectedly imploded. The 'new world order' that came after the end of the cold war, did not eliminate threat or end war; the peace dividend was short, if not ephemeral. Predictions of imminent decline, of structural change, have often been wrong.

Those who deny that the 'unipolar moment' is over argue that US military, technological and economic capabilities are so formidable that they discourage would-be competitors from even attempting geopolitical competition.[29] Nor, they claim, does the United States directly threaten other rising powers, for they all have secure second-strike nuclear deterrent forces that serve to immunize their homelands from conquest.

Neither of these two arguments is persuasive. The first misses one of the principal fault lines in the global system, namely the disconnect between deepening economic globalization and 'military deglobalization'. Economic and military systems no longer coincide as they did throughout the nineteenth and twentieth centuries.[30] The strategic competition between the United States and the Soviet Union was global. Unlike the cold war, the period since 1990 has been one of military deglobalization. There is no longer global military competition, but distinctly regional and predominantly local conflicts; transnational networks can inflict significant damage on powerful states, using inexpensive and locally made weapons.

New forces, non-states, are exploiting these asymmetries to challenge the status quo through low-intensity warfare. Militias, gangs and transnational networks can use chemical, biological and electronic warfare to exploit open societies; and states can support transnational networks in asymmetric warfare. These forces are unable to prevail, but they are exacting punishing costs, especially against democratic states. When offence is cheaper than defence, as it currently is in asymmetrical warfare, violent conflict becomes more likely.

'Hard power', in other words, may not be as valuable in a global system where power is diffusing. Rising powers no longer need military power to secure the resources they need; they can buy resources on open markets or provide governments with easy credit in exchange for what they want. In America's backyard, in Africa, in the Gulf and on its southern and western peripheries, China is making deals for resources with no strings attached. Its overseas investments are growing as its trade surplus is mounting. And tens of thousands of Chinese aid workers and dam builders are found in virtually every corner of the globe – and all this without firing a shot.

The most powerful state, the United States, is discovering the limits to the exercise of military power as an instrument of foreign policy. It is simultaneously the strongest and the most overstretched, with a limited capacity to respond. It can neither quell the insurgency in Afghanistan nor effectively constrain Iran. The longer these conflicts continue, the 'weaker' the United States appears and the greater the strain on its overstretched military and its stressed economy. The United States may well be trapped in the classic dilemma of 'imperial overreach'.[31] These disconnects between military and economic globalization are made worse by weak governance. 'Geogovernance of military globalization,' argues Joseph Nye, 'still lags far behind the dynamic changes in the technologies of destruction and the increasing roles of transnational actors'.[32]

Even more problematic is the assumption that the United States is widely seen as benevolent. Continuing US dominance is premised on the assumption that the United States is widely seen as a benevolent hegemon. But all the data contradict this assumption. Surveys done by the Pew Charitable Foundation demonstrate consistently that in many parts of the world, the United States is now seen as the greatest threat to world peace and security, far more so than China and Iran. A threatening hegemon provokes low-intensity violence by the weak and 'leash-slipping' by great powers. It also provokes nuclear proliferation by those who fear they may be the object of an attack by the United States.[33]

It is not only that the United States is widely perceived as a threat. It is that the 'soft power' of 'the rest' has become more attractive. The European Union trumpets economic development, governance and rights, and attracts those who wish to join its society, to travel without borders, and share its prosperity. It is the world's largest outward investor and its presence far beyond its borders is formidable. Europe is spending its money and political capital locking peripheral countries into its orbit.[34] And, in the East:

> where American policy makers champion the Washington Consensus, the Chinese talk about the success of gradualism and the 'Harmonious Society.' Where the United States is bellicose, Chinese policy-makers talk about peace. Whereas American diplomats talk about regime change, their Chinese counterparts talk about respect for sovereignty and the diversity of civilizations.

In most of the world, the Chinese message is more appealing.[35]

A World of Many Gullivers

'All great empires set too much store by predictions of their own demise,' argues Ian Buruma.[36] Many of the voices warning of the decline of the United States are, not surprisingly, American and much of the frenzied debate is taking place in Washington. Undoubtedly, it reflects the gloomy mood of a capital in transition, with a new president who certainly faces enormous challenges. Nevertheless, much of this debate reflects a tendency to focus on the challenges confronting the United States and minimize the challenges of others.

China is an obvious case in point. It is dynamic, industrious, disciplined and has lifted millions of people out of poverty. The story of China is stunning, yet it faces enormous challenges. With two elderly people for every young person and a striking imbalance between boys and girls it has a demographic problem that will become acute in the next three decades. In China, 70 million boys will not find wives. Normally, 103 boys are born for every 100 girls, but in some provinces of China, the ratio is 128 to 100. China also faces a catastrophic environmental problem that is now affecting public health, as well as immense rural poverty, which makes it the incubator for disease and epidemics. Its future is far from assured.

The European Union too is getting old at an alarming rate. Maintaining a steady population requires a birth rate of 2.1 and in western Europe the birth rate currently stands at 1.5, or 30 per cent below the replacement rate. The current birth rate in Germany is 1.3, and in Italy and Spain it is 1.2. In Japan, it is 1.3 and Japan will lose up to 60 million people over the next 30 years. It has already closed 2000 schools and continues to close 300 a year. By 2020, one Japanese in every five will be 70 years old. Europe and Japan, two of the world's economic engines, are slowly shutting down. A resurgent Russia is richly endowed in natural resources. Yet, the birth rate of Russia is so low that by 2050 its population will be smaller than that of Yemen. There is no road map for sustainable economic growth with these demographics. Only the United States has a birth rate of 2.0, close to replacement. These differences in demographics have profound implications for relative economic growth over the next several decades.

Not only demographics differentiate the United States from the others. Immigration, for example, could partly mitigate the demographic constraints, but Europe is deeply preoccupied, in a way that the United States and Canada simply are not, by the global movement of people and the presence of large numbers of non-Europeans within its borders. The debate on 'multi-culturalism' is sharp and deep in Europe; and a continent that is obsessively preoccupied with this kind of debate is unlikely to be a global beacon much beyond its periphery. Beyond its deepening struggle with immigration, Europe continues to struggle to resolve its disagreements and to pool its resources so that it can act collectively on global issues. The whole is still less than the sum of its parts.

The definite trends of the future are difficult to predict. Most likely there will be uneven multipolarity, laced with newly prominent transnational networks (non-polarity) that can provoke violence and severely, albeit temporarily, disrupt a balance that is unstable because of the sharp disconnections between military and economic power.

In this kind of system, the great powers will have less incentive to manage or resolve conflicts, unless they directly threaten their strategic interests. Asymmetric conflict between non-state actors and states is likely to persist for long periods of time, given the disparity between the costs of offence and defence. Violent low-level conflict within states will continue to be the most prevalent form of conflict.

In this emergent multipolar world, no single power will be able to set the rules unilaterally either for global governance or for conflict resolution. The United States is likely to be first among equals for a considerable period of time, but it will need to build consensus with the other powers to make and enforce the rules. In this much messier, more fractured and diffuse system, governance will be critical. How the United States leads, whether it can share power and build consensus, whether it can open international institutions to those who are rising, will shape the prospects of conflict resolution around the world. That the rules and practices of conflict resolution will evolve is certain, but how they evolve and how they will work will be very much a function of how the United States leads in the new 'post-American' world. Fareed Zakaria put it well:

On every dimension other than military power – industrial, financial, social, cultural – the distribution of power is shifting, moving away from US dominance. That does not mean we are entering an anti-American world. But we are moving into a post-American world, one defined and directed from many places and by many people.

The United States must come to recognize that it faces a choice – it can stabilize the emerging world order by bringing in the new rising nations, ceding some of its power and perquisites, and accepting a world with a diversity of voices and viewpoints. Or it can watch as the rise of the rest produces greater nationalism, diffusion, and disintegration, which will slowly tear apart the world order the United States has built over the last 60 years.[37]

PART II

THE INTERNATIONAL ROLE IN CONFLICT RESOLUTION

2

Same Agenda, Different Results: The UN Interventions in Cambodia and Somalia after the Cold War

Chen Kertcher

In this chapter, the reasons for the different results of UN interventions in Cambodia and Somalia in the early 1990s are examined. Since the end of the cold war there has been a surge in the use of UN peacekeeping operations to resolve local conflicts. Instead of resolving conflicts through the traditional formula of international diplomacy and peace treaties, a complex attitude that called for the execution of multifunctional peace-keeping operations as part of a local peace process was adopted. These operations not only involve the supervision of an existing peace – the way they usually operated during the cold war – but they are also part of a sophisticated technique that tries to solidify the local conditions towards peace. The new operational objectives included enhancing democratic values, supervising government activities, demobilizing armed factions and providing humanitarian relief and economic aid. In the early 1990s there was hope that this multifunctional recipe would end intra-state conflicts and solidify peace around the world.

To carry out multifunctional peacekeeping operations, the UN was required to deploy thousands of soldiers in addition to hundreds and often thousands of civil police forces and international civil personnel. Sustaining such large-scale operations had financial consequences. For example, UN efforts in Cambodia (1991–93) and Somalia (1992–95) cost the UN approximately 1.6 billion dollars each. In comparison, the UN's yearly peacekeeping budget in the 1980s was about 300 million dollars. Accomplishing these complex objectives also required novel organizational and management approaches involving multiple layers of coordination with additional international, regional and local non-governmental organizations.[1]

Experts in the field of peacekeeping usually point to two multifunctional peacekeeping operations at the beginning of the 1990s as a success and a failure.[2] The UN operation in Cambodia from October 1991 to October 1993 is usually portrayed as a success. In this context, studies emphasize that the operation ended the horrible civil war that had raged in that country since the early 1970s. After the end of the operation, there were calls in UN corridors to make it a model for future operations and to learn from this operation about the importance of international political cooperation, clear mandates and collaboration between military and civil personnel and management.[3] In sharp contrast, it is generally accepted that the UN intervention in Somalia from April 1992 to March 1995 was a failure. Conventional academic literature claims that the intervention in Somalia failed to bring peace to the country because of poor international political cooperation, unclear and often changing mandates, poor coordination between military and civil personnel, and inefficient management. Some scholars also point out that these faults played into the hands of local clans who tried to undermine the peace process.[4] While these studies are comprehensive and offer rich insights into UN peacekeeping operations, to my knowledge there is no study that compares the two cases.

The primary objective of this chapter is to evaluate the similarities and differences between the UN operations in Cambodia and in Somalia. In particular, I show that while the outcomes were very different, there were many similarities between the two operations, specifically with respect to their objectives and to the managerial and organizational problems they encountered. Moreover, contrary to what the literature on these cases claims, I shall argue that the main reason for the success in Cambodia and failure in Somalia was related to the varied effects these interventions had on the major local factions.

In the next part of the chapter I reject commonly-held notions about the major differences between the Cambodian and Somalian operations with respect to their objectives, international support and lack of will on the part of local factions. I then go on to examine how the UN operations affected the major local factions involved in the Cambodian conflict. In the last part I analyse the ways in which UN operations affected the major faction in central and southern Somalia.

Similarity between UN Operations in Cambodia and Somalia

The UN interventions in Cambodia and Somalia were advanced as 'state-building' efforts. Today, possibly the best known 'state-building' operations are UNMIK in Kosovo and UNTAET in East Timor. Both operations began in 1999.[5] Like these subsequent missions, UN operations in Cambodia and Somalia had multiple objectives involving peacemaking, assistance to the political process between rival factions, disarmament, advancements of human rights, massive humanitarian assistance and investments in economic development.[6]

While some scholars suggest that the UN intervention in Somalia was led by humanitarian concerns, this view is a reduction of the operation's objectives. The UN intervention in Somalia began officially in April 1992 with an emphasis on diplomatic peacemaking and military observers. The humanitarian operation gained dominance for only a short period from the end of December 1992 to the beginning of May 1993, under a US-led military coalition titled 'Operation Restore Hope'. After March, the UN Security Council's focus shifted to state-building for the two following years.[7]

Executing both operations posed considerable challenges to the UN, with a number of striking similarities. The UN Secretariat managed both the Cambodian and the Somali campaigns. However, because the Secretariat had experience only in managing small peacekeeping operations, it was unprepared to handle the highly complex demands that a multifunctional operation required. In his memoirs, Marrack Goulding – who was in charge of UN peacekeeping operations from 1987 to 1993 – described how, despite the growing demands of the various operations involved in the two interventions, he only received a very meagre increase in budget, manpower and other crucial aid from contributing states.[8]

From December 1992 to March 1994 the operation in Somalia, like the operation in Cambodia, received wide support from foreign powers. Even after March 1994 when most Western states withdrew their forces from Somalia, the major problem was lack of logistical support such as command and control capabilities, and not lack of troops. At its peak, in the summer of 1993, the UN operation in Somalia had twice the number of troops deployed in Cambodia – approximately 30,000 soldiers and civil personnel in comparison with approximately 15,000 soldiers and civil personnel in Cambodia. Providing for this level of deployment posed a substantial financial burden on the UN, as evidenced by the constant complaints the Secretariat made to the Security Council. In addition, both operations suffered from poor coordination and lack of expert civil staff. Exacerbating the challenges were the ongoing political pressures by many members of the Security Council and many contributing states to accomplish the operations' objectives in as short a time as possible so as to reduce their costs.[9]

The similarities between the two cases in both objectives and resource management challenges raise the question of why, if they were similar, were the results so different? The following discussion will show that the answer to this question lies in the effects of the UN interventions on the most powerful factions in Cambodia and Somalia, the CPP and the United Somali Congress (USC)/Somali National Alliance (SNA) respectively.

UN Intervention in Cambodia

After the defeat of the Khmer Rouge genocidal regime in 1979 to Vietnamese armed forces, a civil war developed in Cambodia. On one side there was the Kampuchean People's Revolutionary Party (KPCP), which was in control of the State of Cambodia (SOC) under the supervision of the Vietnamese occupation forces. The KPCP held approximately 90 per cent of the country's territories. In 1991 the KPCP reorganized as the Cambodian People's Party (CPP). A loose coalition of royalists (FUNCINPEC), democrats (BLDP) and radical communists, the Khmer Rouge (DK) factions, which operated from the Thai border and received support from Thailand, China and the USA, fought against the CPP.[10]

Under international pressure to resolve their conflict and the threat of stopping the aid to them, the four factions were pushed to sign a peace agreement on 23 October 1991 known as 'The Final Act of the Paris Conference on Cambodia'. Central to the peace agreement was a call for the UN to execute a multifunctional peacekeeping operation named United Nations Transitional Administration in Cambodia (UNTAC). The operation, the various sides argued, was to support the peace process through the management and monitoring of a democratic election to choose a legitimate government in Cambodia. To support this state-building objective, the operation was given other objectives like advancing democracy and human rights, demobilizing 70 per cent of the armed forces of all four factions, aiding the return of refugees and assisting in rehabilitation and reconstructing the country's economy.[11]

On signing the peace agreement, the four Cambodian factions entered a major and long disagreement over the question of how the state apparatus should be administered pending the formation of a legitimate democratic government. In the end the CPP and the three opposition factions had to compromise. Originally, the three factions opposing the CPP advocated a full international transitional administration in Cambodia. In their view, if a democratic election followed by the formation of a government was to take place, the UN needed to force the CPP to relinquish all its control over the state apparatus. The CPP's leaders, by contrast, wished to preserve the faction's political, military and economic superiority over the other three groups, so wanted minimal international intervention. Therefore, the question was not only if supervision of the election could be successful, but rather if UN intervention in Cambodia could loosen the CPP's hold on the state apparatus.

Daunting tasks confronted the UN. It needed to manage a democratic election in a country that had not held an election for almost four decades. Cambodian society was very traditional, people's relationships with one another were based on rigid hierarchies and the vast majority of the citizens were illiterate. In addition, the infrastructure had been ruined. Many bridges and roads were not useable and the country was covered with mines. Above all, the civil war that had raged for two and a half decades, along with the brutal genocide by the Khmer Rouge, which caused the deaths of one-fifth of the country's population, had left Cambodians in a dire state with no prospects of rehabilitation. The chances of organizing an open, democratic election appeared doubtful.

To make things worse, the UN never managed an election until its involvement in Cambodia.[12] As mentioned earlier, a battery of resource management difficulties also confronted the operation. These problems got worse when from May 1992 the DK (Khmer Rouge) refused to cooperate with the demobilization process that was supposed to enhance security and build confidence between factions. Instead, fighting between the DK's and CPP's armed forces continued intermittently, causing lack of security, a flood of thousands of new refugees and a threat to the presence of UN military and civilian forces.[13]

Despite these difficulties, UN officials registered potential voters, managed political campaigns and conducted the election in May 1993. The results of the election gave FUNCINPEC 58 and the CPP 51 of the 122 seats in parliament.[14] Since Cambodia's new constitution required a government composed of a two-thirds majority, the FUNCINPEC and the CPP formed a coalition and created two prime-ministerial posts. With the formation of a Cambodian government that the international community recognized, the rationale for the UN's operation in Cambodia ended and by November 1993 the last component of the operation had left the country in what seemed at the time to be a successful closure.

However, close examination of UNTAC's actions suggests that to succeed with the management of the election and the transfer of power to a newly elected government, the UN force sacrificed many of its objectives, including the supervision of the work of civil government, advancing democratization and human rights norms, demobilization of all four factions' armed forces and rehabilitation and reconstruction of the economy. Top UN officials recognized the limited accomplishment. For instance, the UN secretary-general, Boutros-Ghali, claimed that the conditions for the departure of UN forces were far from ideal because the organization failed to establish democratic norms in Cambodia. But the Security Council, the states that contributed to the operation, as well as local Cambodian elites, especially the CPP leadership, ignored his reservations.[15]

The effects of the UN's early departure were soon visible. In 1997 the CPP staged a coup against its coalition partner, FUNCINPEC, easily crushing the small resistance. A year later the CPP defeated the last remnants of the Khmer Rouge opposition. Since then, CPP representatives have tightened their grip on local politics all over Cambodia, while also abusing human rights. Their leader, Hun Sen, has been ruling the country as prime-minister since 1985. The international community has not taken any decisive action on these matters since the early 1990s, despite harsh criticism by the special representatives of the secretary-general on human rights in Cambodia.[16]

I shall now turn to examine the effects that UN intervention had on CPP control of domestic institutions. Reviewing the limited efficacy that the international efforts had on the CPP's hold over Cambodia's political, military and economic institutions offers important clues about why the CPP cooperated with UN forces during their intervention.

For UNTAC, the supervision of civil government institutions – like local government offices and country provinces – was essential in furnishing the democratic climate in Cambodia. Since the CPP controlled over 90 per cent of Cambodian territory through SOC institutions, the UN's main focus was on supervising the work of the SOC government offices. UN secretary-general Pérez de Cuéllar (1982–91) and his aides, however, felt worried about their magnitude and lack of precedence.[17] In addition, the UN did not have a concrete plan for implementing the supervision of civil institutions, and the assistance they received from other governments was negligent.[18] The slow arrival of international civil personnel aggravated the problem. Five months after the official launch of the UN operation, UN forces included only 215 civilian government supervisors for the entire country of 180,000 square kilometres with a population of approximately ten million people.[19] And, as the date for the national democratic election approached, the CPP further reduced its cooperation with UN officials.

A UN report to the Security Council in early March 1993 revealed some CPP strategies. It used the 'state apparatus to conduct political campaign activities of the Cambodian People's Party (CPP) in which state employees – police, armed forces and civil servants – are mobilized for CPP electioneering.'[20]

The other three factions could not fail to notice how ineffectively UNTAC forces were supervising the CPP's hold on government institutions. After all, the supervision – rather than the international transitional administration they would have preferred – was one of their basic conditions for signing the peace agreement. This requirement was especially important for the DK leadership and in May 1992 Khmer Rouge leaders voiced their doubts about the fairness of an election in which the CPP kept its hold on 90 per cent of the country and there was minimal international supervision of the state's institutions. As a result, the

DK stopped cooperating with the disarmament process and refused to participate in the election.[21] Under international pressure the other two parties (FUNCINPEC and BLDP) continued to participate in the political process, but CPP agents constantly harassed their activists. With a view to countering CPP dominance, FUNCINPEC and BLDP leaders asked the UN to grant expatriate Cambodians the right to vote, but their request was denied on the grounds that it was not specifically part of the peace agreement.[22]

Because there were almost no UN supervisors, the monitoring of local governments was meagre and, as a result, the CPP maintained all its posts in these institutions. The CPP leadership immediately blocked the efforts of the relatively few UN civilian supervisors to enhance UN involvement in the CPP's decision-making process through gaining access to all government documents. In March 1993, the CPP leader, Hun Sen, wrote to the SRSG (special representative of the secretary general) in Cambodia, Yasushi Akashi, as follows: 'UNTAC's method of control was so rigorous and intrusive that it resembled the method used by Pol Pot!'[23] When the DK stopped cooperating with UNTAC, the CPP reduced its cooperation with UNTAC supervision mechanisms.[24] Even at the highest levels, as in the foreign affairs office where the UN was generally satisfied with its actions, achievements were minimal. The UN representatives' main achievement was to issue passports and visas, which in retrospect seems minor to their overall tasks.[25] In general, the CPP officials cooperated with the UN on minor issues (such as passports) while maintaining their control on the SOC state apparatus.[26]

Lack of cooperation from the CPP and poor results pushed UNTAC's head of the civil component, Gerard Porcell, to resign in February 1993.[27] A month later, an UNTAC expert on public information stated that:

> In Seam Reap, as observed elsewhere, CPP and SOC structures are inseparable, and that there seems to have been no attempt whatsoever to at least make them look even formally separate. It appears that, on the contrary, CPP's control over SOC structures has been reinforced to the point of total fusion, SOC's structures being CPP's instrument to implement its policies and achieve its objectives.[28]

Efforts at disarmament attained similarly poor results. It was initially planned that UNTAC would disarm 70 per cent of the armed men of all four factions in the first few months of the operation, a process that was considered fundamental to the peace agreement. Early assessments of the entire armed forces of the rival factions had put them at 200,000 soldiers, not including a potential quarter of a million militia men. Most of these forces were affiliated with the CPP.[29]

The expectations of the disarmament plan failed to materialize. As mentioned earlier, the Khmer Rouge feared that the CPP would maintain its stronghold over local institutions, and from May 1992 the faction leaders refused to disarm. Until that date, the CPP disarmed only minor parts of its huge armed forces. The few thousand who were disarmed were poorly equipped militiamen who were soon supposed to be released to go back to their farms.[30] Instead of disarmament, the Khmer Rouge and CPP carried on with sporadic fighting during the international intervention.[31]

The UN did not use force to compel the two factions to comply with the demobilization process. UN officials decided to redeploy their forces in Cambodia, but Security Council Resolution 792 ordered UNTAC to concentrate its operations on defending the electoral political rallies – the centres of registration and voter's centres – and not on disarmament.[32]

Another security issue was observation of the work of the SOC's civil police who were under CPP control. UN civil police cooperated with other arms of the UN and also trained local policemen and judges.[33] As in the supervision of government work, the UN's achievements were minor. The deployment of international civil police reached its target of 3000 officers only in January 1993, more than a year after the signing of the 'Peace Agreement'.[34] Although they had a mandate to supervise the work of the civil police, the UN police forces concentrated on supporting the election process. For instance, before the election more then half its forces were deployed in assisting the registration of voters.[35]

UN activities did not have a noticeable impact on public security. Khmer Rouge forces mounted ferocious attacks on Vietnamese minorities that caused the death of dozens. Political attacks on FUNCINPEC and BLDP political activists by CPP agents were frequent. These attacks included sporadic fire by machine guns and grenade throwing. Furthermore, there was a sharp rise in crime and violence in the country.[36] The destabilization of public law and order forced the head of UNTAC, Yasushi Akashi, to issue a statement on 19 November 1992 stating that in such grim conditions human lives, personal security and property were in jeopardy and that there could be no free or fair election.[37]

The UN's failure to loosen the CPP's hold on the state apparatus can also be seen in relation to the country's economy. At the time of the UN intervention, the CPP was in dire straits. Inflation and unemployment were high, and many Cambodians blamed the CPP government for the situation. Fearing that the economic situation would undermine the election, the UN decided to help stabilize the economy by flooding Cambodian markets with massive amounts of rice; this stopped the economic crisis and helped improve the stand of the CPP towards the people.[38] Furthermore, the people in charge of the UN development projects worked with CPP government officials. These projects injected hundreds of millions of dollars into state institutions that the CPP managed and used to its own ends. Moreover, the UN failed to stop the CPP's unlawful trafficking in wood, which was a major source of income to the faction.[39]

In summary, while UN intervention in Cambodia is seen as a model UN multifunctional operation, the main cause of its 'success' was not a result of clear mandates or managerial and organizational excellence. The emphasis on the electoral process – while not trying to enforce the mandate and not meddling too much in CPP institutions and actions – created the impression that the operation had succeeded, while at the same time creating an exit strategy for the UN that allowed it to leave the country with the dominant CPP in power and dysfunctional fledgling democratic institutions. In the following part of the chapter we shall see how UN intrusiveness in Somali politics, security and the economy, combined with its enforcement operations against the USC/SNA, the most powerful faction in the southern and central part of the country, caused contradictory results in comparison with Cambodia.

UN Intervention in Somalia

The fragile Somali democracy established in 1960 ended in 1969 when General Siad Barre formed a dictatorship. In 1988, the Somali National Movement (SNM), which represented the northwestern clan, Isaaq, openly challenged Barre's rule. In the following years a full-scale civil war developed in Somalia. Other factions joined the SNM struggle, such as the Somali Salvation Democratic Front (SSDF) (Majerteen/Darod), the United Somali Congress (USC) (Hawiye) and later the Somali Patriotic Movement (SPM) (Ogaden/Darod). When the faction's coalition finally defeated Barre's forces at the beginning of 1991 they turned against each other. During 1992 the different factions dismembered the state. In the northwest the Isaaq clan formed Somaliland. In the northeastern territory an autonomous region was declared mostly populated by the Majerteen, a subclan of the Darod (SSDF). The south-central region, which was the most populous, was dominated by the Haber Gedir, a subclan of the Hawiye. The Haber Gedir split from the USC and formed the most powerful faction the USC/SNA. This faction was headed by General Mohamed Farah Aidid. The continuation of fighting among the different factions crushed whatever remained of Somalia state institutions and infrastructure, threatening the well-being of hundreds of thousands of Somalis who were suffering from starvation, disease and daily violence.[40]

During the fighting in 1992 the UN tried in vain to mediate a peace agreement between the local factions. Finally, only after the continuous fighting had caused a major humanitarian crisis, the US government decided to lead a 'Unified Task Force' (UNITAF) for a five-month humanitarian operation titled 'Operation Restore Hope'.[41] With intensive international pressures and under UN auspices, leaders from 15 Somali factions signed a peace agreement in March 1993 – 'The Addis Ababa agreement'. The agreement called for the establishment of a Transitional National Council (TNC) under the supervision of the UN operation UNOSOM II, disarmament of the warring factions, assistance in the establishment of civil institutions and the reconstruction of infra-structures, as well as the repatriation of 300,000 refugees.[42]

Somalia at the beginning of the 1990s was a country with no recog-nized government structures or authorities and the infrastructures were in ruin. The Addis Ababa agreement set to the UN the objectives of supporting a political process in this 'collapsed state'.[43] Until the operation in Somalia, the organization had never executed an operation in places where there were no state institutions with which to work. As I mentioned at the beginning of the chapter, the lack of infrastructure and the ambitious mandates caused organizational and managerial difficulties that, though different from the ones in Cambodia, were similar in the view of the UN Secretariat.

Barre clung to power with the support of the Marehan/Darod and Ogaden/Darod, while employing brutal tactics against rival clans. In a society divided along tribal lines, these actions alienated the other clans. During the civil war the animosity further intensified when armed militias formed along clan lines. The continuous fighting left a suspicious society and anxious political leadership. Furthermore, the fighting between the different clans did not end the numerous militia forces and armed gangs (*mooryan*) have made rebuilding state political and civil institutions a daunting task.

According to some analysts, the UN's failure to quell the continuous fighting among armed gangs and clans was the main reason for the collapse of the peace arrangement. A different view suggests that the United States failed to commit the resources the UN needed to build a civil society.[44] There is general agreement, however, that the engagement of UN forces with the most powerful faction in south-central Somalia, the USC/SNA under Aidid between June and October 1993, caused the Western states to withdraw their forces until March 1994. After this event the operation disintegrated until the final withdrawal of all UN forces from Somalia in March 1995.[45] Several UN delegations and the secretary-general, however, wanted to continue the operation. They feared that a

UN withdrawal might have a catastrophic effect on the country, but their arguments were ignored.[46] Since 1995, the fighting between armed militias has continued in south-central Somalia. Despite several national peace initiatives, the awaited peace that most of the population expected after the ousting of Barre remains to be seen.[47]

I believe that the UN forces undermined rather than stabilized the political and security situation in south-central Somalia and reject the commonly-held argument that the lack of will by local factions, or limited support of the international community led to the UN failure in Somalia.

One of UNOSOM II's major objectives was to assist the newly created TNC formed from 15 Somali factions. Originally, UN support was meant to solidify cooperation between Somali factions and create an atmosphere of trust that would help rehabilitate state institutions and create the right conditions for a democratic civil state. In practice, UN representatives ignored the fact that their peacemaking efforts undermined the political integration of Somali factions. Their approach encouraged small clans to create new political factions in order to obtain international political and financial support. Instead of stopping the political disintegration they supported it. Thus, from the four most dominant factions *circa* 1992, there were 15 at the Addis Ababa conference in March 1993. In November 1993 some 16 factions participated in the UN peace process. A year later the UN representative noted 28 factions, excluding the self-proclaimed state of Somaliland in the northwest of the country.[48]

UN relations with Ali Mahdi are symptomatic of the organization's failed peacemaking efforts in Somalia. A dubious political body purporting to represent the Somali opposition to Barre declared Mahdi interim president in January 1991.[49] From then on, he behaved as if he were the elected president of Somalia, whereas in fact he probably only represented the Abgal subclan that lived mostly in north Mogadishu. Mahdi's vocal support for UN intervention[50] was intended mainly to weaken the dominant Haber Gedir clan that controlled most of the main facilities in south-central Somalia, especially Mogadishu harbour and airport. He encouraged UN forces to take over USC/SNA assets in the name of neutrality.[51] The UN envoys seemed oblivious of the real motives of Mahdi and other leaders, mainly factions of the Darod clan. UN recognition of factional leaders empowered the latter in the local political process and, by the time the UN convened the Addis Ababa peace conference, its officials regarded Aidid as only one among 15 other factional leaders. Therefore, although the UN took the role of an unbiased peacemaker, in practice it challenged Aidid's superiority in sheer force and control of political and economic assets.

At provincial and district political levels, the UN made an effort to establish new civil institutions. Their efforts were concentrated in the main areas of UNOSOM II deployment in central and southern Somalia. Because these were the areas under the control of Aidid and his allies, UN operations undermined his rule. Furthermore, many of these UN local civil institutions were corrupt and competition between subclans made it impossible to operate a working local administration.[52]

The border dispute in the centre of the country around the vicinity of Galcayo is yet another example of the adverse influence UN intervention had on Somalia's stability. When Aidid tried to advance local peace initiatives with Abdulahi Yusuf, leader of the SSDF, on the question of borders between SSDF-controlled areas and USC/SNA territories near Galcayo, the UN representatives insisted on taking part in the peace negotiations and tried to impose their norms and preferences on the peace deal devised by Aidid and Abdulahi Yusuf. For example, they wanted the agreement to include leaders of other factions, against the wishes of Aidid and Yusuf. Their intervention almost destroyed the local peace talks, but Aidid and Yusuf circumvented these obstacles and reached an agreement that remained valid years after UN forces had left the country.[53]

Because, as in the Cambodian case, Somalia was overwhelmed with arms, security was a central concern for the UN. While many of the weapons were put in authorized arsenals under UN supervision, thousands of Somalis affiliated with various rival factions still owned light weapons. The UN did not, however, have an international mandate to disarm these factions forcefully. When it did exert pressure to disarm, it focused on Mogadishu, the USC/SNA's main base for operations. The overall result was an imbalance in which the USC/SNA force became much weaker in comparison with other factions.[54]

Aidid was concerned that the international operations would destroy his gains from the war to oust Barre. Between January and March 1993 Aidid's ally Omar Jess (Ogaden/Darod of the SPM) fought Mohamed 'Hersi' Morgan, Barre's son-in-law (Majerteen/Darod of the SNF), for control of the important port city of Kismayu in the south of the country. When Omar Jess was routed from Kismayu after a surprise attack by Morgan, the international forces prevented Jess from launching a counter attack.[55] Furthermore, the deployment of the multinational forces denied Aidid control of areas in south-central Somalia, which his forces occupied during the campaigns of 1991 and 1992.

Aidid saw the international stabilization measures as worsening his position compared with that of other factions. He reacted to his diminishing status by stretching his already strained relations with the UN even further by organizing demonstrations, operating an anti-UN campaign over his faction's radio station and encouraging attacks on UN soldiers. The toughness of UN representatives in Somalia towards Aidid's faction resulted in a war that raged between UN forces and the USC/SNA from June to October 1993.[56] With hundreds of casualties, this war destabilized the factions' already fragile political cohesion. Subclans that suffered from the war began to fight one another, questioning Aidid's leadership as well as his control of political and financial assets. The results devastated the peacemaking objectives. From early 1994 numerous lethal armed clashes accompanied the factions' accelerating disintegration, destroying infrastructures and creating thousands of refugees.[57]

As these conflicts took place, the UN tried to establish a civil police. However, this hesitant initiative gained momentum only after most of the Western states that contributed forces to the intervention had left the country in March 1994. The focus of the police work was on Mogadishu, as it had been in the case of the disarmament process, and these activities mainly included confiscating light arms from civilians. Since many of these operations targeted potential fighters for the USC/SNA, they undermined Mohamed Aidid's position. Therefore, when the UN began its withdrawal from the country the civil police did not receive any support from the rival faction and quickly dissolved.[58]

Finally, the UN's intervention in Somalia had adverse economic implications, especially for Aidid's USC/SNA faction. The tens of thousands of tons of aid in food, medicine and basic equipment that the international community donated and sent to Somalia from 1992 onwards saved tens of thousands of Somali lives. It also dramatically improved living conditions in the southern and central regions of the country.[59] Despite these positive outcomes the operation of humanitarian aid agencies, such as the ICRC and WFP, suggests that their work had negative effects on security and overall political stability. Many aid organizations operating in Somalia hired armed guards from different clans, paying vast sums by Somali standards. Indeed, clans often fought each other to obtain these coveted jobs. This put further pressure on Aidid as many of his allies from other subclans constantly demanded access to the versatile economic resources that his control of aid organization centres in Mogadishu and other cities gave him. Another negative effect of humanitarian aid for Mohamed Aidid's faction was the encouragement that UN officials gave to hundreds of thousands of displaced refugees to go back to their former homes, which clearly threatened to destabilize the more homogenous clans' areas.[60] Instead of peace and stability the international community aid operations helped to disintegrate the factions and ignite war.

In conclusion, UN operations in Somalia most negatively affected Mohamed Aidid's USC/SNA political, military and economic position in comparison with those of other factions. At the same time, UN activities benefited the factions headed by Ali Mahdi or the Darod clan. The last straw for Aidid's faction was the Pakistani UN contingent's inspection on 5 June 1993. The UN command officials ignored the USC/SNA's formal request to delay the inspection, for the latter had reason to believe that the procedure was intended to inflict damage on the faction's radio station. The inspection led to the beginning of a war that harmed both UN forces and Aidid's faction. The decisive battle, sometimes known as 'Black Hawk Down' on 3–4 October 1993, which took place in the streets of Mogadishu, caused the deaths of hundreds of Somalis, 18 American soldiers and one soldier from Malaysia. By the time the UN and Aidid decided to end their feud, the UN's local credibility had been damaged beyond restoration, and political fragmentation in Somalia had intensified.

Conclusion

Comparing UN operations in Cambodia and Somalia in the early 1990s has, in both cases, led me to question common academic measurements of success and failure as well as the underlying causes of the conflicts. First, we have seen that the UN's objectives were similar in both cases. Second, because managerial and organizational problems dogged both operations, we cannot accept that they were the main reason for success or failure. In both cases UN strategies provoked local factions either to cooperate or to oppose the international forces. In Cambodia, UN actions often helped the CPP – the most powerful faction – to increase its control over the state apparatus, thus gaining the faction's support for the peace process. In Somalia, similar objectives and actions under UN auspices worked to undermine the hold on local government and security of the most powerful faction in the southern-central part of the country, the USC/SNA, and in the end pushed it into waging a four-month war against the UN, which severely undermined the peace prospects. With historical hindsight the consequences are clear: In Cambodia Hun Sen's CPP has ruled continuously since the 1980s, while in Somalia constant efforts are still being made to reverse the ongoing political deterioration.

I described the important effects multifunctional interventions have on local political players. These suggest that the policy-makers who define operational objectives as well as the officers in the field responsible for executing the mandates, should try to understand how their operations – whether applying military force or distributing aid to refugees – influence the main local actors. If their actions are helpful to major factions, they tend to cooperate with the international forces, often in the belief that when the UN leaves they will sustain their internal political advantage. If they are harmful to them, local groups may take a hostile stance, even if they make symbolic cooperative gestures.

Managers of multifunctional peacekeeping operations should take into account the potential effects of their actions on the main factions and form decisions on a number of crucial questions. They need to ask who gains from the intervention. Is this gain in accordance with the neutrality of the multinational forces? Should the international community find ways of balancing the forces of the local factions or maintain the existing balance of power between them? Addressing these questions may help to clarify the objectives and actions of the operations with respect to local factions.

If it is likely that one or more of the major factions will stop cooperating with the multifunctional operation, strategies of enforcement or withdrawal should be re-evaluated. In these cases planners of a multifunctional operation should consider in advance if the international community is ready to deal with potential non-cooperation on the part of a major faction and try to enforce political order. How will enforcement influence the balance of power between local factions and other objectives of the operation? Do the different enforcement actions correspond to the operation's final objective of solidifying peace?

3

External Mediation and Internal Ownership: The Belfast and St Andrews Agreements Compared

Adrian Guelke

Understandably, the extraordinary sight on 8 May 2007 of former enemies, the firebrand preacher Ian Paisley and the former IRA chief Martin McGuinness, taking up office as first minister and deputy first minister in a new Northern Ireland executive, captured the imagination not just of people in Britain and Ireland but of people around the world as well. This miracle coincided with significant developments in both British and Irish politics. In the case of Britain, it was the announcement of the date of the long anticipated resignation of Tony Blair as prime minister after ten years in office. For Blair, the miracle of Belfast was a much needed success to offset the issue that had dominated his premiership and forced his resignation, the war in Iraq. At the same time, the establishment of devolved government in Belfast took place in the midst of a general election campaign in the Republic of Ireland, with the Irish prime minister correctly anticipating that credit for his role as a peacemaker would pay electoral dividends when the Irish went to the polls on 24 May 2007.

The date of 8 May 2007 looked set to be seen as a major turning point in Northern Ireland history from the moment in March 2007 that the two former antagonists, Ian Paisley and Gerry Adams, announced that they had agreed on this date for the devolution of power to Northern Ireland. However, history has been made before in Northern Ireland. The Good Friday agreement of 10 April 1998 was supposed to usher in devolved government on a power-sharing basis and for that David Trimble and John Hume, representing the majority party within each community at the time, jointly received the Nobel Peace Prize. At the time, this agreement was hailed as just as much of a miracle as the events of May 2007.

The first version of the Good Friday agreement failed to live up to its promise and, rather than there being a devolved government in place from

June 1998, when the first Northern Ireland Assembly was elected, the province was governed after 1998 mainly under direct rule from London. Indeed, politics in Northern Ireland for the last decade has had some similarity with the scenario in the American film, *Groundhog Day*, in which a weatherman finds himself stuck in a time warp, so that he lives through the same day over and over again and wakes each morning back where he started. Alternatively, it can be compared with the game of snakes and ladders. Gigantic steps towards a new future have been followed by equally large setbacks that have necessitated that history be made again. People in Northern Ireland are understandably more aware of the ups and downs of the peace process than the outside world. Consequently, they tend to be more cautious about current prospects than those ignorant of the history of past breakthroughs. In the last years of the violent conflict in the early 1990s, it was common, with good reason, to refer to war weariness as a factor in the situation. The peace process has been going on for 14 years and a certain amount of fatigue has set in.

Has the establishment of devolved government under the St Andrews agreement finally broken the spell? It might help to examine how we arrived at this point and to consider, in particular, the significance of the terms under which the parties have agreed to share power. The key document in this context is the St Andrew's agreement, which the British and Irish governments unveiled on 13 October 2006. It paved the way for the formation of the Executive on 8 May 2007. The St Andrews agreement might reasonably be described as the second version of the Good Friday agreement. It has also been described as 'the long Good Friday agreement' and, more jocularly, as 'the Good Friday agreement in a kilt'.[1] Whether the St Andrews agreement should be seen as a new agreement at all is a matter of political dispute, since it is the contention of most supporters of the Good Friday agreement that St Andrews simply provided a face-saving mechanism for the Democratic Unionist Party (DUP) to switch from an anti-agreement to a pro-agreement position.

This is a difficult dispute to settle, since, on the one hand, the St Andrews agreement did introduce significant and substantive changes to the rules governing the functioning of the political institutions, while, on the other, it is evident that the essential architecture of the settlement remains unchanged from the Good Friday agreement. However, in any event, issues other than the precise terms of the two agreements explain the DUP's shift from an anti-agreement to a pro-agreement position. In particular, when the DUP entered into government with Sinn Féin in May 2007, the Provisional Irish Republican Army (IRA) had put all its weapons aside to the satisfaction of the Independent International Commission on Decommissioning (in September 2005), and Sinn Féin had accepted the arrangements for the criminal justice system and for policing in Northern Ireland (in January 2007).

Where there appeared to be a large difference between the two agreements was in how they were reached. On 10 April 1998, the chairperson of the multi-party talks, the former majority leader in the US Senate, George Mitchell, announced that the eight parties participating in the negotiations had reached an agreement. The announcement was greeted with euphoria because expectations that a political settlement would be achieved had been relatively low. Thus, at the beginning of the same week, the deputy leader of the Ulster Unionist Party (UUP) had declared in relation to draft proposals that he would not touch them with a 40-foot barge pole. The timing of the agreement – Good Friday – seemed a favourable augur for ushering in a new dispensation. In contrast, when in 2007 the British and Irish governments announced their plan for the future of Northern Ireland and called it the St Andrews agreement at the close of difficult negotiations among the parties, it seemed like their last roll of the dice to save the Good Friday agreement. There was no euphoria in Northern Ireland at the announcement of this agreement, since the two main parties, the DUP and Sinn Féin, immediately made it clear that they had not consented to its text and that as far as they were concerned St Andrews was merely a deal between the two governments. For the superstitious, the publication of the St Andrews agreement on Friday the 13th was a poor omen for its success.

However, the Good Friday agreement and the St Andrews agreement had more in common than was immediately apparent. Each was the product of close cooperation between the British and Irish governments – an aspect of the Irish peace process that has been a complete success. It should also be said that their collaboration predates the peace process. Thus, the basis for the cooperation between the two states on Northern Ireland can ultimately be traced back to the early 1970s when both the United Kingdom and the Republic of Ireland became members of the European Community. Because of its potential effect on cooperation in other areas, this relationship gave both states a strong incentive to prevent the conflict in Northern Ireland adversely affecting their relations. After some ups and downs in the relationship between the two governments and in the context of threatening developments in Northern Ireland, the two governments decided to institutionalize their cooperation in an international treaty, the Anglo-Irish agreement of November 1985. While the Good Friday agreement was presented as a deal among the parties in Northern Ireland, in reality, like the St Andrews agreement, it too represented the two governments' best guess about what the Northern Ireland parties could be persuaded to accept. In short, the two governments were the real authors of both agreements, but that is their potential weakness, for it means that there has been relatively little sense of local ownership in either deal.

This is an appropriate point in the chapter to address the issue of what counts as 'external mediation' in the Northern Ireland peace process. If by 'external mediation' is meant (or includes) the role played by the British and Irish governments, then one would be bound to conclude that it has played a dominant role in the Irish peace process. However, if one confines the term 'external mediation' to the role played by actors outside the British Isles (or islands of Britain and Ireland), such as successive American administrations or the South African government, then one would have to conclude that external mediators have had relatively little substantive influence on the political settlements to date. Further, their mediation has almost invariably been conducted at the behest of or with the consent of at least one of the main parties (including for the most part the British and Irish governments, but also at times one or other of the Northern Ireland political parties). But if the substantive impact of external mediators has been slight, this does not mean that their role has been unimportant. They played a valuable role in assisting the two governments' effort to legitimize the Good Friday agreement. They also played valuable roles as intermediaries in the negotiations that permitted the two governments, for example, to float proposals and then to retreat without loss of face when it became evident that without amendment their wording would be a deal-breaker.

In particular, George Mitchell's chairmanship of the multi-party negotiations that led to the Good Friday agreement helped to put enough distance between the agreement and the two governments to avoid any impression that the agreement was a diktat; an impression that might have proved fatal to its endorsement by the electorate in Northern Ireland. His presence also made it possible for the governments to fine-tune their proposals to fit what the Northern Ireland political parties would be prepared to swallow, as Mitchell was a reliable sounding board on how far any of the parties could be pushed on the various issues. Mitchell, perhaps understandably, gives a rather different impression of his role and emphasizes the constructive contribution of the Northern Ireland political parties to the outcome, while underplaying the influence of the two governments on the process. This is Mitchell's account on learning that the Ulster Unionist delegation was prepared to accept the agreement.

> I took a deep breath and felt tears welling in my eyes – tears of exhaustion, tears of relief, tears of joy. I had to sit down.
>
> As majority leader of the United States Senate, I had learned

that when you've got the votes, you vote. Delay can only hurt. After long and difficult negotiations, the votes were there for the agreement.[2]

Mitchell does not mention that Sinn Féin reserved its position on the agreement at this moment of the decision or that one of the reasons that the Ulster Unionist Party had accepted the agreement had been its expectation that 'Sinn Féin was unlikely to sign up to the GFA'.[3] Mitchell's account can be contrasted with some of the salient points in Eamonn O'Kane's careful reconstruction of the negotiations from a wide variety of sources and extensive interviews of how the agreement was reached.

> By December [1997] the talks had not even led to agreement on an agenda. … In an attempt to break the logjam in January 1998 the two governments drew up and distributed to the parties the document, *Propositions on Heads of agreement* (HOA). … The document did give the talks a certain momentum, providing a focus for the discussions and marked the start of the serious negotiations leading to the GFA. … The next major intergovernmental draft of a possible agreement was that issued by Mitchell late in the night on Monday 6 April, 3 days before the proposed deadline for an agreement. The contentious aspect of this draft was the Strand 2 section, dealing with North–South bodies. Although Mitchell presented the whole document as his work, the two governments had drafted Section 2 and he was told he could not alter it.[4]

Another important dimension in arriving at the agreement was the element of 'constructive ambiguity' involved in the process. This meant that the Ulster Unionist Party could point to the assurance the party had been given by Tony Blair that decommissioning of IRA weapons had to begin straight away, while Sinn Féin was able to claim that the wording of the agreement did not require decommissioning to take place ahead of their entry into government.

Much of the architecture of the Good Friday agreement remains intact under the St Andrews agreement. The main feature of both is devolved government in Northern Ireland under an executive chosen proportionally on the basis of the parties' number of seats in the Northern Ireland Assembly. A controversial aspect of these arrangements is that not merely is the number of ministries determined in this way, but the parties choose the ministries they wish to run, with first choice going to the largest party, the second choice to the party with the next largest number of seats and so on, employing the d'Hondt mechanism.[5] Similarly, there is a North–

South Ministerial Council for the promotion of cross-border cooperation in Ireland, as well as a Council of Britain and Ireland as a forum for cooperation across the whole archipelago, as there was under the first version of the Good Friday agreement. The major change between the Good Friday agreement and the St Andrews agreement lies in the mechanism for the appointment of the first minister and deputy first minister. The Good Friday agreement provided that 'The First Minister and Deputy First Minister shall be jointly elected by the assembly voting on a cross-community basis.'[6] What a 'cross-community basis' entailed in this context was 'a majority of the unionist and nationalist designations present and voting'.[7] Incidentally, the first order of business in the assembly was the registration of members in terms of the designations (of Unionist, nationalist and other).

The provision in the Good Friday agreement was designed to secure the election of the first minister from the largest designation and the deputy first minister from the second largest designation. The joint vote was intended to convey to the Northern Ireland electorate that it was the start of a new era of cooperation across the province's sectarian divisions. The difficulty encountered in securing Trimble's re-election (with Mark Durkan as deputy first minister) in 2001 persuaded the two governments that a more automatic system for the election of the first minister and deputy first minister was necessary to avoid having to ask DUP members to elect someone from Sinn Féin or vice versa. Consequently, the St Andrews agreement stated the following:

> An amendment would be made to the 1998 Act on appointment of Ministers in the Executive. The Nominating Officer of the largest party in the largest designation in the Assembly shall make a nomination to the Assembly Presiding Officer for the post of First Minister. The Nominating Officer of the largest party in the second largest designation shall similarly nominate for the post of Deputy First Minister.[8]

However, when the legislation to implement the St Andrews agreement was being put through the British parliament, a very significant and remarkable change was introduced. The rule was simplified so that the largest party in the entire assembly (not the largest party in the largest designation, unless of course the same party) would get to nominate (and hence appoint) the first minister. However, this simplified process was stated in a convoluted manner in the fine print of the legislation. And yet, despite the confusing language, the Northern Ireland political parties had no difficulty understanding the implications of the legislation. The new rule meant that if Sinn Féin managed to become the largest party in the assembly, it would get to appoint the first minister. Given the symbolic importance of the position of first minister in the government of Northern Ireland, this provided a massive incentive to Unionists to vote for the DUP in order to prevent such an eventuality, which was a point the party fully exploited in the March 2007 assembly elections. The poor showing of both the UUP and the SDLP in the assembly elections reflected the rule's impact on their support (see election results below). Indeed, it was the outcome they sought under those circumstances, despite their previous commitment to support the centre ground of political opinion. The fact that the British government was ready to rig the electoral system in this way for the benefit of the radical parties was an indication of its conversion to the strategy of promoting an alliance of the extremes.

Another change the DUP insisted on for the St Andrews agreement was that there should be less scope for individual ministers to make decisions without reference to the executive than was the case in the previous brief periods of devolved government under the Good Friday agreement. The party wanted to prevent what has been dubbed 'solo runs' by ministers. However, with more decisions being referred to the executive and requiring cross-community support, there was an obvious danger that deadlock would be more frequent. A test of the new dispensation will be whether political paralysis can be avoided. This has occurred in other situations where the representatives of two communities have each been armed with a veto over decision-making. The most notable example is Cyprus in the early 1960s. Before the elections to the Northern Ireland Assembly on 7 March 2007, the stance of the major parties was that they expected devolved government to be a battle a day, but there was a marked softening of this rhetoric after devolution became a reality on 8 May 2007.

However, there are already some indications that the radically different positions of the two main parties have slowed decision-making, raising concerns that the system will freeze as a result of each side using its veto. Thus, the DUP has refused to introduce the Irish Language Act envisaged in the St Andrews agreement. The party has also made it clear that it has no intention of facilitating the transfer of policing and justice powers to the devolved government by the target date set in the St Andrews agreement of May 2008. Further, the party has rejected the proposal to build a sports stadium for Northern Ireland at the Maze because of plans to use part of the prison at the Maze site as a museum and conflict transformation centre. The DUP, which is determined to prevent it, has dubbed this plan a potential 'terrorist shrine'. Given these circumstances it seems probable that one of the main parties will seek to involve the two governments if a complete political impasse over these issues continues. In short, further mediation by the two governments cannot be ruled out. The obvious implication would be that the situation has not become normal and requires continued mediation. However, even in the worst case scenario of a political breakdown necessitating the resumption of direct rule, a return to the political violence of the years of the Troubles would be most unlikely.

At this point, it might be helpful to outline briefly the historical background to the current situation in Northern Ireland. The creation of Northern Ireland as a separate political entity within the United Kingdom dates back to the 1920 Government of Ireland Act, which unilaterally partitioned the island of Ireland. However, the negotiations that had taken place during the First World War between the British government, Unionists and representatives of the Irish Parliamentary Party, which favoured home rule, foreshadowed the partition of Ireland on the basis of a division of six and 26 counties. In this context, home rule meant the devolution of power to a parliament in Dublin.

The Government of Ireland Act established a parliament in Belfast to rule over the six counties of Northern Ireland. It also provided for the establishment of a devolved parliament for the 26 southern counties. The legislation also provided for a Council of Ireland to consider matters of mutual concern between the two parts of Ireland. However, due to the radicalization of opinion among Catholics during the course of the war that was reflected in the triumph of Sinn Féin candidates across Ireland in the general election of 1918, the provisions of the act were a dead letter as far as the southern counties were concerned. Violent conflict between British security forces and Irish nationalists culminated in negotiations that resulted in a treaty between the British government and Irish nationalists establishing the Irish Free State.

Civil war between supporters and opponents of the treaty ensued in which the pro-treaty forces emerged victorious. A common misunderstanding is that the civil war was fought over the issue of partition. In fact, partition was already a *fait accompli* by the time of the treaty and opponents of the treaty were more exercised about the issue of the sovereignty of the new state than about partition. A further factor reducing the salience of partition during the civil war was the treaty's provision for the establishment of a Boundary Commission to determine what the border between Northern Ireland and the new entity should be. That raised nationalist expectations that areas contiguous to the border with the Irish Free State that had nationalist majorities would be transferred to southern rule. In the event, these expectations were disappointed. The chairman of the Boundary Commission, Justice Richard Feetham, employed the argument of economic viability to propose only very modest changes on both sides of the existing boundary. So unsatisfactory were these proposals from a southern perspective that the Irish government quickly agreed with the Northern Ireland government that the commission's recommendations should be set aside in favour of the status quo. Unionists commonly refer to this agreement of 1925 as representing southern acceptance of partition. They argue that the 1937 constitution that de Valera enacted dishonoured this southern commitment to accept the border through laying claim to Northern Ireland in Articles 2 and 3 of its provisions.

The issue of the legitimacy of partition has been at the centre of conflict in Northern Ireland. Unionists wish Northern Ireland to remain part of the United Kingdom, while nationalists wish to see the dissolution of Northern Ireland as a political entity and the creation of a united Ireland. What gives added force to this political division is its coincidence with the sectarian divide between Protestants and Catholics. The primacy of the Unionist/nationalist divide means that all proposals for the governance of Northern Ireland have tended to be viewed first and foremost from the perspective of whether they seem likely to advance or to retard the possibility of a united Ireland. A difficulty for Unionists and for that matter for the British government is how partition tends to be viewed in the rest of the world. There is widespread sympathy for the view that Ireland should be a single political entity, as is also the case, for example, with regard to Cyprus. A further difficulty is that even if the principle of partition is accepted on the basis that Catholics and Protestants had different national identities (Irish and British respectively), it is hard to justify the particular border that was imposed on Ireland. On the basis of a provincial opt-out, the whole of Ulster and its nine counties should have been excluded from the southern entity, while an opt-out on a county-by-county basis would have resulted in a four-county Northern Ireland.

At the time of partition, Protestants outnumbered Catholics by roughly two to one within the borders of Northern Ireland. From a Unionist perspective, maintaining Protestant unity appeared to represent the safest way of ensuring the continuance of the union with the rest of the United Kingdom and this was the strategy that successive Unionist governments adopted from 1921 until the early 1960s. The consequence was a further reinforcement of the divisions between Protestants and Catholics that had consolidated into an ethnic divide during the course of the nineteenth century. In the period between 1921 and 1963 the Unionist government, with the help of local security forces, defeated a succession of violent challenges to its rule from the Irish Republican Army (IRA). Another factor that helped to keep the Irish question out of British politics was a constitutional convention that anything within the remit of the parliament in Northern Ireland should not be discussed in the House of Commons at Westminster. Consequently, issues of discrimination against Catholics and similar issues did not receive an airing in London. The people of Northern Ireland elected 12 representatives to the House of Commons, but throughout the first 40 years of Northern Ireland's existence these representatives, for the most part, formed an unnoticed addition to the Conservative benches and had little impact on British national politics.

Change came in the 1960s with a reformist government in Northern Ireland, which led to political divisions among Protestants and raised but failed to satisfy Catholic expectations. The result was increasing Catholic mobilization behind a civil rights movement, in imitation of the African-American civil rights movement in the United States, pressing for an end to discrimination. A Protestant backlash and violent clashes on the streets followed. This culminated in the onset of what is known in Northern Ireland as the Troubles, the term used to describe a prolonged period of violent disturbances between Protestants and Catholics. The beginning of the Troubles is generally dated from 5 October 1968 when clashes between civil rights demonstrators and police occurred in the city of Londonderry/Derry following the banning of the demonstration by the Stormont minister of home affairs. It is worth emphasizing that this violent breakdown of the political system preceded the deployment of British troops to Northern Ireland to aid the civil power. This followed in August 1969.

The beginning of the Troubles also preceded the formation of what was to become the main Republican paramilitary organization in Northern Ireland, the Provisional IRA. This group was formed in December 1969. The main Loyalist paramilitary organization, the Ulster Defence Association (UDA), was formed in September 1971. The term 'paramilitary' is used in Northern Ireland to describe private armies, not official agents of the state. Indeed, the term 'paramilitary organization' can be regarded as a less pejorative way of referring to terrorist groups, though it should be said that some of the activities in which paramilitary organizations engaged during the early years of the Troubles, such as patrolling their own neighbourhoods, did not amount to terrorism. The terms, Republican and Loyalist, are used to refer respectively to militant nationalists and militant Unionists, though the peace process has tended to undercut the implication that a readiness to use physical force or engage in acts of communal deterrence distinguishes them from their less militant counterparts.

The 1970s were the most violent years of the Troubles. At the beginning of the Troubles the British government sought to limit its involvement in Northern Ireland to reforming the security forces and maintaining the Unionist government while pressing it to introduce reforms. This approach failed. It radicalized Catholics who feared that, after the limited reforms, the situation in Northern Ireland would disappear from the international limelight and they would be left to face continuing Unionist domination of the political system. Following further violence in response to the introduction of internment without trial in August 1971, the British government introduced direct rule from London in March 1972.

Direct rule paved the way for a major political initiative by the British to reshape government in Northern Ireland. The Sunningdale agreement of December 1973 led to the establishment of a power-sharing government in Northern Ireland, which took effect in January 1974. However, the experiment in power-sharing lasted only five months before a general strike by Protestant workers brought down the executive. The provision in the Sunningdale agreement for the establishment of a Council of Ireland especially angered the Protestant community, which widely represented the deal as a slippery slope to a united Ireland. The resignation of the executive's Unionist members, in response to clear indications that the Protestant community rejected power-sharing, feared the Council of Ireland and preferred the alternative of direct rule from London, precipitated the collapse. A prolonged period of direct rule followed.

A crisis in the prisons in the early 1980s further polarized opinion. The denial of political status to Republican prisoners after 1976 prompted protests in the prisons, which the Republican prisoners escalated into hunger strikes in 1980 and 1981. Strong Catholic backing for the prisoners appalled the Protestants who viewed it as support for terrorism. The crisis in the prisons also precipitated the intervention into electoral politics of Sinn Féin, the political wing of the Provisional IRA. The British government's response to the rise of Sinn Féin was to address Catholic alienation through involving the Irish government on a consultative basis in the governance of Northern Ireland. To the Unionists' fury, in November 1985 the British government signed the Anglo-Irish agreement with the government of the Republic of Ireland, which enshrined the basis of cooperation with the republic in an international agreement. When protests on the streets of Northern Ireland failed to bring about the demise of the agreement, the Unionists were forced to contemplate negotiations to secure its removal and helped to create the basis for talks among the constitutional parties in the early 1990s.

Talks among the constitutional parties (those without paramilitary connections) did not result in an agreement, but nonetheless provided the impetus for a broader peace process. By 1992 there were signs that the Republican movement was seeking an alternative to continuing the Provisional IRA's 'long war'. Talks between SDLP leader John Hume and Sinn

Féin president Gerry Adams prompted the British and Irish governments to issue a joint declaration in December 1993. This promised that if the Provisional IRA brought its campaign of violence permanently to an end, a path would be opened for Sinn Féin's participation in negotiations for a new political dispensation for Northern Ireland. The response from the Republican movement was to seek further clarification of the government's stance, but finally at the end of August 1994 the Provisional IRA announced an indefinite cessation of violence. This was followed by a ceasefire declaration from the principal Loyalist paramilitary organizations in October 1994.

The paramilitary ceasefires did not, however, immediately lead to negotiations among the parties. Indeed, the delay was a factor in the Provisional IRA's abandonment of its ceasefire in February 1996. Elections for the purpose of establishing the parties to the negotiations were held at the end of May 1996. Despite the end of the IRA ceasefire, Sinn Féin fared well in the elections to the forum, as it was termed, though the party remained excluded from the negotiations. However, in Sinn Féin's absence, negotiations among the remaining parties made little headway. Following the election of new governments in both the UK and in the Republic of Ireland, there was a resumption of the IRA ceasefire in July 1997. This paved the way for negotiations among the parties, including Sinn Féin, but excluded two Unionist parties that left the talks when Sinn Féin joined the process. Ultimately, these talks led to the achievement of the Belfast agreement – commonly referred to as the Good Friday agreement – on 10 April 1998.

In referendums held in both Northern Ireland and the Republic of Ireland large majorities endorsed the Good Friday agreement. In Northern Ireland, however, this did not reflect a cross-community consensus because the basis on which the Ulster Unionist Party (UUP) sought support for the agreement was that it strengthened the union with Britain. Sinn Féin, by contrast, campaigned for the deal as a stepping stone to a united Ireland. Furthermore, the size of the 'Yes' vote in Northern Ireland – more than 70 per cent of those who voted – tended to mask the fact that whereas Catholics voted almost unanimously for the agreement, Protestants were evenly divided between 'Yes' and 'No'. This became evident in the voting for the Northern Ireland Assembly in June when pro-agreement Unionists achieved only a narrow victory over anti-agreement Unionists. Indeed, while slightly more pro-agreement than anti-agreement Unionists were elected, in terms of first preference votes, the anti-agreement ones actually outpolled the pro-agreement ones. That the anti-agreement forces contained within their ranks a number of members of the UUP, the leading pro-agreement party, complicated the picture. Henceforth, anti-agreement members of the UUP waged a relentless campaign against the pro-agreement leader of the party, David Trimble.

Disagreements over interpreting the Good Friday agreement on the question of decommissioning paramilitary weapons was an obstacle to its implementation and the disputes that followed exacerbated divisions within the UUP. Republicans rejected Unionist demands for the Provisional IRA to start decommissioning its weapons arsenal as a precondition for Sinn Féin's entry into government. A devolved power-sharing government eventually came into existence in December 1999, but because the IRA failed to start decommissioning it lasted only until February 2000. Following an IRA initiative to allow inspection of some of its arms dumps, the devolved government was re-established in June 2000, but the decommissioning issue continued to cast a shadow over its existence. Other IRA activities and not decommissioning as such, however, eventually brought the power-sharing experiment to an end in October 2002. Thus, after the IRA was accused of spying on the Northern Ireland government, the secretary of state suspended the institutions ahead of expected Unionist resignations from the executive over the spying scandal. By this time, the IRA had carried out two acts of decommissioning.

From the start of the peace process, the trend in electoral politics has been towards the two radical parties on either side of the sectarian divide, Sinn Féin and the anti-agreement Democratic Unionist Party (DUP) of Ian Paisley. Because of the different rules applying to elections at different levels, the elections are best examined as separate sets. The details are set out in the tables below. To avoid unnecessary complexity only the results for the main parties are included, except where there is an important reason to include the votes for the minor parties.

Election Results

Table 3.1 Assembly elections in 2007, 2003 and 1998: results for five main parties in terms of percentage of first preference votes and seats

Party	% vote 2007	Seats 2007	% vote 2003	Seats 2003	% vote 1998	Seats 1998
DUP	30.1	36	25.71	30	18.01	20
Sinn Féin	26.2	28	23.52	24	17.63	18
UUP	14.9	18	22.68	27	21.25	28
SDLP	15.2	16	16.99	18	21.96	24
APNI	5.2	7	3.67	6	6.50	6

Elections to the Northern Ireland Assembly took place in 18 six-member constituencies, with MLAs elected on the basis of the single transferable vote system of proportional representation.

Table 3.2 Westminster elections, 1992–2005 for main parties

Party	05%	Seats	01%	Seats	97%	Seats	92%	Seats
DUP	33.7	9	22.5	5	13.6	2	13.1	3
Sinn Féin	24.3	5	21.7	4	16.1	2	10.0	0
UUP	17.7	1	26.8	6	32.7	10	34.5	9
SDLP	17.5	3	21.0	3	24.1	3	23.5	4
APNI	3.9	0	3.6	0	8.0	0	8.7	0

The electoral system in Westminster elections in Northern Ireland is the first past the post or plurality system. Throughout the period, 1997 to 2005 Northern Ireland has had 18 constituencies. In 1992, there were 17 constituencies. In both 1992 and 1997, the constituency of North Down elected a Unionist candidate who did not belong to either of the two main Unionist parties.

Table 3.3 European Parliament elections, main parties' percentage of first preferences

Party	2004	1999	1994	1989	1984	1979
DUP	32.0	28.4	29.2	29.9	33.6	29.8
Sinn Féin	26.3	17.4	9.9	9.2	13.3	–
UUP	16.6	17.6	23.8	22.2	21.5	21.9
SDLP	15.9	28.1	28.9	25.5	22.1	24.6

The DUP candidate from 1979 to 1999 was Ian Paisley. He topped the poll on each occasion. In that period, one DUP candidate, one SDLP candidate and one UUP candidate were elected. In 2004, the SDLP failed to win a seat and Sinn Féin won a seat for the first time.

For the purpose of electing members to the European Parliament, Northern Ireland as a whole functioned as a three-member constituency electing three members by the single transferable vote system of pro-portional representation.

For the forum elections each of Northern Ireland's 18 parliamentary constituencies elected five representatives from closed party lists using the d'Hondt formula. In addition, each of the ten parties with the most votes across Northern Ireland as a whole was allocated a further two seats. For four of the parties, these 'extra' seats were the only seats they won. The forum as a whole had 110 seats.

Table 3.4 Forum election of 30 May 1996

Party	% Vote	Constit. Seats	Extra Seats	Total Seats
UUP	24.2	28	2	30
SDLP	21.4	19	2	21
DUP	18.8	22	2	24
Sinn Féin	15.5	15	2	17
APNI	6.5	5	2	7
UKUP	3.7	1	2	3
PUP	3.5	0	2	2
UDP	2.2	0	2	2
NIWC	1.0	0	2	2
Labour	0.9	0	2	2

Table 3.5 Main parties' share of votes and seats in local elections of 2001 and 2005

Party	% vote in 2005	Seats in 2005	% vote in 2001	Seats in 2001
DUP	29.6	182	21.45	131
Sinn Féin	23.2	126	20.66	108
UUP	18.0	115	22.95	154
SDLP	17.4	101	19.42	117
APNI	5.0	30	5.12	28

The elections to 26 local councils took place on the basis of multi-member wards using STV (single transferable vote). Voting took place on the same day as the Westminster general elections of 2001 and 2005.

The polarizing trend is evident in each of the sets of elections. Some of the detail is worth highlighting. In the Westminster elections of 1992 that preceded the peace process, the two main radical parties, the DUP and Sinn Féin, together won 23.1 per cent of the vote. By the Westminster elections of 2005, the two radical parties' share of the poll had risen to 58 per cent. It is worth noting that even when the DUP was not the dominant Unionist party, in elections to the European Parliament its candidate, who was Ian Paisley until the 2004 elections, topped the poll. A complication for the DUP was that the candidate elected to the European Parliament in 2004, Jim Allister, left the party over the St Andrews agreement and founded a new anti-agreement party, Traditional Unionist Voice, which made a considerable impact by winning 19 per cent of the vote in a local council by-election. Unlike the DUP, Sinn Féin fared relatively poorly in European elections until 1999. It first secured one of the Northern Ireland seats in the European Parliament in 2004 when John Hume stood down as the SDLP's candidate. Sinn Féin first overtook the SDLP in share of the vote in the Westminster and local council elections of 2001, though the gap between the parties was small and the SDLP won more local council seats than Sinn Féin.

The assembly elections of November 2003, in which the DUP clearly established itself as the Unionists' majority party and Sinn Féin entrenched its position as the nationalists' majority party, were crucial in terms of polarizing opinion in Northern Ireland. This had important political implications because a consistent principle in the British government's approach to Northern Ireland since 1972 has been that devolved government in Northern Ireland is only possible with the support of majorities in both communities. That meant that the chief focus of the government's efforts after November 2003 was inevitably on securing a deal acceptable to both the DUP and Sinn Féin. Only after others had already written off David Trimble as being unable to deliver a fresh deal, did the British government finally came to terms with the fact that his day was done, politically speaking.

While in December 2004 the government came close to establishing the basis of a deal between the DUP and Sinn Féin, subsequent events, most notably a major bank robbery the IRA was accused of carrying out and a murder during a bar brawl in which members of the Republican movement were involved, hardened opinion among Unionists and delayed an agreement on power-sharing between the DUP and Sinn Féin until 2007. This position was only reached after major changes in the positions of the Republican movement, including, as mentioned previously, the completion of the decommissioning of the IRA's arsenal of weapons to the satisfaction of the Independent International Commission on Decommissioning in September 2005 and Sinn Féin's agreement in January 2007 to give full-hearted support to the Police Service of Northern Ireland. The decommissioning was a major step towards persuading the British government to put pressure on the DUP to agree to power-sharing. This was on the understanding that if the party failed to do so by the deadline the government set, the latter might abandon any further attempts to achieve devolution and thus marginalize Unionists from the exercise of any political power in the process. In practice, the DUP had considerable success in delaying the day of reckoning, but after Sinn Féin's acceptance of policing, it had no further room for manoeuvre. Ultimately, DUP leaders faced a choice between either agreeing to a date for devolution with Sinn Féin, or precipitating the dissolution of the newly elected assembly in which the DUP had emerged as the largest party.

Two aspects of the Irish peace process commonly cause puzzlement to external observers.

(1) Why has the Republican movement (Sinn Féin and the IRA) settled for playing a role in British rule in Northern Ireland? Or, to put the point another way, why have the sworn enemies of British rule in Ireland signed up to be junior partners in the administration of the British part of the island?

(2) Why have Unionists resisted for so long a peace process that guarantees that Northern Ireland will remain part of the United Kingdom as long as that is the wish of a majority of people in Northern Ireland? Or, to put this point more sharply, why have Unionists been so unenthusiastic about agreements that involve nationalist acceptance of this principle of consent?

A popular joke in 1998 was that the Republicans had lost but were too smart to admit it, while Unionists had won but were too stupid to recognize it. That joke has lost some of its force as a result of the electoral success of Sinn Féin through the course of the last ten years. And much of that success has been built on Republicans' continuing commitment to Irish unity as their long-term objective and their confidence that with demographic change they will eventually achieve this through politics rather than the long war they abandoned in 1994. So that helps, in part, to explain the first puzzle.

The Unionists see the British government as having moved from actively supporting their membership of the United Kingdom to a position of effective if not rhetorical neutrality in which the British government has been willing to make numerous concessions to Republicans to ease their entry into the democratic process. While this falls far short of seeking to force Unionists to accept a united Ireland or threatening them with expulsion from the United Kingdom, it is not surprising that Unionists feel disadvantaged by the change and let down by the British government. Unionists were particularly disappointed that the British government did not abandon the peace process after the events of 11 September 2001. They would have been happier if the British government had treated the situation in Northern Ireland as part of the global war on terror and had abandoned the peace process. To be fair, Unionist attitudes have mellowed since 2001 as a result of the IRA putting its weapons down in 2005. Many Unionists now accept that as far as the current leaders of the Republican movement are concerned the war is over and consequently they make fewer speeches these days comparing Gerry Adams with Osama bin Laden. And that change of attitude does form part of the context of the miracle of 8 May 2007.

However, although lethal political violence is now largely a thing of the past, that does not mean that Northern Ireland has ceased to be a deeply divided society. Paradoxically, the divisions grew deeper during the course of the peace process. In answer to a parliamentary question in April 2007, a government minister acknowledged the existence of 57 peace lines in Northern Ireland – 46 mini-Berlin walls and 11 gates – to separate Protestants and Catholics from each other in the belief that in certain places, physical barriers are needed to stop low-level violence between the communities. The subject of peace lines received further attention a couple of weeks after the formation of the power-sharing executive in May 2007, when it was announced that the government was spending £100,000 to construct a new barrier across the playground of one of Northern Ireland's very few integrated schools because of the incidence of sectarian attacks in the area.[9] In terms of where people live, Northern Ireland is a highly segregated society and has become more segregated since the paramilitary ceasefires. It also remains socially and politically polarized, with an almost total correspondence between the categories of Protestant and Unionist, and Catholic and nationalist, and the domination of radical parties in each community. It is possible to admire how well the British and Irish governments have managed the situation in Northern Ireland in the last few years, while regretting that Northern Ireland is very far from reaching a point where the skills that the governments have demonstrated would not be required.

Some analysts of Northern Ireland, most notably Brendan O'Leary and John McGarry, have described the present situation as a triumph of consociationalism and extolled it for vindicating their long-term advocacy of an enhanced consociational settlement for Northern Ireland, which Brendan O'Leary has dubbed 'consociationalism plus'.[10] It is possible that if the St Andrews agreement provides the basis for stable government in Northern Ireland for the next ten years, such a stance may be justified, but we have certainly not reached that position yet. Approximately 15 years have passed since the initial paramilitary ceasefires in 1994. In that time, devolved government has been in place for five of those years. Clearly, under such circumstances the success of the Northern Ireland peace process cannot reasonably be attributed to the existence of a consociational settlement. In fact, it makes much more sense to regard consociationalism as an instrument of conflict management by the two governments rather than as having an independent role in its own right. It is worth noting that the achievement of a consociational settlement was not a priority of any of Northern Ireland's main political parties. A case might be made that such a settlement is broadly in line with the SDLP's pursuit of a political dispensation embodying political accommodation among the people of Ireland. However, not too much should be made of that. An anecdote making the rounds in Northern Ireland is that when presented with a piece of research on the role of the SDLP in the negotiations leading to the Good Friday agreement, the former leader of the SDLP John Hume pointed to the word 'consociational' and complained that it is not a word in the English language.

It might be thought that the fact that Northern Ireland remains politically polarized and residentially segregated would disqualify it from being a model of conflict resolution that anyone would want to export. That it is promoted as a model reflects how much importance the two governments, as well as Northern Ireland's pro-agreement parties, attach to the legitimization of the settlement through imitation of aspects of the Irish peace process elsewhere. The Northern Ireland case is by no means unique in this context. South Africa also sought to legitimize its transition through exporting its negotiated revolution as a model for conflict resolution in other cases and achieved a measure of success in influencing the Irish peace process. Now it is Northern Ireland's turn to influence peace processes from Kashmir to Iraq with official encouragement. (It may be noted that the Basque case is different because the Basque nationalists themselves took the initiative in trying to apply lessons from the Good Friday agreement to their own situation in the Lizarra Declaration.)

An obvious problem in promoting the Northern Ireland model in many but not all contexts is that Northern Ireland is not an independent state, but merely a region within a much larger state. An Iraqi parliamentarian made that point very forcefully in a seminar at Queen's University in March 2008. He was a member of an Iraqi delegation visiting Northern Ireland at the invitation of the British Foreign Office to learn the lessons of the Irish peace process, with the implication that it would be of benefit politically to Iraq. Understandably, a number of the Iraqis expressed the view that the problems Iraq faced were of a completely different order from those that Northern Ireland faced. They particularly stressed the importance of the regional context of Iraq's political difficulties. The problem of trying to compare Northern Ireland with deeply divided societies that are independent states is compounded when due weight is given to the dominant role the British and Irish governments have played in the process. It recedes somewhat if the emphasis is placed on Northern Ireland as an example of the success of consociationalism. The absence of local commitment to the consociational settlement makes it difficult to justify that emphasis, at least as yet.

4

International Engagement and the Yugoslav War of Dissolution

James Gow

International efforts, first to prevent the break-up of Yugoslavia and then to manage it and end the War of Dissolution, resulted in the emergence of the six formally sovereign states that formed the Socialist Federative Republic of Yugoslavia, and later one contested territory, which was part of one of those states, declaring independence in February 2008. It also resulted in a compromise on key principles, with the central objective in the first phase of major armed hostilities apparently contradicted in the second. Thus, there could be little argument that international diplomacy failed in notable ways, while securing significant achievements in others.

The initial well-meaning but hurried and ill-planned venture of the then European Community (EC) led seemingly ineluctably to the expansion of the EC role to include the Organization for Security and Co-operation in Europe (OSCE), the Western European Union (WEU) and the United Nations in various ways, and eventually to incorporate the North Atlantic Treaty Organization (NATO) and the United States. With each inevitable increase in international involvement, the international stake rose.

The Yugoslav war moved from being an important question for European stability and security and a test of the then CSCE's brand new Conflict Prevention Centre, to being a test of the future of EU common foreign and security policy. From there it moved to being a test of UN diplomacy and UN peacekeeping; then to a test of European, transatlantic and East–West relations and post-cold-war cooperative security. Finally, it became a test of NATO credibility and with that of international and particularly US credibility, culminating first in the conclusion of armed hostilities in Bosnia and then in the handling of Kosovo. Taken as a whole, the handling of the Yugoslav war demonstrated that it was possible for international action to be instrumental in ending the conflict and generating arrangements for peace. The latter had to be underpinned by the same type of engagement and commitment, for without commitment to the follow on, securing agreement was likely to be futile.

The international record on the Yugoslav war confirms that the conditions for obtaining a settlement, or for allowing failure, rest on five fundamental characteristics – timing, appropriateness, cohesion, armed force and political will.[1] I shall approach these in four stages, three of which concentrate on the first phase of the war (1991–95) in the western theatre of the region with a particular focus on Bosnia, which became central to international involvement and where, eventually, the end of hostilities in this theatre was secured. In the first of these sections I offer an overall assessment in which I elaborate the five fundamentals just identified in the context of failure and qualified success in the region. I then go on to consider the linked issues of political will and the use of force, particularly with regard to Bosnia. In the third section – again taking note of the five factors already identified – I investigate why an early major peace initiative failed while a later phase of peace talks with a different plan met with eventual success. In the final section I consider international engagement over Kosovo in the southern theatre in the light of the preceding analysis, exploring the ways in which the same five fundamental features applied.

A Peacemaking Assessment: The Fundamentals of Failure and Qualified Success in the Western Theatre

Five fundamental features characterized the international handling of the Yugoslav war – bad timing, inappropriate measures, incoherence, absence of political resolve and lack of preparedness to use armed forces. The most important of these was political nervousness about the use of force to back policies and ensure respect. The dissipation of the Contact Group during 1994 and subsequent moves towards a potentially more robust use of force demonstrated the indispensable need for both cohesion and political will. Bad timing was always a problem. International efforts suffered from the start because by the time the EC arrived to mediate between Belgrade and Ljubljana, the declarations of independence had been made and it was too late. The EC later tried to broker an agreement based on the republics' confederal positions – Belgrade had rejected their declarations of independence – but once force had been used against Slovenia and Croatia, there was no real prospect of their being able to accept reintegration into a Yugoslav state. This involvement came late in the day considering that for several months, if not three years, there had been clear signals that a situation was developing that required attention.

The international community generally reacted to, rather than anticipated, events. Consequently, action that could have made a difference three or six months earlier came late and usually with too little commitment. The clearest example of this was the fate of Bosnia, where there had been unmistakable signs that the republic was teetering on the brink of war for over a year. By August and September 1991 the Yugoslav army had started to deploy tanks at major communications points throughout the country, had all but abandoned barracks in the major towns in non-Serbian populated areas and had dug in heavy artillery on high ground around the towns. It is important to recall that international recognition did not cause war in Bosnia, though the Serbian camp used it as a pretext and to fuel its campaign. When the Serbian arsenal began to destroy Bosnia in March 1992, the international response was meagre in that there was an internationally coordinated move to recognize the country's independence. The Bosnian Serbian leader, Radovan Karadzic, had been explicit about the threat of widespread violence. Also, the EC and other parts of the international community were clearly aware of the threat because from February 1992 onwards the EC Conference and other international efforts were geared towards avoiding war in Bosnia. The EC adopted the Serbian camp's idea of ethnic territories or 'cantons'.[2] While its negotiators saw it as a way of appeasing the Serbs and avoiding war, it was in reality a charter for 'ethnic cleansing': ethnically designated cantons created the basis for ethnically pure territories.

Some months later, in the wake of the terror that swept the country in the spring and summer, the EC–UN backed International Conference on Former Yugoslavia (ICFY) in Geneva came up with a plan that might have accommodated any genuine fears in the Serb communities in Bosnia. A working group under the Finnish diplomat Martti Ahtisaari came up with a constitutional plan that took ethnicity into account as a factor rather than a starting point. Its end product was a set of regions containing ethnic majorities but constitutionally designed to be multicultural (see below). However, by the time the Ahtisaari plan (now called the Vance–Owen plan) was placed on the negotiating table, 'ethnic cleansing' had already taken place.

A further example of inappropriate measures was the decision to declare 'safe areas' in Bosnia and make a commitment to implementing them. Two, Srebrenica and Zepa, were never going to be viable, while two others, Gorazde and Bihac, were on crucial strategic axes in the war and therefore always unlikely to be left alone as 'safe areas' by the Bosnian Serbs. In so far as they were left alone, they would be zones in which elements of the Bosnian army could prepare for action. Sarajevo and Tuzla, for reasons of size and either international presence or degree of control by Bosnian government forces, would remain the focal points of fighting, but were unlikely ever to become completely vulnerable to military operations. It was certain, however, that without secure logistics lines and a large UN presence, the isolated enclaves in eastern Bosnia would be indefensible. They would therefore be hostages to fortune and no more than symbolically 'safe'. This placed the UN on a hook for a variety of reasons. First, the Security Council had made a commitment to protecting these areas; second, the United Nations Protection Force (UNPROFOR) was unable genuinely to deter attacks purely by a presence in the 'safe areas'; third, deterrence relied on the threat of using close air support to defend the troops, or possibly air strikes, in response to bombardment of the areas; and fourth, the vulnerability of the troops on the ground in those areas, deployed in small pockets and cut off from the main force, neutralized the threat of using air power. In such a situation there would always be calls to take action, as in Security Council declarations, and then inevitable and bitter criticism when the amalgam of UN, NATO and other international instruments failed effectively to implement the ill thought out 'safe area' concept.

The 'safe area' concept was drafted almost on the back of an envelope at the time of the Washington Declaration of 22 May 1993 as a face-saving device for foreign ministers seeking to overcome the divisions within their ranks presenting a positive front. This was a deformed manifestation of the importance of cohesion in the international response to the war. Indeed, the inappropriateness of steps taken and the way in which the international response lagged behind events can be explained largely in terms of the nature and composition of the various bodies involved. All were intergovernmental organizations, all required discussion and agreement between member states, and some required consensus before decisions could be taken. Therefore, over a controversial question such as the collapse of Yugoslavia there was much disagreement between the individual governments that made up the international agencies. This made quick responses impossible in situations that required them.

Differences of opinion were most notable on the questions of recognition, the deployment of military personnel and the use of armed force. Even where there was agreement on what to do, there were different perspectives on implementation. Once it had been decided that the European countries would offer troops to support the UN's humanitarian effort in Bosnia, there were differences of emphasis between the French, who wished to use the WEU to plan the operations, and the British, who favoured NATO for that role. Later, on the question of enforcement of a UN air exclusion zone over Bosnia, the USA wished to have the right to strike targets on the ground and in Serbia, whereas the French preferred to limit operations to Bosnia and, if possible, to aerial targets. This was a reflection of the general tension between the aerial bullishness of the USA and the greater caution of those carrying out the humanitarian mission with troops on the ground.

The crucial problem concerned compliance and the use of force. The pattern of international activity indicated that, although there were numerous efforts to mediate, progress towards either ceasefire or political agreement only emerged after some form of coercion had been applied, usually against the Serbian camp. However, the logic of this pattern was not readily extended to the use of armed force.

Even after almost a year of war, the Vance–Owen plan, despite its complexity, had a role to play in ending hostilities in Bosnia. The plan involved creating ten provinces in a single Bosnian state, in each of which there would be a multiethnic government and, in nine of the ten, a governor nominated by one of the three constituent ethnic groups (the capital, Sarajevo, would have a separate status). Both in January and in May, agreement on all elements of the Vance–Owen plan appeared close, and on each occasion an apparently growing threat of US-led air strikes helped to induce Serbian cooperation. However, the cooperation proved short lived when it became clear that the organization of a force to implement the plan was still subject to debate and that some crucial countries, notably the USA, were reluctant to get involved if their ground troops would be required or if it appeared morally unacceptable to them.

The reluctance of relevant governments to commit their armed forces in the Balkans (or for good or bad reasons to commit them more extensively where commitments had been made), had the effect of giving a green light to those who would go to the limits of what they could do without being brought to account. As one senior UN official engaged in handling the Yugoslav break-up observed: 'Force is the ultimate arbiter and any diplomatic policy that does not rely on carrots and sticks will not really get you very far. Without a club in the closet, without a credible threat of force, policy becomes bluff, bluster.'[3] From the outset, categorical declarations that there would be no use of force stripped diplomatic efforts of one of their key instruments: the threat of force in circumstances where other means proved inadequate or unpersuasive.

Using Force: The Political and Military Equations

There were many aspects to the international debate on using force. The issues used in arguments included history, ethics, interest, the basis for armed action (both political and legal), the nature of the conflict and the resources required, available or in use.[4] From the point of view of those in Western capitals facing the question of an armed intervention, the matter was not clear cut. While it was evident that Belgrade had been responsible for initiating large-scale organized campaigns of violence in Bosnia (which the UN Security Council Chapter VII resolutions recognized, especially on sanctions against Serbia), the aggression was not a classic cross-border adventure involving a well-established member of the UN, as with Iraq and Kuwait. It was, rather, a hybrid war. The continuing presence in Bosnia after independence of the JNA (the Yugoslav People's Army), loyal to Belgrade, meant that although there were significant incursions across the River Drina between Serbia and Bosnia, there were also 80,000 troops already based in Bosnia. Their presence there was a consequence of Bosnia's predicament as a state emerging to independence from the Yugoslav federation.

The transitional nature of the situation in Bosnia confused some of the questions relating to the basis of intervention. So too did the fact that it was only in part a war of external aggression. That the bulk of the JNA and later its successor, the army of Republika Srpska, comprised Serbs from Bosnia, gave the war a strong element of internal conflict. Civil wars are conventionally (and to some extent prudentially) judged to be matters internal to the state and therefore subject to the general proscription of interference in domestic affairs, though in reality there is often external backing for the different sides. Even though there was a critical question over the inviolability of the state's borders, the internal dimension was a counterweight to the need to take similar action, particularly where there was little appetite for doing so.

However, for all the factors of practicability and principle, which complicated the question of military intervention in Bosnia, the crucial matter was the politics of intervention. Experts and officials generally recognized the complexities of the situation in Bosnia and the region, but there was also a general awareness that only the use of force, or perhaps the threat of it, would decisively affect events on the ground. While much was made of military figures' comments about their fears of sending troops to Bosnia, those fears were generally less to do with the strictly military factors involved than with concerns about the relationship of the use of force to political objectives.

For example, when Field-Marshal Sir Richard Vincent, chair of the Military Staff Committee at NATO, took the rather unusual step of publicly voicing his worries, he was widely reported as having said that, without a proper political dynamic, military intervention in Bosnia could parallel the Charge of the Light Brigade. Less attention was given to the fact that his point concerned not the use of force but its link to a political objective. Even less noticed was his reported private assessment that intervention was possible and necessary at different levels.[5]

That opinion could be heard in private discussion from many, if not all, corners of officialdom, both civilian and military. The assessment was that politicians were the major constraint on policy. In a different way, Douglas Hurd conceded this when he sheltered his own rather timorous record and reluctance to lead the way behind the failure 'of other governments to propose committing an expeditionary force'.[6]

More strikingly, the understanding the then NATO secretary-general Manfred Wörner expressed was that the reason there had been no military intervention was that the politicians making up those 'governments lacked "political will"'.[7] Various plans had been made and policies recommended of a more interventionist nature, but ministers had not had the stomach for them. If there was an overall policy failure, its central feature was the absence of armed force as a bottom line. The reason for that absence was the lack of 'political will' to act forcefully in a transitional situation that appeared to be both laced with risk and not absolutely essential.

Because politicians in almost every significant country decided from an early stage of the Yugoslav break-up that the situation was practically and politically uncertain, unclear, complex, danger-ridden and potentially costly, they were unlikely to resort to armed intervention. Also, since the only clear common perspective to emerge was that the problem was too difficult to be dealt with using the kind of armed force that might be made available, it was more or less ruled out. It was that mixture of no intelligible political aim and political queasiness that most prompted the fears of senior military personnel.

With Western political leaders concerned mainly about popular opinion and the need to win votes at the next election, the prospect of the mission going wrong made them reluctant to contemplate intervention seriously enough, especially given the complexity of the problem and its apparently intractable nature. The fear of another Northern Ireland, Dien Bien Phu or Vietnam weighed heavily on politicians' minds. Particularly critical in this respect was the shadow of Vietnam hanging over US political and military leaders. Because of the USA's key role in NATO, as well as the size of its armed forces, no substantial military intervention with ground forces was conceivable without its involvement. Of course, much of this discussion was based on the prospect of large-scale intervention. One alternative for the future use of armed forces, from countries like the UK and France, would be a modernized return to past imperial practices – small, high-quality forces designed to strike at the heart of the enemy, which could have been relevant had there been a decision to use force in Bosnia.

Had the USA been prepared to commit its ground troops, then there would have been every prospect that the UK, despite all the worries of its foreign and defence secretaries, would have served alongside them.

Likewise, whatever French rhetoric might suggest, France was committed in practice to international operations in a way that made it hard to imagine Paris not being associated with any intervention there might have been in Bosnia.

The USA was therefore the linchpin of any concerted international military operation. Both the Bush and Clinton administrations were hamstrung by domestic considerations – the need to deal with the country's economic difficulties; lack of confidence that there would be public support for an intervention, especially if it went wrong; absence of a perceived interest significant enough to overcome the Vietnam legacy to commit forces; and the absence also of a political campaign to explain such a commitment to the public.

In the final analysis, the critical factor in the Western countries' failure to intervene was the USA's refusal to put ground troops into the ring. Only when Washington was forced to accept the inevitability of placing troops on Bosnian soil – either to underpin international withdrawal and complete failure or to implement a peace accord – could international diplomacy begin to address all the fundamentals of its failure. The same attributes of international diplomacy were appropriate for Vance–Owen and Dayton. The conditions for success of both were the same. Dayton was concluded where Vance–Owen was condemned because there had been crucial changes in those conditions. As I shall argue in the following section, apart from securing an end to the war, the international community gained less from the agreements negotiated at Dayton than it would have done from implementing the Vance–Owen plan. The conditions for implementing both plans were, however, the same. Dayton succeeded where Vance–Owen failed because there was a willingness to use force and, crucially, because the USA supported rather than opposed the plan, which I shall demonstrate through a comparison of the two. The analysis relies on drawing out the elements that characterized the failures of international diplomacy prior to Dayton.

Comparing Peace Plans: Vance–Owen and Dayton

The Vance–Owen and Dayton plans were two major international attempts to achieve a settlement in Bosnia and to bring the Yugoslav war of dissolution to an end. In attempting to assess why one worked and the other did not, I shall weigh up the plans themselves, as well as the aims, situation and resources of the four main groups involved – the Serbs, the Bosnian government, the Croats and the international community. The terms 'the Serbs' and 'the Croats' have been explicitly adopted here to include Serbia and the Serbs outside Serbia, and Croatia and the Bosnian Croats. As indicated, the most important difference between the two plans was the US position. Although there were several differences between the plans and the conditions under which they were discussed, this was the critical one.

A peace plan needed to represent the desires of the international community as well as to present arrangements for an accommodation between the Bosnian belligerents. Any plan, therefore, had to be understood in the context of the aims of all concerned. At the heart of this was the essence of the war – the clash of state projects between the Serbs wanting to establish new borders through force, and other Yugoslav republics, notably Croatia and Bosnia, seeking to uphold the integrity of the existing borders.

There were changes in the aims of the parties involved between the pre-Vance–Owen and Dayton periods. In the early stages of the conflict, the Serbs had three aims – to establish the borders of a new entity (whether a mini-Yugoslavia, a Great Serbia, or a Union of Serbian States); to establish the territorial contiguity of Serb areas; and to make those areas ethnically pure. By the time of the Dayton talks, it was clear that there were divisions among the Serbs. The Bosnian Serbs still sought new borders, meaning either independence or union with Serbia, or both. Serbia, however, appeared to have abandoned this project, at least temporarily. The common Serb aim continued to be contiguous and ethnically pure territories.

At the beginning of the war, the Bosnian government was interested in Bosnian state integrity; promoting a multicultural society; protecting the position of Muslims in the country; and gaining international support. Although the emphasis on maintaining a multicultural society continued to be declared, as the conflict progressed the Bosnian government's unstated aim became increasingly concerned with the Muslim position. While the overall aim continued to be the maintenance of Bosnia as a state, as far as a divided leadership had a core aim, it was to maximize the weak Muslim position *vis-à-vis* territory, political influence and military capability.

The Croats were always in a more ambiguous position. Their aim, like that of the Bosnian government, was to preserve the territorial integrity of Croatia; however, like the Serbs, they were also inclined to seek new borders by seizing parts of Bosnia; their desire to keep on the right side of the international community explained these contradictory aims. By the time of the Dayton talks, however, Croatian aims, while still ambiguous, had at least become a little more coherent. The importance of Croatia's territorial integrity had been established as a priority and much done in connection with that intention. The trade-off for foregoing their ambition to establish new borders was a substantial increase in their influence in

Bosnia. Finally, in addition to having their cake and being able to eat most of it, the Croats were able to establish good international ties, particularly with the USA.

Finally, the international community's aims at the time of the Vance–Owen plan fell into two categories. Over Bosnia, three objectives were considered desirable – uphold the principle of state integrity and resist attempts to change borders through force; resist ethnic purification; and deny the Serbs contiguous territories. The international community also wanted to maintain common positions and avoid making commitments judged too great, including the use of force. The Vance–Owen plan was designed to accomplish the three objectives on Bosnia and to square a circle by satisfying the international community's self-focused aims.

Although all three of the goals in the first category remained aspirations, after the demise of the Vance–Owen plan and certainly by the time of the Dayton one, international aims no longer opposed territorial contiguity and (*de facto*) ethnic cleansing. Even the desire to maintain a unified Bosnian state was weaker in the Bosnian peace settlement agreed at Dayton. While the Vance–Owen plan envisaged demilitarizing Bosnia, the Dayton one accepted that the state would have at least two armed forces for the foreseeable future. This was more realistic as an approach and the issue was to be dealt with in the talks on regional stability agreed at Dayton. It also lent continuing encouragement to ideas of permanently dividing the country. On the international side, while US criticism under-mined the chances of a common front on the Vance–Owen plan, that did not apply to the Dayton process. Most critically, the decision to avoid using force had given way to a decision to use force, or its potential, constructively.

These changes in aims reflected changes in the situation and resources. In 1993 the Serbs had more than enough weaponry but relatively little manpower. As a result of their initial superiority, they controlled up to 70 per cent of Bosnia and 22 per cent of Croatia. This gave the Serbs in both countries a strong psychological advantage. However, their position relied on support from Belgrade. As the Bosnian Serb leadership attempted to pursue a separate line, backing from Belgrade, while never completely cut off, was greatly reduced and this had a serious impact on capability, morale and the renewal of some resources.

For the Serbs, however, the most critical change in situation apart from their own intra-Serbian problems concerned the amount and effectiveness of force used against them. The Bosnian Serbs were able to defy Milosevic and the international community over the Vance–Owen plan because there was no use of force available to encourage them. As the Vance–Owen plan anyway ran counter to their aims, they had no desire to accept it. Under duress, the plan was signed, but carried the chance of eventually being rejected because there was no prospect of its being enforced. By the time of Dayton, both the Croatian and Bosnian Serbs had, by contrast, faced a substantial use of force by their enemies in the war, as well as by the international community, which was also now prepared to provide a strong ground force under NATO command to implement the deal. In this situation, being psychologically and physically diminished and without backing from Belgrade for resistance, the Bosnian Serbs were forced to accept terms and to allow Milosevic to negotiate for them.

The Bosnian government's situation and resources had also changed. Its army had huge manpower potential, but was short of weapons. Although enough weapons had been smuggled into the country to increase the number of troops, these had mostly been quite small. The Bosnian government had developed a large infantry force, but lacked the heavy calibre weapons with which to damage the Serbs seriously. That there was relatively little territory under government control compounded the situation and what territory there was often had to be defended on all sides and was cut off from easy access to arms supplies.

In a weak position militarily, the Bosnian government had no option but to rely on international support; therefore, constrained by the need to sustain international sympathy, it always directed its actions towards an international audience. Although probably unhappy about a plan that envisaged a division of Bosnia, the Sarajevo government was likely to go along with it to keep on the right side of international opinion. Aside from international opinion, the Bosnian government was in a difficult position psychologically. During the course of the war, particularly in the early stages, it had lost control of most of the country in which it represented the decimated and displaced Muslim community. This placed the government in the position of a victim and apparent loser. The sense that any agreement might be regarded as an admission of defeat encouraged the Bosnians to fight on, even were this to prove futile, for the sake of dignity.

By the time the Dayton plan materialized, the Bosnian government's situation had been modified. It had been able to arm many of its manpower reserves and had been carrying out operations jointly with Croatian forces. As a result, the Bosnian Serbs had been forced off substantial tracts of land and Bosnian pride repaired a little. Even more significantly, the combined use of force by NATO planes in the air and the artillery of the Rapid Reaction Force supporting UNPROFOR on the ground, dealt the Bosnian Serbs a substantial physical and psychological blow. In doing this, it provided a boost to the Bosnian government and made it far easier psychologically to make terms. It was also encouraged to do this by the fact that although Sarajevo might have preferred to continue the war in order to press the Bosnian Serbs further, its dependence on both Croatian and international, especially US, support meant that it was in no position politically or militarily to do so when Zagreb and Washington had decided it was time to call a halt. (Indeed, to have tried to continue alone might only have opened the way for the Croats to turn on the Muslims again.) The Bosnian government was constrained from going further, but had achieved enough to find honour in a settlement.

The Croats, consistent with their ambiguous aims, were in an equivocal situation. Croatia, like Bosnia, had begun the war in a significantly weaker position than the Serbs. However, it had been able to acquire weapons, including heavy weapons and aircraft, via its maritime and continental, non-Yugoslav borders. As a result, by the second half of 1995, the Croats had a better ratio of men to arms than either the Serbs, excluding Belgrade, or the Bosnian government. Whereas the former had weapons and the latter manpower, Croatia had men and weapons (albeit fewer men than the Bosnian army and fewer weapons than the Serbs). Zagreb was able to use this capability, with Washington's muffled approval, to restore control over most of Croatia. It was then able to press its position with the USA and with the Bosnian government by giving assistance to the Bosnian government in western Bosnia. Thus, despite some international criticism of Croatian army behaviour in the campaign in Croatia, Zagreb had been able to offer itself as a strategic pivot for the Americans. Psychologically, the Croats were confident of their usefulness to the Americans, of their victory within Croatia's borders and of their influence in Bosnia, whatever happened.

The biggest changes between spring 1993 and autumn 1995 were in the international sphere. When the Vance–Owen proposal was put forward, the military presence in Bosnia was not geared towards a major use of force and, deployed as it was in small packages along long communications lines, was vulnerable. However, among the more significant contributors to UNPROFOR, was a NATO command prepared to take on the role of implementing the Vance–Owen plan. However, Washington was dead set against using US troops, either as part of an operation while the conflict continued, or to implement an agreement. By the end of 1995, in terms of manpower and military capability, there were two significant differences. First, the insertion of a UK–France–Netherlands Rapid Reaction Force, in the summer of 1995, along with a force reconfiguration, which began as a result of the hostage taking crisis at the end of May, meant that there was a less vulnerable force on the ground with a greater capability for using destructive force purposefully. Second, crucially, the USA had accepted that it would have to place its forces on the ground in the event of a settlement. That made a settlement both more likely and more credible.

These movements on the military side reflected significant political and diplomatic shifts. The Vance–Owen plan was designed to serve international interests without making too many international sacrifices. In the end, although it had some degree of political backing from most parts of the international community, it was clear that there was an absence of coherent approval for the plan, with the USA leading the way with an attitude that was to make implementation of the plan impossible and so allow the Bosnian Serbs the luxury of being able to reject it. A lack of political commitment to making the plan work reinforced the USA's lack of cohesion. Where the USA opposed the plan, no European government was sufficiently committed to it to carry it forward; and the Russians, who did try, were easily rebuffed by Washington – with important consequences for Russian attitudes in the future.[8]

Circumstances were radically different for the Dayton plan. The whole international community, including the major players in the Contact Group, were behind this American initiative, which reflected the strong political commitment of all involved, particularly the USA. It also signalled the willingness to commit troops to a settlement implementation regime – that is to back diplomacy with force if necessary.

The Vance–Owen and Dayton plans were very different from one another. The Vance–Owen one offered more in terms of the international community's original aims. Its system of provincial governments maintained a single Bosnian state; its provision of ethnic proportionality in government maintained the principle of multiethnicity; and its placing of Province 3 denied the Serbs any sense of territorial contiguity. Beyond providing a mechanism with which to secure international aims, the requirement for demilitarization, though making implementation more difficult, enhanced the chances of reconstituting a unified Bosnia. In these senses, it was a better plan than the one achieved at Dayton.

It is ironic that the Clinton administration effectively destroyed Vance–Owen through allegations that it rewarded aggression and condoned ethnic cleansing. The Dayton accords accepted the principle of an ethnically-defined Serbian territory that ran contiguously from eastern Bosnia across the north and onto the northwestern part of the country. The principles of resisting ethnic cleansing and Serbian territorial contiguity had been conceded. Although Washington condemned the Vance–Owen initiative for such concessions, the plans and its negotiators had made significant formal efforts to avoid them. Having refused even to try to implement the Vance–Owen plan on these grounds in 1993, the USA was prepared to oversee and contribute significantly to a deal that was worse in respect of the principles at stake.

The Dayton plan did, however, secure the absolute minimum for the international community, namely agreement on Bosnia's territorial integrity and on its continuing independent, political and legal international personality. This secured the principle of resisting attempts to change borders through force. However, the future of that partitioned Bosnian state would be fragile for some time to come and would depend almost entirely on international, especially US, commitment. One major shadow was the continuing presence of more than one armed force – another significant and unfavourable contrast with the demilitarization envisioned by the Vance–Owen plans in terms of principle.

The Dayton plan had two advantages over the Vance–Owen one. First, it was easier to implement. The numerous boundaries of the Vance–Owen provincial map were replaced with one single (albeit long and winding) border between two entities. This certainly won more favour in US military thinking than the Vance–Owen one had. It is difficult, however, to see this as overwhelming compensation for abandoning the principles involved when the Vance–Owen plan, for all its complexity and imperfections, could have been the framework for an implemented settlement.

The most significant advantage of the Dayton plan over the Vance–Owen one was, of course, its success. It was agreed and implementation begun almost immediately. This, in itself, was a substantial and welcome achievement. All credit was due to the American diplomatic team that had engineered this outcome. Peace at the cost of some principle was, by this stage, both inevitable and preferable to continuing a war in which ethnic lines of division would become more pronounced and bitterness deeper. However, it is difficult to avoid the conclusion that similarly strong US support for implementing the Vance–Owen plan in 1993 would have ended the war two and a half years earlier and on better terms.

There were important differences in the conditions prevailing between the Vance–Owen and Dayton plans. By the time the Dayton one materialized, the situation on the ground was such that no party had sufficient interest or prospect in prolonging the fighting and therefore had some interest in a settlement. This was true in terms of territorial control, strategic position and psychological attitude. However, without these changes and despite the belligerents' reluctance, a settlement could have been agreed in 1993.

The changes that made a real difference were at the international level. On the ground in Bosnia, the salient changes flowed from the appointment of General Smith as UNPROFOR commander and the force reconfiguration and reinforcement, which occurred in 1995. However, these shifts were only indications of what might have been possible in 1993 had there been strong moves towards implementing the Vance–Owen plan. In the final analysis, the critical differences between 1993 and 1995 lay in the degree of diplomatic cohesion behind the initiatives and the preparedness to use force. The US position was central to both of these. With the USA at the heart of diplomacy, those it had criticized gave their backing and entrusted it to accomplish the task. In doing so, they were more confident in the possibility of using force and moving towards implementation of a settlement because the United States had placed a major stake on the outcome and committed a good deal of political capital to achieving it. It was unfortunate that this US commitment had not been present in 1993 to forestall a further two and a half years of war. This US commitment was sustained into the peace to prevent a return to war in Bosnia, until the point where most US troops could be withdrawn and NATO handed over formal responsibility to the EU (although many of the same forces remained in the smaller EUFOR).

The Kosovo Coda: Different Details, Common Characteristics

In 1995, many players in the international community considered the Yugoslav war to be over, at least provisionally. Yet, in 1998–99, there was another major international engagement, this time over Serbia's southern province of Kosovo. Because of its formal status as a province – under the Yugoslav federal constitution Kosovo was not a federating sovereign state – it was not treated on the same terms as those states in the process of dissolution, either internationally, or among the states feuding on the basis of that constitution. While it is possible to see this as a separate armed conflict, it was in reality the continuation and conclusion of what had gone before. Slobodan Milosevic's Serbian project to create new patterns of populations and borders through ethnic cleansing in Belgrade's western theatre (Croatia and Bosnia) had spun to its southern theatre, its province of Kosovo, a historical Serbian homeland with an overwhelmingly ethnic Albanian population. There, in line with the record in the western theatre, the strategic solution to competing claims of statehood was to remove a substantial part of the ethnic Albanian population through ethnic cleansing – a mixture of killing, forcible expulsion and fear-induced flight. The core of international involvement lay in two linked sets of action. The first was an attempt, at EU-sponsored talks in Rambouillet and Paris in early 1999, to negotiate an agreement on arrangements for self-government and security in Kosovo. In the Western design, these talks would provide the basis for an agreed deployment of a NATO-led Kosovo Force (KFOR), which would underpin security and be a physical obstacle to further ethnic cleansing and which also, Western analysis concluded late in 1998, Belgrade was planning to extend with a major new campaign the following spring. The second area of action was a NATO threat to bomb Serbia with air power if it stood alone in refusing to accept the Rambouillet document – perhaps the biggest real incentive for the Kosovo Albanians to agree to the terms proposed.

Many observers saw Kosovo as where the Yugoslav federation first began to unravel in the 1980s when there was unrest among young ethnic Albanians and repression by the Serbian authorities. It was also where many thought that the business would finally be concluded. While this might appear to be the case (and we certainly hope that the armed struggle is over) there was still a possibility in 2008 that the international community – more particularly, major Western countries – had made a gamble aimed at securing peace and security in the region that could well have snatched a failure from the opening jaws of a success. Time, driven by future events, would tell. Meanwhile, the same five features that shaped the first phase of international engagement in the war, albeit with different dimensions and details, can be judged to have determined the relative successes and failures, including the latest step that might yet turn gold into base metal. Here I shall assess the issues of timing, appropriateness, cohesion, force and will regarding Kosovo in the light of previous experiences in the western theatre and during the first phase of the Yugoslav war, which, for better or worse, significantly informed international diplomacy in the second.

Timing was a crucial factor in the international handling of Kosovo. Three notable examples stand out. First, the major international impetus at the Rambouillet peace talks in early 1999 to gain agreement on political and security arrangements for Kosovo, including an international presence there, came too late in the day to offer any real prospect of success. The Kosovo question had rightly not been on the agenda at Dayton when the Bosnian peace accords were struck and the necessary parallel issues concerning Croatia handled in the margins. Kosovo had nothing to do with the Bosnian peace process directly and the scale of business there was such that it could not have been accommodated. As it was, the Dayton plan almost failed at the last moment. None the less, many observers and Kosovo Albanian activists thought that the Kosovo question should have been dealt with there. While this judgement is wrong, it hints in the right direction. Kosovo was not a matter for the Bosnian peace accords, but rather than being allowed to slip into the background as international diplomats, having secured a peace deal for Bosnia, breathed sighs of collective relief, Kosovo should have been given concerted attention before the armed conflict began in 1998. By the time that concerted effort emerged, it was quite probably too late: the newly emerging Kosovo Liberation Army, Serbian security forces and even major NATO countries had already cast the die of armed conflict.

A second example of poor timing was the introduction of Annex B, concerning military implementation, to the Rambouillet accord part way through the proceedings. Securing agreement to deploy an international security force that would block ethnic cleansing was a good reason to make a concerted international effort, but given the need to discuss issues, it probably could not have been made explicit at the outset. However, if it had been introduced earlier, there might have been more time for it to be explained and understood better – and, failing that, to make clear that Milosevic, as was probably the case, had no intention of reaching an agreement. Alternatively, had it been introduced only after agreement had been reached on all other matters, when it would probably have been too late, there might have been more chance of by-passing the issues it raised. As it was, the question of military implementation was introduced part way through the proceedings, giving Belgrade a chance to present it as a plan for occupying Serbia and an infringement of Serbian sovereignty that no country could accept. The reality was that it was a limited document – far more limited than the terms Belgrade eventually agreed for international military deployment in Kosovo; it had only two areas of activity for the force (cantonment and forced separation), by contrast with the all-encompassing security mission of the Kosovo Force (KFOR) that was eventually deployed. The Serbian objection focused on clauses drawn straight from the equivalent Status of Forces agreement for Bosnia, where war had affected the whole country and the provisions were unavoidable; these clauses made sense in terms of communications and access through narrow Serbia to Kosovo. However, the crucial thing in this was that US envoy Christopher Hill told Milosevic that he could suggest whatever changes he wished, but that Milosevic rejected his offer.

The third major case in which timing was an important issue involved the US-led push to support a declaration of independence by Kosovo, which eventually came in February 2008. It will be some time – perhaps decades – before the full repercussions of this post-Milosevic initiative settle. Time alone will tell whether it was another example of bad timing or a gamble played at just the right moment. However, it is possible to say that it was potentially risky. When it came in early 2008, there was a good prospect of the region's problems being well on the path to settlement in an EU context within a decade.[9] Initially, the chances of such an outcome appeared slim, or mixed. The assessment by those leading the process was that Kosovo was so unusual that its *sui generis* characteristics justified an approach that ran against the grain of the basic ordering of international society and of the diplomatic handling of the Yugoslav war and dissolution up to that point, namely sovereignty and upholding territorial integrity. This position was not easily maintained, except in the very narrow sense that a number of major Western countries agreed collectively to treat it that way, which they would not consider doing for any other case.

The period following the declaration of independence, at least at first, appeared to confirm that not only was the timing awry on coordination, but that the step itself was misjudged. This also makes it the first item to consider under the heading of inappropriateness. As General Raul Cunha, military adviser to the UN mission in Kosovo noted, the EU set too much store by the EU 'carrot' for Serbia, misjudging the extensive negative impact the handling of the issue in Brussels would have there; instead of the peace and security that EU security envoy Javier Solana predicted that Kosovo's declaration would bring, Cunha asserted that the EU position was 'hypocritical' and taking Kosovo in the 'other direction' on peace and security.[10] It was evident within two months of Pristina's declaration of independence, and its recognition by the USA and 18 of the EU's 27 member states, that the move enhanced neither the course of Serbian and regional integration with the EU nor the prospects of peace and stability in Kosovo. In both cases, there were setbacks that more patience might have averted.

With the court of history 'out' on the issue of Kosovo's independence, perhaps the greatest example of misjudgement over it was the mixture of false analysis and ultimatum that preceded NATO air action over Kosovo in 1999. With the diplomatic process of managing Kosovo and the EU-sponsored talks at Rambouillet in France as a focal point, the US-led coercion of Serbia – or more accurately attempted coercion of its leader Slobodan Milosevic – was profoundly misjudged. To a large extent, this approach was driven by US secretary of state Madeleine Albright's assessment that the Serbian leader was a bully who only responded to force. In significant part, the approach to Kosovo was predicated on the false conclusion that NATO air action over Bosnia in 1995 had forced Milosevic into ending the war there and going to Dayton for peace talks. The analysis in 1999 was, in effect, that similar coercion, whether or not it required an actual use of destructive force for effect, would lead to a desirable outcome at the Rambouillet talks. Thus, the USA and NATO issued an effective ultimatum to Serbia that it should agree terms or NATO would be prepared to use its air power.

The assumption was that Milosevic would either accept terms or need a show of force before doing so. Accordingly, operations for up to a week were envisaged. These assumptions were woefully misplaced. The least part of the mistaken analysis concerned the streak of self-defeating (sometimes spiteful) defiance in political culture that regards bowing to ultimatums as unacceptable – witness the triggers of the First World War as a whole and the Second World War in the region.

More major errors in this analysis concerned Milosevic's position and his relationship to the troubled territory in question. Bosnia was not his country, despite attempts to annex parts of it, but Kosovo was. There is a major difference for any political leader between defending a homeland – especially when the areas in question have great symbolic and historical importance for a country and its people – and adjusting interventionist behaviour elsewhere to strategic realities. More significant than this, however, was the false analysis that bombing had brought Milosevic to the negotiating table in 1995. The reality then had been his wanting an end to the war and being able to achieve that because the NATO air action removed the military commander General Ratko Mladic's control of events in Bosnia for 13 days – in effect, delivering him and the Bosnian Serb political leader, Radovan Karadzic, into Milosevic's hands. As a result, it was he, not they, who negotiated on behalf of the Bosnian Serbs at Dayton, reflecting, of course, his overall sway, which the NATO action had consolidated. Thus, using NATO air power over Bosnia served Milosevic's purpose of ending the war in the Western theatre. The threat and use of NATO air power over Kosovo had a different context and completely different effect, albeit one that Milosevic welcomed because it gave him cover for accelerated ethnic cleansing of Kosovo. Also, because NATO's action was seen as precipitating events on the ground, it was possible mistakenly to blame NATO for his forces' actions in Serbia and outside.

As with Bosnia, international, particularly Western, cohesion was an important factor at key moments. It was important in shaping the international approach to Kosovo's prospective independence, although never expressed in quite such clear or strong terms. It was only when international cohesion began to break down and policy making also ran into difficulties (although the policy being pursued was what prompted that breakdown) that some actors, most notably Russia, realized what the real agenda was. In the course of 2005–06, UN special envoy Maarti Ahtisaari worked on a plan intended to result in Kosovo's independence under international supervision by the EU, but here again explicit reference to Kosovo's independence was avoided in case it derailed the process. Development of the Ahtisaari proposal and talks around it were able to proceed in an apparently unified international environment. The only points of disagreement in the discussions were between Serbian and Kosovo representatives.

Wider disagreements emerged in spring 2007 when Belgrade and Russia understood the real agenda, which was Kosovo's independence rather than supervision, made explicit through references to sovereignty and territorial integrity in the replacement of UN Security Council Resolution 1244 (1999) and its binding status in international law under Chapter VII of the UN Charter. Sovereignty was a highly sensitive issue for China, which preferred generally to see Kosovo as a European problem and to let Europeans handle it, unless an issue of real interest came into play. China had been content quietly to allow Ahtisaari to proceed with his mission. Once it was clear that sovereignty and territorial integrity were to be questioned, China was only saved from having to make a stand by Russia, which began strongly to insist that only when there was full agreement to the Ahtisaari plan, including from Belgrade, could there be a new Security Council Resolution to endorse it and to replace 1244.

With the USA and EU set on a course of transferring responsibilities from the UN to the EU, as foreseen under the plan, it was with reluctance that adoption of the Ahtisaari plan was delayed and further efforts undertaken to achieve agreement from Belgrade. The determination not to delay indefinitely resulted in a messy approach and situation in which the EU collectively (with an element of disingenuousness) agreed through a silent decision-making process to deploy its mission to Kosovo on what was known to be the eve of Kosovo's declaring independence. The less than confident mechanism by which this decision was taken allowed the EU to make a collective decision, while formally the position under UN Security Council Resolution 1244 remained unimpaired. This immediately weakened the authority of the prospective mission. However, once the declaration of independence came, divisions between the EU member states, which were already known, became evident, with only two-thirds of the EU's 27 members recognizing the declaration that the EU had worked to coordinate. This less than convincing position was weakened as the official 15 June handover date approached, when EULEX, the EU police and security mission, was supposed to replace the UN. Tensions between EULEX and UN officials, especially military commanders, became evident, as did the realization that the UN mission would have to continue and work in partnership and in parallel with EULEX, even though EULEX leaders were steadfastly opposed to it. This international disarray did not bode well for security and development in Kosovo, at least in the shorter term.

The strong degree of international cohesion while Special Envoy Ahtisaari was preparing Kosovo's 'supervised independence' was an indicator of both the importance of international coherence – as marked by the subsequent absence of that factor – and of the dangers of excessive cohesion. In a sense, too great a consensus for too long resulted in poor assessment, poor judgement and a poor outcome. While there was a clear division between Russia and NATO countries over the threat to use force against Serbia in 1999, there was substantial agreement among the NATO members on the course of action. Again, a policy, strategy or approach that proved to be misguided and based on incorrect analysis, could be seen as the product of strong Western cohesion.[11] However, the generally greater value of international cohesion, if it can be achieved, should not be dismissed because of reservations such as this. Indeed, once armed force had been committed in 1999, one of the most important factors in its eventual success was the surprising degree of unity among NATO members, even when events did not go as foreseen. This was a surprise, in some regards to the members themselves; it was also a surprise to Belgrade, which, it might be presumed, had calculated that, once the initial week of operations had not achieved the imagined outcome, discord within NATO would undermine the alliance's capacity to act, with divisions among members meaning that the use of force would be stopped, or impaired, to Serbia's advantage. The coherence in NATO meant the opposite in practice.

Cohesion was an important aspect of NATO's eventual success in using force over Kosovo. However, the excessive degree of cohesion going into operations meant that the use of force was less well judged than it might initially have been. The issue of miscalculation regarding the mind of Milosevic has already been treated. Reference has already been made to planning that did not extend beyond one week for operations that actually continued for 78 days. However, these were not without problems, given unexpected weather conditions, for instance, and factors pertaining to the characteristics of the operations themselves.

There were three main problems associated with the operations – the limitations that political leaders imposed on them and the need for joint agreement on issues such as targeting; public perceptions of the operations and their purpose; and the commitment to use ground forces. On the first of these, NATO leaders had agreed that operations would be restricted to particular types of target. This meant there were disagreements between France and the USA over targeting bridges in Belgrade, which US air chiefs wanted to destroy but France's political leaders felt was against the humanitarian character of the action and would not achieve anything of real value. Another significant restriction on air operations concerned the decision to avoid targeting Serbian military personnel, as well as civilians, as far as possible. This complemented an approach that sought to separate Milosevic and his political leadership from Serbia and the Serbs as a whole, and recognized that the more Serbian citizens they killed the harder a successful outcome might be. However, from mid-May, which turned out to be the final two weeks of operations, there was a crucial change on this question. A new approach was taken in which a form of cooperation with the Kosovo Liberation Army on the ground would be used to flush out Serbian forces, creating 'kill boxes' for NATO aircraft. Thus, the restriction on killing Serbian military personnel was lifted. One indirect effect of this appears to have been word-of-mouth doubting of the official position in some parts of Serbia, as public gatherings questioned whether the number of official dead being buried tallied with the actual number of dead. Serbia could have continued its defensive operations, while withstanding such losses militarily. However, when word-of-mouth questioning began to undermine state television news, Milosevic could no longer maintain his official story and the confidence of the people in core constituencies.

The character of the operations also affected Western, international and Serbian perceptions of them. The ostensible aim of operations was 'humanitarian' – to impede and, if possible, stop, the commission of gross abuses of human rights by Belgrade's forces. This required elements of subtlety – hence the political restrictions already noted. It also required new thinking and creativity, which created tensions. The needs for restraint and creativity that such operations required particularly inhibited the US Air Force and led at times to a dialogue of the deaf between General Wesley Clark, supreme allied commander at NATO, who indicated a need to generate targets rather than simply work down a preordained list, and US Air Force chief General Mike Ryan, who wanted a list of targets to bomb. Had Ryan been allowed to bomb according to the standard US air power menu, the negative perceptions would have been greater than they were. As it was, the strategy of targeting the decision-making points of the ethnic cleansing campaign in Belgrade and northern Serbia, in particular, though making sense to those involved, was at odds with the general view that the place to stop ethnic cleansing was in Kosovo, with tactical operations to interdict the commission of criminal actions. There were, of course, tactical air operations over Kosovo, but these were incapable of intercepting every Serbian action and, had they been able to do so, would almost certainly have caused collateral deaths and wounding (as happened, on occasion, anyway).

The only feasible interception would have required the use of ground forces, the initial absence of which is the third characteristic of the operations to be discussed. For both political and operational reasons, ground forces had been ruled out. Politicians were reluctant to use them for fear of potential casualties and were relieved to receive military assessments to the effect that the time frame would be too short to deploy a suitable ground force. Also, the infrastructure for such a build-up was unavailable and would need to be constructed in Albania and Macedonia, which in turn would generate further political and diplomatic difficulties and be seen as NATO preparing to invade Serbia rather than as a response to ethnic cleansing. When, in mid-May, NATO leaders suggested introducing ground forces in a non-permissive environment (their initial intention had of course been to negotiate the deployment of such a force in a permissive environment), a decision that, in the end, was never taken formally, the scenario changed. The determination to use ground forces in combat, if necessary, while not singularly decisive in Milosevic's decision to sue for peace at the end of May, was a contributing contingent factor.

As in the western theatre in general and in operations related to Bosnia in particular, in the end diplomacy and force had necessarily to be linked and the key to success in both was political will. Any political conviction linked to the issue of cohesion could have been overwrought and produced miscalculations on Kosovo's independence, but resolute political will was at the core of success both at the peace process in France in 2008 and in the initial decision to use destructive force in 1999. Despite problems and negative perceptions, it was the will to persist and the determination to get the mission right, including being prepared to deploy ground forces if necessary, both to block Serbian action and to underpin the subsequent 'peace', that made the difference in 1999.

Thus, with different detail, the same factors that underpinned international engagement in the first phase of the Yugoslav war in the western theatre were also at the forefront in the later involvement in the southern theatre for Kosovo. These were timing, appropriateness, cohesion, the use of armed forces and political will. If these were aligned, international involvement prospered. In other instances, there could be elements of success, but these would be offset by the need to make adjustments in one or more of the other areas.

Conclusions and Considerations

There were important ways in which the work of institutions concerned with European and international security made a positive difference to the course of the Yugoslav conflict. In difficult circumstances and often with limited means, some of the bodies achieved more than their critics credited to them. However, they were not up to the challenge. Overall, for five reasons international action was ineffective or only of limited effect. The timing was wrong; there were inconsistencies; a lack of coordination and agreement; ever-present weakness over the linked issues of ensuring compliance and the use of force (or deployment of ground forces); and finally the question of political will, which underpinned all the other elements. Conversely, it was the correlation of these factors that underpinned success when it came. Ultimately, it was the political will, or lack of it, to back initiatives with the possible use of force that gave the Serbian leadership the scope to act and to seek to achieve, or obstruct, its goals. Where will was lacking, this severely impaired the credibility of collective approaches to regional crises and conflicts. A consequence of this was a greater propensity to use force by regional actors seeking either to change the political and territorial order or to preserve it.

It was evident in the demise of the Vance–Owen plan that, in the grand scheme of things, international efforts in Bosnia had failed. While the Dayton plan successfully ended the war, it cast a revealing light on the overall failure, for it exemplified what could have been achieved earlier for want of the political will that in the end drove the Dayton diplomacy. That commitment, including being prepared to deploy a ground force to ensure implementation of the accords, meant that a stake had been placed from which neither the USA, the EU nor any of the international bodies through which it had been managed could walk away. With slightly different contours, the same applied to Kosovo. The international strategic stake placed in these places and their futures, as well as the countries of the surrounding region – including Serbia, the mainspring (though not the sole source) of conflict in the region – meant that political commitment would have to be maintained indefinitely, or at least until the situation could be judged a permanent success. Success, where it came, at different stages, always coincided with strong US diplomacy, coordinated with others in a cohesive Western or international approach. Ironically, once more, this only underlined the scale of general failure, at other points, confirming, as it did, the way in which the lack of political will, especially in Western capitals, was the mainstay of international deficiency.

Like losing gamblers, the masters of international involvement in the Yugoslav crisis constantly hoped that they would strike it lucky. Having laid one losing bet after another on half-measures, diplomacy and non-violent pressures that failed to achieve their prime objective of resolving the conflict, the major powers and principal bodies responsible for European security, played double or quits. International diplomacy, with the USA at its heart, finally came through and the Dayton agreement was signed, but only in the ironic shadow of past failure and a present surrender of principle.

In this sense, both the USA and various European countries, even though they sometimes had radically different ideas about the situation in former Yugoslavia, knew and understood most of the detail. However, they still failed, individually and collectively, to gain a sharp focus on events in Bosnia and establish a perspective on its political future. Without such a perspective none of them could clearly analyse the situation or seriously address the question of military intervention. Probably there was no desire to do so. This was why the best opportunity to stop the war was missed with the demise of the Vance–Owen plan. Full or partial implementation of the Vance–Owen agreement was one of five obvious points at which a different international response might have made a crucial difference.

The same five features that run throughout the preceding analysis can be related to an important, though not yet raised, aspect of international affairs on which it would be appropriate to conclude. This concerns war crimes prosecutions at the International Criminal Tribunal for the former Yugoslavia (ICTY). When the UN Security Council set up the body in 1993, it was mainly a diplomatic gesture with little international consensus, except that the mantra of 'never again' was being uttered and some awareness of this had to be shown. Over the years, the initial bad timing of creating an ineffectual body in the middle of an armed conflict has been set in the shade.

While question marks remain about the ICTY's work, there can be little doubt that its record in raising and settling cases (only two of the 161 individuals indicted remain at large, though one of these, General Ratko Mladic, are among the most notorious) had been a success. Also, the tribunal has been instrumental in fostering peace and security in the region, in at least two major ways. Over Kosovo, without the indictment of Milosevic at the end of May 1999 (ironically, against the better judgement of international diplomacy, which would at that stage not have endorsed the chief prosecutor's move), it is unlikely that the Kosovo question would have come to the conclusion it did – and it would certainly not have done so at that stage. Milosevic sued for peace when he did because the accusation ran against his expectations and he needed to look for a quick way out of the Kosovo conflict in the hope that it would overturn the indictment. Its other more widespread impact was across the region, but with greatest effect in Bosnia. This was the way in which indictments and enforcement helped to transform the political and security landscape.

As a result, individuals associated with the misdemeanours of the past (and not only those publicly indicted, as it turned out) could be excluded from political processes. They could be physically removed as obstructions to peace, could remove themselves from the scene, or their political leaders and others could have them transferred to the custody of the tribunal with a view to taking the countries involved and the region as a whole forward. The role of justice and its instrumentalization, which became an essential part of settling the Yugoslav war, also depended on correlating the same five characteristics of success and failure that determined international engagement as a whole.

The Reactive Crisis Management of the European Union in the Western Balkans: Policy Objectives, Capabilities and Effectiveness

Stefan Wolff and Annemarie Peen Rodt

The member states of the European Union individually, as well as the EU as a collective of its members, have for some time been approaching ethnopolitical conflicts by trying to mediate in and facilitate negotiations, and help to implement and manage settlements. Nowhere is this more obvious than in the western Balkans, especially since both abysmal failures and remarkable successes characterize EU engagement in that region. This mixed record can be analysed from different perspectives. The EU and its predecessor organizations has always prided itself in being, among other things, a community of values in which democracy, human rights and the rule of law take on concrete meaning for the benefit of all citizens in each member state, regardless of ethnic, linguistic or religious background. This normative perspective has informed the EU's non-discrimination directives and policies, and has thus been one instrument of the management of minority–majority relations within EU member states. Yet, its success in addressing ethnopolitical conflicts within the EU itself, and even more so beyond its boundaries, has been limited.

Conflicts in Northern Ireland, the Basque region and Corsica persist at different levels of violence and intensity, causing loss of human life and material damage. For the states directly affected by these conflicts, and for others outside the present boundaries of the EU, there is therefore a second, more pragmatic area of concern in relation to ethnopolitical conflicts – security. This not only relates to the physical security of individual citizens and the state, but also involves a wide range of other dimensions of security. Ethnopolitical conflict also has immediate and longer-term consequences for socio-economic and environmental security, and is often intrinsically linked to other security challenges, including drug trafficking, weapons smuggling and illegal migration.

While conflicts within the EU as it existed before the 2004 enlargement were relatively well-contained, that is they did not pose major threats to the security and stability of the EU *per se*, the perception of far graver threats in post-communist Europe, large parts of which had aspired to EU membership since the early 1990s, prompted the EU to adopt a more proactive policy of managing ethnopolitical conflicts outside its boundaries than within them. This approach was, from the viewpoint of policy makers in Brussels, necessary because of the greater risk posed by such actual and potential conflicts in likely new member states and the EU's 'new' neighbourhood. It was made possible as a consequence of the collapse of communism, the end of the cold war division of Europe and the greater political and economic leverage that the EU gained over the respective countries. The fact that internal threats had remained relatively contained for decades, that member states facing such conflicts generally resented and actively blocked EU involvement in their management[1] and that conflicts outside the EU were perceived as potentially dangerous, has resulted in the EU beginning to create a framework of policies and institutions for the management of ethnopolitical conflict aimed primarily at non-member states.

In the following, we shall focus primarily on the European Union's evolving capabilities in the field of conflict management and offer an assessment of the current state of affairs. Yet, rather than just focusing on this 'internal' dimension of EU involvement in the western Balkans, we will also consider the EU's effectiveness from the point of view of the actual conflicts in which it became involved. We begin with a brief overview of the EU's early attempts to develop its own mechanisms and policies in this area and then examine in more detail the acceleration of this process in the aftermath of the Kosovo conflict in 1999. Since it has reached a status of being operational, the European Union has carried out five operations in Europe in 2003 and 2004, three of which are still ongoing. Two of these fall under military crisis management operations, and three under the category civilian crisis management.[2] Following a brief assessment of the EU's performance in managing ethnopolitical conflicts in the western Balkans to date, we shall conclude by drawing some more general conclusions about the EU's ability to meet present and future challenges of ethnopolitical conflict management in Europe and beyond.

The EU and its Balkan Failures: Institutional Reform and Capability Development since the 1990s

Institutional Reforms

Based on its respect for state sovereignty and its own experience of ethnic conflict, the initial response of the EC (later EU) to the Yugoslav crisis in the early 1990s was to attempt to contain the problem by seeking to keep Yugoslavia intact. European countries faced with ethnic conflicts of their own feared that if they supported the dissolution of Yugoslavia, it might encourage ethnic minorities elsewhere to push for independence. The EU therefore sought a neutral role as negotiator between the belligerent parties and was reluctant to recognize any one side as the aggressor. These negotiation efforts failed repeatedly, as violence broke out first in Slovenia and later in Croatia, Bosnia and Kosovo.[3]

The EU's further failures to respect its self-set criteria for the recognition of Slovenian and Croatian independence and its inability (along with that of the rest of the international community) to prevent the increase in and extent of the violence and large-scale disasters such as the 1995 atrocities in the 'UN protectorate' Srebrenica,[4] illustrate the continued failures of EU conflict management efforts in the former Yugoslavia throughout the 1990s.[5] These failures were largely due to the EU's internal struggle with its own inexperience in providing 'soft' as well as 'hard' security; it lacked the institutional structure and the military strategy and strength to back up its infant CFSP, which was simply not ready to deal with a challenge as complex as Yugoslavia.[6] What the EU as a conflict manager lacked more than anything in the 1990s, however, was the political will to act – and to act in unison.[7]

Lessons from these failures of the EU and the broader international community during the ethnic conflicts in the western Balkans throughout the 1990s were gradually learnt and a new European security architecture started to emerge in which different international organizations played their part and contributed to a cooperative, rather than merely collective, security order.[8] Characterized by principles of task and burden sharing, this new cooperative security structure emerging at the beginning of the twenty-first century, involves the same principal security institutions – UN, OSCE, NATO and EU – but with a new set of mandates, instruments and policies that (in principle) enable them to face existing and emerging security challenges. Within this new European security architecture, the EU occupies a central role. It is strengthened in its political weight through the enlargements, accession and association processes, and is diplomatically and militarily more capable as a result of the development of its security and defence identity and policy.

For the EU, lesson learning happened within an existing institutional framework – the Treaty on European Union (1992) revised by the Treaty of Amsterdam (1997) – in which crisis management is regarded as a policy area within the CFSP pillar and Common European Security and Defence Policy (CESDP), but owing to the complexity of the tasks, it also requires input from policy areas in pillars 1 and 3 (see Figure 5.1). Specifically, the Treaty of Amsterdam expanded a range of EU responsibilities to include 'humanitarian and rescue tasks, peacekeeping tasks and tasks of combat forces in crisis management, including peacemaking' (Article 17). These so-called Petersberg tasks have their origin in the June 1992 ministerial council of the Western European Union (WEU) at which the WEU member states agreed to make available military units for tasks conducted under WEU authority.[9]

Figure 5.1: The Place of Crisis Management in EU Policy

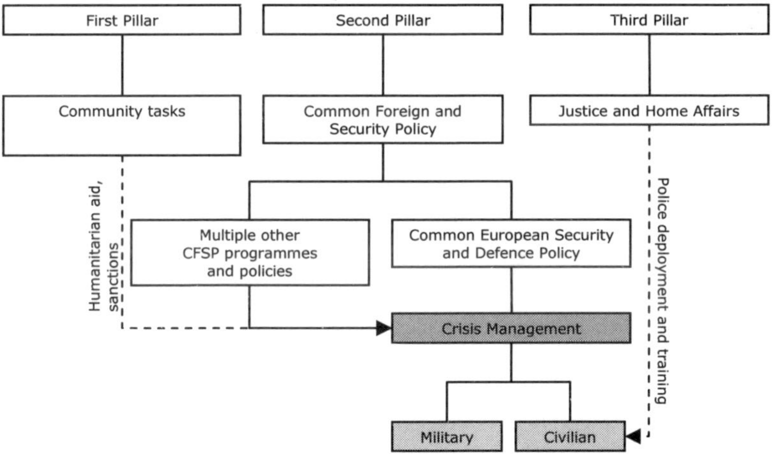

For the military component of crisis management, the European Council in Helsinki (1999) followed up on the decisions made at the Cologne meeting earlier the same year.[10] Comparing existing capabilities with the ambitious Petersberg tasks, the heads of state and government agreed on the Helsinki Headline Catalogue, which determined 144 areas in which capabilities and assets needed to be developed in order to enable the EU to fulfil the Petersberg tasks:

- commitment by member states to make available 50,000–60,000 military personnel deployable within 60 days and sustainable for up to 12 months;
- establishment of coordinating political and military structures within the Union's single institutional framework;

- development of a cooperation framework with NATO and third states.

Subsequent meetings of the European Council contributed to the further development of EU crisis management policy, particularly in relation to the improvement of its civilian component. The 2000 Feira European Council determined four priority areas for the improvement of the EU's civilian crisis management capabilities:

- police (commitment to the deployment of up to 5000 officers and training of local forces);
- strengthening of the rule of law (identification of 200 experts readily available for deployment, development of common training modules for human rights monitors);
- civilian administration; and
- civil protection.

The Treaty of Lisbon, which EU leaders signed in December 2007 reiterates the EU's continued commitment to 'assist populations, countries and regions confronting natural or man-made disaster' and 'promote an international system based on stronger multilateral cooperation and good global governance'. In particular, it confirms the EU intention to 'develop a special relationship with neighbouring countries, aiming to establish an area of prosperity and good neighbourliness, founded on the values of the Union and characterized by close and peaceful relations based on cooperation'.[11]

Four key innovations in the treaty seek institutionally to improve CFSP capabilities and may thus have an effect on the EU's future role as a manager of ethnopolitical conflict in the western Balkans and beyond:

- a new high representative of the Union in foreign affairs and security policy, also the vice-president of the commission, is to increase the impact, coherence and visibility of EU external action;
- a new European external action service, is to provide support to the high representative and work in cooperation with the member states' diplomatic services. The external action service shall comprise officials from the relevant departments of the general secretariat of the council and of the commission as well as staff seconded from the national diplomatic services of the member states;
- a single EU legal personality is intended to strengthen the Union's negotiating power by making it a more visible partner for third countries and international organizations; and

- special decision-making arrangements are to pave the way to reinforced cooperation among a smaller group of member states in the CESDP.[12]

As far as the decision-making process is concerned, the commission will no longer be able to make proposals in the area of CFSP, but should support specific initiatives of the high representative, who because he or she is also vice-president of the commission shall ensure consistency of the EU's external action. At the same time, the principle of unanimity is largely confirmed for CFSP, thus, preserving member states' ability to cast a veto on specific policy proposals. The Lisbon treaty limits the available CFSP instruments to European decisions (on actions, positions and arrangements for implementation). The so-called common strategies under the TEU are preserved in the Lisbon treaty as strategic guidelines set by the European Council and further elaborated by the Foreign Affairs Council.[13]

Civilian and Military Capabilities Development

Lord Robertson, the secretary-general of NATO (until the end of 2003) shortly after taking office in October 1999 emphasized that the three most important elements for securing the future of the alliance were 'capabilities, capabilities, capabilities'. What is true for NATO, the most powerful military alliance (albeit largely dependent on the USA in this context) is equally valid for the EU's crisis management capabilities, be they military or civilian in nature. In the EU context, the 'capabilities, capabilities, capabilities' dogma can be broken down into three main areas: capabilities to act, capabilities to fund and capabilities to cooperate and coordinate (see Figure 5.2).[14]

Figure 5.2: The EU's 'Capabilities, Capabilities, Capabilities' Problem

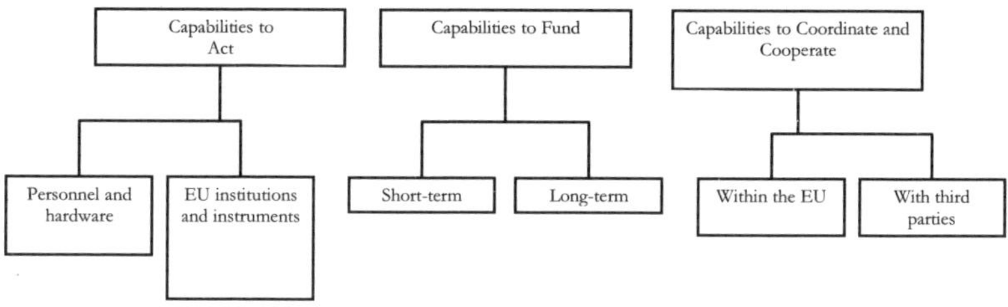

In terms of capabilities to act, issues of personnel and hardware were addressed at several European Council meetings following the inauguration of crisis management as a distinct policy under CESDP in Cologne in 1999. Specifically, the Helsinki European Council in 1999 agreed to the Helsinki headline goal, which was to set up the rapid response capabilities needed to fulfil the Petersberg tasks (see above). By the time the heads of state and government of EU members met again in Laeken in 2001, the headline goal had, in their view, been partially met, and they found that:

> through the continuing development of the ESDP, the strengthening of its capabilities, both civil and military, and the creation of appropriate structures within it and following the military and police Capability Improvement Conferences held in Brussels on 19 November 2001, the Union is now capable of conducting some crisis management operations.[15]

However, the council also recognized that there were a large number of deficiencies in areas crucial for the EU's ability to take on more demanding operations and emphasized that it had to improve coordination between the resources and instruments of military and civilian crisis management, strengthen its military capabilities, finalize agreements with NATO to gain access to resources (planning, military assets, command options) and implement already existing arrangements with other non-NATO partners.[16] NATO–EU cooperation has subsequently made significant progress in the form of the Berlin Plus agreement, a framework agreement on the EU–NATO partnership and an agreement on security of information.

The development of appropriate institutions and policy instruments also progressed significantly. The creation of the post of secretary-general of the European Council and high representative for CFSP (and the appointment of former NATO secretary-general Javier Solana to the post) was a significant step forward and indicated that the EU was prepared to follow up on its intentions with substantive commitments.[17] The new institutional structure, made permanent under the Treaty of Nice (see Figure 5.2) has to date proved reasonably efficient and effective. As for EU policy instruments, and emphasizing the multi-faceted nature of CFSP, Hill has aptly summarized the situation: 'the arrival of Joint Actions, Common Positions and now Common Strategies in the CSFP has spawned new initiatives such as the Stability Process in South-East Europe.'[18] In addition to these three policy instruments, 'statements' also form part of the range of options available to the council for the conduct of its CFSP.

Capabilities to fund various crisis management operations in the short and long term do exist within the EU. The provision of long-term funds for CFSP activities is normally not a problem; it certainly has not been a shortage of financial means that has impeded EU policy in the western Balkans. However, the complicated system within the EU to make the use of its funds transparent and accountable has, until two years into the existence of crisis management as a distinct EU policy, often hindered their rapid disbursement. An important contribution to the improvement of the EU's short-term funding capabilities, therefore, was the creation of the Rapid Reaction Mechanism (RRM) in February 2001. Its main aim is to 'allow the Community to respond in a rapid, efficient and flexible manner, to situations of urgency or crisis or to emergence of crisis'.[19] The RRM covers six dimensions of EU crisis management: 'assessment of possible Community responses to a crisis, conflict prevention in countries and regions showing significant signs of instability, acute crisis management, post-conflict reconciliation, post-crisis reconstruction and the fight against terrorism'.[20] Actions financed with funds from the RRM may be carried out by 'authorities of Member States or of beneficiary countries and their agencies, regional and international organizations and their agencies, NGOs and public and private operators with appropriate specialised expertise and experience' (Article 6) and must be implemented within six months. The RRM has a fixed amount of funds at its disposal each year, determined annually by the budgetary authority (Article 8). This was €20 million in 2001, €25 million in 2002 and €30 million in 2005. Of the 2001 funds, 64 per cent were spent on Macedonia alone, while in 2002 all new activities financed by the RRM took place outside the western Balkans, since then only one programme took place in Macedonia, while the rest of the RRM programmes were launched outside the Balkans. This underlines clearly the importance of the Balkans experience to other areas in which the EU is engaged in conflict management: institutions created in direct response to EU conflict management needs in the Balkans now form an integral part of the EU's broader approach to conflict management beyond this region, including in the ENP area.

Coordination and cooperation capabilities here relate to EU internal processes as well as to the EU's relations with third parties. Within the EU, these have two dimensions: a horizontal one (coordination among the three pillars) and a vertical one (between the EU as a supranational organization with its own institutional structures and the EU member states). At the external level, coordination and cooperation is essential in particular with NATO (see above) and, while potentially increasing EU dependency on NATO resources, has so far worked well. Especially in the western Balkans there has been a longer tradition of cooperation anyway (Bosnia and Herzegovina, Macedonia, Kosovo), and the EU took over SFOR in 2004 after having already assumed responsibility from an earlier

NATO force in Macedonia. The EU accords high priority to cooperation with third countries (namely non-EU and non-NATO members) and international organizations (UN, OSCE, UNHCR, NGOs). This is the case for two reasons: the EU is strongly committed to a multilateral approach and it recognizes the mutual benefits of cooperation with organizations that 'specialize' in different crisis management tasks. In the case of cooperation with NATO, permanent consultation structures have been created in the wake of the Berlin Plus agreements; in the case of cooperation with third parties the EU has clear procedures for coordination, including the establishment of so-called committees of contributing countries meant to give third parties an adequate role in the day-to-day running of a particular crisis management operation while leaving responsibility for overall strategic direction with the relevant institutions inside the EU. In addition, as recent experience in the western Balkans indicates, the EU also uses its ability to conclude bilateral agreements with third parties to put any crisis management cooperation on solid legal foundations.

The changes in the Treaty of Lisbon are intended to improve the EU's institutional capability to cooperate and coordinate better internally and externally and to act in a more coherent and efficient manner with regard to the CFSP. Furthermore, the amended article 28 of the Lisbon treaty states that the council shall adopt a decision establishing the specific procedures for guaranteeing rapid access to appropriations in the EU budget for urgent financing of initiatives in the CFSP framework, and in particular for preparatory activities referred to in Article 28 A(1) and Article 28 B; namely, joint disarmament operations, humanitarian and rescue tasks, military advice and assistance tasks, conflict prevention and peace-keeping tasks, tasks for combat forces in crisis management, including peace-making and post-conflict stabilization. The treaty also states that preparatory activities for such tasks that are not charged to the EU's budget shall be financed by a start-up fund made up of member state contributions. In this way the Lisbon treaty also increases the EU's short-term capability to fund its conflict management efforts.[21]

Testing Capabilities in the Western Balkans: EU Missions to Date[22]

The EU Police Mission in Bosnia and Herzegovina

The 2003 EU Police Mission (EUPM) in Bosnia and Herzegovina (B-H) was the first ever CESDP mission. It is part of a comprehensive pro-gramme of measures aimed at establishing rule of law in B-H and is envisaged to accomplish its tasks by the end of 2008. It succeeds the UN's International Police Task Force. EUPM's annual budget is €38 million (50 per cent provided directly by Brussels); personnel consists of 207 staff from 34 EU and non-EU countries. EUPM derives its legitimacy from Security Council Resolution (SCR) 1396 and a decision by the Peace Implementation Council (PIC) to accept EUPM to follow the UN Mission in B-H. EUPM is a crisis management operation and as such has a unified command structure within the single EU institutional framework, comprising the European Council and its SG/HR, the Political and Security Committee (PSC) and the EU Special Representative (EUSR) for B-H. The head of mission/police commissioner, who leads EUPM and is in charge of day-to-day operations, communicates with the SG/HR through the EUSR. The EUPM has two key priorities – fighting organized crime and ensuring the security of returnees. Apart from technical and professional assistance and training, EUPM is therefore also involved in the creation and consolidation of new institutional structures. Following an invitation by B-H authorities the EUPM refocused its mission in 2004 to support the B-H police reform process to develop and consolidate local capacity and regional cooperation in the fight against organized crime.[23]

Operation Concordia in Macedonia

Operation Concordia also followed on from a previous international mission, in this case NATO's Operation Allied Harmony. The background of this mission was to ensure sufficient levels of security and stability in Macedonia to enable the implementation of the 2001 Ohrid agreement. Concordia derived its legitimacy from a request by Macedonian President Trajkowski and UN SCR 1371. The operation fell within the remit of EU military crisis management operations and was the first ever CESDP deployment of military forces. It comprised 400 soldiers from 26 countries, again including non-EU contributor states. Operation Concordia was the first case for EU–NATO cooperation under the Berlin Plus agreements, that is the EU made use of NATO capabilities. Initially only assumed to last for six months, Operation Concordia was extended at the request of the Macedonian government until December 2003. Command of the operation rested with EUFOR headquarters.[24] Contributions to Operation Concordia were made by EU member and non-member states, the budget of €6.2 million was contributed by the EU with non-common costs borne by the participating states. As part of the day-to-day management structures, a committee of contributors had a consultative role in its decision-making procedures.

Operation Proxima in Macedonia

Operation Proxima became the second EU police mission in the Balkans. The mission was established at the invitation of Macedonia's prime minister. Its implementation was closely linked to the implementation of the Ohrid agreement. The mission was extended beyond its initial 12-months following another request by the Macedonian prime minister and was completed in December 2005. The mission personnel comprised staff from EU member and non-member states. Operation Proxima was deployed to five locations across Macedonia to monitor, guide and advise Macedonia's police force and promote European policing standards. The budget was €7.3 million for start-up costs and €7 million for 2004 running costs to be financed from the community budget. For the 12-month extension a budget of €15.95 million was agreed.

Operation Althea in Bosnia and Herzegovina

In 2004, the European Council decided to take over responsibility from NATO for securing the conditions for the implementation of the Dayton peace agreement.[25] The initial budget for common costs was €71.7 million to be administered by the Athena mechanism, which relies on financial contributions by EU member states determined on a GDP basis. EU member and non-member states participate in this operation. Perhaps more than any other ESDP operation to date, Operation Althea exemplifies the importance of cooperation among the international organizations making up Europe's security architecture. The EU takeover from NATO was only possible following the work of NATO's SFOR and the resulting improvements in the security environment on the ground.[26] The EU was able to rely on NATO assets and capabilities. NATO's deputy supreme allied commander for Europe was appointed as the operation commander for the military component of Operation Althea, and SHAPE simultaneously became the EU operation headquarters.[27] The command structure of Operation Althea again stresses close cooperation between NATO and the EU, which is under the political control and strategic direction of the EU's PSC, the EU operation headquarters at SHAPE in Mons, the EU command element at the Allied Joint Forces Command in Naples, and the headquarters of EUFOR at Camp Butmir in Sarajevo. The EU command element at the Allied Joint Forces Command is a crucial element in the coordination with NATO, for it ensures that EU operations in the Balkans conform to the EU's regional approach and cooperate closely with NATO operations in the Balkans. In addition, the EU closely coordinates its military mission with its police mission. As both are meant to contribute to the implementation of the Dayton agreement, cooperation with the PIC, the Office of the High Representative (OHR) and other international actors engaged in the region (primarily the UN and OSCE) is essential.

The Effectiveness of Ethnopolitical Conflict Management in the Western Balkans

In 1993, Christopher Hill predicted six future functions of the then European Community (EC) as an international actor, including that of 'regional pacifier' and 'mediator of conflicts'.[28] In each case, he made explicit reference to former Yugoslavia and pointed out that it fell to the EU 'to act as mediator/coercive arbiter when the peace of the whole region seems under threat' and that there had been 'considerable diplomatic effort and creativity in the early stages of the Yugoslav imbroglio'.[29] However, it was only after the NATO intervention in Kosovo in 1999 that the EU started to play a really important role as regional pacifier and mediator of conflicts in the western Balkans, albeit with varying success over time. No matter which perspective one takes on the EU's conflict management policy in the western Balkans, it is the largest donor and the organization with the biggest presence in the region, having contributed significantly (partly in cooperation with third parties) to the stabilization of the countries in the region and their reconstruction to date. This general view at least partly testifies to the existence of EU conflict management capabilities in the western Balkans. A closer look at the operations conducted there will, however, allow us to make better informed statements about the status of capability development in general.

Current EU capabilities appear to be sufficient to take on tasks of the kind required in the western Balkans at present. The EU was able to mobilize sufficient personnel, hardware and funds to sustain them. It had the institutional framework and enough instruments available to make the necessary decisions and proved capable of a certain level of cooperation and coordination within its own structures as well as with third parties. This relatively positive assessment of EU crisis management capabilities in the western Balkans after 1999, however, cannot necessarily be taken as a general indication of the readiness of the EU to manage conflict elsewhere and with a similar degree of success. While it is undoubtedly true that the 'CFSP, through the position of the HR for CFSP, has experienced in a very short time a substantial improvement in its coherence and visibility',[30] improved coherence and visibility do not necessarily translate into effectiveness. With respect to the western Balkans one could question whether the EU has indeed been successful. In Macedonia, for example, it could be argued that early-stage conflict management, despite the mobilization of significant resources, failed, and that it was only once the violent conflict had erupted that the EU (through conflict management measures) succeeded in brokering a deal between the fighting factions.[31]

Taking into account the complexity of the situation the EU had and still has to deal with in the western Balkans and the intensity of the conflicts it had to manage (in post-Dayton Bosnia and Herzegovina and in Macedonia) the EU has demonstrated that it has developed an institutional framework and set of policies that enable it to make decisions quickly, to provide adequate funds and personnel, and to cooperate and coordinate activities with third parties in ways that enhance its own capabilities and maximize the chances of successful crisis management. It is equally important in this context to bear in mind that since the failure of conflict management in the early and mid-1990s, the EU's capabilities have been improved significantly, enabling it now to undertake both civilian and military operations. In other words, it is able to back up its diplomatic efforts with credible threats of force where necessary. This evolution of expertise both at headquarters and ground level demonstrates a significant process of lesson learning at the institutional and operational level of EU conflict management capabilities.

However, the EU's relative success of late in the western Balkans not only derives from improved capabilities. In our view, its experience in the western Balkans cannot be generalized or easily exported. The distinct advantage the EU has in this region is that its policy of conditionality is much more effective *vis-à-vis* countries in which the promise of closer association with, and potentially accession to, the EU is credible and where both political elites and the general public are ready to make significant compromises to attain what many believe to be the only option for a viable future, even though there is now growing Euroscepticism in Croatia, Serbia and Bosnia-Herzegovina because the imagined solutions are not happening as quickly as envisaged. In other words, the success of EU conflict management in the western Balkans must be seen in a wider context in which conflict management is only one element in a comprehensive EU approach to a region. As Javier Solana pointed out as early as 2000, 'the European Union is uniquely placed for comprehensive action in the Western Balkans' and is 'the only institution capable of comprehensive action, ranging from trade, economic reform, and infrastructure, humanitarian assistance, human rights and democratization, justice and police to crisis management and military security'.[32] Without the clear long-term commitment of the EU to the western Balkans' prospect of EU membership, the incentives for political elites and the various ethnic groups they represent would be less powerful and thus the EU's ability to elicit short- and long-term compliance, which has been a major factor in the success of its conflict management operations so far, diminished.

A second note of caution regarding the EU's readiness to engage successfully in conflict management operations elsewhere concerns the availability of personnel and especially military assets. The commitments that EU member states made have not yet been tested to the full – the two police missions in Bosnia-Herzegovina and Macedonia have required only about 10 per cent of the total number of police officers committed by EU member states, and the two military operations Concordia and Althea have similarly required only around 12 per cent of the total committed troops. At the same time, the EU is now, for better or worse, locked into a framework of cooperation with NATO, which will perpetuate its dependency on NATO resources.[33] This may significantly decrease the EU's capability of autonomous action in situations where NATO resources are stretched or where disagreement within NATO prevents the use of certain resources by the EU.

A final factor limiting the generalizability or indeed transferability of the relative success of recent EU conflict management operations in the western Balkans is at the same time one of the very reasons for this success – the increasing familiarity with, and sensitivity towards, the situation in the region and the countries concerned, a long-standing network of information sources (EUMM), and previous experience in dealing with the political elites and populations in the area. One of the main shortcomings of EU capabilities, identified by the director general of the European Union military staff, General Rainer Schuwirth, namely 'shortfalls in all areas of intelligence gathering' and a lack of a 'common system for intelligence fusion', could thus be at least partially neutralized.[34]

Nevertheless, even the limited conflict management operations that the EU is currently conducting in the western Balkans are very valuable for its future role as a serious international actor. While it might be too early to proclaim the overall success of EU conflict management in the region, there are some indicators that a certain degree of success might not elude the EU on this occasion.[35] First of all, they have proven the success of institutional reforms within the EU and of the development of credible policies and instruments for conflict management. Second, they underline that the overall approach of the EU to the conduct of international affairs is fruitful – commitment to multilateralism (within the EU and with its partners elsewhere),[36] constructive and long-term engagement with conflict regions, combining short-term crisis management with long-term structural conflict prevention, and a fair balance between civilian and military strategies to maximize the short- and long-term impact of its policies. Third, by highlighting remaining deficiencies in EU conflict management capabilities, the EU now has an opportunity to draw lessons for the future before engaging in more ambitious and demanding operations elsewhere.

PART III

AMERICAN AND EUROPEAN EXPERIENCES IN THE MIDDLE EAST

6

American Middle East Strategy and the Bush Legacy

Robert J. Lieber

The foreign policy and grand strategy of the George W. Bush administration are often depicted as a dramatic departure from those of prior governments, both Democratic and Republican, yet historical continuities exist not only with post-Second World War administrations, but earlier eras as well.[1] Of course, the 11 September 2001 attacks on New York and Washington indelibly shaped the Bush policies. These events manifested an enduring and lethal threat to the United States and its national interests and brought to an end a post-cold war decade in which the international environment seemed no longer to pose grave dangers. The national security strategy documents of September 2002 and March 2006 embodied this threat perception. Their elements of pre-emption and the maintenance of American primacy have received the most attention, but it is important to understand that both multilateralism and democratization were also key components of these documents.

Not surprisingly, the Middle East occupied a central place in Bush's foreign policy. Outside observers have focused on differing and sometimes competing priorities in the State Department, National Security Council and Department of Defense, as well as among senior foreign policymakers and neo-conservative advocates. This approach does not, however, take the impact of 9/11 sufficiently into account. Moreover, many of the differences with previous administrations have been more of degree than of kind. With reference to the Israeli–Palestinian conflict, Bush's 24 June 2002 speech offered more explicit support for the creation of a Palestinian state than any of his predecessors had done, though the idea was already implicit in the approaches of President Clinton and the elder George H. W. Bush. The younger President Bush's insistence on Palestinian abandonment of terrorism and his unambiguous support for Israel's security were comparable too, though the demand to replace Arafat's corrupt and dictatorial rule as a precondition broke new ground.

Significant continuities are evident in other dimensions of Middle East policy as well, for example in approaches toward Saudi Arabia, the Gulf states, Lebanon and Iran. In addition, the commitment to democratization is rooted in a long tradition of American exceptionalism and embodies themes that can be identified in the statements of presidents since at least the time of Woodrow Wilson almost a century ago. The momentous decision to invade Iraq was fateful, but even here it is as well to recall that in 1998 Congress had overwhelmingly approved, and President Clinton had signed, the Iraq Liberation Act calling for regime change. Indeed, prior to the start of the Iraq war in March 2003, substantial majorities in Congress and the public supported the use of force.

In assessing Bush's Middle East policy, I do not attempt in this chapter to encompass the entire region, but instead shall focus on three key elements – the relationship with Israel and policy toward the Israeli–Palestinian conflict; democratization and the Bush freedom agenda; and, more briefly, strategies to confront the threat of radical Islamist terrorism.

America, Israel and the Israeli–Palestinian Conflict

Some 60 years after the founding of Israel, America and the Jewish state maintain a close and unique relationship.[2] The majority of Americans tend to accept this as something natural and long-standing. Foreign observers, however, do not always comprehend the nature of this connection, its durability and the deep-seated continuities on which it rests.[3] Some are merely puzzled or curious, others may reach for far-fetched explanations or – in worst cases – embrace sinister conspiracy theories to account for this bond.

To understand the basis of the relationship it is necessary to appreciate the uniqueness of Israel, the particular characteristics of the USA and the manner in which these legacies interact. For many Americans, Israel's creation in 1948 was an extraordinary accomplishment for a people who had sustained a religious and communal identity through the ages and who had managed to survive and overcome centuries of dispersion, oppression and powerlessness, as well as the ultimate horrors of the Holocaust. Their achievement constituted not only a remarkable historical and human saga, but one that harked back to the origins of the Old Testament and engaged the imagination and sympathy of many non-Jews.

For their part, the American founders saw themselves as creating a country free of the heavy burdens of the European past and that would be 'a light unto the nations' or, in the words of the Massachusetts Puritan leader, John Winthrop, in 1630, a 'city upon a hill'. Both expressions were drawn from Hebrew Bible references to Jerusalem and reflected aspirations for America to become a 'New Jerusalem'. Alexis de Tocqueville, writing in the 1830s, described how American society differed from its European counterparts and the way in which a 'nonconformist' Protestant religious tradition reinforced the country's sense of mission and identity. In the past century, as well as in more recent times, this sense of exceptionalism with its legacy of religiosity, liberalism and special purpose, can be found in the language of successive presidents: Woodrow Wilson's democratic idealism, Franklin Delano Roosevelt's four freedoms, Harry S. Truman's words in introducing the doctrine that would bear his name, John F. Kennedy's inaugural address, and remarkably similar expressions of purpose and belief in the speeches of Ronald Reagan, Bill Clinton and George W. Bush.

While these religious and historical inheritances are not the only basis for the US–Israeli connection, in subtle ways they reinforce it. The unique national origins of both Israel and the United States contribute to a relationship between the two countries that is both special and different from the kinds of impersonal international interactions commonly assumed among certain scholars, diplomats and foreign policymakers. As a result, observers who insist on narrowly conceived definitions of national interest may wrongly assume that a faulty strategy, lack of understanding or even nefarious motive must underlie a relationship that fails to conform to their deductive logic. In reality, the intimate Israeli–US bond results from a complex combination of past and present history, national interest, public opinion, shared values and religious beliefs.

This special relationship, however, took many years to develop. At the time of Israel's founding, leading American diplomats were mostly unsympathetic. President Harry S. Truman overcame the objections of the State and Defense Departments and of Secretary of State George C. Marshall in making the historic decision to recognize Israel moments after Israel's own declaration of independence on 14 May 1948. Truman was well read and had a keen historical sense. Reflecting on his role, he later remarked, 'I am Cyrus', invoking the name of the Persian king who had liberated Jews from their Babylonian exile some 2500 years earlier.

In its early years, Israel received only limited US support. Despite Truman's historic decision, the USA did not initially lift its arms embargo and eight months of bureaucratic delays stalled Israel's request for an urgently needed loan. In 1952, the Truman administration granted its first real economic aid, which amounted to $86 million. The Eisenhower administration, however, which took office in 1953, was quite cool toward the Jewish state. It pushed for a peace plan that Israel saw as jeopardizing its security and then engaged in forceful arm-twisting to secure Israel's withdrawal from the Sinai Peninsula after the 1956 war with Egypt. During these years, however, relations between non-governmental and civil society organizations expanded and intensified. These contacts were by no means limited to Jewish organizations. For example, the AFL-CIO developed a strong relationship with its Israeli counterpart, Histadrut.

To the extent that the Israeli state enjoyed a special relationship with another country, for the first two decades it was less with the United States than with France. Leaders in Paris and Jerusalem regarded Egyptian President Nasser and his promotion of Arab nationalism as a serious threat. Israel and France collaborated with Britain in the October 1956 Suez crisis and war, and France provided the original technology for Israel's nascent nuclear programme. Though President Charles de Gaulle broke with Israel and tilted toward the Arab states at the time of the June 1967 Six Day War, Israel was armed mostly with French weapons when it achieved its stunning victory.

American policy shifted only gradually, beginning with the July 1958 Middle East crisis. After the pro-Western monarchy of Iraq was overthrown, Israel allowed use of its airspace and provided other support for American and British efforts to stabilize the situation in Jordan and Lebanon. For the administration of President Eisenhower and Secretary of State John Foster Dulles, Israel became a significant regional asset in the face of increasing Arab nationalism and Soviet pressure.[4] The relationship grew closer in 1962 with the Kennedy administration's decision to sell Hawk anti-aircraft missiles to Israel to counter-balance Soviet arms flowing into Egypt and Syria. This collaboration intensified after the 1967 war and even more so after the Yom Kippur war of October 1973. The provision of arms and foreign aid increased markedly during these years and enjoyed broad public and congressional support. Moreover, during the cold war decades of the 1960s, 1970s and 1980s, Israel proved to be a significant source of foreign intelligence and of captured Soviet weapons, tactics and military technology.

The Egyptian–Israeli Peace Treaty, signed at the White House in March 1979 exemplified just how important the American role in the Middle East and the bond with Israel had become.[5] President Anwar Sadat of Egypt, who had come to office after Nasser's death in 1970, broke with his Russian patron after the October 1973 war and established close ties with the United States. From 1977 onward, Washington played a crucial part in helping to bridge Egyptian and Israeli differences. President Jimmy Carter presided over key negotiations resulting in the Camp David accords in September 1978, and with the support of Congress his administration provided large amounts of economic and military aid to Israel and Egypt as a means of ensuring implementation of the peace treaty. For Israel, this meant assurances that its security would not be jeopardized and that the costs of relocating bases from the Sinai Peninsula could be offset. For

Egypt, there was major economic aid plus re-equipping of its armed forces with American weapons.

The close relationship between America and Israel meant that only the United States could serve as the indispensable intermediary in the region.[6] This was not only because of its position as the leading external power in the Middle East, but also because of its credibility and importance to Israel. No other country or international organization was in a position to undertake such a task. Russia, Britain and France as the former colonial powers, the European Union, and the UN could at times play contributory roles, but none possessed these key capacities.

With the end of the cold war, the relative strategic importance of Israel for the United States appeared to lessen, but the close ties between the two countries remained undiminished. The ongoing centrality of the US role continued to be evident in every significant crisis and negotiation. For example, the elder Bush administration's 1990–91 response to Iraq's invasion of Kuwait, culminating in Operation Desert Storm, led to the historic Arab–Israeli Madrid conference of October 1991. Less than two years later, in September 1993, President Bill Clinton presided over the White House signing of the Declaration of Principles (the Oslo agreement) between Israel and the Palestinians. In the following year, the Israeli–Jordanian peace treaty of October 1994 was based on an agreement reached in Washington three months earlier and Prime Minister Yitzhak Rabin, King Hussein and President Clinton all signed the treaty. Disengagement agreements between Israel and the Palestinian authority in the mid-1990s involved a key US role, as did intense (though ultimately unsuccessful) efforts to broker peace between Israel and Syria and between Israel and the Palestinians in 1999–2000.

President George W. Bush's speech of 24 June 2002 offered explicit support for the creation of a Palestinian state, while requiring that the Palestinians first abandon terrorism and select new leadership not compromised by corruption, autocracy and terrorism. In this respect, his words were remarkably explicit:

> I call on the Palestinian people to elect new leaders, leaders not compromised by terror. I call upon them to build a practising democracy based on tolerance and liberty. ...
>
> And when the Palestinian people have new leaders, new institutions and new security arrangements with their neighbors, the United States of America will support the creation of a Palestinian state, whose borders and certain aspects of its sovereignty will be provisional until resolved as part of a final settlement in the Middle East. ...

> The United States will not support the establishment of a Palestinian state until its leaders engage in a sustained fight against the terrorists and dismantle their infrastructure.[7]

The subsequent 'Roadmap' for peace developed later in 2003 in coordination with the European Union, Russia and the UN (the Quartet), as well as the Annapolis conference of November 2007 aimed at relaunching the peace effort and seeking to advance a framework for final status negotiations, both took place under largely American aegis.

ഇ)രു

Foreign policy ultimately rests on domestic foundations. For the United States, the relationship with Israel is a product of multiple factors. American exceptionalism provides an important dimension of sentiment and belief. The Judeo-Christian heritage takes on added importance here, as seen in the enormous support for Israel by tens of millions of evangelical Protestants. Indeed, they far outnumber the 2 per cent of the American population who are Jewish. History is vital too. The indelible memory of the Holocaust and the development of ties over 60 years provide another source of support and affinity, as does the fact that Israel is a democracy and a long-term ally of the United States. Support for Israel in the US Congress remains deep and bipartisan, and has shown no evidence of diminishing.

Both Jewish and non-Jewish political groups have played an active role in the American political process (though in the case of assertions about the 'Israel lobby' this has been much exaggerated), and where they are effective it is because they advocate policies that are consistent with national beliefs and largely supported by public and elite opinion. Throughout the 1990s, despite the end of the cold war, support for Israel among policy elites and the wider public remained consistent.[8] Recent American opinion continues to be strongly sympathetic, and the ups and downs of the peace process, war and terrorism, the rise and fall of Labour and Likud governments, and changes in the Arab world have had relatively little effect. Asked to list the countries with which they feel most sympathetic, Americans rank Israel behind only Canada, the UK, Germany and Japan, and ahead of France and India.[9] Between two-thirds and three-quarters of Americans continue to regard Israel as an important ally. In addition, the public typically supports Israel over the Palestinians by margins of four to one or even more. For example, during the August 2006 war in Lebanon the ratio was 52 per cent versus 11 per cent,[10] and in a March 2008 poll a record 71 per cent versus 8 per cent.[11] And, despite increasing criticism from the political left and among portions of the academic community, substantial majorities of

Democrats and even higher proportions of Republicans continue to report positive views.

During the 2008 presidential campaign almost all the candidates adopted strong pro-Israeli positions. The only exceptions were on the outer flanks of each party – left-wing Democrat Dennis Kucinich and right-wing Republican libertarian Ron Paul. Both favoured foreign policies of retreat and disengagement, and neither emerged as a serious contender. Meanwhile, the leading candidates, John McCain, Barack Obama and Hillary Clinton advocated strong and unequivocal support for Israel. For example, their May 2008 statements commemorating Israel's sixtieth anniversary employed such similar language that without the name of the candidate it would have been difficult to tell one statement from another.

That peace efforts both during the Bush administration and under Clinton were unsuccessful illustrates both the necessity and the limits of the US role. Over the years, virtually every significant agreement between Israel and its Arab adversaries has involved the United States in some essential capacity as intermediary, supporter, guarantor or source of legitimacy. Yet, any durable peace requires that the parties themselves should be prepared and willing to end the conflict. Despite often repeated urging from Europe and the Middle East, what the United States cannot do is *impose* peace, and when it has put forward proposals that have not gained Israel's consent, the result has been stalemate. Cases include, for example, the 1969 Rogers plan, a 1977 Carter administration idea for multilateral talks in Geneva (rejected by Egypt as well as Israel), the 1982 Reagan plan, and a 1989 proposal by Secretary of State James Baker.

To be sure, both sides to the conflict need to be held to their commitments, and the United States along with others is in a position to support the transparency and reciprocity that are essential for any lasting agreement. Yet, the tragedy of recent years, and especially since the 1993 Oslo agreement, is that the Palestinians have been unwilling to abandon the conflict, halt virulent incitement and drop their maximalist and unattainable demands.

The majority of Israelis, by contrast, have come to terms with the idea that peace will ultimately mean relinquishing most of the West Bank with only limited border adjustments, some kind of accommodation for Palestinians in Jerusalem, and acceptance of a Palestinian state. In fact, Israeli opinion is dynamic, not static. When presented with a credible and unambiguous partner for peace (Anwar Sadat or King Hussein), Israel has been willing and able to respond decisively. However, in the face of security threats, suicide terrorism and the absence of a partner able and willing to negotiate to deliver a genuine peace, Israelis will not make significant concessions. As a case in point, consider the consequences of

Israel's withdrawal from southern Lebanon in May 2000 and from Gaza in October 2005. In the former case, Hezbollah turned the area into a heavily armed enclave with thousands of Iranian and Syrian supplied rockets targeted against Israel, which ultimately triggered the war of July–August 2006. In the case of Gaza, after Israel removed 8000 settlers and relinquished the territory to Palestinian control, the firing of short range Qassem and then longer range Grad rockets into Israel continued virtually without interruption until Israel acted militarily in Operation Cast Lead. The Hamas takeover of Gaza in June 2007 put the area under the domination of a movement committed to the most fanatical anti-Jewish and anti-Israel policies. For the majority of Israelis, these cases discredit the concept of land-for-peace and are likely to do so until a Palestinian leadership emerges that has the capacity to speak authoritatively for its entire community, to monopolize the means of legitimate violence among its people (the political test long ago described by Max Weber), and to be unambiguous in its willingness to end the conflict.

Following the failure of strenuous attempts by the Clinton administration in its final year (at Camp David, Sharm el-Sheikh and the White House), the Bush administration in its first year launched initiatives by former Senator George Mitchell, CIA director George Tenet, Secretary of State Colin Powell, and retired marine general Anthony Zinni. These were followed by the president's June 2002 speech, the Roadmap in 2003, and later the Annapolis summit of November 2007. Whether the Bush administration could have been more active and effective in seeking an Israeli–Palestinian peace remains open to debate, but the evidence of unsuccessful undertakings suggests that the greatest obstacles are those on the ground in the region rather than a lack of diplomatic effort.

Seen from abroad, the character of the US-Israeli bond is often poorly understood. Even those who appreciate its depth and breadth can misconstrue its policy consequences. America's role as well as its influence on Israel is unique. Yet the achievement of a much-desired peace is not a matter of the United States putting pressure on Israel or imposing a settlement. There is little domestic support for such a policy, but even if there were, it would neither provide a viable solution nor be accepted by the Israelis. Thus, foreign leaders could have greater and more positive effect by using their political and economic leverage to encourage the Palestinians to make the necessary changes, as well as to bring home the message that outsiders cannot impose peace. The Arab states affected by the ongoing Israeli–Palestinian conflict also need to provide much more decisive diplomatic, political and economic support for peace than they have been willing to offer in the past.

Two additional points are worth emphasizing. First, it is impossible to accommodate the demands of radical Islamists and extremist Palestinian and Arab groups. No amount of concessions are likely to deflect them from their ultimate objective, which remains the destruction of Israel. The willing suspension of disbelief has been all too common in the recent past; even under Yasser Arafat's corrupt and duplicitous leadership, Western audiences were too often willing to take his pronouncements at face value while ignoring his actions and contradictory messages to Arab audiences. The second point is that even the disappearance of Israel would not greatly lessen the problem of Middle East regional instability. As Josef Joffe has observed, even in a 'world without Israel', Sunni–Shia conflicts, inter-state rivalries, bitter differences between modernists and reactionaries, despotism, radical Islamism and political oppression would guarantee the continuation or intensification of conflict.[12] One can now add to this list the disruptive regional role of Iran and the ongoing violence within Iraq. To be sure, a viable peace involving Israel, the Palestinians and Syria is greatly to be desired, but it will not be achieved through wishful thinking about intransigent Arab or Islamist intentions, misunderstanding the American role, or failing to appreciate the fundamental nature of the US–Israeli relationship.

Democratization and the 'Freedom Agenda'

With criticisms from a wide range of different political perspectives, few foreign policy efforts have been subject to as much mischaracterization or hyperbole as the Bush administration's attempts to promote democracy and freedom. The left has portrayed the Bush doctrine and Iraq war as ill-considered attempts to 'impose' democracy; foreign versions of the same stance add neo-colonial and imperialist labels to the characterization. Realists of various varieties and some on the political right believe that the policy is naïve, disruptive and greatly over-reaches. Democracy theorists and some NGOs warn, with more effect, that democratization and elections can be counterproductive if undertaken in an unstable political environment and without the necessary institutions and practices of civil society.

Democratization figured significantly in Bush's grand approach, most notably in his September 2002 national security strategy, which ranked it alongside the needs to maintain American primacy, use pre-emptive force when necessary and pursue multilateralism where possible. It is also included in the US-led coalition's effort (under a UN mandate) to establish order in a post-Saddam Hussein Iraq, though what drove the fateful decision to use force was the apprehension of a strategic threat rather than a crusade to impose democracy.[13]

The second inaugural address of 20 January 2005 stands out among statements and speeches made during the George W. Bush presidency as the central expression of democratization policy and it is useful to examine it both for what it does and does not say.[14] First, it is important to note that the commitment to democratization does not represent a dramatic departure, but instead follows in the tradition of previous presidential addresses. Historically, the inaugural provided a newly elected or re-elected president with a unique opportunity to go beyond political partisanship and the ordinary business of governance to speak to the entire country and to embody what President Abraham Lincoln described in his first inaugural as the 'better angels of our nature'. For generations, Democratic and Republican presidents have invoked the loftiest ideals in speaking about America's purpose, the religious foundations of these beliefs, and the indispensable role that the USA plays, both as an example and in helping other people achieve the fundamental ideals of freedom and democracy. These beliefs reflect the uniqueness of the United States. Americans are immigrants or their descendants and are not unified by a shared ethnicity, race or national origin. Instead, to be American is to subscribe to the beliefs in democracy and liberty embodied in the Declaration of Independence, the Constitution and the Bill of Rights.

For example, in January 1961, President John F. Kennedy uttered the memorable words, 'Let every nation know, whether it wishes us well or ill, that we shall pay any price, bear any burden, meet any hardship, support any friend, oppose any foe, in order to assure the survival and the success of liberty.' Two decades later, in January 1981, Ronald Reagan spoke of America as 'the exemplar of freedom and beacon of hope for those who do not now have freedom.' And Bill Clinton proclaimed in his 1993 inaugural that, 'Our hopes, our hearts, our hands, are with those on every continent who are building democracy and freedom. Their cause is America's cause.' Moreover, Bill Clinton used his January 1997 inaugural address to speak of America's role as an 'indispensable nation'.

Each of the these presidents, as well as their predecessors including Wilson, Roosevelt and Truman, invoked liberty as a God-given right, an idea that goes back to the original founding of the USA. Throughout the centuries, US presidents have not only viewed freedom and democracy as an example to other people, but have encouraged and supported those who suffer oppression and seek to free themselves. But this is not tantamount to mounting an international crusade to impose democracy through force of arms or other profoundly interventionist actions. Thus, in his speech, Bush proclaimed, 'it is the policy of the United States to seek and support the growth of democratic movements and institutions in every nation and culture, with the ultimate goal of ending tyranny in our world.' This statement embodies a key insight: real democracies neither make war on other democracies nor nurture terrorists.

Yet some foreign observers have misunderstood or even distorted the meaning of this statement, claiming that it signals an imperial crusade to impose democracy by force. This kind of criticism misstates the meaning of the Bush speech. Indeed, the president made clear that:

> This is not primarily the task of arms, though we will defend ourselves and our friends by force of arms when necessary. ... America will not impose our own style of government on the unwilling. ... Our goal instead is to help others find their own voice, attain their own freedom, and make their own way.

The universality of this message is expressed in the words, 'America will not pretend that jailed dissidents prefer their chains, or that women welcome humiliation and servitude, or that any human being aspires to live at the mercy of bullies.' At the same time, however, the president was explicit in saying that America 'will not impose our form of government'.

Democratization is regarded as fundamentally important, but as something that can take a very long time to achieve. Bush acknowledged that the 'great objective of ending tyranny' is a long-term task, 'the concentrated work of *generations*'. Though the effort is often arduous and failure not uncommon, there has been considerable success in increasing the number of democratic countries in the past half century. In this process, the United States has often played an indispensable role in encouraging or helping others to liberate themselves and to establish or strengthen free institutions and the rule of law. The list of countries includes Germany, Japan, Italy, South Korea, the Philippines, parts of Asia and Africa, most of eastern Europe, much of Latin America and Ukraine. Moreover, even where the task remains dangerous and uncertain, as in Afghanistan and Iraq, the ousting of despotic regimes and the holding of free elections remain historic achievements.

For all its uncertainties, democratization is linked to a broader sense of purpose related not only to the freedom agenda but also to the wider war on radical Islamist terrorism. Though policy documents might contain inconsistent or even deliberately ambiguous wording and political officials use innocuous language, President Bush's approach was apparent in his observation that: 'The survival of liberty in our land increasingly depends on the success of liberty in other lands. The best hope for peace in our world is the expansion of freedom in all the world.' More specifically, as he added in a weekly radio address just two days later, 'We will continue to promote freedom, hope and democracy in the broader Middle East – and by doing so, defeat the despair, hopelessness and resentments that feed terror.' In short, for the president and his closest foreign policy advisers, vital interests, ideals and security remained closely linked, and to some extent his words echoed those of Wilson, Kennedy, Roosevelt and Reagan as they confronted the First World War, Second World War and cold war. Indeed, in places, Bush's language was so like that of previous presidents that, had the name on the text been removed, the identity of the speaker would not have been evident.

Policy implementation, however, is a demanding and exceedingly difficult task and expectations, both at home and abroad, tended to extend beyond the limits of what was immediately possible. Whatever the subsequent judgement of history about the George W. Bush presidency, it is useful here to observe that previous presidents were far from consistent and not infrequently made decisions on grounds of practicality or through political or military necessity that were at odds with their stated ideals.

Initially, Bush's Middle East policies seemed to be producing encouraging results, but many turned out to be short lived. In the Palestinian territories, the government of President Mahmud Abbas proved weak and the Fatah movement he inherited from Arafat remained corrupt, authoritarian and inept in meeting the needs of its population. In the parliamentary elections that followed in January 2006, Hamas won the majority of seats in the Palestinian Legislative Council, not least as a protest vote against Fatah, but its subsequent armed seizure of power in Gaza marked an ominous turn of events. In Lebanon too, initial hopes ran high. The assassination of former Prime Minister Rafik Hariri on 14 February 2005 led to massive public demonstrations and American and French support for the reformist 14 March coalition and the withdrawal of Syria. Unfortunately, Hezbollah, with Iranian and Syrian backing, was able to frustrate the hope for real improvement and to plunge the country into civil war. In Iraq, the three unprecedented free elections, each with a larger number of voters and with members of the public defying terrorist death threats to vote, did far less than had been anticipated to dispel deep seated problems of murderous communal antagonism, weak or failed governance, insurgency and terrorism.

In responding to these tumultuous events, the Bush administration made mistakes in judgement and implementation. For example, in the Palestinian and Iraqi elections, it violated Weber's classic dictum. Armed militias portraying themselves as political parties were allowed to take part in the election process when their disarmament should instead have been a precondition. Paying insufficient heed to the dangers, the Bush administration, partly led by misleading poll results that suggested that Hamas would lose, put pressure on both Israel and the Palestinian Authority to allow the elections to take place.

In Iraq, the administration turned a blind eye to the implications of a party list system a UN representative had designed even though the result was certain to exacerbate rather than bridge sectarian conflicts. The absence of security in large parts of Iraq prior to the January 2007 shift to the 'surge' strategy also contributed to a dire political climate. In addition, while courageous and dedicated people led some of the important development and democratization projects in Iraq, and risked their lives to bring progress, others were run carelessly or incompetently, and with personnel ill suited for the demanding tasks at hand.

Still other obstacles loomed. Authoritarian regimes often deliberately intensified the tradeoffs between stability and democracy. In Egypt, for example, the Mubarak regime made a point of repressing its moderate opposition, and then pointed to the fundamentalist Muslim Brotherhood, with its base in the mosques, as the principal anti-regime force. After initially providing rhetorical support and encouragement to the nascent democratic forces, the Bush administration backed off in the face of Mubarak's recalcitrance, as well as reversals and security threats elsewhere in the region.

Yet another problem underlying the promotion of democracy is that it can sometimes elide the important distinction between two of its very different components, popular sovereignty and liberty. Originally, and especially prior to the last century, democracy was often understood in terms of popular sovereignty and critics saw it as bringing the risk of mob rule. In more recent times, democracy became associated with liberty and the two conceptions tended to run together in common discourse. But the older forms of liberty, including the rule of law, could sometimes be found in polities without popular sovereignty (like ancient Athens, the Roman Republic, and England in an earlier age), where courts or other institutions might exist to protect the rights of the individual. Thus, James Madison could warn about the danger in a democracy (as opposed to a republic with separation of powers) to personal security and rights of property.[15] This distinction is akin to the one that Isaiah Berlin made in differentiating between negative and positive liberty, and is thoughtfully discussed by Michael Mandelbaum in *Democracy's Good Name*.[16]

The freedom agenda exists along a continuum of power and values. American policies rarely embody an exclusive focus on either power or, conversely, on values alone. Instead, the mix of these two elements tends to vary with the intensity of security dangers and their urgency. In the context of the threats from radical Islamist jihadism and terrorism, greater emphasis will tend to be placed on power considerations, but the values and purposes represented by the commitment to democratization will not disappear. The freedom agenda remains rooted in a long American tradition, and it embodies a long-term vision of what may ultimately be required if there is ever to be a successful and peaceful transformation of the Arab and Muslim Middle East.

Threats from Radical Islamism and Terrorism

The years from 11 September 2001 to the present now extend over a period of time longer than the entire time span of the Second World War. The 9/11 attacks, their symbolism, aftermath and legacy, consumed nearly the entire George W. Bush presidency. Fundamental elements of this threat did not just emerge on a September morning, they had been developing and increasingly visible during the two decades prior to 9/11, but the shock of that event, the casualty toll and the uniqueness of this most deadly foreign assault ever carried out on American soil were bound to give it a unique centrality in strategy and foreign policy.

Three factors both shaped the resultant Bush grand strategy and are likely to have a strong impact on his successors' policies.[17] First, there is a profound lethal threat to the vital interests and national security of the United States and its allies, as well as to the liberal international system that has evolved over the past six decades. This peril emanates from a combination of radical Islamism, terrorism and the prospect of chemical, biological, radiological and nuclear weapons (CBRN). The sources of danger include not only radical jihadist and terrorist groups but also states that sponsor or support terrorism and/or proliferation, especially Iran, North Korea, Syria and Venezuela. There are also, as Azar Gat has cogently argued, potential great power challengers like Russia and China.[18]

Second, international organizations present a problem. The United Nations can play a crucial role in certain realms, as in the operation of some of its specialist agencies and in peace keeping, if there is a peace to be kept. All too often, however, on the most urgent and deadly problems, the UN and prominent regional bodies such as the European Union, Africa Union, the Arab League and others are politically or institutionally incapable of acting on a timely and effective basis. Two conspicuous examples from the contemporary Middle East are Darfur, where ethnic cleansing and death from starvation, disease and murder have taken place with near impunity, and Iran, which has been running the clock out on the often well meaning but ultimately ineffective efforts of the UK, France, Germany, the International Atomic Energy Agency (IAEA) and the UN Security Council.

This leads to the third factor. Despite its considerable problems and burdens at home and abroad, the United States continues to possess and exercise unique power in the world. This is enhanced when it can act in concert with other countries or institutions, including the EU and UN. Indeed, the alternative to American leadership or involvement in confronting the most urgent problems is not that some other country, group or organization will take the necessary initiatives, but that none will. Thus, as Robert Kagan aptly observes, 'American predominance, therefore, does not stand in the way of progress toward a better world. It stands in the way of regression toward a more dangerous world.'[19]

Insofar as the Middle East is concerned, these facts dictate that the United States should continue to exercise an assertive and interventionist role. This is not only in its own national interest and security, but also because no other country or organization has the capacity to do so.

The Future of the Middle East after the Bush Administration

It is sobering to attempt an assessment of Bush's complex Middle East record, not least because discourse on this subject is so weighted with conceptual landmines and political agendas. Even more daunting are the yet unresolved or unknown answers to some of the most profound questions. On the Israeli–Palestinian conflict, despite widespread criticism abroad and at home, it is not at all obvious that a more activist Bush policy could have produced tangible results in the absence of a viable Palestinian leadership prepared to make peace and to end the conflict.

On the freedom agenda, despite initial signs that the wave of democratizations that had swept large parts of the world in the half century between 1950 and 2000 might at last be touching the shores of the Arab Middle East, the Arab spring proved a disappointment. In addition, the presence of massive oil and natural gas resources and the enormous revenues they bring generally serves to work against democratic trends in petrol states in the Middle East and elsewhere.[20] Nonetheless, as Fouad Ajami has noted, the democratic currents stirred by the Bush policies have not gone away, and it is likely that pressure for change will continue to ferment.[21]

The Bush administration, *vis-à-vis* Iraq and Afghanistan, accomplished an extraordinary task in ousting two of the most reprehensible and dangerous regimes in the region. The resulting instability and insurgencies in both countries should not obscure this considerable achievement. In turn, this leads to the question of whether Iraq eventually will stabilize in a way that does not jeopardize the security and stability of its neighbours, let alone the well being of its people. If yes, then the enormous human, material and geopolitical war costs may yet prove to be counterbalanced. If not, then the fate of Iraq and the immediate region are likely to be grim.

In the meantime, the United States serves as the ultimate source of order in the region and the principal balance against an Iranian regime that, in the absence of a powerful and dangerous Iraqi state acting as a counterweight, has become an increasing threat to the entire region. In the years since Saddam and his Ba'thist regime were ousted, Tehran has intensified its campaign to transfer arms, training and terrorism to Iraq, Lebanon, Gaza and elsewhere. Without the US presence, moderate and Sunni regimes lack the capacity and will to provide a balance on their own, and the dangers not only to Israel, but also to a much wider world and to the United States would be far more serious.

The intractable regional circumstances are likely to provide President Barack Obama with less room for manoeuvre than he might wish and, even though he seeks a rapid withdrawal of forces from Iraq, the need to remain engaged in the region will continue. If the situation in Iraq were to worsen, so too would the pressures confronting a new president. Yet, even if Iraq were to improve, the urgency of Middle East issues is likely to remain demanding. The Israeli–Palestinian problem, political instability and the threats posed by Iran to its neighbouring countries and through its nuclear proliferation and missile programmes will all demand close attention. In addition, the need to ensure the flow of oil and natural gas will continue, and – last but not least – deadly threats from radical Islamist groups are unlikely to disappear. In view of these regional realities, though names, tactics, rhetoric and diplomacy will surely change, the strategies followed by the next president may well exhibit some significant continuities with the Bush doctrine.

7

Reflections on French Experiences in the Middle East

Jean-Pierre Filiu

France tried over the years to promote its vision of peace in the Middle East, not just through diplomatic action but also through a combination of military involvement and political initiatives. In this chapter I shall try to reflect on two major past experiences, namely the French evacuations of the PLO leadership from Lebanon in 1982–83, and the French contribution to signing and monitoring the April 1996 truce between Israel and Hezbollah. Those two experiences have to be put in perspective through a brief survey of French involvement in the Middle East since Charles de Gaulle's presidency.

In 1982–83, France under François Mitterrand twice saved Yasser Arafat and the PLO leadership from a deadly siege in Lebanon. In summer 1982 the Israeli army besieged Beirut and in autumn 1983 the Syrian army, with the help of Libyan units and Palestinian 'dissidents', besieged Tripoli. Paris tried to promote a comprehensive peace settlement to both these open conflicts, while at the same time mobilizing its forces to safeguard the PLO evacuation from Lebanese soil. The partnership with Egypt was crucial in both cases.

In spring 1996, France helped end the 'Grapes of Wrath' crisis in southern Lebanon. The ceasefire established a monitoring group of the truce between Israel and Lebanon, co-chaired by Washington and Paris with Syria as an 'observer'. The new feature of this group was that only civilian casualties were taken into consideration as violation of the truce, while military targets went unreported. During the four years of this group, informal channels were developed and escalation of the crisis was repeatedly neutralized.

∞⟩⟨∞

French support of the UN partition plan for Palestine was crucial to its endorsement by the international community in November 1947. At that time Paris saw Arab nationalism as the main threat to its colonial control of North Africa (Morocco and Tunisia were protectorates while Algeria was officially a 'French' territory). The Quai d'Orsay, the French ministry of foreign affairs, was wary of the Arab League, founded in Cairo in 1945, and saw in it little more than a British tool for regional influence. At the same time there was strong popular feeling in favour of the Zionist movement and some socialist militants were actively supporting illegal immigration to Palestine (the *Exodus* sailed from southern France and the French press echoed this collective adventure). Paris did not last long in establishing friendly ties with Israel, while it never accepted the UK-sponsored Jordanian annexation of the West Bank.

The French Fourth Republic at its top level was very sympathetic to the young Jewish state and the close relationships between the French socialist party and the Israeli labour movement were at the core of this bilateral intimacy. When the FLN (*Front de Libération nationale*/National Liberation Front) launched its guerrilla war against France in Algeria, many French leaders tended to think they were sharing with Israel not only political values but also the same enemy – Arab nationalism, with Gamal Abdel Nasser its rising star in Cairo. That set the stage for France and Israel secretly to plan a joint offensive against Egypt, which eventually included Great Britain and ended up with the tripartite aggression on Suez in November 1956. The military victory turned into a political disaster for France, which had to withdraw its troops under direct American pressure. Angry rioters attacked French embassies, consulates and institutions all over the Middle East and French influence in the Arab Levant was in a shambles. Beirut was alone in keeping its diplomatic relations with Paris.

When Charles de Gaulle took power in May 1958 and established the Fifth Republic, he pursued intense military cooperation with Israel and even greeted David Ben-Gurion when he visited Paris in May 1961 as a 'friend' and 'ally'. But de Gaulle's focus was on cutting French losses in Algeria, acknowledging the Algerian people's right to self-determination and then opening negotiations with the FLN. Algerian independence in July 1962 paved the way for the resumption of French diplomatic ties with the Arab world and opened a new chapter for France in the Middle East. But France was still a critical arms supplier to the Jewish state.

When at the end of May 1967 the crisis in the Middle East escalated, Abba Eban, the Israeli minister of foreign affairs, stopped in Paris on his way to Washington. De Gaulle sternly warned Israel against opening hostilities and declared publicly that the party eventually responsible for a conflict could not expect French assistance. When the war started, however, France only suspended new supplies to Israel and, in any case, the latter's arsenals were not exhausted during the six days of operation. It took the destruction of Lebanese civil aviation, during an Israeli raid against Beirut airport in December 1968, for de Gaulle to order a fully-fledged military embargo on Israel.

The main political dispute between France and Israel erupted in the United Nations in November 1967 with the approval of Security Council Resolution 242. US diplomats insisted on the request for an Israeli 'withdrawal from occupied territories', but their French colleagues defended the French version of the withdrawal. English and French languages had the same legal value in the UN system, but Israel, backed by the United States, rejected the French interpretation, which implied that the withdrawal from the West Bank, Gaza, the Golan Heights and the Sinai Peninsula had to be negotiated in modalities, not in principle.

Israeli opposition to France sharpened when Georges Pompidou, de Gaulle's successor at the Elysée in 1969, officially endorsed an 'Arab policy', mixing the historical relations with North Africa and the Levant with active support for the rights of the Palestinian people. Paris developed a new partnership with Riyadh and, after the October 1973 Arab–Israeli War, this French–Saudi axis became the basis of an unprecedented 'Euro–Arab dialogue' between the nine-member European Community on the one side and the Arab League on the other.

Israel expected a lot from the end of the Gaullist era and election of Valéry Giscard d'Estaing in April 1974, but the continuation of the 'Arab policy' and launching of French–Palestinian contacts shattered these hopes: the French foreign affairs minister met Yasser Arafat in Beirut and the PLO opened an 'information and liaison office' in Paris. Even in Lebanon, despite French historical ties with the Maronite community, Paris refused to favour the Christian militias and clashed with Israel on that regard. France was consistent in its support for Lebanese unity and, when Israel invaded south Lebanon in March 1978, France joined the newly formed UNIFIL (United Nations Interim Force in Lebanon). The first armed incidents involved French soldiers and Palestinian guerrillas in Tyr, but UNIFIL's main challenge was related to Israeli refusal to evacuate Lebanese territory fully and to let the Lebanese Army along the border.

Giscard d'Estaing was openly critical of the Israel–Egyptian peace process that started with President Sadat's visit to Jerusalem in November 1977 and led to the US-brokered treaty signed at Camp David in March 1979. France resisted the logic of separate peace and supported a comprehensive settlement that would include the PLO and address the right of the Palestinian people to self-determination. Paris convinced its European partners to endorse this position at the Venice summit in June 1980. Prime Minister Menachem Begin and his Likud government vehemently attacked the Venice declaration and the pro-Israeli militants in France called for a 'sanction vote' against Giscard d'Estaing during the coming presidential campaign. His socialist challenger, François Mitterrand, was one of the staunchest friends of the Jewish state in France and promised to bridge the gap that had deepened between France and Israel.

∽◌◠

François Mitterrand was elected president in May 1981. He had promised to visit Israel during his first year at the Elysée and he kept this promise, becoming the first French head of state to visit the Holy Land, more than seven centuries after Louis IX (Saint Louis) had done so. Mitterrand immediately ordered the dismantling of any kind of French economic boycott against the Jewish state. And France stayed silent when Israel decided to annex the Syrian Golan in December 1981. This pro-Israeli bias, far from neutralizing Mitterrand's Palestinian drive, induced him to be even more active. During his speech to the Knesset in March 1982, Mitterrand mentioned not only the PLO but also the prospect of a Palestinian state.

Through his two terms as president of the French republic, François Mitterrand committed France in the Middle East in an unprecedented manner. Twice, in 1982 and 1983, he sent the French navy and commandos to protect PLO fighters faced with annihilation in Lebanon and to guarantee the safety of their evacuation. The first time this was from Beirut besieged by Israel, and the second time from Tripoli surrounded by the Syrian army and its followers. Twice, in 1982 and 1990, he proposed a new approach to UN resolutions to engage the PLO in a political process with Israel. Receiving Yasser Arafat officially in Paris in 1989, he persuaded him to declare the PLO charter 'obsolete' (*caduc*).

During all these years, Mitterrand looked for the closest cooperation with the USA in the Middle East. As an early and warm supporter of the Camp David agreements, he never disputed America's leading role in the region. He deployed French troops along with the US Army in Beirut or Iraq, and he thought that this military exposure would provide him with an exceptional leverage to act in favour of a lasting peace between Israel and the Arabs. He hoped also that his longstanding friendship with the Jewish state would be taken into consideration, not only by the Labour Party, but also by the Likud.

When 100,000 Israeli soldiers invaded Lebanon in June 1982, launching the fifth Arab–Israeli war under the name of 'Peace in Galilee', Mitterrand was hosting the G7 summit in Versailles and, along with President Reagan, appeared ready to buy the Israeli decoy: this invasion was only intended to 'cleanse' a 40-kilometre deep pocket into Lebanese territory from the PLO military presence. He even coined the concept of the 'three occupations' of Lebanon, creating a new equivalence between Israeli, Syrian and Palestinian 'occupations'.

The French president felt even more betrayed when the Israeli army, far from stopping 40 kilometres away from the borders, entered deep into the Chouf mountain, took over the city of Saida after a bloody battle, and besieged west Beirut in mid-June. Arafat became trapped in the surrounded capital where PLO fighters and Lebanese allies had decided to resist. Syria agreed to a ceasefire and from now on the war opposed a guerrilla force to Israel. The political impact of this new confrontation was tremendous in the West as well as in the Arab world. In France, the images of Israeli bombings shocked the public and galvanized the leftist parties and unions against the war.

Mitterrand could have turned a blind eye to the restoration of 'security' on the northern border of Israel. However, the risk of bloodshed in Beirut, which might ruin the future of Lebanon and jeopardize stability throughout the Middle East, outraged him. Moreover, the Israeli deception incensed him and he confided to his advisers: 'Begin lied to me.' But the Israeli plan, designed to liquidate the PLO and roll back Syria, appealed more and more to the neo-cold-war warriors of the Reagan administration. Their interpretation of the Arab–Israeli conflict in strict East–West categories matched Begin and Sharon's rhetoric perfectly. So, when Mitterrand proposed the 'neutralization of West Beirut under the monitoring of UN observers', the US veto rejected the French resolution at the UNSC on 26 June.

After this UN humiliation, Mitterrand worked on two levels to maintain a diplomatic momentum: first, among the ten-member European Community; second, in close cooperation with Egypt. Presidents Mitterrand and Mubarak nurtured the same fears about the mid-term impact of the siege of Beirut all over the region. They were also convinced that this military crisis could only be solved through a political opening, by offering the PLO a diplomatic trade-off for disarming the bulk of its fighters. On 2 July Paris and Cairo together drafted the project of a UNSC resolution that would enhance the scope of resolution 242 (which only mentioned the Palestinian 'refugees') by including the right of the Palestinian people to self-determination. The very same day, Nahum Goldmann, Philip Klutznick and Pierre Mendès France met in Paris to urge Israel and the PLO to negotiate. While Arafat welcomed this call from besieged Beirut, the French–Egyptian attempt to link the current crisis to a broader peace process was countered by Israel's rejection, US bias and Arab fears that any delay in solving the Beirut showdown could ignite the whole region.

Even though this diplomatic option was blocked, Mitterrand adamantly insisted on preserving Lebanon's sovereignty and the PLO's dignity in any settlement. When Reagan wrote to him on 9 July to bypass the UN and send immediately a joint intervention force to Beirut, the French president responded by demanding a formal request from the Lebanese government, an explicit PLO agreement and a UN endorsement. Despite repeated all-out assaults on west Beirut, which included bombing several French diplomatic and cultural symbols, Israel failed to break the military stalemate. Philip Habib, Reagan's special envoy, brokered a global 'plan', but never dealt directly with the PLO; on 6 August France received Lebanese and PLO approvals to its intervention. On that same day, the socialist and communist parties, along with all the major leftist unions and associations, emphatically supported Mitterrand's position and called for the establishment of a 'fully-fledged sovereign Palestinian state'.

On 9 August, a terrorist attack in the heart of the historically Jewish neighbourhood of Paris left six dead and 25 wounded. Israel immediately accused 'the anti-Israeli climate prevailing in France since the beginning of the war in Lebanon' and Begin put the blame on Mitterrand, who met a hostile crowd when comforting the families of the victims at the nearest synagogue. Arafat uttered his 'absolute condemnation of this beastly act' and Mitterrand sent him his personal thanks for this message. The tension between France and Israel was extreme, but on 17 August Mitterrand declared that 'nobody, nothing, not even Mr Begin's statements, will turn me into an enemy of Israel'. On 18 August the so-called 'Habib plan' was finalized and, the next day, the Lebanese government formally requested France, the USA and Italy to form a multinational force. The first units to be deployed were French and they landed in Beirut harbour on 21 August.

Over the following ten days, approximately 14,700 fighters were transferred from Beirut. Three out of four of them were PLO commandos, who, along with Arafat, mostly left Beirut by sea for Tunisia, Algeria, Yemen or Sudan. The remaining Syrian armed personnel reached Damascus by land. Despite much friction between French and Israeli soldiers, the whole operation was a technical success. On 23 August, Bashir Gemayel, Israel's historical ally in Lebanon, was elected president of the republic and, on 1 September, Reagan proposed a peace plan for the Middle East that mentioned neither the PLO nor a Palestinian state. By mid-September, the multinational force had left Beirut. Mitterrand could believe that Lebanese sovereignty and Palestinian dignity had been saved against all odds, but the killing of Bashir Gemayel and ensuing slaughters in the Palestinian camps of Sabra and Chatila shattered all these hopes.

Mitterrand immediately agreed to send 2000 soldiers back to Beirut within the framework of a new multinational force. Their mission would be twofold — to protect the Palestinian survivors of the massacre in the refugee camps and to assist the stabilization of Lebanon under its new president Amin Gemayel, Bashir's brother, elected on 21 September 1982. But, while the Italian contingent stuck to its presence in the Palestinian camps, the US forces, concentrated around the airport, basically backed the Lebanese army in restoring law and order in west Beirut, formerly run by pro-PLO militias. The contradiction between the two dimensions of the French mission became obvious after the signing, on 17 May 1983, of an Israeli–Lebanese peace agreement. The text, which the USA brokered without any consultations with its allies, brought to a head violent opposition to Gemayel's regime. The mainly Druze (PSP) and Shiite (Amal) militias could rely on massive Syrian support.

Meanwhile, to Egypt, Jordan and the Israeli Labour Party's dismay, Begin fiercely rejected the logic of the 'Reagan plan'. France kept its political dialogue with the PLO and engineered fruitful anti-terrorism cooperation with Abou Iyad's intelligence apparatus. But the diplomatic horizon was bleak, for the internal dissidence (*inchiqaq*) that Syria fuelled in spring 1983 further weakened the PLO. Pro-Damascus 'rebels' progressively took over the Palestinian camps in the parts of Lebanon the Syrian army occupied. By the end of the summer, the elimination of PLO loyalists was nearly complete and Arafat sneaked into Tripoli, the main city in northern Lebanon, to galvanize 4000 of his armed supporters in their last stronghold.

Once again, the PLO chief and his fighters were besieged in a Lebanese harbour, but this time by an Arab army and even Palestinian 'revolutionaries', who denied Arafat's legitimacy to lead his people in front of Israel. The threat of annihilation was no less dangerous than during the Beirut blockade and Mitterrand committed himself to deter it one more time. On 26 October, he praised Arafat as 'an intelligent and brave leader' and expressed compassion with the Palestinian people 'so unhappy, so ignored', but the pro-Syrian 'rebels' reacted vehemently by denouncing French 'interference' in 'Palestinian internal affairs'. The assaults on Tripoli became more deadly throughout November and Mitterrand demanded that the 'manhunt' stop.

Northern Lebanon's capital city was now completely surrounded – on land by the Syrian army backed by Libyan units and pro-Damascus guerrillas; at sea by the Israeli navy, ready to crush Arafat who had escaped its grip in 1982. But the PLO, which had captured six Israeli soldiers in Lebanon, had sheltered them in Tripoli and was negotiating through the International Committee of the Red Cross (ICRC) their exchange with thousands of Palestinians and Lebanese held by Israel. The fighting in Tripoli urged all the parties to settle the deal, which French logistical and military support guaranteed.

On 24 November, the PLO transferred the six Israeli prisoners aboard French vessels close to Tripoli. Meanwhile, 4683 Arab detainees were released from Israeli prisons in Israel and Lebanon. Some 1117 of them, mostly Palestinians, travelled from Tel Aviv to Algiers on three Air France Boeing 747s. The remaining lot, half Palestinian, half Lebanese, were bussed into the main cities of south Lebanon. France delivered the six former PLO prisoners to the Israeli navy. Arafat and Shamir, who had replaced Begin as Israeli prime minister, publicly thanked Mitterrand. The whole exchange was a great political victory for the PLO, which had demonstrated its ability to deal with Israel for the sake of the Palestinian people. Syria understood at last that the fall of Tripoli was beyond its political and military reach.

By the end of November, everything seemed in place to organize a new evacuation of the PLO fighters and stop the bloodshed. Arafat requested UN intervention and Secretary General Pérez de Cuéllar guaranteed his endorsement of the operation. France had to act on its own, albeit under the UN flag, and Mitterrand weighed seriously the risks of such a solo operation. A PLO terrorist attack against a bus in Jerusalem on 4 December further inhibited the French president, who was anxious to avoid any clash with the Israeli navy, which repeatedly bombed Tripoli. It was only two weeks later that the French army transferred 4326 Palestinians, including many women and children, out of Tripoli on Greek civilian ships. The operation was completed in one single day and the French navy escorted Arafat and his followers to their new exile. While going through the Suez Canal, the PLO leader left ship to meet President Mubarak and close the Palestinian–Egyptian rift that had existed since Camp David.

Mitterrand had succeeded for the second time in saving the PLO as a partner for a future political process and the Arafat–Mubarak summit reasserted the PLO's peaceful stand against all rejectionists. But the Likud government clung to its vision of a 'Greater Israel' and even the Labour Party ruled out any contact with the PLO. Mitterrand was concentrating on avoiding the worst for French troops in Lebanon: they had been the targets of a massive suicide bombing on 23 October 1983 that also killed hundreds of US marines, and the French soldiers were now taken in the crossfire of the military escalation between the warring Lebanese factions. On 6 February 1984, west Beirut fell into the hands of the pro-Syrian militias and the US contingent was 'redeployed offshore'. This American withdrawal quickly left the French units by themselves in Beirut, where they stayed until the end of March, leaving a country superficially reconciled by the repeal of the peace agreement with Israel. After more than two years of intense involvement in the Middle East, Mitterrand longed for some respite and left the Palestinian issue on the backburner.

All the loyalty Mitterrand showed Reagan (support for Camp David, suspension of any European initiative that could hinder US plans, direct military exposure in Lebanon) was insufficient to allow US administrations to bring France into any political settlement in the Middle East. Mitterrand's militant friendship and solidarity with Israel was not enough to soften Likud rejectionism and only Israeli leftist circles and their supporters in the diaspora took the PLO evolution that France encouraged into consideration.

While Mitterrand's commitment to the Middle East process was deeply Israel-centred, Jacques Chirac's involvement stemmed from his personal relationships with Arab leaders, especially in Lebanon. In his attempt to revive the Gaullist 'Arab policy' through a solemn speech in Cairo in April 1996, he felt directly challenged by the 'Grapes of Wrath' Israeli offensive a few days later. He therefore took the unprecedented initiative to send his minister of foreign affairs, Hervé de Charette, on an open-ended assignment in the Middle East, no return to France being conceivable before a ceasefire in Lebanon. The French envoy, based in Damascus, started shuttle-like trips to different parts of the region and eventually contributed to the end of the hostilities. The Syrian regime appreciated the fact that de Charette had chosen Damascus as his operational base and that, contrary to Secretary of State Warren Christopher, he took into consideration the Iranian connection with Hezbollah.

The differences between French involvement in the summer of 1982 and in the spring of 1996 were important: during the Israeli siege of west Beirut French diplomats were dealing directly with the PLO and explored different ways to associate the Palestinian movement with the political process; during Operation Grapes of Wrath, French added value to US efforts in the region came through its contacts with the Syrian and Iranian regimes and not via a French dialogue with Hezbollah. There is, however, one striking similarity between French proactive choice during both crises – Paris wanted to spare Lebanon a new round of destruction and violence and it mobilized, in 1982 as well as in 1996, its regional and international network to prevent further escalation and ruin.

On 26 April 1996, the USA made public an arrangement whereby Hezbollah was only mentioned under the name of 'armed groups based in Lebanon' and agreed to stop firing Katyusha rockets on Israeli territory. The conflicting parties did not renounce their legitimate right to self-defence, but they agreed to avoid targeting civilians and civilian infrastructures. This partial ceasefire was established under the sponsorship of a monitoring group, co-chaired by the USA and France, where Israeli and

Lebanese officials were assisted by a Syrian 'observer', in fact a powerful general from military intelligence. The operational details of the monitoring group were finalized only in July 1996 in Washington and the Clinton administration showed great difficulty accepting that it had to share joint responsibility for the truce with France. This was nevertheless a significant improvement on the US-sponsored verbal agreement brokered in south Lebanon in August 1993 that did not prevent the April 1996 crisis.

Over the next four years, the American and French chairmen, often based in Nicosia, met at times of crisis in Nakura in south Lebanon in up to 48-hour-long sessions. During these intense and even exhausting meetings, US and French diplomats carefully avoided siding with any one party, while the Syrian 'observer' withdrew at times of heavy Israeli–Lebanese dispute, only to come back for the long-awaited compromise. The UN Interim Force in Lebanon (UNIFIL), which had been sent to southern Lebanon in 1978 but was unable to fulfil its mandate on the Israeli–Lebanese border, provided logistical help and field reports to the monitoring group.

The committee's only weapon was to issue public statements blaming one party or the other for violating the truce. Israel had pressed the USA into imposing the unanimity rule to avoid being put in the minority against a possible coalition of France, Syria and Lebanon. But, contrary to Israeli fears, France had supported the unanimity rule to promote integration instead of dissent. The logic of consensus meant that the accused party had to tacitly endorse any blame before going public.

This was only made possible by a parallel and unbalanced illusion at the very heart of the truce. Israel would not agree to blame being placed on its own military institution, but could not veto a statement pinning down the South Lebanon Army (SLA), the local militia it had been training and organizing. The Lebanese government, whose army was not deployed in the south, could let the 'Islamic resistance', Hezbollah's military wing, be publicly criticized, if the Syrian 'observer' tacitly approved such a criticism.

The other interesting aspect of this truce, with far-reaching implications, was that the ceasefire was in fact limited to attacks on civilians. The military operations between Israel and Hezbollah were tacitly legitimized for the sake of 'security' on one side and 'resistance' on the other. The monitoring group was not concerned with military casualties, but with civilian ones, with a permanent debate about the use of populated areas by Hezbollah to shell IDF or SLA positions.

In this framework, the monitoring group was efficient in limiting the 'collateral damage' of the conflict, while the military cost of a continuous Israeli presence in south Lebanon became even more obvious. The monitoring group also helped to prevent the escalation of the crisis, especially after the SLA bombing of Saida in April 1997, which could have triggered a full-fledged war. While the Likud government had suspended the peace talks with Damascus, the monitoring group became the only place where Israeli and Syrian officials could meet. The group activities came to an end with the Labour government's unilateral decision to evacuate south Lebanon in May 2000.

೫)೮೩

While American narratives on Beirut in 1982 or south Lebanon between 1996 and 2000 are quite different from the lessons drawn in Paris, these two French experiences could be studied anew in the light of the present conflict, keeping in line the following points:

- In both cases, the UN framework was systematically discarded (the UNSC resolutions were not implemented, and UNIFIL or the UN observers were not directly involved) to promote a *de facto* agreement with new political parameters (the 1982 Habib plan or the 1996 south Lebanon arrangement).
- The US administration, and not only Israel, was basically reluctant to include any outside partner in the management of the ceasefire and only after a new outburst of hostilities was France eventually accepted. This prejudice was equally strong in Republican and Democrat administrations.
- The protracted diplomatic process aimed basically in both cases to address two parallel denials of legitimacy: Israel consistently referred to PLO fighters in 1982 and Hezbollah militiamen in 1996 as 'terrorists', while the PLO at that time and Hezbollah still denied Israel's right to existence.
- The 1982 and 1996 agreements were presented as humanitarian break-throughs to spare the civilian population, while they were truly political commitments, and their main weakness probably derives from this unaccomplished political dimension.

Throughout the years and under several successive presidencies, Lebanon remained the main local arena from which France deployed a wider Middle Eastern policy. It was because of the Israeli raid on Beirut airport and civil aviation in December 1968 that de Gaulle finally decided to impose a military embargo on the Jewish state. It was in Beirut that a French minister of foreign affairs met Yasser Arafat for the first time in October 1974. It was in south Lebanon that France deployed a major peace keeping contingent under the banner of the United Nations Interim Force in Lebanon (UNIFIL) in May 1978.

We saw how in 1982 and 1983 Mitterrand twice sent the French navy and infantry to Lebanon to ensure the safety and preservation of the PLO leadership. But once the Palestinian issue became disconnected from the Lebanese environment, France gradually lost its political leverage and was mainly an observer during the Oslo process and its aftermath on the West Bank and Gaza. The same Lebanese focus led France to stay heavily involved between 1996 and 2000, but it did not help Paris play a significant role in the Syrian track of the peace process – that remained under strict US supervision.

In 2004 and 2005 France and the USA coordinated a political campaign against the Syrian military presence in Lebanon. Paris had always supported the full restoration of Lebanese sovereignty, but in the 1990s Washington had seemed to condone Syrian hegemony over Lebanon. UN Resolution 1559 proved in August 2004 that Damascus could no longer rely on, even tacit, international approval of its occupation of part of Lebanon. The assassination in February 2005 of former Prime Minister Rafiq Hariri sent shock waves through the country and well beyond. The mass demonstrations of the Cedar Revolution, supported by US and French-inspired international pressures, compelled the Syrian troops to withdraw from Lebanon in May 2005.

The '33-day war' that raged between Israel and Hezbollah in the summer of 2006 offered France, in close cooperation with Washington, a chance to contribute significantly to the drafting of UN Resolution 1701 and to its implementation in south Lebanon, along with its European allies, mainly Italy and Spain. A beefed-up UNIFIL, nicknamed 'UNIFIL plus', was deployed along the Lebanese border with Israel, to which the Lebanese army could eventually return for the first time in two generations. In a significant evolution, France had helped restore this dimension of Lebanese sovereignty under the flag of the UN and as a catalyst for an unprecedented European involvement.

Lebanon stood at the heart of the Gaullist presidents' Middle Eastern choices – Charles de Gaulle himself and certainly Jacques Chirac. François Mitterrand followed a different path, both intellectually and politically. His intimacy with Israel drove him to stand against the Likud's military adventures and to defend the national Palestinian leadership. French commitment to UN resolutions and missions in the region was strongly asserted throughout the Fifth Republic. Despite a greater European Union (EU) visibility in the region, the bilateral framework remained the privileged channel of action, with a lot of energy devoted to the dialogue with Washington.

8

The Reagan–Bush Administrations and the Middle East: Institutional and Bureaucratic Rivalries

Robert David Johnson

Suggesting that domestic forces influenced US policy in the Middle East is hardly a novel thesis. Yet, during the administrations of Ronald Reagan (1981–89) and George H. W. Bush (1989–93), domestic matters had an impact on the administrations' approach to Middle Eastern affairs in novel ways. The two Republicans entered the White House after a decade of congressional attempts to impose restrictions on the executive's freedom of action in the international arena. Both were strongly committed to reversing this pattern. Yet both enjoyed, at best, mixed success in this regard.

The Reagan–Bush years taught us three lessons about institutional rivalries over Middle East policy. First, the executive's frontal challenges to congressional authority almost always failed, sometimes with disastrous results, as in the 1982–83 Lebanon intervention in which institutional rivalries so distracted the government and media that they failed to examine the shortcomings in US policy. Second, the occasional willingness of Republican administrations to set aside their constitutional scruples and work within the framework of a more powerful Congress often solidified popular support for the president's policies – as in the covert aid to Afghanistan, or the first Gulf war. Finally, as in the Saudi AWACS sale, congressional actions provided a reminder that in the foreign policy of a democracy, an erratic approach to international affairs sometimes cannot be avoided.

⁍⁌

Ronald Reagan came to office after a period of intense congressional activism in foreign affairs, and amid conventional wisdom that a more powerful Congress had pushed US foreign policy to the left. In the decade before Reagan's election, Congress had used the appropriations power on several occasions. These included the 1970 Cooper–Church amendment on Cambodia to cut off funding for US military operations; the 1973 Kennedy–Fraser amendment to deny military aid to Augusto Pinochet's regime in Chile because it violated its citizens' human rights; and the 1975–76 Tunney and Clark amendments to prevent covert operations in Angola. Beginning in the late 1960s, Congress more aggressively used its oversight power to tackle major national security questions; in 1969–70, the Symington subcommittee provided high-profile oversight of US policy towards Thailand and Spain. And, in 1973, with the passage of the War Powers Act, Congress sought to reclaim the warmaking power that many members believed Lyndon Johnson had improperly seized to send US troops to Vietnam.

Most of these 1970s congressional initiatives focused on Southeast Asia, sub-Saharan Africa, or Latin America, but a few involved the fringes of the Middle East. Stuart Symington (D-Missouri) led the effort to reduce military aid to Pakistan after the 1971 India–Pakistan war, and his increasing involvement in Southwest Asian issues led him to question the merits of continued military assistance to the Shah of Iran's regime as well. In 1974, Symington's Missouri colleague, Thomas Eagleton, led a successful effort to cut off military aid to Turkey, as punishment for the Turkish invasion of Cyprus.[1]

As the 1970s progressed, the idea of an empowered Congress became linked with a liberal, pro-human rights agenda that grew increasingly unpopular. The sponsors of the two amendments to cut off covert aid to Angola – Senators John Tunney and Dick Clark – both lost their re-election bids. In 1978, Congress also repealed the Eagleton amendment, even though Turkish forces remained in Cyprus. From the intellectual right, Jeane Kirkpatrick launched a powerful attack on the congressional human rights agenda in a 1979 article in *Commentary* that posited a distinction between totalitarian (communist) regimes and authoritarian (right-wing) governments. She reasoned that authoritarian regimes often evolved into free ones – and in any case were friendly to the United States. From this framework, Kirkpatrick argued that human rights diplomacy had retarded the cause it claimed to promote by making authoritarian regimes more vulnerable to takeover by the totalitarian left.[2]

In the 1980 campaign, GOP presidential nominee Ronald Reagan embraced the Kirkpatrick argument to considerable political effect. He and Republican Senate candidates also strongly criticized the 1970s efforts to bolster congressional power. In a symbolic move against the decade's institutional activism, the 1980 Republican platform advocated repeal of the Clark amendment; Reagan also denounced the War Powers Act as unconstitutional. With incumbent Jimmy Carter increasingly besieged by the Iranian hostage crisis, double-digit inflation and rising unemployment, Reagan easily prevailed, capturing 44 of 50 states.

Little doubt existed that the new administration would seek to assert presidential authority in foreign affairs. Even before Reagan took office, the incoming secretary of state, Alexander Haig, denounced the Clark amendment as 'a self-defeating and unnecessary restriction'.[3] (Congress would eventually repeal it, in 1985.) Reagan's first foreign policy fight, however, came on most inhospitable turf – confronting not only the remnants of an empowered Congress but also the Israel lobby.

Near the end of his presidency, in a move that reflected the Nixon/Ford strategy of showering the shah's regime with US weapons, Gerald Ford had proposed selling to Iran seven Airborne Warning and Control System (AWACS) aircraft. (At the time, the United States had supplied only Britain with AWACS, the most advanced surveillance aeroplanes the air force possessed.) Ford left office before the sale was completed, but despite his promise of a foreign policy geared to human rights, Jimmy Carter initially sought to move forward with the sale. Congressional opposition delayed matters and the collapse of the shah's government in late 1978 terminated the plan.[4]

With the US strategic position in the Middle East weakened by the Iranian revolution and the Soviet invasion of Afghanistan, Carter looked for an alternative buyer. In his 1980 State of the Union address, the president proclaimed what came to be known as the Carter Doctrine:

> Let our position be absolutely clear: An attempt by any outside force to gain control of the Persian Gulf region will be regarded as an assault on the vital interests of the United States of America, and such an assault will be repelled by any means necessary, including military force.[5]

The policy essentially committed the United States to defending the territorial integrity of Saudi Arabia – even though, in the era before the establishment of CENTCOM, the United States lacked the military capability to enforce Carter's pronouncement. To symbolize US support for the Saudi regime, Carter offered to sell Saudi Arabia five of the seven AWACS aircraft originally intended for Iran. But, faced with congressional criticism, Carter shelved the sale just before leaving office.[6]

Congress could involve itself with the proposed Saudi arms sale because of the Nelson–Bingham amendment, passed in 1974. The amendment applied to all foreign military sales of more than $25 million (the Saudi arms package, at $8.5 billion, was the largest US arms sale in history until that time), and blocked any sale for which a majority in both houses of Congress passed resolutions of disapproval.

On 21 April 1981, Reagan revived what he termed the 'Royal Saudi Air Force Enhancement Package' announcing that he intended to sell the five AWACS along with conformal fuel tanks, AIM-9L Sidewinder missiles, and KC-3 aerial tankers. For the new president and his advisers, the move served two interrelated purposes. First, as Secretary of Defense Caspar Weinberger explained, the sale would forward US 'vital national interests' by binding the Saudi regime more closely to the United States and minimizing the likelihood of a domestic revolt against the Saudi regime. Enhanced coordination between the US and Saudi air forces, moreover, would 'increase the effectiveness of our own military capabilities if we were ever called upon to deploy US forces to the area'. And since the Saudis promised to share all intelligence gathered by the AWACS planes with the United States, the sale would lay the foundation for a US–Saudi strategic partnership that would extend into the 1990s.[7]

Second, and perhaps equally important, the sale provided a chance to weaken the congressional restrictions imposed in the 1970s. The AWACS sale would set a precedent – by 1980, 60 per cent of US foreign military sales went to the Middle East – that the Nelson-Bingham amendment established no real check on the president's international freedom of action.

Both sides knew that the House would pass a resolution opposing the sale. The American Israel Public Affairs Committee (AIPAC) led the public opposition, citing the possibility that the AWACS could threaten Israeli security. (The Saudis rejected a US request for US and Saudi pilots to staff the aircraft jointly.) The administration's position in the House, where the Democrats retained control, was also weaker politically than its standing in the GOP-majority Senate. On 14 October 1981 the resolution of disapproval passed the House by an overwhelming margin of 301 to 111.[8]

Since 54 senators (a majority of the body) had co-sponsored the Senate resolution to disapprove the sale, it appeared as if Reagan would experience a crushing defeat. In fact, North Dakota freshman Mark Andrews foresaw a 'diplomatic Bay of Pigs'.[9] As *Time* reporter George Church explained in early October, 'In the eyes of much of the Arab world, the AWACS deal – rightly or wrongly – has become a test of Israeli influence over Washington. If it should be voted down, many Arabs would conclude the US will not, perhaps cannot, pursue an evenhanded Middle East policy.'[10] Moreover, 'If Congress turned down the Administration's plan … Reagan's ability to conduct any effective foreign policy at all would be called into serious question. If he could not deliver on this promise, how could foreign leaders trust any other commitment he might make?'[11]

An intensive lobbying effort from the administration, headed by chief of staff (and future secretary of state) James Baker and White House counsellor Edwin Meese, helped reverse the tide.[12] Reagan himself held 44 one-on-one lobbying sessions with senators.[13] The new Saudi ambassador, Prince Bandar, worked effectively behind the scenes.

In the end, however, the outcome of the vote depended not on grand strategy or the power of the administration's arguments but on the peculiarities of politics. The turning point came with Roger Jepsen (R-Iowa), who was initially one of the Senate's most outspoken critics of the arms sale. But Jepsen also had a reputation for being politically and intellectually weak, so administration officials targeted him. 'We just beat his brains out,' remarked White House aide Ed Rollins. 'We stood him up in front of an open grave and told him he could jump in if he wanted to.'[14] In a meeting of the Republican caucus, Jepsen complained about the pressure before breaking down in tears. Soon thereafter, he remarked that he and his wife had prayed over the issue and decided that he should change his mind and vote in favour of the sale.[15] Jepsen's high-profile defection provided cover for other Senate Republicans to reverse their positions; in the end a bare majority of 52 senators backed the president, allowing the sale to go through.

In the long term, the sale had considerable effects, helping to solidify the US–Saudi strategic partnership. The outcome also all but nullified congressional control over foreign arms sales. If even the strong support of AIPAC was not sufficient for Congress to check the president's ability to negotiate sales, it seemed unlikely that the legislature would ever pass a resolution of disapproval to block a sale.[16]

Yet at the time, the outcome, dependent as it was on the fickle nature of a lightweight Iowa senator, raised doubts about how the United States formulated its policy towards the region. The Israeli government unsurprisingly perceived the vote as a major setback. As one close aide said to Prime Minister Menachem Begin: 'We realize what the Saudis can do in the White House. They can do anything they want.' The Saudis privately complained about the difficulty of the fight, while a British cabinet minister observed, 'The disarray and doubletalk at the higher levels of American foreign policy has become so pronounced as to make us wonder who really is in charge.'[17]

Reagan's next major Middle East initiative featured a similar problem of the administration seeking simultaneously to neutralize a key piece of 1970s legislation while upholding the US position in the region. But, unlike the AWACS sale, in this instance the administration failed in its efforts.

The United States first intervened in Lebanon in 1958 to implement the Eisenhower Doctrine, which gave to the president the right to send troops to the Middle East to counter a perceived Soviet threat. The affair ended badly. When it quickly emerged that the chief threat in the country was not communism but the ambitions of Christian president Camille Chamoun, US forces helped install a new (Christian) president and pulled out.[18]

Lebanon further destabilized politically when the PLO leadership migrated to Beirut after Jordan expelled Yasser Arafat and his advisers. The subsequent outbreak of sectarian fighting prompted incursions from both Israel and Syria; UN Security Council Resolution 425, passed in 1978, supposedly addressed the problem through a multinational peacekeeping force. Yet the basic goal of US policy remained unclear. Was Washington intent on propping up the central government, brokering a deal among foreign powers, or reforming Lebanese political institutions to give the majority Muslim population more power?

In June 1982, amid terrorist attacks on its northern border, Israel moved into the vacuum. The decision badly strained US–Israeli relations. Secretary of State George Shultz recalled a phone call with the Israeli prime minister: 'At the very moment he [Begin] was reassuring us [that Israel Defence Forces were not attacking], we could hear the noise of the Israeli guns' on the line from Beirut. As a result, 'High US officials … began to assume that reports from Israel were simply not accurate, whether through confusion or purposely.'[19]

The Israeli intervention generated a UN Security Council resolution designed to create a multinational force that would ensure the PLO leadership's safety as it moved from Beirut to Tunis. The United States contributed 800 soldiers; France sent the same amount, while Italy offered 400. Once Arafat and his comrades had left Beirut, the troops were withdrawn; Secretary of Defence Caspar Weinberger worried about needlessly keeping US forces on the ground in a war zone.[20] Soon thereafter, the Lebanese political situation collapsed. President-elect Bashir Gemayel was assassinated and, in response, Christian militia, operating under the protection of the IDF, moved into Palestinian refugee camps at Sabra and Shatila.

The Sabra and Shatila massacres prompted a round of fingerpointing in Washington. Shultz blamed Weinberger. The defence secretary blamed both Shultz and the national security adviser Bud McFarlane, claiming they had done insufficient diplomatic work to ensure stability once the multinational force withdrew. McFarlane blamed Weinberger and State Department special envoy Philip Habib. Amid this bureaucratic disarray, Reagan authorized US participation in a second multinational force, this one with the vague task of stabilizing the Lebanese capital, and sent nearly 2000 marines to Beirut.[21]

By any measure, an indefinite stationing of US forces in war-torn Lebanon appeared to require the president to invoke the War Powers Act.[22] Yet, Reagan refused to do so lest such an action concede the measure's constitutionality. Instead, the president publicly dismissed the possibility that the troops could be involved in combat activities, a necessary finding to trigger a war powers resolution.[23] Reagan could not avoid Congress permanently: in early 1983, he submitted an emergency appropriations measure to fund the Lebanon operation. Congress approved, but with the caveat that 'for any substantial expansion in the number or role in Lebanon of US Armed Forces ... the President shall obtain statutory authorization from the Congress.'[24]

In a sign of potential political problems for the administration, Senator Gary Hart (D-Colorado), who had just launched what seemed at the time like a long-shot bid for the Democratic presidential nomination, seized on the issue. After Hart threatened to organize a filibuster until the administration consented to a war powers vote, other leading Democrats – former Vice President Walter Mondale, the front-runner for the nomination, and also Senators John Glenn and Alan Cranston – seconded his demand. The administration countered that nothing in the War Powers Act could 'infringe upon the constitutional authority of the President as Commander in Chief, particularly with respect to contingencies not expected in the context of the multinational effort to strengthen the sovereignty and independence of Lebanon.'[25]

During the spring and summer of 1983, then, debate over Lebanon focused more on the constitutionality of Reagan's decision to send troops than on the merits of the administration's policy. Democrats saw the intervention as an opportunity to portray the president as constitutionally reckless; Reagan viewed Lebanon as a test case for establishing executive freedom of action in the international arena. Several months passed before the two sides compromised; Congress passed a resolution, citing the War Powers Act, granting Reagan the authority to keep troops in Lebanon for up to 18 months, after which point he would need an additional authorization. While Reagan informed the House Foreign Affairs Committee chairman Clement Zablocki (D-Wisconsin) that 'if our forces are needed in Lebanon beyond the 18-month period, it would be my intention to work together with the Congress with a view toward taking action on mutually agreeable terms,' he also denied 'any acknowledgement that the President's constitutional authority can be impermissibly infringed by statute.'[26]

Reagan signed the compromise Lebanon authorization on 12 October 1983. Then, 11 days later, a suicide bomber attacked the US marine barracks in Beirut, killing 241 service members. Popular support for the Lebanon intervention collapsed; a February 1984 Gallup Poll showed that only 38 per cent approved of Reagan's foreign policy, with 49 per cent disapproving.[27] The next month, the United States withdrew the last of the marines from Lebanon.

The multinational force bequeathed a no-man's-land; within 18 months, Hezbollah took hostage six Americans (along with around two dozen other foreign nationals). The administration's efforts to obtain the hostages' release helped trigger the most serious confrontation between the Congress and the executive that occurred during the 1980s.

Though Reagan had campaigned in 1980 on a promise of no negotiations with terrorists, as president, the hostages' personal ordeal touched him deeply, and he strongly pressed his advisers on the issue. The result was a plan theoretically intended to send arms to Iranian 'moderates', who would then attempt to influence Hezbollah to release the hostages. The effort quickly devolved into an arms-for-hostages scheme, capped by the bizarre sight of national security adviser McFarlane travelling to Tehran to present a cake baked in the form of a key and a Reagan-autographed Bible intended to show the sincerity of the president's wish for a deal with the Iranians.[28]

The Iranian arms initiative, which occurred without congressional knowledge, soon became entangled with the administration's efforts to bypass congressional restrictions on US aid to anti-communist rebels in Nicaragua. Reagan described the contra rebels as the 'moral equivalent of the Founding Fathers', but most Democrats and independent observers had a very different view of a force comprised mostly of former members of deposed dictator Anastasio Somoza's National Guard. In late 1982, intelligence committee chairman Edward Boland (D-Massachusetts) introduced an amendment, which the House unanimously passed, severely restricting the scope of the covert operation.[29]

By prohibiting aid for the purpose of overthrowing the Nicaraguan government, the Boland amendment set the stage for four years of battles between the White House and Congress over Latin American policy. In 1984, Congress resumed aid, only quickly to cut it off again after revelations that the CIA had helped the contras (illegally) to place mines in Nicaragua's harbours. The next year, the house considered a bewildering array of measures, prompting the *Wall Street Journal* to complain that a 'preoccupation with the *procedure* of the aid is merely designed to hide the fact that what's at issue is the *substantive* imperative of getting help to the contras.'[30] On the key question of military assistance, the administration's request fell short by a mere two votes.[31] Reagan, enraged by the result, announced that he would 'return to the Congress again and again to seek a policy that supports peace and democracy in Nicaragua.'[32] He did not need to wait long: Nicaraguan president Daniel Ortega ostentatiously left for Moscow shortly after the aid was cut off, prompting the house to resume what was deemed 'humanitarian' assistance for the contras.

By this point, in any case, the president had assigned his NSC staff the constitutionally dubious task of finding alternative sources for contra funding. For 1985, Lieutenant-Colonel Oliver North secured one-off donations from Saudi Arabia and Brunei to keep the contras afloat; for the next year, North and his new boss, the retired admiral John Poindexter, decided to use the profits from the Iranian arms sales to fund the contras – despite the Boland amendment's prohibition on military aid. The scheme collapsed in late 1986 after a Beirut newspaper broke word of the Iranian arms sales and a plane carrying military equipment to the contras crashed in Costa Rica. Lengthy investigations by a joint congressional committee and independent counsel Lawrence Walsh concluded that Reagan did not know of North's decision to transfer funds from the Iranian arms sales to the contras.[33]

Reagan's Lebanon policy provided a low point of the administration's record in the Middle East. In first the 1983 military intervention and then the outgrowth of the Iran-contra affair, Reagan and his advisers focused excessively on bypassing Congress, even at the expense of maintaining dubious policies. The end result was disastrous.

Given his administration's consistent efforts to weaken or bypass congressional power in foreign affairs, Reagan, ironically, achieved one of his greatest (short-term, in any case) international victories by cooperating with established congressional procedures. The result was one of the most unusual alliances of the 1980s – the team of CIA director William Casey, a conservative Catholic and hard-line anti-communist; and Texas congressman Charles Wilson, 'Good Time Charlie', a man who had graduated with more demerits than any cadet in the history of the Naval Academy, and after coming to Congress was known for his partying and beautiful women. He joked, 'I'm the only one of the [ethics] committee who likes women and whiskey, and we need to be represented.' Yet, Wilson was also an accomplished legislator, whose position on the defence appropriations subcommittee, which had jurisdiction over CIA funding, gave him considerable influence over covert operations.[34]

What many Western observers considered a pattern of Soviet expansionism in the Third World came to a head in 1979 when Leonid Brezhnev sent Soviet troops across the border into neighbouring Afghanistan. The strategically located central Asian state had experienced several years of political instability following the overthrow of its last king, Zahir Shah, in 1973. In 1978, Afghan communists seized power, but their anti-religious attitudes generated widespread opposition. So, on 25 December 1979, elite Soviet forces invaded, killing Afghan president Hafizullah Amin and installing the more pliable Babrak Karmal in his place. To justify its action, Moscow cited the Brezhnev doctrine, first proclaimed after the Warsaw Pact invasion of Czechoslovakia in 1968. The doctrine held that the Soviet Union could use any means necessary to prevent a socialist country from passing out of its orbit. As occurred with the United States in Vietnam, outside intervention inflamed nationalist sentiment against the superpower. The *mujahidin* resisted the invaders with surprising effectiveness.[35]

Despite their differing personalities, both Casey and Wilson were deeply committed to assisting the *mujahidin*. For Casey, Afghanistan provided an opportunity to implement his plan to roll back Soviet power by aligning the United States more closely with religious groups, whether Roman Catholics in eastern Europe or Islamists in Southwest Asia. For Wilson, Afghanistan provided a new focus for a figure who in the 1970s had involved himself mostly in Israeli and Nicaraguan affairs. Wilson also had a personal connection to the region: his new girlfriend, Democratic fundraiser Joanne Herring, had come to the attention of the Pakistani embassy in Washington, and had grown friendly with the fiercely anti-communist Zia regime.[36]

With Wilson using his position in Congress to ensure that funds went to the covert operation, Casey coordinated efforts with Saudi and Pakistani intelligence. By the time Reagan left office, the covert operation was viewed as a great success − although, of course, subsequent events would produce a differing interpretation. In the short term, however, Afghanistan showed the merits of a cooperative approach between the executive and Congress, even at the expense of trimming back the administration's crusade to weaken legislative power.

‼)(‽

When Reagan left office the international environment was very different from the one that had existed in 1981. Reform-minded Soviet leader Mikhail Gorbachev, who came to power in March 1985, understood the link between Soviet domestic problems and the empire's aggressive foreign policy derived from its centralized, isolated and heavily militarized economy dating to the late 1920s. Gorbachev's programme of domestic reform (*perestroika*) therefore depended on two other initiatives − an internal opening of the Soviet political system (*glasnost*), and a re-evaluation of Soviet foreign policy based on principles of non-intervention, arms control and peaceful integration into the international system. Gorbachev and his newly appointed foreign minister, Eduard Shevardnadze, who was committed to withdrawing the Red Army from Afghanistan, proposed the abolition of all nuclear weapons and decreased the number of Soviet front-line forces in eastern Europe by 500,000. Most important, they allowed eastern European societies economic and ultimately political freedom. By 1987, Hungary and Poland had effectively severed their ties with the Soviet bloc and, by 1989, with the fall of the Berlin Wall, the cold war had ended.[37]

The end of the cold war shattered the balance of power in the Middle East. In 1988, a savage eight-year conflict between Iran and Iraq ended inconclusively. Saddam Hussein's Iraqi regime was left deep in debt, largely to the oil-producing kingdoms of the Persian Gulf – Saudi Arabia, Kuwait and the United Arab Emirates. Iraq owed roughly $75 billion to foreign interests. For much of the cold war, Iraq was a client state of the Soviet Union, but the decline of Soviet power left Saddam to fend for himself. Throughout 1989, he asked the Gulf states to write off the war debt, arguing that the funds helped to defend their territory from Iran's theocracy. When they refused, he accused neighbouring Kuwait of stealing Iraqi oil. In early 1990, he threatened to annex the nation he now termed 'Iraq's 19th province'.[38]

Despite Saddam's reckless policy, the United States seemed eager to develop a *rapprochement*. Reagan's vice president, George H. W. Bush, had prevailed in the 1988 election, and promised to retain both his predecessor's increasingly pragmatic approach to world affairs and his aggressive pursuit of maximizing executive power in foreign policy. But Bush departed from Reagan's approach in one significant effect. The new administration's National Security Directive 26, which defined policy for the Persian Gulf, abandoned Reagan's stated hands-off stance towards Saddam's regime and instead urged the development of 'normal relations' with Iraq.[39]

Some forces in Congress welcomed the new policy. Farm state senators, led by Bob Dole (R-Kansas) and Alan Simpson (R-Wyoming), saw Iraq as a potentially important market for US agricultural goods. Dole and Simpson travelled to Baghdad in 1990, as part of their effort for warmer ties with Saddam's government. Dole sought to reassure Saddam: 'If there is a campaign against Iraq, President Bush is not a part of it. He wants better relations, and the United States wants better relations with Iraq.'[40] Simpson went even further, telling the Iraqi leader, 'I believe that your problems lie with the Western media and not with the US government.'[41] But the Bush policy also drew sharp attacks. Senator Howard Metzenbaum (D-Ohio) had long criticized Saddam's record of human rights violations. In the house, banking committee chairman Henry Gonzalez (D-Texas) explored the troubling relationship between US agricultural assistance, Saddam's weapons-building programme and money-laundering through an Atlanta-based bank, BNL.[42]

With Congress divided on the question and high-profile Republicans still committed to undoing what they perceived as the institutional excesses of the 1970s, the administration avoided legislative involvement in Iraqi policy. As had occurred with Reagan and Lebanon, this approach backfired. The US ambassador in Baghdad, April Glaspie, seemed nonplussed by Saddam's increasingly belligerent rhetoric toward Kuwait, and Western intelligence agencies believed that Saddam was bluffing when he stationed his army on his neighbour's border. They were wrong. On 2 August 1990, Iraqi troops invaded Kuwait, which fell within a matter of hours. Bush, bolstered by a visit from British Prime Minister Margaret Thatcher, publicly promised that the invasion 'will not stand'. Four days later, Saudi Arabia's King Fahd formally requested US military assistance; and more than 200,000 US troops would arrive in the Arabian Peninsula.[43]

Throughout the US mid-term election campaign, Bush consistently characterized the goal of 'Operation Desert Shield' as defensive. But shortly after the election the mission dramatically changed. On 8 November 1990 Bush announced that the troop level would rise to meet a new objective – providing 'an adequate offensive military option' that would, if necessary, liberate Kuwait. Secretary of Defence Dick Cheney seconded the wording, indicating that US forces should be prepared 'to conduct offensive military operations'.[44]

Bush had not invoked the War Powers Act before sending the troops to Saudi Arabia, and he refused to do so when their mission changed. Instead, he cited his authority as commander-in-chief, and in addition turned for support from the UN. Throughout the cold war, the UN's collective security provisions had been a dead letter; the threat of either a US or Soviet veto in the Security Council ensured that the international organization would not sanction aggressor states. But with the Soviets embracing a newly cooperative course and the PRC eager to repair relations with the United States after the Tiananmen massacre, the UN could act. On 29 November 1990, the UN Security Council passed a measure authorizing the use of 'all means necessary' to eject Iraq from Kuwait.[45]

In 1945, debate over approving the UN Covenant, the Senate's two delegates to the San Francisco conference that created the United Nations, Arthur Vandenberg (R-Michigan) and Tom Connally (D-Texas), made clear that nothing in the Covenant could override the power of Congress to declare war. With Bush now implying the opposite, 45 members of the House, led by Ron Dellums (D-California), took the highly unusual move of filing suit in the district court for the District of Columbia. 'Only the Congress of the United States,' declared Dellums, 'has the capacity to declare war.' White House spokesman Marlin Fitzwater countered, 'We believe that this lawsuit is unnecessary in the sense of the commitment by the President and the Administration to work with the Congress at every opportunity in this matter and to keep them informed.'[46]

Attorney General Dick Thornburgh made clear that the administration would strongly oppose the lawsuit: 'We will indicate quite clearly what we think the President's responsibilities are and what limits, *if any*, exist [emphasis added].' Briefs filed on Thornburgh's behalf rejected the applicability of the War Powers Act, dismissing as 'remote and conjectural' the possibility that US troops could be involved in combat. Administration filings also suggested that the president, as commander-in-chief, had sole discretion on determining when or if any particular offensive military operation constituted an act of war.

US District Judge Harold Greene rejected this sweeping conception of executive power. He ruled:

> The Court has no hesitation in concluding that an offensive entry into Iraq by several hundred thousand United States servicemen under the conditions described above could be described as a 'war' within the meaning of ... the Constitution. To put it another way: the Court is not prepared to read out of the Constitution the clause granting to the Congress, and to it alone, the authority 'to declare war'.

Despite these findings, Greene dismissed Dellums's suit, holding that the judiciary

> should not decide issues affecting the allocation of power between the President and Congress until the political branches reach a constitutional impasse. Otherwise we would encourage small groups or even individual Members of Congress to seek judicial resolution of issues before the normal political process has the opportunity to resolve the conflict. ... It cannot be said that either the Senate or the House has rejected the President's claim. If the Congress chooses not to confront the President, it is not our task to do so.[47]

The combination of political pressure and Greene's harsh wording about Bush's claims of executive freedom helped bring about a shift in the administration's strategy, and Bush decided to request from Congress a resolution authorizing him to use force. In the House, moderate and conservative Democrats sided with the administration, and the measure easily passed. In the Senate, however, majority leader George Mitchell (D-Maine) resisted strongly. Presenting a Wilsonian viewpoint against the administration, Mitchell argued that in the post-cold war world, Iraq provided a test case of whether non-military options could deter aggression. He and other Democrats counselled Bush to permit more time for economic sanctions to work. But Mitchell failed to hold his own caucus, and ten Senate Democrats – John Breaux (Louisiana), Richard Bryan (Nevada), Al Gore (Tennessee), Bob Graham (Florida), Howell Heflin (Alabama), J. Bennett Johnston (Louisiana), Joe Lieberman (Connecticut), Harry Reid (Nevada), Chuck Robb (Virginia), and Richard Shelby (Alabama) – sided with the president. The Senate voted 54–46 for the war resolution.

By this stage, Saddam's only support came from Jordan, which depended on Iraq economically; a few rogue states such as Libya; and the PLO. The Iraqi ruler nonetheless still refused to withdraw, and war commenced on 17 January 1991. International forces began their campaign with massive aerial bombardment, designed both to limit coalition casualties and to soften up Iraqi resistance. After more than 40 days of bombing, coalition troops crossed the border into Kuwait. They routed the poorly trained and ill-equipped Iraqi conscript army.

Now the question became whether the conflict would conclude with the toppling of the Iraqi regime. Bush encouraged the Shiite majority in the south and the Kurdish minority in the north to rebel, seeming to promise US protection. But he then agreed to a quick cease fire, allowing Saddam's regime to suppress the Shiite insurrection. By the mid-1990s, nonetheless, the Kurds had established a *de facto* autonomous state in the north. In addition, Iraq had to operate under stringent UN sanctions designed to compel it to disarm.

As with Reagan and Afghanistan, Bush's decision to prosecute the Iraq campaign without challenging Congress' foreign policy authority helped to prevent an institutional backlash against his policy. It also avoided distracting debates over which branch should coordinate policy towards the region – as had occurred in Reagan's approach towards Lebanon and, to a lesser extent, in the handling of Iraq during the early Bush years.

Yet, even while frontal challenges to congressional authority rarely succeeded, the foreign policy process bequeathed by the 1970s reforms worked awkwardly, at best. The Wilson–Casey partnership united two figures whose personal agendas, rather than acceptance of the institutional status quo, led them to cooperate. And the AWACS sale showed how the foreign policy of a democracy could antagonize regional allies and make the United States look foolish internationally.

9

EU Efforts to Resolve the Palestinian–Israeli Conflict

Georg Simonis

The European Union tries to stabilize and resolve the Israeli–Palestinian conflict through a variety of security missions (such as UNIFIL, BAM and EUCOPPS) as well as by providing political, economic and financial assistance and support. The political actors in the EU want to maintain the tense peace in the Middle East and help local actors deal with the entrenched conflict.

The EU is only one among other external actors to influence the Israeli–Palestinian conflict and to try and reduce its violence and negative effects on world peace. Over the last few decades, despite the Madrid and Barcelona processes, the EU has not been a dominant player in the region compared with the United States and Israel's Arab neighbours. The widening and deepening of the EU, however, have significantly increased its weight and possible influence in the eastern Mediterranean. The question therefore is whether the EU can, beyond its current efforts, offer a special European contribution to solving the Middle East conflict.

I base my analysis on four assumptions:

- The complex structure of the Israeli–Palestinian conflict as well as the entrenched attitudes and behaviour patterns of the various parties involved do not allow any easy or quick solution of the conflict.
- There seems to be no plausible alternative to the idea of 'land for peace'. However, its realization is extremely difficult because it requires a basic solution to the conflict before the implementation of a peace-building programme.
- The nature of the conflict is such that it cannot be solved by external actors. In the last resort, only political actors who are directly involved in the region have the capabilities to manage and resolve the conflict.
- However, the external environment (institutions, conflict situations and historical conjunctures) and the external actors' strategies are not

without influence. They also shape and mould the forms in which the conflict develops. They can influence local conditions – perceptions, resources and potential action – and may modify the strategies and action programmes in the direction of more peaceful and less violent behaviour.

Once these assumptions are accepted, it should become easier to discuss what political moves might actually or potentially modify the incentive structures of the local partners to the conflict than to give a detailed overview of EU activities in the Middle East.

If one understands the EU as a complex governance structure with quality actors, it would be useful to look at its institutional arrangements for countries in the European sphere, as well as at the tools and activities of its Common Foreign and Security Policy (CFSP), especially those pertaining to security and defence. As I shall show, in the last resort the institutionalized incentives of the EU's governance system offer more potential to shape the Israeli–Palestinian conflict than do the strategic instruments of the CFSP. With its enlargement and deepening since the end of the cold war, the EU has further developed its governance structure concerning relations between neighbouring states. The EU formulated the European Neighbourhood and Partnership Instrument (ENPI) to offer states in the neighbourhood a chance to become better integrated into the EU.

The European Union is not a state, but a special confederation of states. It forms a multi-level system in which responsibility for some policies lies completely, for others partially or not at all, with the community. The political nature of the EU is difficult to determine and up to now it is not firmly fixed. Further integration and successive enlargements have changed its political character. With the accessions of Romania and Bulgaria on 1 January 2007, the EU has 27 members. The Republic of Cyprus, only about 100 nautical miles away from Israel, now forms its eastern outpost in the eastern Mediterranean and since 2004, Israel has been one of the EU's closest neighbours. In October 2005 Turkey was invited to start official accession negotiations. If in ten or so years' time Turkey is deemed ready to be accepted as a member of the European Union, the institutional weight and political influence of the EU in the eastern Mediterranean might grow substantially.

As Jan Zielonka put it,[1] the European Union bears a closer resemblance to an empire than a neo-Westphalian state. It can be conceived as an open political system that other European states can join should they fulfil the Copenhagen accession criteria and the EU is prepared to welcome them. It is important to note that member states have the right to withdraw from the EU. Because member states have this option, to a remarkable extent the community has to respect the interests of everybody. In this context it is important to remember that the EU is a community of states and people. Without the consent of the people no state can accede to the EU or remain a member. This means, without perceived benefits, however they may be defined, the stability of the EU will be precarious.

Guiding Principles of European Foreign Governance

The position of the EU in the international system is determined largely by its characteristic structure as an open multi-level system.

> The Union's action on the international scene shall be guided by the principles which have inspired its own creation, development and enlargement, and which it seeks to advance in the wider world: democracy, the rule of law, the universality and indivisibility of human rights and fundamental freedoms, respect for human dignity, the principles of equality and solidarity, and respect for the principles of the United Nations Charter and international law.
>
> (Article 21)

Basically five structural properties shape the foreign relations of the EU.

To act in the sphere of international relations on behalf of the EU the Brussels institutions (the European Council, Commission and Troika) require a strong legitimacy base. The observance of community law can produce what Niklas Luhmann called procedural legitimacy,[2] but this would not be enough to convince the people of the EU of its benefits. As it is laid down in the preamble of the treaties, the EU will help overcome divisions in Europe and the long lasting hostilities between European people that have led to two world wars. The foreign activities of the EU thus have to be measured against this high standard. The governance structures (regimes, networks, cooperatives and associations) the EU has established with third states operate through governance mechanisms (such as soft power, conditionality, functional cooperation or multi-lateralism) that pursue the interest of the EU without resorting to the traditional instruments of power politics in the sense of 'Realpolitik'. With limited means the EU has to optimize its output legitimacy.[3] The policy results must convince the European people of the benefits of the EU not only in the areas of growth and economic policy but also in the domain of foreign policy. If they do not appreciate the outcomes of the integration project, if the opening of frontiers and establishment of freedom makes them feel insecure, they can stop the deepening processes. In times of economic and social crises, in which the short-sighted national interests of states and people come to the forefront, the whole integration project may come under great pressure. One cannot rule out the possibility that in a time of crisis some European states may resort to the dangerous instruments of power politics. Regression remains an option.

After the awful experiences of the Second World War, based on the neofunctional conception of Jean Monnet and Robert Schuman, the abandonment of traditional power politics and development of integration politics occurred under the influence of an international system that was dominated by the escalation of the East–West conflict and the deployment of nuclear weapons. During the 1950s and 1960s of the last century the six founding countries of the European Union were able to concentrate on the institutionalization of economic integration and to overcome old enmities because the Western alliance, the North Atlantic Treaty Organization (NATO), guaranteed security. At the same time, the Council of Europe advanced the value base (human rights and democracy) of an open and cosmopolitical European identity.[4]

With the establishment in the 1970s of the pan-European Conference for Security and Cooperation, which, after the collapse of the Soviet empire was renamed the Organization for Security and Cooperation in Europe (OSCE), European security architecture was extended to eastern Europe. At that time of radical change at the beginning of the 1990s, some European-centred political actors, as well as leftist groups and representatives of the peace movement, hoped that the OSCE would reduce Europe's dependence on NATO. However, this political conception of a Europe more independent of the United States turned out to be an illusion. In fact, NATO gained in importance. Central and eastern European countries like Poland, the Czech Republic, Slovakia, Hungary and the Baltic states applied for membership and the pre-Maastricht European Union proved to be incapable of handling the dissolution of Yugoslavia in a peaceful way. So, in the first instance, the functional division of labour between the EU and NATO prevailed. However, since the mid-1990s, mainly as a result of the dissonance – namely the disintegration of Yugoslavia, especially the Bosnian war of 1995 – induced in the EU, through the treaties of Amsterdam and Nice the EU stepped up its efforts to institutionalize its own conflict-prevention and crisis-management capacity.

The terrorist attacks on 11 September 2001, the changing global security environment and the increasing engagement of the USA outside Europe accelerated European activities to establish a Common Foreign and Security Policy (CFSP) based on operational capacities. At its December 2003 Brussels meeting, the European Council adopted the European Security Strategy, which 'can be seen as an innovative conceptual framework for the whole of EU external action, based on the notion of comprehensive security'.[5]

The CFSP is still in the EU's intergovernmental domain, though in some cases since the Amsterdam Treaty (1997) qualified majority votes have been possible. The Lisbon Treaty (which the European Council signed in December 2007) will not basically change this situation. Each member of the EU, including both the nuclear powers, members of the Security Council, Germany, Poland and the Mediterranean countries, will pursue its own foreign and security policies. This means that the international environment of the EU has to interact with different, sometimes incompatible foreign policy options. The formal instruments of the CFSP (general guidelines, common strategies, common positions, joint actions, international agreements, declarations, contacts with third countries and systematic cooperation) will not suffice for harmonizing all substantial differences in the perception of national interests. One can, however, expect that the foreign policy *acquis communitaire* will slowly but continuously gain in relevance.

Beside the CFSP, and its military component the CFDP, the European Union has established a new type of foreign policy called integration policy or integrative foreign policy. This new foreign policy area is the natural offspring of the European unification project. According to its founding principle, to build a unified Europe to which all European states can in principle apply for membership, the EU has a duty to accept an application so long as the candidate complies with a set of special criteria, the so-called Copenhagen criteria – recognition of human rights, established democracy, a stable market economy, and acceptance and implementation of the *acquis communautaire*. But, besides these conditions, all member states have to agree to accept the applying state (principle of unanimity). Today, after the great enlargement round in 2004, the accession of Bulgaria and Romania (1 January 2007) and the start of membership negotiations with Croatia and Turkey, a sceptical mood has developed in some of the old member states over further enlargements because they might endanger the cohesion of the EU.

Even before the big bang enlargement, the European Commission, at that time still under the presidency of Prodi, began to outline a new foreign policy instrument, the so-called European Neighbourhood Instrument, which would be offered to all states in the neighbourhood of the enlarged EU that at present are not eligible for full membership. Some of these states unquestionably are European, for example Ukraine and Moldavia; others are not, such as the Maghreb states or the countries of the eastern Mediterranean. The EU thus divides its neighbourhood into different categories of states and only some of them have any real prospect of accession in the years to come. The EU conceived of the neighbourhood policy to keep neighbouring states interested in deepening their relations with the EU to build, as Prodi said, 'a ring of friends' around it. With the Neighbourhood Policy Instrument the EU offers its neighbouring countries a set of incentives 'aiming to establish an area of prosperity and good neighbourliness, founded on the values of the EU and characterized by close and peaceful relations based on cooperation'.[6] Within the framework of the ENPI, *inter alia* the EU offers special access to the common market, financial assistance for joint activities and support for adapting to the *acquis*.

After successive rounds of broadening and deepening its membership, the EU has developed a complex multi-layered structure. It interacts with its international environment in three different legal forms – as a supranational actor, as an intergovernmental (coordinating) actor, or as a mixed, partly supranational partly intergovernmental, actor. Because the EU is endowed with a highly differentiated legal form based on international treaties, each foreign policy instrument, be it an instrument of the CFSP integration policy (accession, neighbourhood, association) or common trade policy, has its own specific legal form defined in the treaties. This means that individuals acting in the name of the EU (president of the European Council, high representative, president of the Commission or commissioner of foreign relations) behave in a narrow framework of legal (supranational and international) norms, established procedures and principles, agreed guidelines, common strategies and positions. Both supranational and intergovernmental actors are forced to generate this form of institutionalized and highly legalized external policy structure when they undertake to secure legitimacy and the support of the principal, namely the community of states and people it represents. To prevent conflicts, reduce transaction costs and ensure legitimacy, the institutionalization and legalization not only of the instruments but also of the substance of external policy are unavoidable. Inevitably, the foreign policy process of the EU is at the same time rather complex and highly transparent, at least for all who want to know what the EU intends and what obligations it has accepted. The international partners of the EU thus possess the possibility to weigh their advantages and disadvantages when they decide to cooperate with the EU within the framework of a special foreign policy instrument. For the EU, offering cooperation is not without self-interest, the partners have to choose. On the new neighbourhood the interests of the EU are quite clear – to build a 'ring of friends' around the community.

Forms of External Governance in the Middle East

Not all EU member states ratified the Lisbon Treaty, now scheduled to come into force on 1 January 2010 to provide different rights, obligations and capabilities for the community as an international actor in different foreign policy areas. The treaty, like all other EU treaties before it (Maastricht in 1993, Amsterdam in 1996, Nice in 2001 and the non-ratified constitutional treaty in 2004) still differentiates between communitarized (supranational) action space for external policy activities, so-called external actions under Article 205, and the not fully communitarized classical domains of foreign policy that are regulated under Common Foreign and Security Policy (CFSP) headings in Articles 24 and under Common Foreign and Defence Policy (CFDP) in Article 42. In the Lisbon Treaty, the CFDP is viewed as an integral part of the CFSP but is treated in a special section because the deployment of military capabilities requires an unanimous vote of the member states:

> Decisions relating to the common security and defence policy, including those initiating a mission as referred to in this Article, shall be adopted by the Council acting unanimously on a proposal from the High Representative of the EU for Foreign Affairs and Security Policy or an initiative from a Member State.
>
> (Article 42, 4)

Besides these three foreign policy areas, the Lisbon council inserted a new article in the treaty on the relationship with neighbouring countries. In Article 8,1 it said: 'The Union shall develop a special relationship with neighbouring countries, aiming to establish an area of prosperity and good neighbourliness, founded on the values of the Union and characterized by close and peaceful relations based on cooperation.' The insertion of this article in the Treaty of Lisbon means that the EU has built up a new action space for a special form of external policy and that it can institutionalize new foreign policy instruments, as for example the European Neighbourhood Instrument, designed for the establishment of special relationships with its neighbours.

Without going into too much detail, we can ascertain that the EU has developed and legalized in its treaties a broad spectrum of functionally and sectorally differentiated foreign policy instruments. The establishment of these instruments and action spaces reflects the historical evolution of the EU on the one hand and the complex compromises that shape and characterize the European integration process on the other. Some areas of foreign policy, united under the heading 'external action', are organized supranationally; other areas, especially the CFDP, are organized inter-governmentally and still others have both an intergovernmental and supra-national component (CFSP and relationship with neighbouring countries).

It has to be noted here that inside the EU the so-called *Kompetenz-Kompetenz* still lies with the sovereign member states who remain in the last resort the masters of the treaties.

Based on these four different fields of action the EU has established foreign policy instruments and institutionalized special forms of external governance (see Table 9.1). The concept of governance is here used to elucidate a neo-institutional perspective of analysis. In the frame of this analytical perspective external governance[7] can be defined as an institutional arrangement established between an international actor and third parties to regulate problems of interdependence or – in other words – to solve common problems.

With the concept of external governance, it is possible to gain insights into the specific governance problems of a governance system's institutionalized structure (actor constellation, principles and objects of cooperation, issues, legal form, working institutions), capacity for problem solving (resources/financial instruments, incentives, commitments to undertake, political or governance mechanisms), contributions (input) towards mastering a governance problem and impact on resolving the problem.

To address the conflict in the Middle East, in the course of the last 15 years the European Union, sometimes in cooperation with other international actors, embarked on three different political initiatives, which led to the establishment of new forms of external governance. They are the European Mediterranean Partnership (EMP), the Middle East Action Strategy (MEAS) and the European Neighbourhood Policy (ENP), each with its distinct institutional setting and each with special activities and capabilities.

In Table 9.1 I show, in the form of a matrix, that each of the three Middle East governance systems has been founded on a special pattern of foreign policy instruments of the European Union. The primary focus of the EMP, which emerged from the institutions and activities of the 1995 Barcelona process, is on measures to establish a free trade zone between the states of the Mediterranean and the EU. Communitarized policy instruments, especially common commercial policy, technical and financial assistance and development cooperation, dominate this arrangement of external governance.

The MEAS, however, which grew from an early twenty-first-century EU initiative to revitalize the stagnating peace process and led to the institutionalization of cooperation in the so-called quartet between the UN general secretary, the EU high representative and the governments of Russia and the United States, is an offspring of the only partly communitarized CFSP instruments that include the action possibilities of the CFDP.[8] Finally, motivated by the 2004 enlargement round in which eight

Table 9.1   EU foreign policy intruments and forms of external governance in the Middle East

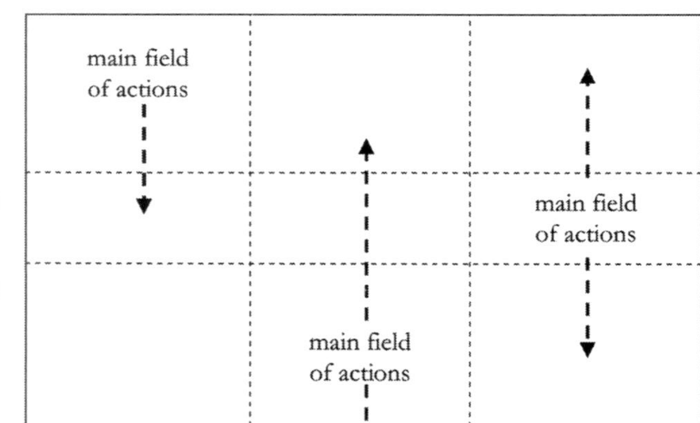

Table 9.2:   Schematic overview of three forms of external governance of the EU in the Middle East

	EMP *(1995–2005)*	*MEAS* *(since 2002)*	*ENP* *(since 2003)*
Governance problem	regional integration	conflict resolution	interdependency management
Structure, actor constellation	multilateral (bilateral)	trilateral (international)	bilateral
principles	free trade	land for peace	joint ownership, differentiation
objectives	security community	comprehensive peace	prosperity, democracy, security/stability
issue areas	three baskets	mediation, support/peace building	ten key sectors
legal form	Barcelona declaration, association agreements	declarations, agreements (road map)	association agreements, Action plans
working institutions	association committees, EuroMediter-ranean c'ttee	Quartet meeting, special envoys	association committee, subcommittees, joint managing authority, political dialogue
Capacity of problem solving resources	MEDA I/II	donors conference	ENPI, GF (ENPI), RIP (ENPI), NIF
incentives	assistance, preferential trading relations, projects/ programmes	security guarantees, support	assistance, preferential trading relations, participation in EU activities/ programmes, political support, joint programming
commitments to undertake	democracy, human rights, rule of law, transformation/ rule adaption	implementation of agreements	democracy, human rights, rule of law, transformation, good governance, regulatory harmonization
political mechanisms	negative conditionality, hierarchical procedures	bargaining, mediation, monitoring, conditionality	negative and positive conditionality, bargaining, dialogue, joint programming, twinning/TAIEX, monitoring

Middle and Eastern European countries along with Cyprus and Malta became new members of the EU, the ENP not only focuses on the Lisbon Treaty's new Article 8 on relations with neighbouring countries, but is also connected with the instruments of External Action and the CFSP.

In the next part of this chapter I provide a short overview of the three types of external governance that the European Union has established with its partners in the Middle East in an attempt to make its own contributions towards resolving the Israeli–Palestinian conflict (see Table 9.2). Without access either to the decision making processes or to the methodological tools with which to differentiate between the different factors externally influencing and conditioning local actors, it is not possible to assess the exact impact of these governance systems on mitigating the conflict.

European Mediterranean Partnership (EMP)

The direct influence of the EMP (Barcelona Process) launched on 27 November 1995 by the then 15 EU member states and 12 Mediterranean countries on the Middle East peace process has been disappointing. Its successful predecessor, the Helsinki Process, with the Commission on Security and Cooperation in Europe (CSCE) and the Organization of Security and Cooperation (OSCE), largely determined the organizing principles of the Barcelona Declaration's founding document. Like its model, the EMP was composed of three baskets, namely (1) the Political and Security Chapter, (2) the Economic and Financial Chapter and (3) the Social, Cultural and Human Chapter. Yet, the idea 'of turning the Mediterranean basin into an area of dialogue, exchange and cooperation guaranteeing peace, stability and prosperity' through regional cooperation failed.[9] The Middle East conflict overshadowed the multilateral approach and impeded the establishment of regional projects between Israel and the Arab states of the Mediterranean.[10] Only in some minor but not totally unimportant areas could regional cooperation be implemented (Malta seminars for young diplomats, the Euro-Mediterranean Study Commission research network).[11] On the positive side it can also be said that the EMP is besides the UNO the only forum where diplomats and foreign policy actors of the conflicting parties meet rather regularly.

If the EMP has made any further contribution to the peace process, then it is of an indirect nature. In its first phase the Barcelona Process was concentrated on the erection of a free trade zone in the Mediterranean. For its establishment the conclusion of bilateral association agreements has been necessary. So, interestingly, the multilateral conceptualized EMP got a bilateral performance. The projects supporting trade liberalization and the transformation of the economies, in so far as they were developed and organized on a bilateral basis, reinforced that bias. After the first five years of implementing the financial instrument of the EMP, the MEDA programme, the bureaucrats of the EU Commission's Middle-East and Southern Mediterranean directorate were not the only people who were dissatisfied with the results of the steering effects of this governance system.

> It is an open secret that the pace of reforms in the Mediterranean is not rapid enough. ... Encouragement by the EU will henceforward be more differentiated than in the past. But strategic choices will be made in partnership. ... In this respect under MEDA II we will strive to intensify economic dialogue with the Partners at bilateral as well as regional level.[12]

Insufficient progress in regional cooperation and the modest improvement in the efficiency of the EMP strengthened economic issues at the expense of political and cultural ones, and bilateral forms of coordination at the expense of multilateral ones. Table 9.2 gives a general view of the characteristic features of the EMP governing structure without taking into account slight modifications between its first (1995–99) and second (2000–05) financial regulation periods.[13] As a result of the bilateralization and economization of relations inside the EMP governance structure,[14] the unsolved problems of the Middle East conflict fell into the background. Also, depoliticization at the regional and bilateral levels meant that the European Union could not employ the instrument of negative conditionality. Although clauses on human rights and democracy were included in all the assistance programmes, the EU did not in any case return to them. 'All this means that, even if the Barcelona process, at both bilateral and multilateral level, attaches great importance to progress on democracy and human rights, in practice the EU has not shown any determination to see that such undertakings are respected.'[15]

So, we can take it as a provisional finding that during its first ten years the EMP was unable to influence the peace process directly. Also, the indirect effects of the EMP were minimal. Because of its depoliticization the EU renounced *de facto* use of the instrument of negative conditionality to support the observance of human rights, democratic liberties and good governance. The EU relied only on the indirect effects of economic liberalization and long-term transformation to develop good neighbourly relations. However, in recent years several factors have caused a general reorientation of the EU's Mediterranean policy. The EU had to react to new developments:

In the wake of September 11, the second Intifada and the war in Iraq, the Barcelona Process has gradually put more emphasis on the first chapter of the Barcelona Declaration, in particular political and security cooperation. Issues related to justice and home affairs, border control, the fight against terrorism and crime have come to the forefront in the Euro-Mediterranean Partnership.[16]

In addition to these issues, the accession in May 2004 of the new states to the EU raised the question of how the community should in future manage its relations with its new neighbours, especially the neighbours of the new member states. After two years of discussions, almost at the same time as the accession of eight eastern European countries and two Mediterranean states, Malta and Cyprus, in May 2004 the Prodi Commission presented the strategy paper, *European Neighbourhood Policy*,[17] to the EU, which the Council and the European Parliament later approved.[18] The Prodi Commission proposed establishing privileged relationships with all EU neighbours not eligible for full membership. From the neighbouring states at that time only Romania and Bulgaria were waiting for full membership, while the west Balkan countries and Turkey awaited a perspective for future membership. Therefore, to manage the complex interdependencies with new and old neighbouring states on the one hand and to elude the formation of new hitches in Europe on the other, the commission invented a new external governance system, the European Neighbourhood Policy (ENP).

According to this fundamental decision, between ten and twelve Mediterranean countries that were members of the Barcelona Declaration and of the EMP had to be integrated into the new governance system. Malta joined the EU and Turkey gained the status of an accession state. But the transition from a multilateral and regional form of organization shaping the European Mediterranean Partnership to a bilateral form of organization shaping the European Neighbourhood Policy was a rather complex operation.[19] It resulted in a typical European compromise whereby the two governance systems were amalgamated. To the bilateral structure of the ENP a regional component was added. This was not so difficult because the EMP had, as mentioned above, continuously strengthened its bilateral elements. Therefore, the reorganized Mediterranean partnership is predominantly bilateral in structure. But the regional traits of the EMP survived and now complete the neighbourhood policy. Interestingly, the regional component of the Barcelona Process continued not only because of problems associated with the growing interdependence of Arab states (migration, climate change, terrorism and trade liberalization) but also because of the special accomplishments of the

Middle East peace process. As the EU Commission put it: 'In the political domain the Barcelona Process constitutes a unique regional forum to further mutual understanding with a view to abating tensions in the Middle East, even if it is not the forum in which a political settlement will be reached.'[20]

For the period 2007–13, the regional strategy paper, now within the framework of the ENPI, which replaced the previous MEDA financial instrument for the southern Mediterranean and Middle East channels, divided the contents of the five-year work programme into three priority objectives:

- a common Euro-Mediterranean area of justice, security and migration cooperation;
- a common sustainable economic area, with a focus on trade liberalization, regional trade integration, infrastructure networks and environmental protection; and
- a common sphere of socio-cultural exchanges, with a focus on cultural and people-to-people exchanges, and raising awareness of the partnership through the media.

The Regional Indicative Programme (RIP) 2007–10 transposes this policy response into concrete action programmes representing a total of €343 million, while the political objectives of the Barcelona Process are all together sustained by a budget of more than €3.3 billion.[21]

Besides its forum function (political and security dialogue at ministerial conferences and at Euro-Med senior officials meetings) the RIP contributes to the peace process through its Partnership for Peace (PfP) programme established in 2002 as the successor to the 'people-to-people programme' (1998–2002). The RIP states that the objective of this PfP programme is 'to help support the conditions for relaunching the peace process and provide a solid foundation of civil society and inter-governmental level for a just and lasting peace in the Middle East by strengthening and increasing direct civil society relationships and interagency/intergovernmental cooperation'.[22]

That these high and commanding objectives can see the light of day is obviously not just in the hands of the European Commission. The local partners must be prepared to implement them.

Middle East Action Strategy (MEAS)

Unlike the EMP, the external governance system labelled here as Middle East Action Strategy (MEAS) is, according to the EU's latest foreign policy activities to support the Annapolis revitalized peace process, based on the instruments of the European Union's CFSP. Even though there are overlaps between the EMP's institutions and processes, as well as between the ENP and MEAS governance system, the latter has, as Table 9.2 shows, a specific structure and logic of its own. It is concentrated on the peace process and its entire right to existence rests exclusively on its supporting role. At the present time the MEAS governance system seems rather well established, although its institutionalization starting in the 1980s with declarations of principles may not have come to an end.

The institutional centre of the MEAS governance systems is constituted by the international 'Quartet' in which the EU is only one member besides the USA, Russia and the UNO. It was a European initiative[23] that organized the Quartet in April 2002 as an informal meeting of high representatives.[24] Since 2002 the Quartet has convened erratically about fifteen times, most recently at the beginning of May 2008 in London.

Though the EU is clearly only one partner of this international body, it provides the political, financial and human resources to the Quartet's special representatives for disengagement (James Wolfensohn in 2005–06 and Tony Blair since June 2007) and kept it alive when the Bush administration had other priorities than the Middle East peace process. The gains in reputation it received from being globally recognized as a leading international actor working alongside the USA, Russia and the United Nations can only partly explain the EU's great interest in the Quartet's mediation activities. Another and deeper motive for the EU's growing engagement in the Middle East seems to be a change in threat perceptions:

> Even in an era of globalization, geography is still important. It is in the European interest that countries on our borders are well-governed. Neighbours who are engaged in violent conflict, weak states where organized crime flourishes, dysfunctional societies or exploding population growth on its borders all pose problems for Europe.
>
> The integration of acceding states increases our security but also brings the EU closer to troubled areas. …
>
> Resolution of the Arab/Israeli conflict is a strategic priority for Europe. Without this, there will be little chance of dealing with other problems in the Middle East. The European Union must remain engaged and ready to commit resources to the problem until it is solved.[25]

Based on a couple of Middle East declarations,[26] the European Union turned in the 1990s after the Oslo accords towards a more active Middle East policy supporting the Oslo process with its limited capabilites.[27]

Concerning the establishment of an external governance system occupied only with peace building in the Middle East, three factors were essential besides the enlargement of the EU and the effects of the Balkan wars in connection with the dissolution of Yugoslavia:

- the institutionalization of an independent foreign and security competence at the European level through the Maastricht and Amsterdam treaties,
- the creation of the position of a special representative of the European Union for the Middle East peace process, and
- the acceptance of a special responsibility and with that of a special role as financial donor for the building of a 'democratic, viable and peaceful sovereign Palestinian State on the basis of existing agreements and through negotiations'.[28]

As mentioned earlier, the Quartet at the heart of the MEAS governance system was formed in April 2002 because the 11 September 2001 terrorist attacks, the failure of the Camp David II talks and the outbreak of the second Intifada fundamentally changed the international and regional situation in the Middle East. Only with the road map declaration of 30 April 2003 did the Quartet successfully assume the role of an international mediator. Yet, at the start of the Iraq war the Bush administration had priorities other than to resolve the Middle East conflict. Therefore the Quartet was largely blockaded. This situation did not change until the presidential election campaign started in the summer of 2007. Also, during the second Intifada under the Sharon government, the erection of the fence and the withdrawal of the 8000 settlers from the Gaza Strip were at the local level the political conditions for a practically non-existent autonomous European peace policy. The European Union had almost the only chance to pursue a reactive Middle East policy. Within the framework of the MEAS external governance system, the EU pursued five main fields of activity:[29]

- to provide humanitarian assistance to refugees,
- to provide financial assistance to support Palestinian state building (public finance reform, direct financing of the budget, electoral and judicial reform), and to promote security sector reform (since 2005), *inter alia* via efforts to reform Palestinian civil policing (EUCOPPS),
- to support the Israeli withdrawal from the Gaza Strip by establishing, in November 2005, an EU border assistance mission at the Rafah crossing point on the Gaza–Egypt border,
- to extend after the Israel Hezbollah summer war (2006) in Lebanon the

UNIFIL peace-keeping mandate and to deploy up to 15000 soldiers under European command (Security Council Resolution 1701),
- to facilitate political dialogue (including regional dialogue through the EMP; organization of trilateral policy dialogues with the participation of the European Commission and parties on transport, energy and trade; and encounters between civil society actors from Israel, the occupied territories and neighbouring countries) and to accomplish confidence-building measures, including electoral observation activities, in the Palestinian territory.

All these political activities may contribute to the Middle East peace process. However they are not the expression of an autonomous European Middle East peace policy. They react only to local or regional events and are pursued in close cooperation with the Israeli government. While in the 1980s and 1990s European declarations on solving the Middle East conflict often failed to correspond with Israel's policy or ideas about peace, almost all local EU activities designed to ease the conflict or, more precisely, master the social, economic and political consequences of the unresolved conflict, were realized after consultations with and political support from the Israeli government. In relation to the European Union Israel holds a *de facto* veto over practical measures at the local level.

The practical implementation of the latest European initiative that EU High Representative Javier Solana and Commissioner for External Relations Benita Ferrero-Waldner put forward on the Annapolis process (November 2007) to assist Palestinian state building and provide support for the transition period will therefore depend on the results of the bilateral peace negotiations at the local level. The EU has very limited space in which to contribute actively and independently to peace-keeping and peace-building in the Middle East conflict. Although it has a 'strategic objective' in a 'comprehensive peace in the Middle East' it can only call 'on all other interested parties to support the current process, bearing in mind the high cost of failure for everyone involved'. 'Israelis and Palestinians will have to fulfil their responsibilities in that respect, by refraining from measures and decisions which undermine the bilateral process, and by pursuing efforts to improve security and lift obstacles to access and movement'.[30]

The 2007 EU Action Strategy offers the following peace-supporting measures in relation to three issue areas:

1.   Palestinian state building

- Supporting the establishment of modern and democratic police forces, 'in full cooperation with the US Security Coordinator'.

- Comprehensive institution building and good governance 'via ... its work in the Jerusalem based ... Governance Strategy Group'.
- Support for sustained growth of the Palestinian economy 'including credit guaranties, vocational training and trade facilitation'.
- Customs and trade. 'The EU is ready to retune the work of its trilateral trade policy group.'

2.   Support for the transition period

- Support to sustainable PA finances.
- Planning modalities for institution building and economic revival. 'Active involvement of the Palestinian Authority is necessary for these efforts. ... Israeli cooperation is needed for their implementation, in particular with respect to access and movement as a prerequisite for Palestinian economic revival.'
- Emergency and humanitarian support.

3.   Support for conflict resolution

- East Jerusalem. For many years the EU has supported hospitals, schools and community centres for the people of East Jerusalem and 'these activities could be stepped up'.
- Refugees. 'Since 1971 the EU has been providing significant support. ... It is committed to adapting this support as appropriate, in pursuit of a just and equitable solution to the refugee issue.'
- Security arrangements. 'If requested, the EU will be ready in due course to contribute to a system of security arrangements that would be agreed between the parties in the framework of a permanent settlement.'[31]

According to my interpretation of this recent EU Action Strategy on state-building for peace in the Middle East, the EU is making a really big offer. If the local parties are prepared to take advantage of it, the European Union could become deeply entangled in Middle Eastern affairs, which in all probability would imply the return of Europe to the region for a very long time. But are the people of the region willing to accept the reappearance of the old colonial powers, albeit in modernized and democratized form?

European Neighbourhood Policy (ENP)
The ENP was established as a direct result of the big bang enlargement of the European Union in May 2004. The political bodies of the EU,

especially the Commission, had at that time to consider how the enlarged EU should develop its political relations with those European countries that had the right (under the Preamble and Article 49 of the treaties) to file an application for membership of the EU. In other words, these are countries like Ukraine that are seeking access, but do not yet fulfil the Copenhagen criteria for full membership and whose accession would strain the coherence of the EU.[32] The Prodi Commission reacted to this challenge by formulating the ENP, a form of external governance that allowed for the establishment of special relations with the EU and that could be offered indiscriminately to all neighbours, whether new or old. 'When we launched the policy, we had to make it clear that the offer on the table was the same for everyone, with no discrimination.'[33]

The Prodi idea of launching a new policy instrument conducive to building a 'ring of friends' around the EU of countries without membership but highly integrated into the EU, like Norway or Switzerland,[34] was realized and, with Article 8, firmly established in the Lisbon treaty. Although designed for the new eastern European neighbours (Ukraine, Belarus, Moldavia and Russia) the new policy instrument institutionalized in the ENP has been offered indiscriminately to all neighbouring countries, therefore also to states already cooperating within the framework of the Mediterranean partnership as mentioned in the section above on the European Mediterranean Partnership (EMP). In contrast to the EMP, however, the EU's new system of external governance, the ENP, (see Table 9.2) stressed as its basic criteria the principles of:

- bilateralism,
- differentiation,
- joint ownership, and
- responsiveness,

'but always within the common framework of the ENP'.[35] Corresponding to these cooperation principles, in the case of the Mediterranean neighbours, bilateral agreements, association agreements and mutually adopted action plans resulting out of joint programming procedures constitute the institutional basis of the ENP governance system.

The latest action plans for the countries of the Middle East were adopted in winter and spring 2007 (see Table 9.3).

In Table 9.4, I show the principle of differentiation at work in four of Israel's neighbouring Arab countries.[36]

Table 9.3: ENP action plans in the Middle East

Partner countries	Force of contractual relations with EC, Association agreement	Country report	Action plan adoption
Egypt	June 2004	March 2005	6 March 2007
Israel	June 2000	May 2004	11 April 2005
Jordan	May 2002	May 2004	2 June 2005
Lebanon	April 2006	March 2005	19 January 2007
Occupied Palestinian territory	Interim A/7 July 1997	May 2004	4 May 2005

Source: EC.Europe.eu/world/enp/faq.eu.htm 4.1, p 11 (30 April 2008)

With the exception of the PA, the earmarked financial assistance is still rather modest although in the cases of Lebanon and Jordan the inhabitant ratios are more than negligible (see Table 9.5). The currently enacted action plans have, however, to be evaluated as starting points for a possibly deepening partnership with the states in the neighbourhood of the European Union in the future:

> The ENP is a partnership for reform that offers 'more for more': the more deeply a partner engages with the EU, the more fully the EU can respond, politically, economically and through financial and technical cooperation. As the partnerships develop, within the common ENP framework, the policy's operation is becoming increasingly differentiated.[37]

The basic political logic of the ENP is positive conditionality in accordance with the principle of 'more for more'. Because this principle was institutionalized in the ENP's governance structure, the neighbouring states eligible for the programme have by themselves to decide if and to what extent they are willing to accept positive conditionality.

Currently three countries, Israel, Morocco and the Ukraine, are apparently prepared to accept the ENP's offer and conditions.[38] The example of Israel demonstrates how quickly the relations between the European Union and its neighbours can be broadened and deepened if there is the necessary political will. The EU–Israel action plan was adopted in April 2005 for a period of three years. A first ENP progress report was adopted in December 2006. The latest progress report gives a rather positive account of the development of EU-Israel cooperation:

Table 9.4: ENP Country patterns (priority sectors, examples)

	Egypt	*Lebanon*	*Jordan*	*PA*
EC assistance	2006: €127m 2007: €137m	2006: €32m 2006: €91m (additional) 2007: €50m 2008: €50m	2007–10: €265m	EU: lead donor 2005: €500m (EU: €280) 2006: €688m (EU: €340m) 2007: €550m 2008: €486m
education	trained 1500 teachers, 1000 schools		early childhood education in rural areas	
public finance			fiscal reform	
elections				establishment of independent election commission
rule of law, civil society		implementing the AA		revenue collection
trade	modernized customs procedures		facilitated convergence with EU standards	
human rights, civil society		legal support to vulnerable people, intercommunity dialogue	support to organizations, women's participation, labour rights	
good governance		reinforcing capacity of police and judiciary	anti-corruption strategy, environmental governance	
humanitarian assistance		support for Palestinian refugees		relieve socio-economic crisis
local development		micro-credit programmes, development plans, local projects		

Source: European Neighbourhood Policy Conference on 'Strengthening the ENP', 3 September 2007. http://ec.europe.eu/world/emp/documents_en.htm/accessed 18 October 2009.

Israel has been an active partner in the framework of the ENP as demonstrated by the progress made in implementing a large number of priorities of the Action Plan. ... The ENP has clearly enhanced the pace of cooperation between the EU and Israel in a large number of fields: from enhanced EU–Israel dialogue to Israel's involvement in a number of European initiatives. Having agreed a framework protocol with the EC, Israel is the front-runner in making use of the new possibilities for ENP partner countries' participation in Community programmes. It has also sought closer cooperation with EC and EU agencies.[39]

Table 9.5: Regional distribution of ENPI: assistance per inhabitant in Euros (2007–10)

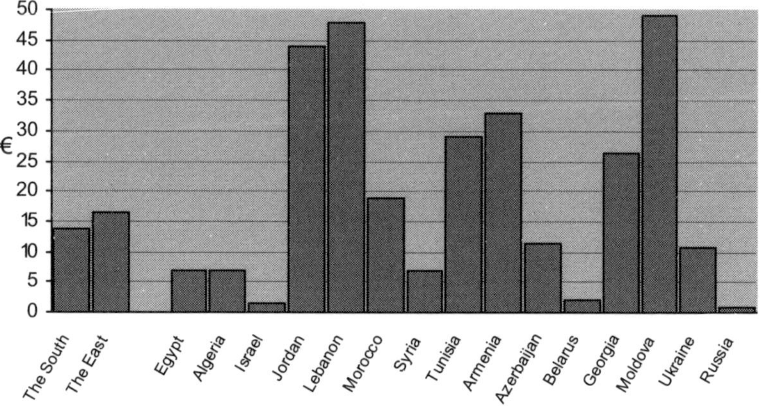

Source: European Commission as well as own calculations; the south = southern ENP countries + regional programme for the European Mediterranean partnership; the east = eastern ENP countries (without Russia) + programme for the East Region.[40]

Because of space limitation it is not possible to describe at length in this chapter the different issue areas of the developing cooperation between EU and Israel in the ENP framework. Three comments concerning possible contributions of the ENP governance system to resolve the Middle East conflict might suffice:

- Owing to the principles of bilateralism, differentiation and ownership, the ENP governance approach is strictly committed to a two-state peace model. Building a viable and sovereign Palestinian state is an integral component of the ENP structure. Yet, the ENP is no more than an offer to cooperate, though a relatively far-reaching offer that consists of establishing privileged partnerships with the European Union.
- The local elites have to decide whether they are prepared to accept the

secondary effects of integration and Europeanization. The principle of positive conditionality is deeply enshrined in the ENP governance system. While the neighbours receive incentives such as access to markets, scientific and technological cooperation, the erection and support of modern infrastructures, financial assistance or the building of common security structures, they have to accept European cultural values (democracy, human rights, women rights and minority rights) and the Europeanization of their economies and societies (environmental regulations and product standards). Europeanization also implies that they respect international and European laws, especially those that renounce using direct force to resolve political conflicts.

- Although in the short run the ENP governance system will be unable to make much contribution towards resolving the Middle East conflict, in the long run it may offer incentives to support modernizing and Western-oriented democratic local elites in their efforts to resolve the conflict. The European Neighbourhood Policy may thereby contribute towards stabilizing the PA and building a viable Palestinian state. Intentionally or unintentionally the ENP supports a conflict resolution model based on far-reaching dissociation of the local conflict partners. Whether this model is compatible with the local conditions, especially local and regional conflict dynamics, is quite another question.

PART IV

THE TANGLED WEB OF REGIONAL CONFLICT

10

Military Intervention and Democratization: Global Order and the Radical Islamist Challenge to Lebanon

Eyal Zisser

On the morning of 12 July 2006, Hezbollah fighters attacked an IDF patrol moving along the Israeli–Lebanese border fence. The Israeli response to the attack was forceful, even unprecedented. The government of Israel decided to undertake an all-out war against Hezbollah. The war lasted 33 days. During that time, the missiles and Katyusha rockets that Hezbollah fired on northern Israel up as far as Haifa and deployed in the ground fighting in south Lebanon killed 153 Israeli civilians and soldiers. The war also brought ruin and destruction on the Lebanese side of the border, all the way from the Shiite towns and villages in the border area up to the Shiite suburbs of south Beirut. During the fighting, 1287 Lebanese civilians were killed together with several hundred Hezbollah fighters. Nearly a million Lebanese – 973,334, according to the official figures the Lebanese government published – became refugees, including most of the residents of south Lebanon, most of whom are Shiites. When the smoke of battle cleared, this multitude of people found that their lives had been spared but that their homes had been turned into mounds of rubble.[1]

The ceasefire declared on 11 August 2006, following the adoption of United Nations Security Council Resolution 1701, gave Israelis and Lebanese a new hope for peace and calm that would enable the residents on both sides of the border to return to their normal routines and repair the damage caused during the fighting. These hopes, however, were accompanied by worries that the lull would only be temporary, rather like a time-out in a campaign that was far from finished.

As time passed, the severity of the blow that Lebanon and its people had suffered as a result of the second Lebanese war became increasingly clear. As soon as the war ended the country was thrown into a lengthy political crisis that threatened to flare into a new civil war, this time with Hezbollah-led members of the Shiite community facing the other religious communities in the country. During the years between 1976 and 1989 Lebanon had suffered a bloody civil war that threatened to destroy the state, and now this threat was emerging once more. The second Lebanese war was not the factor that engendered this crisis. Rather, its origins lie in deeply rooted long-term demographic, social and economic processes. However, there is no question that the war intensified existing tensions, unravelled stitches, and exposed wounds that could only heal with great difficulty. In this sense, the war served as an irritant exacerbating a situation in which a new violent 'struggle over Lebanon' seemed to be on the verge of erupting.

In this sense, a straight line connects the second Lebanese war and the events of May 2008 during which armed Hezbollah fighters forcibly took over the Sunni quarters of west Beirut. Hezbollah's strong-arm tactics ignited violent confrontations all over Lebanon, during which nearly 100 people were killed. The violence eventually subsided and, on 22 May 2008, an all-Lebanon agreement signed at Doha, Qatar, resolved, at least temporarily, the crisis engulfing the Lebanese state.[2] However, it was clear to everyone that the country had embarked on a path that was very likely to descend into a new and bloody civil war, as had happened in the past.

From the Ta'if Agreement to the Second Lebanon War

Representatives of the Lebanese communities signed the Ta'if agreement on 22 October 1989 in Ta'if, Saudi Arabia. The accord was an updated and expanded version of the National Pact of 1943, yet, unlike its precursor, it was set down in writing and signed. It aimed to lay the foundations for the establishment of a new Lebanese order. The Ta'if agreement contained a series of reforms of the governmental structure including reduction of the Maronite president's authority and his placement on an equal footing with the Sunni prime minister and Shiite speaker of parliament, an expansion of parliament, and numerical parity between Christian and Muslim deputies. The Ta'if agreement called for the disarming of the militia and the restoration of the central government's authority in Beirut over all Lebanon, including the south.[3]

At the core of the Ta'if agreement was a recognition by Lebanese leaders – especially those of the Sunni and Maronite communities – that not only would a continuation of the civil war fail to serve their sectarian and personal interests, but that it was also liable to pose a real threat to those interests. This threat came mainly from the Shiite community, which in addition to its military might had, owing to its high rate of natural increase, become the largest community in the country. Various estimates fix the Shiite population in the mid-1990s at around 40 per cent of the overall population compared with only 18 per cent at the previous census taken in Lebanon in 1932.[4]

Sunni and Maronite leaders, and Shiite notables or leaders of the Shiite Amal movement as well, thus felt pressed to bring about a swift conclusion to the civil war before it was too late. The question was who would be charged with getting the job done? There being no other practical alternative, Syria became the natural choice of many Lebanese, as well as of external players such as the United States. Syria had the strength, the determination and especially the military ability to do the job and bring the civil war to an end. Indeed, not long after its signing and initial implementation, Syria made itself the standard bearer of the Ta'if accord, while interpreting and implementing it as it wished and in keeping with Syrian interests.[5]

The Lebanese state that arose, thanks to the Ta'if agreement, from the rubble and ruins of the civil war was not very different from the entity that had collapsed into strife and warfare 14 years earlier, in April 1975. This was because communal identification and family membership continued to serve as the foundations and central pillars of the state. They continued to be the basic factors that determined one's place in the system. In any case, the Ta'if agreement was not geared to resolving Lebanon's fundamental problems, which were what led to the outbreak of the civil war. Nor was the agreement able to resolve the new issues that emerged during and after the war. First among these was the 'Shiite question', that is the increase in the Shiite community's demographic strength and its military and political power, and even more, its rallying around the flag of the 'Hezbollah challenge'. That challenge is anchored in the Hezbollah organization's radical worldview, which argues that the confrontation with Israel must be sustained at any price and under all conditions and that the Lebanese state must be turned into a state governed by Islamic law. The fact that Hezbollah became the most powerful factor in the Shiite community following Ta'if, when that community became the most populous one in the country, only served to increase the impact of the 'Hezbollah challenge'.

Hezbollah made a stormy entry into the centre of the Lebanese political arena toward the end of 1983, when its activists delivered a series of painful blows to the Israeli, American and French military headquarters in Lebanon. The Hezbollah attacks left hundreds of dead and wounded and eventually led to the withdrawal of the American and French forces and, following them, the Israeli forces from Lebanon as well. Hezbollah thus broke into the centre of the Lebanese arena as a radical and militant organization carrying on a violent struggle against the West, and Israel in particular. And it was no less determined against its political opponents domestically. Two major events in the recent history of the Middle East influenced the approach taken by Hezbollah and exerted a formative influence on the organization. The first was the Islamic revolution in Iran, which began in December 1979 and served Hezbollah as a source of inspiration and model for imitation. The second was the Israeli invasion of Lebanon in June 1982, which brought to a peak Israel's lengthy intervention in the affairs of that state. Israel now became an easy target against which much of the enthusiasm and radicalism characteristic of the Lebanese Shiites, and especially the Hezbollah organization, in those years, could be channelled. However, these two events stood in the shadow of a third one, the civil war raging in Lebanon at the time, during which the Shiites became central actors on the Lebanese political stage.[6]

Within several years of its founding, Hezbollah began to make its move to gain a leading role in Lebanese social and political life. The organization's political platform, published in February 1985, outlined its mission and goals. The document concentrated on what it described as the uncompromising struggle with Israel until the destruction of that entity. The platform also focused on the struggle to establish an Islamic republic in Lebanon, on the model of Iran, as a stage on the way to establishing one united Islamic state covering the whole Islamic world. Joining actions to its words, Hezbollah intensified its struggle with Israel in south Lebanon. At the same time, it engaged in a vigorous struggle, sometimes even involving bloody confrontations, with its main Shiite competitor in the Lebanese arena – Amal, and no less importantly, various Palestinian organizations working in the Palestinian refugee camps, mainly in south Lebanon and Beirut.

By the end of the 1980s Hezbollah had become the leading force in the Shiite community, and it seemed to have it within its power to take over Lebanon, or at least those parts of the country inhabited by Shiites, and to establish an Islamic order there on the Iranian model. However, just at the moment when Hezbollah had reached its peak, it got into trouble, and for the first time had to confront a real challenge to its advance, and perhaps even to its very existence. In October 1989 the 'Ta'if agreement' was signed in Ta'if in Saudi Arabia. This agreement ended the civil war that had made Hezbollah's successes possible. A process of rehabilitation of the institutions of the Lebanese state began. This led to the disarming of most of the militias that had been active in the country. The 'Ta'if agreement' also laid the foundations for the establishment of a new Maronite-Sunni order, with the backing and support of Syria. These developments left the Shiite community far behind, even though it had become the largest, and perhaps the strongest, community in the country.

Faced with this threat, Hezbollah proved very pragmatic, taking whatever steps were necessary to survive. The organization looked ready to abandon its ideological positions, or at least to postpone their realization to the distant future. True, at first, it did not hide its opposition to the 'Ta'if agreement', but in the end it resigned itself to the re-establishment of the Lebanese state, the 'Lebanon of Ta'if', and began to act in ways that would enable it to integrate into the state's institutions. Little by little Hezbollah turned from being an armed militia into a social and political movement. In doing this it broadened greatly the scope of its activities among the Shiite population all over the country. From the mid-1980s the organization began – with generous Iranian help, estimated at tens, even hundreds of millions, of dollars yearly – to establish a network of social and welfare services that would draw the support of the Shiite community and provide it with an alternative to the services the Lebanese state provided, or, to be more precise, to the benefits and aid the state should have provided for this population and did not. The Hezbollah network of services expanded greatly over the years as Shiite support became firmer and firmer. To be sure, many Hezbollah supporters today view the organization as simply a convenient framework for political, social and economic activities, without necessarily feeling any commitment to its ideology. However, the leadership, and certainly the hard core, remain as committed to the Hezbollah worldview as in the past, and they are the ones who have power and control over the organization and its members.[7]

The Struggle with Israel in South Lebanon: The Way to Victory

The struggle against Israel, or, more precisely, against the Israeli presence in the south Lebanon 'security zone', continued to be an important focus of Hezbollah activity, though not the only one and perhaps not even the main one, until May 2000. However, in the shadow of this struggle the government of Israel, led by Ehud Barak, decided to retreat from Lebanon unilaterally. During the night of 24 May 2000, the Israel Defense Forces (IDF) carried out this decision and withdrew entirely from the 'security zone' – in a unilateral step taken outside the framework of any agreement or arrangement.

In the eyes of many Lebanese and Arabs and Muslims in general, the IDF's unilateral retreat from south Lebanon turned Hezbollah into the leading force in the Arab struggle against Israel. The organization was now viewed as a rising power with a great future before it, both inside and outside Lebanon. People thought it was destined to play a significant regional role, especially given the lack of leadership and the political and ideological vacuum that characterized inter-Arab relations in those years. Some observers in Israel even expressed concern that Hassan Nasrallah was aspiring to become an all-Arab leader and model worthy of admiration and emulation, like Gamal 'Abd al-Nasir in his day.

Hezbollah's seeming victory over Israel in south Lebanon in May 2000, however, in fact served to intensify the existential dilemma into which the organization had been thrown following the October 1989 Ta'if agreement that ended the Lebanese civil war. From Ta'if onwards, the organization's identity, goals and course were all thrown into question. Should it continue with its close ties and commitments to Iran and the devotion to radical Islam and jihad that went with this? Or should it adopt more consistently the identity it had begun to assume since the end of the civil war, the Lebanese–Shiite identity, with a certain Islamic coloration?

Adoption of the jihadist and Iranian-oriented identity meant, of course, continuation of the struggle with Israel, but also continuation of the struggle to take over Lebanon. The struggle over Lebanon would be a political struggle, but violence would be employed whenever deemed necessary. The aim would be to change the character of the country and turn it into an Islamic state. Adoption of the more moderate Lebanese-Shiite identity meant continuation of the trend towards 'Lebanonization' that had already begun, and turning the Hezbollah organization into a broad-based, deeply-rooted social and political movement acting within the Lebanese system according to the prevailing rules of the game in that country.

Hezbollah resolved this dilemma in practice by adopting a policy that allowed it to have it both ways. In other words, it stuck to its Islamic-revolutionary, even jihad, identity mainly by continuing the struggle with Israel, albeit in a low key, and took on Lebanese trappings by acting as a political organization to all intents and purposes. This was done while cleverly trying to conceal the organization's loyalty to Iran as much as possible and the long-term goal that went with this, namely, turning Lebanon into an Islamic republic ruled by Shiite Islamic law. After all, Hezbollah could take its time, or, more precisely, it seemed as if the organization's leaders, taking into consideration the demographic processes occurring in Lebanon, assumed that time was on their side. They were therefore prepared to wait patiently for the moment of truth and meanwhile act moderately and patiently, as called for by the Lebanese trappings they had assumed and by the constraints they faced both within and outside the country.[8]

In any case, from the mid-1980s Hezbollah was wise enough to build itself up into an organization standing on two legs. One leg was its powerful armed militia that focused on the struggle with Israel. The other leg was the organization's political and social activities, which were aimed at improving the lot of the Lebanese Shiite population and eventually even challenging the existing order in the country in the name of the Shiite community. Most students of the movement naturally focused on its military dimension and tended to underestimate the importance of the social, economic and political aspect. However, as the years passed, two things became clear – the latter activities were no less central in the eyes of the organization than the former, and, even more importantly, they had far-reaching implications for the organization's future.

Indeed, during the 1990s Hezbollah became the leading power among the Lebanese Shiites, thanks to the social, economic and political infrastructure it had developed. It grew much stronger and became much more popular than the other organization competing for leadership of the Shiite community, the Amal movement. A vivid expression of this superiority can be seen in the election results to the Lebanese parliament and the local municipalities since the end of the 1990s. Hezbollah gained clear victories over its opponents in these elections. In the light of this, since the year 2000 many people in Lebanon and abroad have begun to suspect that Hezbollah leader Hassan Nasrallah has set himself the ambitious goal of taking power in Lebanon by democratic means, exploiting the fact that his Shiite supporters constitute the largest community in the country (between 35 and 45 per cent of the total population). Indeed, following the American invasion of Iraq and the establishment of a new regime there, Nasrallah began calling for the implementation in Lebanon of a democratic system such as the Americans had brought to Iraq. The implications of this were that the Shiites should be granted the representation due them by virtue of their numbers and, eventually, they should become the majority in the institutions of the state.[9]

Testimony to the dilemma facing Hezbollah, and in fact the whole Lebanese state and society, is to be found in the 'Cedar Revolution' that erupted in February 2005, following the assassination of former Lebanese Prime Minister Rafiq al-Hariri in the heart of Beirut. This revolution, without a doubt, represents one of the highest points Lebanon has known in the process of rebuilding and restoration since the civil war. Indeed, in mid-February 2005 it seemed as if Lebanon had reached a real turning point and that the country had changed the course of its history in one fell swoop. This was after hundreds of thousands, some observers claim even more than a million, Lebanese from all the ethnic communities gathered in Martyrs' Square (Sahat al-shuhada) on the evening of 14 February 2005 in central Beirut to participate in the largest protest demonstration the Lebanese capital had ever witnessed. The demonstration came in response to the Hariri assassination in the morning of that same day. The murder of the former prime minister shocked the people of Lebanon deeply, since he, more than any other Lebanese political figure, was identified with the Ta'if agreement of October 1989, which aimed to rebuild and restore the Second Lebanese Republic, the Republic of Ta'if.[10]

Like many other people in Lebanon and abroad, the demonstrators in

Martyrs' Square were in no doubt about who was behind the Hariri assassination. They were certain that it was the Syrian regime of Bashar al-Assad and Syria's tool, the Lebanese government, led by President Emile Lahud. Thus, the protesters insisted that the Syrians get out of Lebanon and that Emile Lahud resign, along with the other Syria supporters holding key positions in the Lebanese government. However, the masses demonstrating in the streets of Beirut had their eyes on a much more far-reaching goal than just a change in personnel among Lebanon's political leadership. Their hopes were for the establishment of a totally new order in Lebanon, or, to be more precise, a return to the situation that had existed prior to the outbreak of civil war in April 1975 when the state was open, liberal, democratic and Western.

Syria found it increasingly difficult to withstand the pressure from the side of the Lebanese people to leave their country, especially since this pressure was given backing by the international community, led by the USA and France. Thus, on 5 March 2005, Syrian President Bashar al-Assad announced the withdrawal of Syrian forces from Lebanon.[11] With this, for the time being, Syria's intervention in Lebanon came to an end, an intervention that had begun in the early 1970s and reached its height in the 1990s, when Damascus blatantly dominated the Lebanese state. When it happened, the Syrians' sudden withdrawal left many Lebanese, as well as many scholars and commentators in the West and Israel, gaping. After all, just a few months previously Syria's hold on Lebanon had seemed more solid than ever and it would have been difficult to imagine that it would come to an end so quickly. As soon as the Syrian forces were gone, mobs of Lebanese descended on the bases and headquarters that had served the Syrians and smashed every symbol, sign and reminder of the lengthy Syrian presence, including statues, monuments and pictures of Hafez al-Assad and his sons, Basil and Bashar. Anyone who witnessed these scenes was left in no doubt that an era in the history of Lebanon had indeed come to an end.[12]

The departure, or perhaps expulsion of the Syrians, however, did not mark the end of the storm that engulfed Lebanon in spring 2005, for in the wake of the Syrians' withdrawal a no less dramatic political reversal occurred in the country. In the elections to the Chamber of Deputies (Parliament) held in May and June 2005, about a month after the withdrawal of the Syrian forces, the camp of those who opposed Lebanon's existing political order won a sweeping victory. The Sunni leader and son of recently murdered Rafiq al-Hariri, Sa'd al-Din al-Hariri, and the Druze leader, Walid Jumblatt, headed this camp and a number of important figures and powerful members of the Maronite Christian camp joined them. The elections led to the formation of a new Lebanese government headed by Fouad Siniora, a close associate of the young Hariri. This government adopted a pro-Western, even anti-Syrian, position and it included, for the first time, a representative of Hezbollah. This was because the latter was also among the big winners in the parliamentary elections, thus proving once again its strength in Lebanon's Shiite community.[13]

Hezbollah Goes to War against Israel

Lebanon's underlying structural weaknesses, which continued to exist even after the 'Cedar Revolution', were exposed in July 2006 when fighting broke out between Israel and Hezbollah in the wake of the latter kidnapping two Israeli soldiers. Moreover, the fighting left behind not only physical ruin and destruction all over the country, but also serious ethnic, political and social tensions, which began to intensify significantly even as the fighting was taking place. All this raised new doubts about whether Lebanon could ever return to being a stable and solid state with an open and democratic political and social system and a flourishing and prospering economy. The end of the war between Israel and Hezbollah marked the renewal of the 'struggle over Lebanon', which had seemed to be concluded numerous times in the past, only to flare up anew. This was the old battle over the character and structure of the Lebanese state, and perhaps even over the question of its very survival, but above all else, over the question of who would rule it.

As soon as the war ended Hezbollah secretary general Hassan Nasrallah declared that his organization had won the victory, even a 'divine' victory.[14] After all, Hezbollah had survived the Israeli assault, and it even had quite a few successes in the fighting to its credit. However, when one reckoned the gains and losses, one could not ignore the severe blows the organization had sustained during the fighting. Proof of this is Nasrallah's admission that if he had assumed that there was even a 1 per cent chance that Israel would respond to the kidnapping of its soldiers in the way it did, then he certainly would not have given orders to kidnap the Israeli soldiers.[15]

In both Israel and the West, Nasrallah was largely perceived through a narrow prism as the leader of a terrorist militia with several thousand fighters and with over 12,000 rockets. Those who looked at him through that narrow prism would probably have concluded that as he continued firing rockets into Israel until the last day of the fighting, he was the victor in the confrontation. However, Nasrallah was not only the leader of an armed militia and he did not see his organization as such; in fact, since being appointed leader of the organization in 1992 he has dedicated his efforts towards turning it into something else entirely. As of 11 July 2006, Nasrallah was the leader of a political and social movement, probably the largest in Lebanon, with deep roots in the Lebanese Shiite community. Hezbollah had

14 representatives in parliament, more than 4000 representatives in local municipal councils in the country's Shiite villages and towns, an education system with dozens of schools and around 100,000 students, a health system with dozens of hospitals and clinics caring for half a million people a year, a banking system, marketing chains, and even pension funds and insurance companies. Over the last decade Nasrallah has devoted much of his energy to building up his movement, or empire, as it were. He viewed the creation of such an empire as his life's work, which would take him far, possibly even to a contest over the control of Lebanon.[16]

Israel damaged Nasrallah's efforts badly; only those who had witnessed the destruction and ruin in Lebanon could comprehend just how severely the war affected the Shiites in general and Hezbollah and its leader in particular. One out of every two Shiites living in Lebanon became a refugee during the war, and most of the Shiite community – peasants, merchants and industrialists – returned to their homes, stores and factories in villages and towns in southern Lebanon or in the Shiite quarters of south Beirut to find they had lost their homes and their possessions. Indeed, Hezbollah suffered an estimated damage to its institutions and enterprises of almost three to four billion dollars, while the damage caused to Lebanon during the war was estimated at 20 billion dollars.[17]

In essence, these Shiites had no choice but to rally around Hassan Nasrallah's flag. No one else in Lebanon cared about them – not the UN or international community, not even the Lebanese government whose leaders focused on the interests of the Sunni, Maronite and Druze communities, which barely suffered in the war. This was after all the nature and character of the Lebanese system in which each community took care of itself. As such, members of the Shiite community continued to support Nasrallah. However, the damage inflicted on them clearly reduced Nasrallah's room for manœuvre, as evidenced by his admission at the end of the war, which undoubtedly was aimed at his supporters, that he had underestimated Israel's response to the kidnapping.

The Renewed Struggle for Lebanon

For several months after the second Lebanese war, and perhaps because of the fighting, the various factors wielding power in the country managed to keep matters on a low burner. However, toward the end of the year, after all efforts to engage in quiet dialogue and reach mutual understandings had failed utterly, matters began to get out of hand. There is no doubt that the increasingly bitter rhetoric and accusations over the outcome of the war that Hezbollah and its domestic opponents began to hurl at each other contributed to the failure of negotiations.

On 9 November 2006, the Amal and Hezbollah ministers in Fouad

Siniora's government handed in their resignations. They did so in protest against the 'Cedar Revolution' coalition's refusal to meet Shiite demands to establish a 'national unity government' in which Shiite representation would be increased and in which representation would be granted to General Michel Aoun, who at the beginning of 2006 had become a faithful ally of Hezbollah. On the face of it, this appeared to be an innocuous, perhaps even legitimate, demand aimed to advance dialogue and mutual understanding between the religious communities and various factions holding power in Lebanon. However, it was clear to everyone that if this demand were met, and Nasrallah's representatives and allies were granted a third of the government ministries, they would then constitute a 'blocking third', with the power, according to Lebanese practice, to prevent the adoption of any resolution they opposed, and Nasrallah and Hezbollah would thus acquire the power to veto every decision the Lebanese government might wish to take in the future.[18]

Throughout 2007 and early 2008, Lebanon was in the throes of an ongoing political crisis that paralysed the entire political system. President Emile Lahud's term of office ended on 24 November 2007 and he left the presidential palace in Ba'bda. Up until that moment, and indeed for long weeks afterwards, Lebanese politicians found it impossible to come to an agreement on the identity of Lahud's successor. The speaker of the parliament, Nabih Bari, complicated matters further by using his authority to prevent the parliament convening to elect a president. It should be noted that, according to accepted Lebanese practice, the Hezbollah-led opposition could in any case have boycotted any session of the parliament, thus denying the quorum needed for the parliament's decisions to have any validity or legitimacy.

During the first months of 2008 all efforts to resolve the crisis in Lebanon and to bring about the election of a new president failed. In the meantime, the tension between the rivals increased until a break became unavoidable. Towards the beginning of May 2008 this tension increased further. On 8 May 2008 Hezbollah activists took over the Sunni suburbs of west Beirut. Alongside the occupation of west Beirut, Hezbollah men took over the west Beirut offices of the al-Mustaqbal party, led by Sa'd al-Din al-Hariri, and shut down transmission of its TV station 'al-Mustaqbal' and its radio station, 'al-Sharq' (Orient). In addition, they set fire to a building housing the party's newspaper, *al-Mustaqbal*, which belonged to the media empire run by the al-Hariri family. Hezbollah also surrounded the residences of Sa'd al-Din al-Hariri and Walid Jumblatt, the leader of the Druze community, though they did not try to enter them.[19]

This was an impressive demonstration of Hezbollah's military might, though there was nothing surprising about it. After all, every Lebanese acknowledges Hezbollah's military superiority over all its rivals, including the Lebanese army. It seems that Hezbollah's move was calculated and cautious. Its activists did not appear in uniforms and as organized forces, and avoided attacking government buildings or clashing with the Lebanese army. They were giving a clear message that for the time being they were not interested in bringing about a total destruction of the Lebanese political order. Indeed, after two days the Hezbollah activists evacuated their positions and left the streets of west Beirut, thus enabling the Lebanese army to deploy its forces there. Hezbollah's message was clear — at will it can occupy west Beirut and at will it can evacuate it.

The round of violence of early May 2008, which cost the lives of more than one hundred Lebanese, shows that no one in Lebanon has an interest in a renewed civil war in which all would lose and no one would win. It took place only a few days before an Arab reconciliatory effort had begun that led to an all Lebanese summit in Doha, Qatar. On 22 May 2008, the summit produced the Doha agreement, which paved the way for the election of Michel Suleiman as Lebanese president two days later. Other parts of the agreement dealt with the establishment of a unity government in which the opposition, headed by Hezbollah, would have one-third of the seats and thus the power to veto any government decisions on the election law for the forthcoming 2009 parliamentary elections.[20] The total break had thus been put off until the next time.

Lebanon has sorted out its problems over the identity of the president, the composition of the government and the parliamentary elections, which took place in June 2009. We should view these achievements, however, as a preface to the much more significant questions of who is to rule Lebanon, what identity should Lebanon have and what course should it follow. These questions are being addressed, even if no one has said so openly and even if the discussions are being conducted on a low flame and, for the most part, in the political corridors of Beirut.

This struggle, as is usual in Lebanese history, does not involve the Shiite and Sunni communities exclusively, or even these two plus the Maronite community. The struggle also has clearly regional aspects. The conflict between Israel and Syria and Syria's striving for control, influence and even hegemony in the Lebanese region, perhaps even in the Levant as a whole, also play a role in the struggle over Lebanon. Besides this, there is the clash between Iran and the moderate Arab states, which include Egypt and Saudi Arabia. Saudi Arabia in particular manifests a lively involvement in what happens in Lebanon, which is one of the fronts in the battle today in the Arab world between the Sunnis and the radical Shiite camp led by Iran. Indeed, the tension, even hostility, between Sunnis and Shiites has become one of the keys to understanding developments in the Middle East in general in recent years. Hezbollah seems to have fallen victim to this tension without being able, as in the past, to conceal its links and affinity with Iran, not to say its dependence on and obligations to that country. A characteristic example of this was the angry reaction among Sunni Muslims in the Arab world following the Iraqi government's execution of Saddam Hussein in January 2007. The Sunnis' fury was directed not only against the United States and the Shiites controlling the government in Iraq, but also against Iran and Hezbollah, neither of which concealed its support for the elimination of Saddam.[21] Incidentally, as early as spring 2006, before the outbreak of the Israel–Hezbollah war, an al-Qaeda cell composed of Sunni youths was exposed in Lebanon. According to Lebanese sources, it was planning to assassinate Hassan Nasrallah.[22]

The big question bothering the citizens of Lebanon today is, of course, whether the period of calm, quiet and stability that the country enjoyed following the signing of the Ta'if agreement is coming to an end, just as similar periods of calm in Lebanon's history came to an end, thus revealing that they were simply time-outs between one civil war and another. From this point of view, the 'struggle over Lebanon', over the path the state will take and the future it will have, and even more, over who will control it, did not end with the termination of the civil war and the signing of the Ta'if agreement, nor even with the 'Cedar Revolution' or the cessation of the second Lebanese war. In fact, the struggle had only just begun, and it perseveres like a glowing ember that threatens to flare up at any moment.

The two sides in the struggle are those who support the present Lebanese order, with Western backing, versus those who support Hezbollah, with Syrian and Iranian backing. Hezbollah has decided for the present to engage in the struggle using political means and relying on the increasing demographic weight of the Shiite community in Lebanon. However, Hezbollah has also made it clear that it is liable to resort to the use of force some day to improve its position and advance its long-term goals. The manner in which the Lebanese state, society and ethnic communities cope with the Shiite community in the coming period will determine what direction the Shiites take. The questions are: will this community be given the recognition it deserves, and will what is necessary to integrate it more fully and justly into the Lebanese system be undertaken? The answers given to these questions will determine whether the Shiites choose to live in a framework of coexistence with the other ethnic communities or resort to force and even violent struggle to take control of the Lebanese state for themselves. Several other questions emerge from these considerations: will the members of the Shiite community really be able to conquer for themselves the senior position in the state? Will it be Hezbollah or some other factor that will lead the Shiites to victory in the struggle? Will it perhaps be Hezbollah, in any case, that will determine Lebanon's character in the future? The present 'struggle over Lebanon' is still in its early stages and Hezbollah is weaker than ever in the campaign, but the organization is still on its feet and should not be underestimated.

It must be admitted that the international community has demonstrated helplessness in the face of the current shaky and dangerous situation in Lebanon. In the past the international community has been incapable of saving the situation there. Time after time, the intervention of foreign troops failed in the purpose of helping the Lebanese body politic stand on its feet. The severest failure was that of the three-nation Multinational Force (MNF) sent to Lebanon in the late summer of 1982, with the aim of enabling President Amin Jumayyil to establish a stable government. Jumayyil's regime was pro-Western and, on 17 May 1983, it even signed a peace agreement with Israel, which, however, was never ratified. In the autumn of 1983 Hezbollah activists managed to kill hundreds of US marines and French and Italian soldiers of the MNF in two separate truck bomb blasts. This led to the withdrawal of the Western forces from Lebanon.[23]

In 1976 a previous outside intervention also failed. At that time it was an Arab Deterrent Force (ADF) dominated by Syria and given legitimacy by the Arab League that failed. The ADF was supposed to help bring to an end the civil war that had escalated a year before in Beirut. Dominated by Syria from the beginning, the ADF eventually fell apart, and only the Syrian forces remained in Lebanon.[24]

Following the fighting between Israel and Hezbollah in the summer of 2006, the mandate of the United Nations Interim Force in Lebanon (UNIFIL), with Hezbollah's agreement, was enhanced. However, UNIFIL's experience also indicates the limitations on the international community in playing a really effective role in bringing about stability in Lebanon. After all, prior to the outbreak of the 2006 war the UN force failed to prevent the activities of Hezbollah, and even after the war its effectiveness was greatly limited and it was still dependent on Hezbollah's goodwill.[25]

With all these considerations in mind, it seems clear that for any foreign intervention in Lebanon's bloody domestic conflicts to be successful, it must have the approval of all the parties involved and even an invitation from them. Only with great difficulty did the Lebanese manage to reach such a consensus in the past, after bloody and devastating battles. At the present time it would seem that they have learnt the lesson of the civil war that raged from 1975 to 1989. Who knows for how long this memory will stand them in good stead and defend them against a renewed 'struggle over Lebanon' deteriorating into another bloody episode?

11

The Geopolitical Dimension of Sunni–Shi'i Sectarianism in the Middle East

Uzi Rabi and Brandon Friedman

The global and local have interacted in an important way in the Middle East over the past eight years. The USA, reacting to the events of 9/11, invaded Afghanistan in 2001 and then Iraq in March 2003, removing the Taliban and Saddam Hussein from power. Saddam on Iran's western border and the Taliban on its eastern border had presented the Islamic Republic of Iran with serious security challenges that were transformed by the US incursions. In other words, the pre-9/11 regional balance of power changed following the US military operations and, over time, left Iran in a more favourable position.

As the USA's missions in Iraq and Afghanistan became more challenging and sapped greater resources and manpower, Iran was able to exploit the instability and project its influence using instruments of soft power, such as economic, political and logistical support to its fellow Shi'is in Iraq and Afghanistan. This new geopolitical reality, catalysed by the impact of a global intervention and the threat of regime change, set the stage for a renewed emphasis on regional sectarianism, which has affected regional priorities.

One of the manifestations of the new regional dynamics was the intensification of sectarianism that prompted leaders to invoke labels such as 'Shi'i crescent' or 'Shi'i revival'. Therefore, in this chapter we shall address the roots and expressions of sectarian religious divisions in the region, as well as identify other factors influencing and affecting the new priorities in the region.

In an article published in the *Washington Post* on 29 November 2006, Nawwaf 'Ubayd, a security adviser to the Saudi king, emphasized the urgent need for 'massive Saudi intervention' in Iraq to shield the Sunnis against any Shi'-supported sectarian cleansing should Iraq split up.[1] Nawwaf's Sunni–Shi'i terminology reflected a new perception that was becoming increasingly common while characterizing the changing social and political dynamics in the Middle East.[2] Over the past few years, this 'Sunni–Shi'i' terminology has become a feature of the Arab political discourse, which has been interlaced with uncharacteristically blunt statements by Sunni Arab rulers expressing their concern about the dual loyalty of their Shi'i communities. Egyptian President Hosni Mubarak stated that 'Shi'is in the Arab states (primarily Iraq and its Gulf neighbours) are mainly loyal to Iran and not to the states in which they live'.[3] Saudi Foreign Minister Sa'ud al-Faisal expressed similar sentiments in various contexts. The most prominent expression of such concerns came in December 2004, when Jordan's King 'Abdallah II warned that a 'Shi'i crescent' (*al-hilal al-shi'i*) threatens to split the Arab and Muslim world.[4]

This statement stimulated lively debate in the Arab media. Vitriolic Sunni rhetoric levelled at the Shi'a has become prominent in Arab political discourse, with headlines portending 'the Shi'i wave', 'the Shi'i revival' and 'the Shi'i danger' appearing throughout print and electronic media. The Arab press has outlined the Shi'i crescent as extending from Iran at the head of the Persian Gulf, through Iraq, where Shi'is make up approximately 60 per cent of the population, and including Bahrain (65 per cent Shi'i), Kuwait (30 per cent Shi'i) and Saudi Arabia (13 per cent Shi'i). This Shi'i crescent also includes Iran's client, Syria, as well as politically fragmented Lebanon, where Shi'is constitute 40 per cent of the population.

The summer 2006 Israeli–Hezbollah war fuelled growing concerns about the Sunni–Shi'i conflict. The volume of anti-Shi'i *fatwa*s (religious rulings) was a sharp manifestation of the conflict. The Saudi *ulama* (religious scholars), who adhere to Wahhabism (or *al-muwahiddun*), an extreme form of Sunni Islam, issued numerous *fatwa*s denouncing Shi'i Islam as heresy. The Wahhabi clerics even went so far as to denounce Lebanese Shi'i leader Hassan Nasrallah as an enemy and a 'son of Satan'. The most outspoken Wahhabi cleric was Shaykh 'Abdallah bin Jibrin, a senior Saudi *'alim*, who issued a *fatwa* declaring that supporting Hezbollah was a sin.[5]

In the aftermath of the war, Arab acrimony over the Sunni–Shi'i issue intensified. In August 2006, during a speech he delivered to the Egyptian journalists union, Shaykh Yusuf al-Qaradhawi, an Egyptian religious scholar residing in Qatar, triggered a public debate on the status of Shi'is in Egypt. Qaradhawi warned that the Arab Sunni community should be aware of 'the Shi'i infiltration into the Arab Sunni states. Such an infiltration might ignite a flame and could eliminate every good and pious lot. We could easily witness the recurrence of events in Iraq in other Arab Sunni countries.'[6] The Egyptian press cited Qaradhawi's warnings that Shi'is in Egypt were attempting to legitimize and spread the Shi'i message by claiming that the graves of Shi'i holy figures, Sayyid Hussein and

Sayyida Zaynab, were located in Egypt.[7] Furthermore, Qaradhawi warned that 'the Shi'a used Sufism as a bridgehead to *tashayu'* (preaching in praise of Shi'ism and persuading believers to adhere to it), through which they have managed to infiltrate Egypt in the last few years.'[8]

Qaradhawi was not the only Sunni voice to raise the alarm regarding the Shi'is. An indication of the pervasiveness of Qaradhawi's claims could be seen in many of the Egyptian newspapers and government aligned media outlets, which published reports about supposed conversions of Sunnis to the Shi'i sect.[9] The Egyptian daily, *Ruz al-Yusuf,* may have taken the notion of a 'Shi'i rise' to the extreme when it claimed that the Sunnis should be aware that Shi'is aspire not only to a 'Shi'i crescent', but also to a 'Shi'i Full Moon' (*al-badr al-shi'i*).[10] The level of alarm in Egypt, where the Shi'i population is relatively insignificant in comparison with Lebanon or Iraq – Egypt's Shi'is constitute only a small fraction (1 per cent) of the total Muslim population in Egypt, approximately 650,000–700,000 – illustrates the Sunni perception of the 'Shi'i threat'.

Saudi King 'Abdallah also expressed concern regarding Sunni conversion to Shi'ism (in Arabic, *tashayu'*):

> We are following this matter, and we are fully informed about the extent of this campaign to spread Shi'ism. However, we maintain that this campaign will never achieve its goal, because the overwhelming majority of Muslims, who are Sunni, will never turn away from their creed. ... Ultimately, the decision is in the hands of the majority of Muslims (that is the Sunnis), and other Islamic sects are unable to impinge on their historical authority.[11]

The Saudi king does not grant interviews very often, and certainly not on sensitive topics such as this, so his statement further underlines the serious attention the Arab rulers were giving to the Sunni–Shi'i issue.

It was not just Arab rulers who were expressing their concern about sectarianism but senior religious establishment officials as well. Leading Sunni cleric Shaykh al-Azhar Muhammad Sayyid al-Tantawi stated that, 'The argument between the Sunnis and the Shi'is is focusing on the clauses and not on the essence of faith.'[12] Even Shaykh Qaradhawi has articulated a more moderate message from time to time. The more moderate messages from senior figures were a product of a growing realization in the Sunni religious community that harsh sectarian rhetoric would lead to further escalation. In February 2007, Shaykh Qaradhawi and Ali Akbar Hashemi Rafsanjani, the former president of Iran, issued a joint call to end the war in Iraq and ease tensions between Sunnis and Shi'is.[13]

The quiescent dispute between the two factions exploded rather suddenly in Iraq and quickly spread through the streets of Baghdad and southern Iraq. Signs of sectarian tension were evident everywhere in the Arab world – in speeches, editorials, conversations on the street and in coffee shops, and discussions on the Internet. Arab newspapers were full of headlines, articles and declarations about Shi'i aggression. In January 2007 the Jordanian newspaper *al-Dustur*, which is identified with the royal regime, warned about a master plan that aimed to spread Shi'ism from India to Egypt. An important element on the agenda of the 'heretics' (namely the Shi'is), it was claimed, was to murder 'central Sunni figures'.[14] That same day an Algerian newspaper reported that parents had called on the government to put an end to the preaching of Shi'i beliefs in schools. In Cairo's famous al-Madbuli bookstore, books with titles such as *The Shi'is*, *The Shi'is in History*, *The Twelfth Shi'a* and so on were on display in the front showroom window.

The feelings of alienation separating the Shi'is and Sunnis date back to the early days of Islam, and the struggle between 'Ali and Mu'awiyah during the years CE 656–61, and certainly influence the way modern Shi'is and Sunnis view one another. The differences between Sunnis and Shi'is have evolved through the ages beyond the early Islamic schism and encompass different socio-cultural dimensions. Contemporary Sunni Arab culture in some areas of the Middle East maintains a particularly strong legacy of tribal tradition. The Sunni tribes have always maintained a strong tribal identity that historical lineage and family genealogy govern. This tribal identity is imbued with a sense of cultural superiority with respect to the Shi'is. There is no question that Shi'is in the Arab states (despite differences from state to state) were, and still are, second-class citizens in many respects. The members of the Sunni elite – landowners, tribal dignitaries, senior military men and bureaucrats – were the power brokers throughout the Ottoman period and the post-First World War mandate period and fostered cooperative relations with external powers. Thus, these Sunni elites were able to preserve their status and supremacy from one era to the next. Despite the dynamic changes that engulfed the Middle East during the course of the twentieth century and despite the rise and fall of new political ideologies and regimes, the Sunni elites maintained their supremacy while the Shi'is largely remained marginalized. The Shi'is were able to find opportunities in the lower ranks of the labour force (for example, as oil field workers in Saudi Arabia, or mercenaries in certain units of the Iraqi army during the reign of Saddam Hussein), but they seldom, if ever, rose to senior positions of responsibility or authority.[15]

Arab nationalism, which permeated the region during the period after independence, was also primarily a Sunni phenomenon. Therefore, the states that raised the banner of Arab nationalism – Egypt, Syria and Iraq –

granted senior government positions to Sunnis, in the name of the past glory of the Sunni Umayyad (661–750) and 'Abbassid (750–1258) dynasties. Thus, Arab nationalism, secular and socialist in its roots and Sunni in character, was biased against the Shi'i Arabs. And, despite sharing Arabic as their mother tongue, Shi'is were still considered 'second class Arabs'. There has been a widespread popular belief among Sunnis that Arab Shi'is are ethnic Persians who are sympathetic to Iran. The fall of the shah, the rise of Ayatollah Khomeini, and the efforts of the new regime in Tehran to export the revolution to Arab states transformed a popular Sunni belief into a political calculation that gave rise to the notion that the Shi'is in the Arab states were a 'fifth column'.

The tension between Sunnis and Shi'is has historically been part of the socio-cultural dynamics of the region. However, the intensity and scope of clashes between Sunnis and Shi'is during the past eight years is unprecedented in the modern history of the region.

Shi'i Regional Unity: Perceptions and Misperceptions

What then, is the likelihood that a 'Shi'i crescent' or a greater Shi'i entity is being formed in the heart of the region? It would be a misleading oversimplification to assume that a homogeneous Shi'i framework is coalescing: the story is more complex and nuanced. The Shi'is in the Sunni Arab states are indeed aware of their religious identity and, it can be assumed, even feel certain solidarity with their coreligionists and believers. However, if past experience is any guide, the various Shi'i communities in the Arab states have exhibited local and particularistic loyalties first, and made use of the 'Shi'i flag' primarily as a means of protest, to improve their position in the economic, cultural and political contexts of their respective states.

The Iran-Iraq war of 1980–88 offers a case in point. Fearing that the Iraqi Shi'is would be a 'fifth column' loyal to Iran, President Saddam Hussein tried to use anti-Shi'i rhetoric to gain the support of the Sunni Arab street. However, contrary to the conventional wisdom, the Shi'is of Iraq generally remained loyal to their country, just as the Sunni Arabs of Iran remained loyal to Iran.

Kuwaiti Shi'is also demonstrated loyalty to their state during the 1990–91 Iraqi invasion and occupation of Kuwait, when they participated in the sporadic resistance to Iraqi forces during the initial invasion, while the Sunni ruling family and other elites fled the state. The leading Kuwaiti Shi'i cleric, Sayyid Muhammad Baqir al-Mahri, recently reiterated this point when he said that when put to the test, Kuwaiti citizens responded to the 1990–91 invasion as Kuwaitis and not as Sunnis or Shi'is. He added that those who raise the issue of sectarian loyalty have a hidden agenda that strives to undermine the foundation of the Kuwaiti nation. Al-Mahri indicated that Shi'is were not proselytizing or trying to convert Sunnis to Shi'ism and the Shi'i popularity following Hezbollah's 'victory over the Zionists' was simply a natural reaction and admiration for the 'only group that stood up in the face of Zionism'.[16]

This perception that Arab Shi'is throughout the region were working towards the same objectives and sharing a common agenda is misleading. In fact, Shi'is across the region do not constitute a single, unified entity. For example, even in Iraq, the first Arab state ruled by a Shi'i government, there are differences between Shi'i political and religious figures. The Arab Shi'i cleric Muqtadha al-Sadr, who takes a bellicose nationalist position,[17] and Ayatollah Ali Sistani, who is of Iranian origin and rejects several basic principles of Ayatollah Khomeini's philosophy, including the principle of the *velayat-e faqih* (rule of the jurist), exemplify the diversity of Shi'i opinion across the Iraqi Shi'i community. The Shi'is of Iraq also have competing visions of Iraq's future in particular and of the Shi'is' future in general, and therefore do not share a unified Shi'i vision. In addition, Iranian cleric Mohsen Kadivar, in his *Hukumat-e Velayat (Government of the Guardian)*, argues that all Shi'is do not necessarily follow the principle of *velayat-e faqih*, for different groups of Shi'i clerics adhere to different conceptions of religion and government.[18]

Shaykh Ali Salman, the leader of Bahrain's opposition political party, al-Wifaq, in January 2007, appeared on the Dubai-based television network, *al-Arabiyya's*, 'Point of Order' programme and discussed Shi'i loyalties to the Iranian Supreme Leader, Ali Khamene'i. According to Salman, *velayat-e faqih* does not extend beyond Iran to the people of Bahrain. 'The people of Bahrain have their own decision and their own religious authority, and are not tied to Sayyid Khamene'i (the Supreme Leader of Iran).' Salman added, 'if there are religious authorities in the Shi'i world, be it Sayyid Sistani in Najaf or Muhammad Husayn Fadhlallah in Lebanon, they (Bahrainis) are linked to him (Sistani or Fadhlallah) within the context of religious authority, which is a different arrangement from *wilayat al-faqih* [*velayat-e faqih*].' Salman also completely rejected Egyptian President Mubarak's comments that the Shi'is were more loyal to Iran than to the Arab state in which they lived.[19] In fact, he suggested that Mubarak's comments were aimed at diverting attention away from other kinds of political pressure and 'serve[d] the purpose of maintaining corrupt conditions in our [the Arab] countries so that we can say there is a threat called Iran or Israel'.[20]

While the possibility of a greater Shi'i entity may be remote, the Sunni leaders of the moderate Arab states are behaving as if the issue of a Shi'i entity in the region is more than a possibility. This is not to say that every Sunni Arab state believes that a 'Shi'i empire' is imminent, rather their concerns are primarily based on the assumption that emboldened Shi'i elements in the region might tilt the regional balance of power in favour of Iran. The 'Shi'i crescent' rhetoric should not be perceived solely through sectarian religious principles, but also through the geopolitical prism.

Iran and the Arab World: Troubled Relations

The 1979 Islamic revolution in Iran had far-reaching implications for the Arab states. From its inception, the Khomeini regime represented a threat to the Arab world by communicating directly with its Shi'i communities, many of whose leaders were old acquaintances of the new Islamic government in Iran. In particular, the revolution in Iran marked the opening of a new era for the traditionally passive and cautious Shi'i communities of the Gulf and Lebanon and influenced their political behaviour in various ways depending on the particular state, its demographics and the local political culture. Iran targeted three areas to project its revolutionary message beyond its borders – Iraq, the Gulf and Lebanon.

Khomeini targeted Saddam's dictatorship in Iraq with particularly vitriolic propaganda, which contributed to the atmosphere of hostility that led to the Iran–Iraq war. The birth of Hezbollah in Lebanon in 1982, and the ongoing attempt to enhance the Shi'i role in Lebanese politics, gave Iran a new foothold in the area, from which it could also harass Israel and assume a position of leadership in the Arab–Israeli conflict. In the Gulf, Khomeini also viewed the Gulf monarchical regimes as corrupt American 'puppets' that should be completely uprooted, and he tried to incite the Shi'a inhabiting Saudi Arabia, Bahrain and Kuwait to rebel. In 1981 and 1989 failed *coups d'état* that were carried out in Bahrain (where Iran has territorial claims) were aimed at overthrowing the Sunni al-Khalifa family and establishing an Iranian-style Islamic republic.

The removal of Saddam Hussein in April 2003 created a new opportunity for Iran to reassert its regional claim to hegemony. Following the fall of Saddam's regime, over a million and a half people, according to some estimates, crossed the border from Iran to Iraq. While many were Shi'is who had immigrated to Iran during the reign of Saddam, many who entered Iraq were operating in the service of the *Pasdaran* (Islamic Revolutionary Guard Corps). Others were Iranian activists and clerics seeking to restore Najaf to its eminent position as a centre of Shi'i Islamic learning, and to create new points of leverage for Iran inside Iraq. Indeed, the *Pasdaran* was able to create a power base in Najaf and Karbala and project its influence in the region.

Prime Minister Nuri al-Maliki's government in Iraq is Shi'i-dominated and many of the government ministers, including al-Maliki, have close contacts with Iran. Indeed, al-Maliki is said to converse in Persian with

Iran's Supreme Leader Ali Khamene'i during his visits to Iran. Post-Saddam Iraq is setting a precedent: the Shi'is, for the first time in contemporary history, occupy the leadership positions of an Arab state. US and Iranian involvement in Iraq has altered the historical balance of power between the Sunnis and Shi'is in favour of the Shi'is.

Against the background of these events, the moderate Arab regimes' anxiety has been rising in response to Iran's growing power in the region. This new dynamic is a product of the intercommunal strife in Lebanon, and to a larger extent Iraq, which have become the primary arenas for a bloody interreligious and intercommunal conflict. The Arab Sunni leaders were viewing the Sunni–Shi'i conflict through the geopolitical lens. An Egyptian diplomat encapsulated Arab concerns when he said:

> The Arab allies of the USA, Egypt, Jordan and Saudi Arabia are very worried by the sweeping influence Iran has gained in Iraq, Lebanon and the Palestinian Authority. With the help of the Hezbollah and Hamas organizations – radical and uncompromising forces on the issue of Israel – Iran is propelling the whole region toward a goal the opposite of that which the allies of America want to reach.[21]

For many in the Arab world, the Iraqi saga has blurred distinctions between 'Shi'i' and 'Iranian', and the term 'Shi'i' has turned into a way of describing someone who shares Iranian regional ambitions in the Arab Middle East. This rhetoric reached an absurd level when it spread to the Palestinian Authority, where the two rival parties are both Sunni. Fath activists, hostile to Hamas, derided Hamas activists, by calling them 'Shi'is'.[22]

Sunni Salafi groups have also adopted the same logic and have even taken it to the extreme. In September 2005, Abu Musa'b al-Zarqawi, leader of the al-Qaeda organization in Iraq, announced in a video clip that 'The al-Qaeda Organization in the Land of Two Rivers (Iraq) is declaring all-out war on the *rafidha* (heretics: here, the Shi'is), wherever they are in Iraq.' He added a call to the Sunnis: 'Wake up from your slumber … the war to exterminate Sunnis will never end.' In a video clip dated 2 July 2006, Osama bin Laden accused the Iraqi Shi'is of planning to wipe out the Sunnis in Iraq. He called the Shi'is 'traitors' and 'agents of imperialism', and even claimed that Shi'i religious rites contained heretical elements. Bin Laden concluded that Shi'i heresy would require that Shi'is receive appropriate punishment, in accordance with the *Shari'a* (Islamic law).[23] In late April 2008, Ayman al-Zawahiri, the number two figure in al-Qaeda, accused Iran of collaborating with the USA in the 2001 invasion of

Afghanistan. He also accused Iran of using Hezbollah's al-Manar television station to spread the idea that Israel rather than al-Qaeda was behind the 9/11 attacks.[24] As Zawahiri claimed: 'Iran has clear goals, which is the annexation of southern Iraq and the east of the (Arabian) Peninsula, and to expand in order to be able to communicate with its followers in southern Lebanon.'[25]

Iran views the present circumstances as its hour of opportunity, so to speak, and its chance to establish a firm foothold in the heart of the region. The Islamic Republic of Iran views itself as the regional hegemonic power and acts accordingly. Iran has exerted its influence in Damascus and Beirut for some time, but now it has expanded to Baghdad as well.

What makes Iran's growing influence all the more evident today is the fragmented status of the Arab state system. Iran is well aware of the leadership void that has emerged among these states and is capitalizing on it. Iran, a non-Arab, non-Sunni, Muslim actor, is attempting to fill the regional leadership vacuum, and its hard-line president, Mahmoud Ahmadinejad, has attempted to become the regional standard-bearer for the Palestinian cause by calling for the elimination of the state of Israel.

The possibility of a nuclear Iran has become another dimension of the anti-Iranian discourse that has been gathering momentum in the Arab media. 'Nuclear Iran is Reviving the Dream of the Persian Empire', was the title of *al-Sharq al-Awsat*'s January 2006 editorial, which claimed that Iran's nuclear programme was not intended for an attack on Israel, but was meant to provide Iran with an important tool for further expanding its regional influence. Another claim published by the Arab media is that Iran, facing international sanctions and pressure over its controversial nuclear programme, is exploiting the Sunni–Shi'i conflict in Iraq and Lebanon for political leverage in its negotiations with the international community.

The anti-Iranian tenor of the discussion of the nuclear question stands at the heart of the Arab public debate. Apart from Syria, which supports the Iranian nuclear programme because of its strategic alliance with Tehran, most Arab governments disapprove of Iran's nuclear ambition, believing that Iran is using its civilian nuclear programme as a pretext to develop nuclear weapons. In February 2006, Egypt, which has historically called for a nuclear-free zone in the Middle East, has made it clear that it opposes Iran's nuclear programme by voting to transfer the Iranian crisis from the International Atomic Energy Agency (IAEA) board of governors to the UN Security Council. Furthermore, Iran's nuclear activities have stimulated increasing Arab interest in nuclear energy. Egypt, Saudi Arabia, Bahrain, Qatar, Jordan and the UAE have already sought nuclear partnerships with the USA, Russia and France to acquire nuclear technology.

The moderate Arab states also fear that Iran's nuclear programme could lead to a military conflict between Tehran and the USA/Israel. The 2007 US National Intelligence Estimate (NIE), which declared that Iran gave up its nuclear weapons programme in 2003, may have decreased the chances of a US military attack, but the option of an Israeli attack, similar to its June 1981 attack on the Osirak nuclear reactor in Iraq, remains an option. If Iran refuses to surrender its nuclear programme and the USA or Israel attacks its facilities, Tehran's retaliation could have a major impact on the stability and security of the region. It would be unwise to overlook Tehran's ability to make an impact on the (Arab) oil market. Tehran has joint control of the Straits of Hormuz from which nearly 40 per cent of the world's oil is exported. In January 2008 Tehran's Revolutionary Guards launched five Iranian patrol boats to provoke US ships in the Strait of Hormuz, but they did not respond.

The geopolitical interpretation of the Sunni–Shi'i issue was further underlined in January 2007, when Saudi Arabia publicly warned Iran that its activity in the Gulf could be perilous. 'We advised the [Iranians] not to expose the Gulf Region to dangers,' said the Saudi king, 'Abdullah bin Abd al-Aziz. Furthermore, he reinforced the Saudi position in a strong statement he made to the Kuwaiti newspaper *al-Siyasa*, 'Any country that carries out unwise actions will be held accountable for them by the countries of the region.'[26]

Al-Ahram editor Osama al-Sarayya put it bluntly in stating that:

> Iran wants to spread the Shi'i doctrine in Sunni countries. This is not religion: this is politics. Iran does not care for the consequences of its actions. It only wants to be number one. Are Iran and the USA in cahoots? The claim is preposterous, but their policies seem to be heading in the same direction: that of 'uncreative' chaos. Some say that the Iranians have no ill intentions towards the region. I doubt it. Iran is not just reacting to the Americans. It has always been disruptive in its methods and aims. And yet a US–Iranian confrontation is the last thing this region needs.

Sarayya also said, 'Iran is working actively towards spreading Shi'i doctrine even in countries that do not have a Shi'i minority for reasons ... that have political dimensions, paving the way for reviving the dreams of the Safavids.' Sarayya was referring to the Safavid dynasty that ruled Iran from the end of the fifteenth century to 1720, and converted Iran's population to Shi'ism. 'That some people defend the Iranian position and deny Iranian ambitions over the Arab region, I see only as naivety and stupidity, coated with hatred for the American presence in the region,' explained Sarayya.[27]

Across the Region: A State-by-State Analysis

To get past the rhetoric of generalities such as the 'Shi'i crescent', one has to examine the Shi'i communities on a state-by-state basis, taking into account all the social, economic, political and cultural particularities of the local environment. With mounting anxiety in Sunni Arab states over Iranian regional ambitions, the Shi'i communities in these states came under increased scrutiny and pressure. The current geopolitical environment was renewing historical perceptions that the Shi'is in Arab states were indeed 'lesser Arabs' who sympathized with Iran.

There is no doubt that a whole series of questions and unresolved issues – primarily having to do with the internal politics of these 'mixed' Sunni–Shi'i states – will engage the attention of the region, and the way in which they unfold will have a formative influence on the whole region in the coming years.

Iraq has been the primary theatre for Sunni–Shi'i violence where it threatens to shatter the state into pieces. Iraq's long border with Iran, its social-demographic composition, its Shi'i holy sites, the presence of foreign occupying forces, and its oil resources make it the critical arena for the changing dynamics of the region.

The Iraqi Shi'is' vision of turning the country into a Shi'i Arab state is materializing. It is no surprise that Sunni tribal leaders have expressed concern that Iraq's Shi'i-dominated government will be a satellite Iranian regime. In 2004 a Sunni tribal leader claimed, 'They [Iranians] are increasing the number of their agents every day, and they are spending millions of dollars to brainwash the people to establish a Shiite state.' He also expressed concern that the new Iraqi state will follow Iran's example and combine religion and politics, 'They have different means, offering people money or tempting them with free trips to Iran. They want to convince people about the positive aspects of combining religion and politics.'[28]

Writing in 2006, Kayhan Barzegar, an Iranian scholar, painted a picture of Iran's goals in Iraq in geopolitical terms. As he put it: 'Iran's security challenges in the new Iraq is the result of Iran's legitimate concerns in terms of establishing national security on the one hand and creating opportunities for it to walk out of geopolitical isolation and thus consolidate its credit and influence both regionally and internationally on the other.'[29] In other words, two primary goals defined Iran's foreign policy in Iraq. The first was to prevent the USA from attacking Iran, and the second was to prevent Iraq from becoming a client state of the USA by ensuring a Shi'i dominated government. One might add that a third foreign policy goal of Iran was to maintain a 'managed chaos'[30] in Iraq for use as a point of leverage against US-led international pressure and sanctions related to Iran's nuclear programme. It is clear that for Iran, 'Iraq is the most important country in the world', as the then Iranian minister of intelligence and security, Ali Yunesi, noted in 2004.[31]

Despite widespread Sunni–Shi'i violence in Iraq, Iran's interests in Iraq are guided by geopolitics in conjunction with ideology. Iran has strong national security interests in seeing Iraq succeed as a viable sovereign state. Also, Iran has no wish to see Iraq's Kurds establish an independent state that would, by virtue of its very existence, foment separatist unrest among Iran's Kurdish population. Iran would prefer an Iraqi central government that is strong enough to hold the state together but too weak to constitute a threat on its border. Iran supports a Shi'i-led central government in Iraq, in part, because it believes 'Shi'is don't fight Shi'is.'[32]

Despite Iran's strong geopolitical interests in establishing its influence in Iraq, there is also a strong ideological component that is closely woven into the fabric of its geopolitical interests. Kayhan Barzegar, who in 2006 characterized Iran's involvement in Iraq in almost entirely defensive national security terms, later in 2008 described Iran's influence in Iraq in broader more ambitious terms: 'The advent of new political developments in Iraq counts as a turning point in the strengthening of the Shiite position in the region and the world.' Barzegar described Iran's changing regional position along sectarian and ethnic lines: 'the empowerment of the Shiite element in new Iraq will play an important role in balancing Iran's relations with ... the Arab countries.' Iran's geopolitics are intimately linked to its Shi'i identity, according to Barzegar who compared the renewed Shi'i role in the region with the 1979 Islamic revolution in Iran:

> In fact, the Islamic Revolution encouraged the Shiites of the region to identify themselves and embolden their presence in the region. In the new conditions, the Shiites, as one expert of the Middle East called them the 'Forgotten Muslims' – dramatically enter the Middle East developments as one of the most important effective factors.[33]

In other words, Iran's geopolitical interests converge with its ideological principles in Iraq and provide Iran with an opportunity for an enhanced regional role via its Shi'i influence in the new Shi'i dominated Iraq. Iran has been using its Shi'i identity as a tool through which to exercise soft power to advance its geopolitical interests.

The establishment of a Shi'i-dominated Iraqi government and the strong grip in which Shi'i militias hold southern Iraq up to Baghdad are developments that augur badly for moderate Arab regimes. The Jordanians, Saudis, Egyptians and others are warning about increasing Iranian intervention in the internal affairs of Iraq and view this as a violation of the accepted rules of the game and a real danger to the stability of the region. For their part, the moderate Arab regimes are doing what they can to extend their influence in Iraq by providing financial support to Sunni political and tribal groups and by donating funds and personnel for infrastructure and aid projects like hospitals and schools. There have been unsubstantiated rumours that some Sunni regimes have provided support to radical groups in Iraq to combat Iran's militias, but these reports are anecdotal and difficult to verify or confirm. Indeed, following the US military withdrawal from Iraqi cities in late June 2009, Sunni radicals appear to have made a renewed effort to attack Shi'i targets, particularly visiting Iranians making the pilgrimage to Shi'i holy shrines.[34]

The question of the future of the American presence in Iraq, and the great number of unanswered questions that linger regarding its future, will compel the Arab moderate states to come together on a joint policy for Iraq whose aim will be to block the influence of Iran. Despite these aims, Arab moderate states realize there are few good options for limiting Iran's presence in Iraq.

Iran and Iraq are the two Middle Eastern states with the largest Shi'i populations. However, Shi'is can also be found in large numbers in many of the Arab states of the Persian Gulf – Saudi Arabia, Bahrain, Kuwait, Qatar and the United Arab Emirates (UAE). Shi'is in Bahrain comprise 70 per cent of the citizen population, while in Kuwait the citizen population is 30 per cent Shi'a.[35]

Saudi Arabia, despite its relatively small population, is the largest Arab Gulf state and the most outspoken in attacking Iran's expansionist aims in the region. The Saudi press has issued a number of doomsday scenarios portraying what could happen if Iran succeeded in causing instability in the Arab states. For example, the following was written with regard to the Kingdom of Bahrain, where the demographic situation is particularly complex, with an Arab Shi'i community living beside a Persian Shi'i community and the Sunni al-Khalifa royal family ruling over them all:

> At a time when the USA will soon begin to reduce its presence in Iraq and when all forecasts indicate the outbreak of a civil war there, the Iraqi chaos will give Iran an excuse for strengthening its presence there [in Iraq] and for intervening militarily under the cloak of protecting the Shi'is.[36]

Two case studies, Bahrain and Kuwait, aptly illustrate the similarities, and, more importantly, the serious differences regarding the Sunni–Shi'i dynamic from one Arab state to the next.

In Kuwait, Sunnis are the majority, and constitute approximately 70 per cent of the citizen population, including the Sunni al-Sabah ruling family.[37] Shi'is in Kuwait are not necessarily a cohesive and homogenous socio-religious group.

The recent Sunni–Shi'i violence in Iraq and Lebanon has not appeared in the Arab Gulf states. However, even in Kuwait, where Sunni–Shi'i relations have been relatively tranquil, there have been signs of simmering tension. While relations between Sunnis and Shi'is in Kuwait are generally not characterized by violence, the Salafis (Sunnis who favour a return to an earlier 'purer' form of Islam) are usually hostile to the Shi'is. In March 2007, a Kuwaiti Sunni cleric, 'Uthman al-Khamis, announced plans to launch a new satellite channel to warn Muslims of 'the Shi'i threat'.[38]

In more recent developments, two Shi'i members of the parliament's *popular bloc*, 'Adnan 'Abd al-Samad and Ahmad Lari, participated in commemorations for the assassinated Lebanese Hezbollah commander, 'Imad Mughniyya. Mughniyya, who was killed by a car bomb in Damascus on 12 February 2008, and was believed to have participated in the 1988 hijacking of a Kuwaiti airliner that cost two lives. This public display of Shi'i solidarity by Lari and al-Samad threatened Kuwait's relatively relaxed climate of intercommunal relations. The appearance of hundreds of Shi'is at a rally in Mughniyya's memory provoked widespread Sunni anger. The *Thawabit bloc* secretary, Muhammad al-Mutayri, claimed that MP Abd al-Samad, who went as far as to claim that Mughniyya was a 'martyr hero … whose blood will wipe Israel off the map',[39] had ambitions to become Kuwait's Hassan Nasrallah. Mutayri went on to accuse the Kuwaiti government of ignoring the increasing radicalism of Kuwaiti youth, both Sunnis and Shi'is.

The row over Mughniyya's memorial rally followed a rare outbreak of apparently sectarian violence on the night of 11–12 January 2008, when stone-throwing vandals attacked a dozen Sunni religious bookshops, thus hinting at hitherto unsuspected sympathy for radical ideas among at least a few young Shi'is. A bomb threat against the Kuwaiti embassy in Beirut has since further heightened tension. This follows a period when books and audio-visual material insulting Shi'i beliefs have been circulating, serving as a reminder that even in Kuwait, where stability and sectarian tranquillity is the norm, Sunni–Shi'i relations remain a delicate issue.

Shi'i tactics are pragmatic and conducted within the Kuwaiti tradition of dialogue and compromise. Shi'i cleric al-Mahri's political activism exemplifies the Shi'i *modus operandi*. In March 2005 the Kuwaiti government warned al-Mahri against violating 'the mosque code of conduct' during his Friday sermons. Al-Mahri's sermons drew the attention of Kuwaiti authorities for two primary issues: (1) he criticized the increasing political participation of women in Kuwait, and (2) he was critical of the head of Egypt's al-Azhar University for not condemning Sunni suicide attacks on Shi'is in Iraq. Al-Mahri responded by pointing out his position of independence in Kuwait. He noted that, 'Shi'i mosques do not come under the Ministry of Awqaf. They were built with our money. We are responsible for maintenance work and pay the mosque employees. No one in the Ministry of Awqaf can stop us from giving sermons'.[40] It is also worth noting that Kuwait University's College of Islamic Law does not offer training in Shi'i jurisprudence, requiring Shi'is to travel to Iran or Iraq for the necessary Shi'i education. Al-Mahri articulates the dual nature of the Shi'i position in Kuwait: the Shi'is feel as if they are independent in the religious realm, but at the same time are constantly seeking to increase their political participation and representation in the Kuwaiti government.

Al-Mahri has been careful to advance the Shi'i agenda in terms that respect Kuwaiti political leaders' authority. He has referred to the Kuwaiti government as 'just and fair' and stated that Kuwait's constitution was one of the 'best'. He pointed out that the Shi'a have rights in Kuwait, but were seeking equal opportunity in government and he referred to the small number of Shi'i deputy ministers. Al-Mahri characterized Kuwait as a 'liberal democratic society' and affirmed that the Shi'is allegiance was to their Kuwaiti homeland and its political leadership.[41]

In summary, Kuwait's Shi'is – who account for up to one-third of the Kuwaiti population – are well integrated into society. The multi-layered complexity of the Sunni–Shi'i relationship in Kuwait is different in many respects from its Gulf neighbours. As the Mughniyya incident illustrated, outbursts of intolerance on both sides may be an uncomfortable sign of the pressures and risks for Kuwait as a result of intermittent confrontation between Shi'is and Sunnis in the wider Middle East. However, Kuwait's strong tradition of an open political dialogue combined with a strong sense of national identity should be up to the task of managing the sectarian challenges.

Bahrain is unique among the Gulf states in that it has a majority Shi'i population. According to the best available estimates, Shi'is make up 70 per cent of the citizen population of 700,000. Moreover, the majority of Bahraini Shi'is are followers of the 'twelver' (*ithna 'ashariyya*) branch of Shi'i Islam.

The Shi'is of Bahrain cannot easily be defined as either rebellious or quietist; the picture is more complex, particularly against the background of Iran's revolutionary regime. In the first place, unlike other states in the region, Bahrain carries the burden of an ancient Iranian claim to its territory. The Bahraini–Iranian dispute seemed to have been settled in 1971, when the shah relinquished the claim of sovereignty over Bahrain and recognized its independence, following a United Nations sponsored referendum on independence in Bahrain. But the Iranian revolution revived the issue, albeit in a new form.

In contrast to Kuwait, the ruling al-Khalifa family of Bahrain has not considered the Shi'is worthy of inclusion in its system of alliances. The al-Khalifa regime has been accused of discriminating against and oppressing the Shi'is, including sporadic physical attacks by Sunnis. Shi'is were often not allowed to practice their religious ceremonies, particularly the *'ashura* rites. They were also barred from owning land or joining the army, and could not hold supreme ministerial offices. The Sunni-dominated security forces persecuted them continually as suspects of subversion.

Although deprivation tended to unite them emotionally, the Shi'is of Bahrain are divided along geographic and ethnic lines, by living conditions and even praying styles – all of which have given rise to varied types of political behaviour. The *al-Baharna*, who consider themselves indigenous inhabitants of Bahrain, make up the largest portion of the island's Shi'i population. There are several prominent Shi'i families, such as the Safar, Sharif, Kanu, Fakhro, that form an integral part of the socio-political establishment. In addition, there is a sizeable community of Shi'is, originating from Saudi Arabia's eastern province, al-Ahsa. Mainly small traders and manual and service workers, they have developed a degree of self-sufficiency. They manage the most important Shi'i mourning house (*ma'tam*), where Imam Hussein's martyrdom is commemorated in a totally different style from the Baharna processions.

As Bahrain's political blocs followed sectarian lines, Persian Shi'is ('Ajam) remained separate. At the beginning of the twentieth century Persians constituted the largest foreign group in Manama, the capital city. The Persian *ma'tam* was financially supported by leading Persian merchant families, such as the Bushehri family. Throughout the first half of the twentieth century, the Persian *ma'tam* was instrumental in establishing religious links with Iran. The merchants often hired respected clergymen from Bushehr, Shiraz and Qom as teachers of Shi'i theology. Until 1970, Bahraini 'Ajams held both Bahraini passports and Iranian identity cards.

Iran's claim to Bahrain is an ongoing saga. This became evident again in July 2007 when Hossein Shariatmadari, editor of the conservative Iranian daily paper *Kayhan* and an adviser to Iran's Supreme Leader, Ayatollah Ali Khamene'i, published a controversial editorial. It claimed that Bahrainis supported reunification with Islamic Iran and that such a reunification was 'an indisputable right for Iran and the people of this province [Bahrain] and should not and cannot be overlooked'.[42] Iran may be using its historical claims to sovereignty over Bahrain to entrench its broader regional influence in the Gulf. Meanwhile, it gives the king of Bahrain yet another reason to keep a close eye on Iran's influence on Bahrain's Shi'i population.

The 'spiritual father' of Bahrain's Shi'i political and religious movement Shaykh Abd al-Amir al-Jamri died in December 2006. Jamri had served in Bahrain's first parliament from 1973 to 1975, before it was dissolved by Bahrain's amir. Throughout the 1990s Jamri was a leading Shi'i political activist and the Bahraini authorities gaoled him from 1996 until 1999, but the new king, Hamad bin 'Isa al-Khalifa, pardoned him as part of his new plan of political reform.[43]

Al-Jamri's political activism set the stage for Shaykh 'Isa Ahmad Qasim to re-emerge as the leading Shi'i cleric in Bahrain and one of the spiritual leaders of Shaykh Ali Salman's political group, al-Wifaq.[44] Considered to be the most prominent popular religious figure in Bahrain,[45] Qasim spent eight years of exile pursuing religious studies in Qom, Iran, and returned to Bahrain following the new Bahraini king's reform plan in March 2001. Like al-Jamri, Qasim had been a member of Bahrain's parliament when it was dissolved in 1975. Qasim was also the chairman of the Islamic Awareness Society from 1972 to 1984, when the government shut it down. While in exile in Iran, Qasim developed a hard line towards the Bahraini government and in 1997 went so far as to threaten the Bahraini government with a call to 'holy war' if a group of more than 30 Bahraini Shi'is – accused of being members of Hezbollah-Bahrain and conspiring to overthrow the government – were sentenced to death. The accused were ultimately sentenced to prison.[46] On returning to Bahrain in 2001, Qasim moderated his political rhetoric and said he intended to confine himself to religious matters and guidance, rather than engage in political activities.[47]

Qasim has become one of the main spiritual leaders of the foremost Shi'i political organization, al-Wifaq (Islamic National Accord), which is led by Shaykh 'Ali Salman. Al-Wifaq was formed in 2002 and serves as an umbrella organization for several different Shi'i groups, including the former al-Da'wa, Hezbollah-Bahrain, and the Free Bahrainis Movement (*al-Baharna al-ahrar*). For Shaykh Salman, who has led the Shi'i opposition since the early 1990s, sectarianism (*al-nafas al-ta'ifi*) remains the divisive social-political issue in Bahrain. 'Let me speak frankly', Salman said, 'sectarian prejudice exists in all levels of the government. It strongly exists among influential figures. I can say that most officials are influenced in their programmes by sectarianism, which governs Bahrain on political and economic issues.'

Shi'i clerics were not the only group that believed that sectarianism was destroying the state from within. A political scandal erupted when Salah al-Bandar – a Sunni, who was employed as an adviser to the cabinet affairs ministry – blew the whistle on a government scheme to marginalize Shi'is in the 2006 elections. Bandar released hundreds of pages that document a scheme to keep the Shi'a politically fragmented and weak, while at the same time restructuring the island's political districts to give Sunnis a demographic advantage they could transform into a political victory in the 2006 parliamentary elections. The documents even suggest there was a programme to convert Shi'is into Sunnis.[48] The elections, Bandar warned in his 240-page report, was only part of a five-year plan to give political control of Bahrain to a small group of anti-Shi'i Sunnis. This imbroglio attests to how serious the minority Sunni government views the political challenge posed by the Shi'i majority in Bahrain.

Iran–Syria–Hezbollah Axis

Iran has been active in Lebanon since 1979, and gave birth to Hezbollah in 1982, which has allowed Iran to export its revolutionary ideology and enhance the Shi'i role in Lebanese politics. With this in mind, it is no surprise that Lebanon would be a central arena for the Sunni–Shi'i violence, the struggle for regional hegemony, and more precisely, the struggle between Iran and a number of Arab states.

Hezbollah leader, Hassan Nasrallah, sought to turn the summer of 2006 war in Lebanon into 'the struggle of the Muslim nation'.[49] Hezbollah was determined to carry on the fight against Israel, and its success in bringing about Israel's withdrawal from Lebanon has earned it the sympathy of the Arab public throughout the region. There was thus nothing surprising about large demonstrations showing solidarity with Hezbollah's struggle being held on the streets of Cairo, Rabbat and Amman during the summer 2006 war in Lebanon. For the Saudi, Egyptian and Jordanian regimes, a Hezbollah victory, even a partial victory, would have served as a source of inspiration for the regime's domestic opponents.

The moderate Arab states directed severe criticism at Hezbollah at the start of the Lebanese crisis. They condemned its 'adventurous and hasty policy that could bring disaster down on Lebanon's head'.[50] On the second day of the war, Saudi Foreign Minister Sa'ud al-Faisal, declared that 'there is a difference between legitimate resistance and miscalculated adventurism.'[51] These critical statements reflect the Arab states' sentiments that Hezbollah's defeat could have provided the beneficial effects of weakening their own domestic opposition and exposing the limitations of Iran's power.

A nuanced explanation of what was worrying the Sunni Arabs was not a Hezbollah victory against Israel, but rather its success in spreading its ideology throughout the Arab world. Sunni Arabs feared that a victorious Hezbollah would become an instrument through which Khomeini's successors in Iran could expedite the delivery of the Islamic revolution to the Arab world.[52] In a Middle East where Saddam Hussein has become a thing of the past, and the extent of bin Laden's influence has been drastically limited, the Arab public continued to seek cultural heroes who would stand firm against the West. Shi'i leader Hassan Nasrallah could be the new hero of the Arab street owing to his bold and provocative conduct in defying the West. The increasing sympathy being shown for the values of the 'resistance' (*al-muqawama*), and the pictures of the new cultural hero, Hassan Nasrallah, that were paraded on the streets of Arab cities – not only in Damascus and towns in the Palestinian Authority, but also in Cairo – have become very worrisome phenomena for the moderate Arab regimes.

Lebanon's reconstruction and rehabilitation following the 2006 war also resulted in a competition for influence between Iran and the Arab moderate states. Saudi King Abdullah announced a grant in aid of $1.5 billion as an advance for an Arab and international fund for the reconstruction of Lebanon. The Saudis, it should be remembered, were involved in Lebanon in the past and served as patrons of the Ta'if accord of 1989, which brought about a temporary end to the Lebanese crisis during the 1980s. The Saudis also invested enormous amounts of money in Lebanon in the past, and they were allies of murdered Lebanese Prime Minister Rafiq al-Hariri.

The summer 2006 war in Lebanon should not be perceived as merely an additional chapter in the story of the Arab–Israeli conflict. It was also a confrontation between Israel and Iran, via Iran's proxy, Hezbollah. Moreover, the war shifted the regional balance of power and paved the way for new alliances. One of the most interesting phenomena to appear during the war was the behaviour of the Arab states at the emergency conferences of the Arab League that were convened as the fighting proceeded. For the first time the Arab states did not present themselves as a unified front against Israel in a time of war, which was a departure from a consistent Arab pattern throughout the twentieth century. This is an important new development, indicating that the power configurations in the Middle East are being realigned. The main element in this rearrangement is the struggle for regional primacy, with Iran being pitted against the moderate Arab states. In the campaigns of the twentieth century, Israel was entirely excluded from the regional coalitions. Now, however, it finds its interests converging with those of the moderate, Sunni Arab states.

The May–June 2008 Lebanese political agreement that Qatari Shaykh Hamad brokered in Doha was instrumental in further solidifying Hezbollah and Nasrallah's prominence in the Arab world. Hezbollah was able to demonstrate its military strength and defend its political independence from the Lebanese state authority, effectively placing its institutional apparatus on a par with the state's. However, the violence in June–July 2008 has exacted a high price, and perhaps deepened sectarian divisions in a fragile and fragmented Lebanese society. The *New York Times* noted that Lebanese television stations affiliated with the opposing political groups were broadcasting recorded segments underlining the communal divisions. Sahar Khatib, an anchor for Saad Hariri's television station, which was forced off the air during the conflict, addressed Hezbollah: "'This grudge against us, why?" Khatib shouts, staring angrily at the camera. "I am someone who believes in God, not sects. Now you have awakened this sectarianism in me. Look at your victims, victims like me, one after another".'[53]

The Doha agreement may have ended the political deadlock and sectarian street violence in Lebanon, but it undermined Lebanon's government institutions and ensured that Hezbollah would not be disarmed, as was stipulated in UN Resolution 1701, which was part of the agreement that ended the 2006 Lebanon war with Israel.

The battle for Lebanon's future following the 2006 war has continued, not only internally among Lebanon's sectarian parties, but also regionally, as the Arab states compete with Iran for local influence. The efforts to prevent Lebanon from being turned into a Shi'i stronghold and to retain it as an integral part of the Sunni Arab expanse were at the heart of the struggle leading up to the June 2009 Lebanese elections. This was a struggle in which the victorious pro-Western coalition led by Saad Hariri was reported to be financially supported by the moderate Arab states. Hariri's victory was an important sign that Hezbollah, backed by Syria and Iran, has not achieved political hegemony in Lebanon, even if the government remains incapable of disarming the group and ending its institutional independence from the Lebanese state.

Running parallel with recent events in Lebanon, the Arab moderates, along with Turkey, continue to launch diplomatic initiatives aimed at separating Syria from its 'Iranian connection'. Motivated by their understanding of the Iranian threat and their efforts to reduce Iran's strategic depth, the moderate Arab states and Turkey are working to advance an Israeli–Syrian dialogue. Until recently these efforts have moved forward cautiously and slowly, but the sporadic calls for peace coming from Damascus may be signs of a possible change.

The moderate Arab states seem to be applying a similar strategy in their approach to the question of Palestine. They have been steadfast in their efforts to settle the differences between the clashing sides in the Palestinian Authority, in part, because they view the Palestinian cause as another lever that Iran uses to project its influence and ideology in the region. Many observers interpret Iran's support of Hamas as a factor limiting Egypt's room for manoeuvre in its efforts to mediate among the Palestinian groups. Efforts to form a Palestinian unity government that is more in line with the moderate Arab states in the region proceed without let-up. In February 2007 the Saudis succeeded in bringing the various Palestinian sides to Mecca and to agree on the establishment of a Palestinian unity government, but the unity government ultimately resulted in renewed fighting and the Saudi efforts came to nothing.

The convergence of interests between Israel and the conservative Arab regimes became evident in late December 2008 and January 2009 during Israel's Operation Cast Lead in Gaza, which was designed to end Hamas's rocket-fire directed from the Gaza Strip onto civilian communities in southern Israel. While Iran was said to be providing arms to Hamas (via Sudan and the tunnels from Egypt into Gaza), Egypt sealed the Rafah crossing and did not permit Hamas to use the Egyptian border as a strategic asset. Hezbollah's Hassan Nasrallah, outraged by Egypt's behaviour, delivered a passionate speech on 28 December 2008 denouncing the Egyptian government and in oblique language calling for Egyptian military officers to rebel against Egyptian President Mubarak:

> What we hear and know about the Egyptian officers and armed forces that they are still adherent to their noble Arab descent and still on their anti-Zionist position. … I'm not calling for staging a *coup d'état* in Egypt. I'm not in the position of calling for a *coup d'état* in Egypt but I'm with the generals and officers pressing on the political leadership: that doesn't go with the honour of our military uniforms, and military affiliations to see our people in Gaza being slaughtered while we guard Israel's borders! Let's move today: Egypt, the people of Egypt, scholars, Al Azhar sheikdom, the various armed forces, and political elites – I don't think anyone is excused.[54]

Saudi Arabia remained relatively silent during the Israeli operation, while Iran's Supreme Leader made a series of harsh speeches denouncing Israel and chastising the passive Arab leadership as traitors. On 4 March 2009, in a speech in memory of the Gaza operation Khamene'i said:

> At times some people are heard to say that Palestine is an Arab

problem. What does that mean? ... If it means that the heads of some Arab countries should refuse to pay any heed to the cries of help of the Palestinian people, which are addressed to all Muslims, if it means that they may collaborate with the ruthless usurper enemy in such an important case as the tragedy of Gaza while loudly condemning others who cannot remain indifferent to their call of duty to help Gaza, then no proud and conscientious Muslim or Arab will accept it, nor spare the speaker of disapproval and reproach.[55]

Meanwhile, Iran's Supreme Leader Khamene'i was forced to send a group of Iranian 'volunteers' home from the airport where the group had waited for more than six days in Tehran following President Ahmadinejad's call for martyrs to go to Gaza. This incident illustrates that the Islamic regime was willing to support its Palestinian allies financially and logistically to serve its own strategic interests, but would not risk its own security and become directly involved in the conflict despite its public ideological commitment to the issue.

The rift between the moderate Arab regimes and Iran grew deeper and more profound following Egypt's April 2009 disclosure that it had uncovered a Hezbollah cell operating to undermine the government in Egypt. President Mubarak, using uncharacteristically blunt language to allude to Iran during his Sinai Liberation Day speech on 25 April 2009, said:

We will not allow the interference of regional powers who are antagonistic to peace, and who are pushing the region into abyss, seeking to spread their hegemony and agenda on our Arab world, feeding differences on the Arab and Palestinian arenas and deploying their agents into the region to threaten Egypt's national security, violate its borders and shake its stability. To those I say: We are fully aware of your schemes. We will reveal your conspiracy and we will strike back whenever we are attacked. Stop taking the Palestinian cause as a pretext and beware of the anger of Egypt and its people.[56]

Even if the concerns and worries of the Sunni Arab states over the sensitive issues on the regional agenda have increased greatly, these states still would prefer a diplomatic political outlet that will allay their concerns regarding Iran's perceived 'meddling' in Arab affairs.

Conclusion

The rise in the status of the Shi'is constitutes a significant change in the Middle East. Even if the idea of one large, cohesive Shi'i entity is unrealistic, the Shi'is have gained influence in Middle Eastern politics and shifted the balance of power in mixed states like Iraq, Lebanon and, to a lesser extent, Bahrain, Kuwait and Saudi Arabia.

The sharp rift dividing the Sunnis and Shi'is, which came to light clearly during and after the summer 2006 war in Lebanon, is certainly not a passing phenomenon. For the first time, Shi'is have taken over the leadership of an Arab state, Iraq. Hezbollah, which did not enhance its political position in the June 2009 Lebanese elections, also did not lose any ground and won in the areas where Shi'is predominate. Further, Hezbollah is unlikely to lose its position of military authority in the delicate balance of power in Lebanon anytime soon, while its aspirations are closely linked to the rising status of Iran.

A number of scholars and analysts would refute the notion of a growing Sunni–Shi'i rift, and instead argue that the decisive factors in the Middle East are essentially political, rather than religious or ideological. Such claims were articulated during the recent 'Doha Debates' televised by the BBC. Hisham Hellyer of the Oxford Centre for Islamic Studies, for example, referred to the historical coexistence between sects: 'Sunnis and Shiites, after all, have learned "grudgingly" to tolerate each other for centuries, despite doctrinal differences.' He concluded that, 'those differences have never turned into religious wars like we saw in Europe. They never turned into inquisitions, genocides, or anything like that.'[57]

Those who examine the region through the Sunni–Shi'i lens, according to this school of thought, are drawing on patronizing colonialist conceptions that tend to view the region as a collection of sects, ethnic communities and groups of congregations, rather than vibrant and viable national states. A further extension of this argument would be that the Sunni–Shi'i issue has been overblown, suggesting that the Sunni–Shi'i debate has been propagated as part of a hidden agenda to sow dissent within the Muslim world. Another similar claim, asserts that the Sunni–Shi'i rivalry and rhetoric diverts attention from important fundamental problems in the Middle East, such as the American incursion into Iraq and Israeli policy towards the Palestinians. Shaykh Mohammad Hussein Fadhlallah, the spiritual leader of the Hezbollah, for example, allots a special place in his sermons to the Americans' deeds in inflaming Sunni–Shi'i tension. And he claims that the concepts of the Shi'i renaissance and the *tashayu'* are the result of a protracted American effort to deepen the gap between the two Muslim communities. One of the leaders of the Muslim Brotherhood, Mohammed Mahdi 'Akif, has expressed similar views. He accused the 'enemies of Islam' and the 'foreign conquerors' of deepening the split and spreading the culture of hatred between Sunnis and Shi'is 'that had developed recently'.[58]

The Sunni–Shi'i confrontation in Iraq is influencing developments and perceptions in the Middle East, particularly in the Gulf States and Lebanon. Assessing the tone and mood of events from state to state, rather than referring to a 'Shi'i crescent', one gets the sense that the Sunna and Shi'a provide a window through which to understand better the changing geopolitical picture across the region. It appears – and this is our central claim – that the new dimension of the age-old conflict between the Sunna and Shi'a is less a matter of faith and more a product of geopolitical developments. In January 2007, King 'Abdallah of Jordan explained:

> When I spoke about the 'Shi'i crescent', it was in connection with political coalitions. I had no intention of discussing the term from the sectarian point of view. We relate to things through the lens of regional stability and security, and not from narrow self-seeking considerations. The matter is not one to be understood through slogans, but one that focuses on the imminent challenges and dangers facing the Middle East.[59]

At the beginning of the twenty-first century it would seem that Iran is emerging as the only regional super power in the Middle East, and there is no Arab state capable of challenging its supremacy. Iran finds it convenient to view the issue of the Sunni–Shi'i conflict as 'a plot concocted by America and the Zionist regime with the aim of deepening the conflict between Sunni Muslims and Shi'is in order to increase America's ability to exploit the states of the region and their resources'.[60] Meanwhile, in practice, as it has done for some time, Iran continues to antagonize its Arab neighbours by fomenting divisions in Iraq and Lebanon and by extending material and moral aid to the Hamas and the Islamic jihad in the Palestinian territories. As a result, on the one hand, Iran's Islamic regime has been very successful in its efforts to gain the sympathy of the Arab public, thanks to its anti-Western declarations and policies. On the other hand, its controversial behaviour has deepened the Arab regimes' anxieties.

Despite the moderate Arab states' concern about the aforementioned regional sources of conflict, they still seek diplomatic and political means to lead them out of the morass. In this respect, the role of the global offered a potential route to jump-starting a local diplomatic solution. The January 2008 Annapolis conference, which was meant to revisit the Israeli–Palestinian dialogue, included Israel, the Palestinians, Syria, Saudi Arabia, Egypt, Jordan, other Arab moderate states, the Europeans and the USA. It was an indication of the continued concern among both regional and international players about the changing geopolitical circumstances and Iran's quest for regional hegemony.

Moreover, President Obama's election in late 2008 promised a renewed effort in regional peace making. However, his public effort to reach out to Iran has fed the concerns of the moderate Arab regimes that Obama's desire for a bargain with Iran will come at the expense of the Arab states.[61] There also appeared to be some concern that Obama's inclination to see the region's problems as interlocking may have led him to an overly ambitious approach that sought to address, (1) the nuclear threat posed by Iran, (2) peace between Israel and Syria; and (3) the conflict between Israelis and Palestinians, contemporaneously. According to Obama's comprehensive approach, a US understanding with Syria would entice the latter away from Iran and perhaps bring Iran to the negotiating table with the USA. A US rapprochement with Syria would then give Arab states and the Palestinians the political support needed to negotiate with Israel.[62] Needless to say, the complexities of the region and the particularities of these different issues have not accommodated President Obama's initial vision. Syria has not responded to US overtures, Hamas and Fatah remain bitterly divided, and Iran has shown little if any indication of wanting to sit down with the USA and discuss its nuclear programme, and is unlikely to change its position in the light of the current post-election unrest that is challenging the Supreme Leader's authority.

Years after 9/11, the USA, as the global power, is still struggling to come to terms with local conflict across the Middle East, but finds itself facing a very different regional balance of power due, in part, to the sectarianism that has emerged as part of the war in Iraq and Iran's resurgence. Whether sectarianism is the cause or the symptom of the recent geopolitical changes is hard to say, but perhaps the more relevant question in the short term is how the new balance (or perhaps imbalance) of power between Iran and the Arab states will affect regional as well as global priorities in the near future. As historians are inclined to point out, only time will tell.

12

Egyptian and Saudi Intervention in the Israeli–Palestinian Conflict (2006–09): Local Powers' Mediation Compared

Joseph Kostiner and Chelsi Mueller

Egypt emerged from the 2008–09 Gaza War as the main mediator in the Israeli–Palestinian conflict, when Cairo became the hub of consultations with regional and international players towards the goal of achieving a ceasefire acceptable to Israel and Hamas. In fact, Egypt had been working steadily behind the scenes mediating in Hamas–Fatah matters and in Hamas–Israel matters since Hamas came to power in the 2006 Palestinian Legislative Council elections. Whenever violence flared up between Fatah and Hamas, Egyptian negotiators would intervene in an attempt to prevent their infighting turning into a full-blown Palestinian civil war. At the same time, Egypt negotiated between Hamas and Israel for the release of the kidnapped Israeli soldier, Gilad Shalit. After the violent takeover of the Gaza Strip by Hamas in June 2007, the Egyptians worked tirelessly to reconcile the two Palestinian factions while simultaneously trying to mediate a ceasefire between Israel and Hamas.

For years, Saudi Arabia has also viewed itself as the region's main mediator. Prominent historical examples of Saudi mediation include the Ta'if agreement of 1989, which was signed by warring Lebanese factions, and King Abdullah's 2002 peace initiative for the Arab–Israeli conflict, which became the Arab Peace Initiative. Most recently, in February 2007, the Saudis brokered the Mecca Accord between the warring Palestinian factions and then in March of the same year, they embarked on a diplomatic campaign to garner support for the revival of the Arab Peace Initiative. In fact, these efforts took place as part of a broader diplomatic campaign that the Saudis undertook to cope with the implications of Iran's regional ascendancy: they sought to establish a dialogue with Iran while simultaneously working diplomatically to contain Iran's growing influence in Iraq, Lebanon and the Palestinian territories.

In this chapter[1] we shall compare and contrast two models of local power conflict mediation, namely Saudi Arabia's and Egypt's mediation activities in the Arab–Israeli and inter-Palestinian arenas from the Second Lebanon War in 2006 to the aftermath of the Gaza War in 2009. We shall precede the individual Saudi and Egyptian cases with an analysis of the regional context and the regional pressures, without which the decisions and actions of these two states and the parties being mediated cannot be fully comprehended.

The most noteworthy differences between the Egyptian and Saudi models of mediation emanate from the two states' geographical proximity to the actors, their relationships to the specific actors, and the degree to which each gets involved. Egypt shares a border with the Gaza Strip, has a peace treaty with Israel and directly experiences the volatility of the Israeli–Palestinian arena. Furthermore, Hamas's connection with Egypt's own Islamic opposition poses a threat to Egypt's domestic stability. Egypt has sat down with representatives of each side, or in the case of Hamas and Fatah, has brought them together for talks. It knows each side's respective position, and learns where there is room for compromise. Paradoxically, as much as Egypt's physical border with the Gaza Strip has made Egypt an active mediator in the Israeli–Palestinian conflict, so it has also made Egypt an unwilling party to its own mediation when the parties that were being mediated made any would-be agreement contingent on demands for Egyptian action on its border. Such was the case when Egypt's unwillingness to meet Hamas's demand to open its border crossing and Israel's demand to station international monitors on its border to prevent arms smuggling prevented the Egyptian mediators from securing the Israeli–Hamas ceasefire that they sought in the autumn of 2008.

Egypt's proximity to the actors and its hands-on approach stands in contrast with the Saudis' distance from the actors and hands-off approach. Saudi Arabia, neither sharing a border nor having diplomatic relations with Israel, remains detached from the actors and events in the Israeli–Palestinian arena. In the cases of the Arab Peace Initiative and the Mecca Conference, after having initiated a process, the Saudis avoided involvement in its later intricate procession. Having neither the knowledge nor the experience required to influence the parties, the Saudis left the task of sitting down with the sides and working out the details to the Egyptians. Thus, the Saudi mediation role can be regarded as a 'posture'. Their typical mediation and coordination of activities is designed to attract the attention of international or regional powers with a view to elevating Saudi Arabia's regional position and thus improving the kingdom's security. Such was the case in 2007 when King Abdullah hosted the Mecca Conference and revived the Arab Peace Initiative in the Arab League. These moves were calculated not to solve the Israeli–Palestinian conflict for its own sake, but rather to serve as mechanisms for coping with Iran's regional ascendancy and calming the regional instability that Iran generated while in pursuit of regional dominance.

Thus it can said that while Saudi Arabia's interventions were aimed at gaining the attention of regional and international actors, and coordinating a complex regional scheme, the Saudi strategy does not rely on getting involved in the process or seeing it through to completion. This is in contrast to Egypt, whose interventions in the Israeli–Palestinian arena were intended to produce immediate and tangible (albeit limited) results because failure to influence the outcome bore consequences for Egypt's national security.

Egypt, Saudi Arabia and the Emerging Regional Dangers

Saudi Arabia and Egypt, which have historically been bitter rivals for Arab leadership, both employed mediation in the inter-Palestinian and Arab–Israeli arenas as a means of boosting their own regional standing in the period between 2006 and 2009. The two states jockeyed to gain the coveted position as the region's main mediator, but during this period they neither took steps to thwart each other's mediation initiatives nor aired grievances against each other publicly. This was owing to the two states' shared perception of Iran as the region's main threat.

The prospect of Iran obtaining its long-held aspiration of hegemony in the region was the main regional threat from the vantage point of both Saudi Arabia and Egypt. The two strongest and most influential Arab governments had every reason to fear that Iran was actively pursuing its hegemonic ambitions in the region. Iran lunged at an opportunity to secure a position of influence in the new Iraq. Through its proxy, Hezbollah, it waged a proxy war against Israel in 2006. It also charged down a collision course with the West over its nuclear programme and threatened to 'wipe Israel off the map'.

The post-11 September 2001 milieu has seen Saudi Arabia take up residence in the so-called 'peace camp', which was previously dominated by Egypt and Jordan, the two Arab states that have peace treaties with Israel. Iran, the leading anti-Western, anti-Israel force in the region, has come to the fore as a regional power, rivalling the 'moderate' pro-Western Arab states. This widening fault line stretches across the region between the 'moderate' Sunni Arab states that accept the notion of peace with Israel and the 'radicals' that support violence against Israel, namely Iran, Syria, Hezbollah and Hamas. Thus, two regional camps have emerged – the Iranian-led 'radical' camp and the Sunni Arab 'moderate' camp. The hardening of these alignments, as a result of Iran's becoming stronger in the region, has meant that the Palestinian Hamas has had to lean more on Iran and Syria for sympathy with its cause.

For a radical Sunni Palestinian organization like Hamas, the support of the Sunni Arab states – particularly Egypt and Saudi Arabia – would be preferable to the support of a Persian, Shiite state like Iran.[2] Given the choice between moderating its core principles to have the support of the Sunni Arab states, or accepting Iranian support and maintaining its bellicose stance against Israel, Hamas has opted for the latter. Thus, because Egypt and Saudi Arabia went along with the Western boycott of Hamas in 2006 (however grudgingly), Hamas turned to Iran for financial backing and support for its uncompromising position on Israel.[3] In this way, Hamas has exploited the region's rivalries by selling influence to the highest bidder (of weapons and money).

From Egypt's and Saudi Arabia's vantage points, the policy of isolating Hamas turned the latter into an Iranian instrument that, like Hezbollah, Iran could use to fight Israel and halt the peace process. These states are keenly aware that the Iranian regime's sponsorship of violence against Israeli and Western targets is a means by which Iran can promote itself as the leading Islamic power in the region. The populations of such states as Egypt, Jordan and Saudi Arabia are awed by the exhibitions of militancy, martyrdom and defiance put on by Iran's Arab clients. Meanwhile, Iran continuously accuses the leaders of the 'moderate' Arab states of being collaborators with Israel, and that kind of an accusation resonates on the Arab streets.[4] In this way, Iran makes it difficult for the Arab leaders to condemn publicly the Arab militias who fight Israel or take actions that could be perceived as collaborating with Israel without facing a backlash from their own populations.

Egyptian and Saudi officials have long referred to the 'interference of outsiders' in the Palestinian and Lebanese arenas.[5] As their perception of the Iranian threat has grown, Egyptian and Saudi leaders have become more intrepid in their willingness to blame Iran and its clients for the instability they create. For example, just after the 2008–09 Gaza War, Egyptian Foreign Minister Ahmad Abul Gheit accused Tehran, together with Hamas and Hezbollah, of 'acting to turn Gaza into a battlefield'.[6]

Iran's profile peaked at the end of 2007 when violent conflicts in the Iraqi, Lebanese and Palestinian arenas reached the boiling point. On the Palestinian front, it had become clear that the Egyptian sponsored negotiations for a power sharing agreement were failing. On 15 December intense fighting broke out in the Gaza Strip between Hamas and the Fatah-controlled Palestinian security forces – the most serious escalation in the factional fighting since Hamas came to power.[7] Gun clashes, car bombings and kidnappings left 90 dead in December and January and the

Palestinians teetered on the brink of civil war. The Egyptian security team was mediating ceasefires that were lasting no longer than 48 hours.[8] The Saudis, seeing that President Bush's policy of isolating Iran was only allowing Hamas and its patrons to grow stronger, and fearing that Hamas would become a pro-Iranian regime, decided to break with the Western imposed boycott and try to bring Hamas back into the 'Arab fold'.

Saudi Mediation in the Palestinian and Arab–Israeli Arenas

The Rationale Behind the Saudi Mediation

Saudi Arabia's mediation and coordination in the Arab–Israeli and Palestinian arenas in early 2007 emanated from its leaders' perception of rapidly evolving dangers to the kingdom. Saudi Arabia is imperilled not only by Iran's regional ambitions but also by Iran's ambitions in the Gulf. Saudi Arabia's most strategic area of activity is the Gulf basin, owing to its vast oil wealth and its need to ensure that the oil tankers can travel safely in and out of the narrow Gulf waterway – a waterway shared with Iran. The Saudis fear that Iran's bid to become a nuclear power could trigger an American or Israeli attack on Iran. Saudi Arabia and the smaller Gulf states (which host American military bases), fear that in the event of an American–Iranian military confrontation – that they could find themselves caught in the middle and could even become victims of Iranian retaliation. Not only could such a conflict in the Gulf be costly to the Saudis in terms of their oil exportation, but it could also foment radicalism against the kingdom and against the smaller Arab states. Saudi Arabia, the bastion of Sunni-Wahhabi Islam, has a Shiite minority that constitutes 10 to 15 per cent of the population, and feels deeply concerned about Iran's promotion of Shi'i–Sunni fighting in Iraq and in Lebanon. Many of the smaller Arab Gulf states also have discontented Shi'i minorities (or in Bahrain's case, a majority), and the Saudis fear that these states could collapse or fragment, which would have a concomitant effect on Saudi society, particularly its Shiite minority.

To tackle dangers to the security of the Saudi kingdom and to diffuse conflicts before they can reach the Saudi borders, the Saudis enact a strategy of mediating regional conflicts. Mediation is intended to bestow on the Saudis the image of an Arab patriot, acting for the good of the Arab nation as whole. In addition, playing the role of the indispensable arbiter of disputes will ideally provide Saudi Arabia with immunity from regional attacks.

Saudi Arabia has not fought a war since the mid-1930s. An oil state with a traditional, tribal and puritanical-Islamic social order, a commercial society, a highly developed and technologically sophisticated urban infrastructure and an extensive social welfare programme, Saudi Arabia has consistently chosen to enact a strategy of mediation and negotiation rather than confrontation, which has at times disappointed Washington. For example, when Iranian-stoked conflagrations in the Iraqi, Lebanese and Palestinian arenas dramatically escalated in 2006, the Bush administration hoped that Saudi Arabia would work to forge a regional coalition of Sunni Arab states that would stand against Iran and its proxies and even work together with the United States and Israel to roll back Iran's influence in the region.

At least one prominent member of the Saudi royal family, Prince Bandar bin Sultan (a former national security adviser and ambassador to the USA), seemed to have advocated this course of action in Washington, but Saudi King Abdullah ultimately took a different course of action. Rather than confront Iran, the king opened negotiations with Iran. And rather than continue to go along with the Western-imposed boycott of Iranian sponsored terrorist groups (Hamas and Hezbollah), which Saudi Arabia viewed as a failed policy, King Abdullah opted to play the role of the neutral mediator. Thus, between December 2006 and February 2007, King Abdullah launched a frenetic diplomatic campaign during which he dealt simultaneously with a handful of burning issues. He invited Iran's chief negotiator, Ali Larijani, to Riyadh for talks to negotiate a reduction of temperature in the regional sectarian battles. He undertook trying to persuade the Americans to increase their troop strength in Iraq to curtail the sectarian fighting there. He undertook mediation between Hezbollah and the pro-Western Fuad Siniora government in Lebanon. And he undertook to mediate in the Palestinian arena between Hamas and Fatah.

In the Palestinian arena, mortar fire, gun clashes, abductions, assassinations and car bombings increased daily as both factions prepared for the outbreak of a full-blown civil war. On 28 January 2007 Saudi King Abdullah issued an open letter in which he invited Fatah and Hamas representatives to 'meet immediately … in the Holy City of Mecca, to discuss the issues between them in an objective manner without any interference by outsiders'.[9] Fatah and Hamas accepted the invitation to Mecca the same day it was offered, but nonetheless continued fighting each other on the streets of Gaza.[10]

The Components of the Saudi Mediation

On 8 February 2007, senior members of Hamas and Fatah arrived at a palace in Mecca overlooking the Ka'aba for talks that resulted in the Mecca agreement to form a Palestinian unity government.[11] The Saudi role in the Mecca agreement is a prime example of how the Saudis combine ample financial resources, a non-confrontational public style and cultural, tribal and religious norms to manage regional conflicts. At Mecca, the Saudis offered $1 billion to promote Palestinian reconciliation, effectively supplanting Iran as the Palestinians' main financier. The Saudis chose to conclude the three-day summit with a 'mini-hajj', as if to sanctify the agreement and, to disseminate an image of Sunni Arab harmony, they invited the press to photograph the leaders of the warring factions praying together.[12]

Having set the Palestinian factions on the path towards a unity government, the Saudis revived the Arab Peace Initiative for the Arab–Israeli conflict in the March 2007 summit of the Arab League. To Riyadh's satisfaction, it was duly praised, particularly in the West, for being a worthy peace broker and coordinator of a 'moderate' Sunni Arab coalition poised to counter Iran and its 'radical' clients. However, it is worth looking beyond the praise to examine the logic and consequences of the Saudi strategy. Accepting Saudi Arabia's role as regional mediator means accepting some anomalies in Saudi Arabia's performance.

One anomaly in Saudi mediation concerns the need to adjust its own initiatives to suit a broad, inter-Arab consensus. This can be seen in the manner in which the Saudis valued Syrian support for the peace initiative more highly than the possibility that the initiative could be an effective tool for negotiations. The original Saudi initiative offered Israel normalized relations in return for full withdrawal to the 1967 borders and the creation of a Palestinian state in the territories with East Jerusalem as its capital. The Israelis viewed the wording in King Abdullah's original text with tacit interest. But, in order to turn the Saudi initiative into an inter-Arab agreement at the March 2002 Beirut summit, the Saudis compromised their original plan to incorporate Syria's caveats. The Arab states, led by Syria, ratified the proposal only after it had been modified to include a reference to UN Security Council Resolution 194 on the return of the refugees and explicit mention of the Golan Heights and disputed territories on the Israeli-Lebanese border in the list of 'occupied Arab territories'. From Israel's vantage point, the refusal to negotiate the thorny issues turned the Saudi initiative into a useless tool.[13]

In the run up to the March 2007 Riyadh summit, where King Abdullah aimed to revive the offer of the Arab Peace Initiative, Israeli officials were careful to praise the Saudis' efforts, but urged them to make some modifications to the current proposal to 'strengthen the chances of negotiations between [Israel] and the Palestinians'.[14] Israeli Prime Minister Ehud Olmert told his cabinet that he was ready to 'treat the proposal seriously' and hoped that Saudi Arabia would bolster its 'positive elements' at the Arab summit.[15] Foreign Minister Tzipi Livni expressed cautious optimism for the proposal, but stated that it still contained clauses that were problematic for Israel, namely those concerning the Palestinian refugees. She also said that the issue of borders should not be determined in advance, but handled through negotiations.[16] However, Saudi Foreign Minister Sa'ud al-Faisal rejected the idea of holding talks with Israel or negotiating the proposal; and thus, the Arab Peace Initiative was reaffirmed as a 'take it or leave it' proposal, unmodified and with the foreknowledge that Israel would not accept it.[17]

Another such anomaly found in Saudi mediation concerns the scope of the actual mediation activity. In the aftermath of the Mecca Conference and the revival of the Arab Peace Initiative, Saudi Arabia did not engage in direct mediation between any of the parties and thus, the Egyptians took both mediation dossiers upon themselves. At the 2007 Arab summit, it was decided that the Egyptian and Jordanian foreign ministers (representing the only two Arab states to have peace treaties with Israel) would deliver the offer of the Arab Peace Initiative to Israel.[18] It was also decided that the Egyptians would take over managing the negotiations between Fatah and Hamas towards the goal of a national unity government. The Saudis did not assign themselves the direct role of negotiator with the Palestinians, let alone Israel, and even denied rumours that they were involved in tacit negotiations. At most, their officials planned to meet their Egyptian counterparts for debriefing and reports.[19]

The Saudi leaders' calculations did not rely on their initiation of these processes necessarily becoming an effective and successful reality. Merely the posture sufficed, giving them credit for having played the mediating role, gaining the trust of the parties coordinated, and attracting the attention of United States, Iran and the main Arab parties, particularly Syria. The Saudis used mediation and regional coordination as a means of orchestrating a complex regional scheme to improve the Saudi kingdom's security rather than to pacify the Israeli–Palestinian conflict for its own sake.

The Impact of the Saudi Mediation

The Saudi mediators initially succeeded in getting the Palestinians to agree to form a 'unity government'. The Saudis managed to get a phrase included in the Mecca Accord that called on Hamas to respect the agreements signed by the PLO.[20] The Saudis also managed to get Fatah and Hamas to agree to a preliminary distribution of portfolios in the new cabinet.[21] The effort to reconcile the Palestinians ultimately failed because within months the situation had again devolved into a civil war – this time ending in Hamas's defeat of the Fatah forces in the Gaza Strip and the establishment of a separate Hamas enclave there. While Egypt's first reaction was to declare Hamas's takeover a 'coup on legitimacy' and to issue a statement backing Palestinian President Mahmud Abbas, Saudi Arabia condemned the fighting, but tried to appear neutral in terms of Hamas and Fatah, and did not place the blame squarely on the shoulders of one faction.[22] The Saudis made a point of distancing themselves from both factions, even giving their preferred leader, Mahmud Abbas, the cold shoulder.[23]

To comprehend the Saudis' failure to reconcile the Palestinians and their muted response to Hamas's takeover, it is necessary to take into account that Saudi mediation in the Palestinian arena was just one facet of their complex regional strategy. The Saudis' regional strategy aimed to strengthen pro-Western, Sunni 'moderate' groups, and to diplomatically contain Iran's influence in various arenas while simultaneously engaging Iran in negotiations. Among the various facets of the Saudis' efforts to contain Iran diplomatically was their mediation in the Lebanese and Palestinian arenas where Iranian-fuelled sectarian conflicts roiled. Another facet of this strategy was Saudi Arabia's revival of the Arab Peace Initiative, particularly its efforts to use the plan as a tool by which to lure Syria into the camp of 'moderate' Arab states. By getting Syria on board with the peace initiative, Saudi Arabia served to establish that there were limits to Iran's influence in Syria and Iran's input in the matter of the Palestinian issue. While the Saudis worked diplomatically to contain Iran in these various arenas, they also opened direct negotiations with Iran for a reduction of the temperature in the Iraqi, Lebanese and Palestinian sectarian conflicts. The early part of 2007 saw Ali Larijani, Iran's chief negotiator, scuttling back and forth between Tehran and Riyadh, Saudi Foreign Minister Sa'ud al-Faisal, visiting Tehran, and ultimately Iranian President Mahmoud Ahmadinejad making a state visit to Riyadh.[24]

The Saudis' decision to take a back seat at the US-sponsored Annapolis Middle East Peace Conference is part of the same coin. The Saudis' recent active diplomacy in the Palestinian arena had generated hope in Washington that the Saudis would follow through to become more directly involved in negotiations between the sides with the aim of creating a Palestinian state.[25] However, ongoing Saudi efforts to strike a *modus vivendi* with Iran meant a certain relaxation – or at least the pretence of a relaxation – in the Saudis' cooperation with Washington. That cooling was already evident in King Abdullah's depiction of the American war in Iraq as an 'illegitimate foreign occupation', as well as his cancellation of a state dinner that Washington had planned to hold in his honour.[26] It is also worth noting that the Saudis did not confront Iran over the nuclear issue.

Ultimately, the Saudi attempt to coordinate inter-Arab politics as a means of containing Iran's influence in the region was a failure. Syrian president, Bashar al-Assad, remained firmly entrenched in the Iranian-led extremist camp, even proclaiming that the Arab Peace Initiative was 'dead'.[27] The Saudi mediation in the Lebanese arena failed and left a vacuum that Qatar stepped in to fill. In May 2008, Qatar succeeded in coaxing Hezbollah and the Fuad Sinora government into a political agreement, prompting analysts and the media to declare that Qatar had performed a 'diplomatic coup' – succeeding where Saudi Arabia and others had failed, and gaining recognition as a leading mediator in the Middle East.[28] The Saudis' mediation in the Palestinian arena failed. Hamas's bloody takeover of the Gaza Strip rendered the Mecca Accord dead, and what's more, Hamas continued to torpedo Egypt's attempts to broker a Hamas–Israel ceasefire, boldly firing rockets into southern Israel and ultimately provoking a full-scale Israeli military invasion. Then, on the matter of the Gaza War, the Arab states came out in 2009, once again, divided against each other and lacking the willpower to collectively oppose Iran's regional ascendancy.[29]

The Egyptian Mediation in the Israeli-Palestinian Arena

The Rationale Behind the Egyptian Mediation

Egypt has been eager for an opportunity to re-establish its former role as the leading Arab state. A country with an ancient history, the largest population in the Arab world and a vibrant press, Egypt has long served as the cultural and informational centre of the Arabic speaking world. Egypt also came to be regarded as the leading political and military force in the region, especially under the charismatic leader, Gamal Abdel Nasser. Egypt's regional prominence declined after it made a peace treaty with Israel, but it has continued to play a vital role by serving as the region's indispensable mediator between the Israelis and Palestinians.

The Egyptians have both regional and domestic reasons for their intervention in the Israeli–Palestinian arena. Like the Saudis, they covet the international recognition that goes along with being the indispensible Arab mediator, especially since that role could lend the autocratic regime some legitimacy and insulate it from calls for democratic reform. And, like the Saudis, the Egyptians also perform their role as mediator with an eye to containing Iran's regional ascendancy. Unlike the Saudis, the Egyptians deal with instability at their doorstep. Through Hamas, Iran sits right on Egypt's border and fans the flames of the intra-Palestinian and Palestinian–Israeli conflicts. Egypt, therefore, has a vested interest in quelling any fighting between Israel and the Palestinians or between the rival Palestinian factions.

Domestically, Egypt is suspicious of the ideological connection between Hamas and Egypt's largest opposition group, the Muslim

Brothers – Hamas's parent organization. The grassroots popularity of both Islamist movements is contrasted with Hosni Mubarak's unpopular domestic and foreign policies. Furthermore, both movements claim an Islamic legitimacy, in contrast with Mubarak's secular rule. Finally, Hamas has enjoyed some electoral legitimacy since its victory in the 2006 Palestinian Legislative Council elections, in contrast with the autocratic rule of Mubarak's regime. The Egyptian government fears that if the Hamas movement were to gain momentum, so too would the Muslim Brothers across the border also gain momentum, which would inevitably lead to harsher crackdowns, instability and unrest.[30] In fact, as Egypt prepares for a shaky leadership transition from father to son, the sight of Muslim Brothers' activists turning out in thousands to participate in combat-style parades in support of Hamas has been disconcerting for the Mubarak regime.[31]

The 2007 Hamas coup in the Gaza Strip made matters even more dangerous for Mubarak's regime. Intelligence inside Egypt warned that a Hamas victory could encourage the Muslim Brothers to develop military capabilities that could be used to overthrow the regime.[32] The direction of weapons smuggling and human trafficking that moves through Egypt and into Gaza could one day be reversed to the detriment of the Egyptian government. Therefore, the strengthening of ties between the Egyptian Muslim Brothers and the Palestinian Hamas is something that Mubarak aims to thwart.

Events in the Israeli–Palestinian arena affect Egypt's domestic stability; therefore, Egypt gets involved in the fine points of mediation and stays involved day in and day out. The Egyptian security delegation, placed in Gaza in 2005 as part of the arrangements following Israel's withdrawal from there, facilitated Egypt's active, day-to-day coordination between the parties. Close examination of the details of Egypt's mediation reveals that Egypt is not a disinterested mediator and has even been accused of biased dealing. That is because Egypt's pursuit of its own state interests is part and parcel of its mediation efforts and often the cause of the success or failure of those efforts.

The Components of the Egyptian Mediation

Egypt's mediation between Hamas and Fatah after Hamas's 2006 election victory was aimed at quelling the violence between them and reconciling them to a power-sharing agreement. But the Egyptians' task was no easy one. Palestinian President Mahmud Abbas demanded that Hamas compromise its fundamental principles, agree to recognize Israel and authorize him to negotiate with Israel on behalf of the Palestinians.[33] Abbas made these demands in June 2006 while Hamas launched rocket attacks on

Israeli towns and Israel carried out a military offensive in Gaza.[34] Therefore, before they could move forward on the Hamas–Fatah front, the Egyptians needed to mediate a ceasefire between Israel and Hamas, which they did in November 2006.[35] The 'ceasefire' led to an Israeli withdrawal, but erratic rocket launches out of the strip continued – a proverbial thundercloud over the Egyptians' ongoing mediation efforts.[36]

Following the Second Lebanon War, Egypt assumed the role of mediator in the protracted negotiations for the release of kidnapped Israeli Corporal Gilad Shalit, whose abduction by Hamas had precipitated the fighting in Lebanon. The Israeli government, led by Prime Minister Ehud Olmert, came under enormous domestic pressure to secure the release of Gilad Shalit. Thus, Egypt's means of staving off another Israeli military offensive in Gaza was to keep the negotiations for the release of Gilad Shalit moving forward. The chief of Egyptian intelligence, Omar Suleiman, held alternating talks with Israeli and Hamas officials. Egypt reportedly got the two sides to agree to a deal that would have meant an exchange of Gilad Shalit for more than 1000 Palestinian prisoners held in Israeli prisons.[37] Then the focus of the negotiations turned to finalizing the list of names that would be released.

The list of names was tricky because neither Egypt nor Israel wanted to see a situation in which Israel released Hamas heroes, Hamas declared a victory, threw a defiant celebration in the streets and gained popularity through that. So Egypt cleverly linked the matter of the prisoner list to the matter of power sharing between Hamas and Fatah. The logic was this: if Hamas were serious about sharing power, then Hamas would negotiate with Fatah over the list of names that would be included on the list. And Egypt, working with the parties, did get them to submit an agreed upon list; however, the Hamas–Fatah rivalry was neither the primary obstacle to achieving a deal nor Israel the obstacle. The obstacle was Hamas's refusal to conclude a deal without a green light from the Syrian government.[38]

After many rounds of negotiations, which took place in the autumn of 2006, Egypt notified Hamas that Israel had finally approved a prisoner list and urged Hamas to accept. Hamas leader Khaled Mashal left Cairo for Damascus to consult with the Syrian leadership and, thereafter, the negotiations stalled.[39] Later, in an interview with *Asharq al-Awsat*, Egyptian Foreign Minister Ahmad Abul Gheit explained that, at times, Egypt manages to reach an understanding with Israel, then 'external parties' who have sway over Hamas interfere, Hamas takes an intransigent stand and the negotiations break down.[40]

In fact, Hamas apparently did not get the green light to conclude a prisoner swap until January 2007 when the escalation of violence between Hamas and Fatah raised the spectre of a civil war. Under those circumstances, not wanting to give Hamas any political gains that could tip the scales, Israel decided that the time was not right to conclude a deal.[41]

Egyptians prefer to get the credit for being the main mediator in the Israeli–Palestinian arena, but continue to mediate out of concern for their own national security, even if not in the full glare of the cameras, because instability on the border has the potential to spill over into Egypt. Thus, the Egyptian security team continued to negotiate ceasefires on the streets of Gaza even as representatives of the rival Palestinian factions were departing for the high profile Mecca Conference on Saudi jets.[42] The Saudis' intervention in inter-Palestinian affairs was likely viewed with suspicion in Cairo because, whereas the Egyptians were experienced at mediating between the Palestinian factions, the Saudis came into inter-Palestinian affairs as newcomers and seemed for a time to pose as the region's new inter-Palestinian mediator. Even if the Egyptians feared a 'mediation coup', the fear was momentary. After Saudi King Abdullah was photographed praying in Mecca with the Palestinian leaders, the Saudis failed to pursue further contact with the parties, while the Egyptians resumed the business of sitting down with the sides to hammer out the details of the unity government. The Egyptians also failed in that endeavour but not for lack of trying.

Serious fighting broke out again in the Palestinian territories in May 2007 between Hamas and Fatah, followed by a brief Egyptian-brokered ceasefire. Then, when the fighting started up again in June, less than a week later, Hamas wrested control of the Gaza Strip from the Palestinian Authority. Mubarak pronounced the Hamas takeover of the Gaza Strip a 'coup over legitimacy' and reassured Palestinian President Mahmud Abbas of Egypt's support.[43] He ordered Egypt's embassy to move from Gaza to the West Bank city, Ramallah – Fatah's headquarters – and called the Gaza security delegation back to Cairo.[44]

Given Egypt's hardened stance toward Hamas, it came as a surprise to many observers when at the Sharm el-Sheikh summit on 25 June 2007, President Mubarak became the first Arab leader to call for renewed dialogue between the Palestinian factions after Hamas's bloody takeover of the Gaza Strip. Saudi King Abdullah, whose accomplishment at the Mecca Conference had been torpedoed by Hamas's coup, appeared at the summit as the failed mediator, defeated and without resources to go on, but Egypt decided to restart the Fatah–Hamas dialogue for several reasons. Given the power vacuum the Saudis left when they refused to go on with inter-Palestinian mediation, Egypt saw an opportunity to reassert its traditional role as the region's indispensable mediator and to promote its image as the only mediator capable of handling inter-Palestinian dynamics.[45] In addition, the other options were untenable from Egypt's perspective. Egypt did not want to see a total collapse of the Hamas regime because that would create a power vacuum for another extremist force, like al-Qaeda, to fill. It would also create a humanitarian disaster that would force Egypt to take greater responsibility for the Gaza Strip – a prospect that Egypt diametrically opposed.[46] Finally, Egypt preferred to talk to Hamas because the other alternative – to isolate Hamas – would have pushed Hamas into sole dependence on Iran.

What had not changed after Hamas's takeover was the Egyptians' trademark hands-on approach. Following Mubarak's announcement of renewed mediation at Sharm el-Sheikh, Egypt's head of intelligence, Omar Suleiman, asked each side to present him in writing with their ideas of how to resolve the crisis. His method was to review both documents and then use them to craft his own suggested joint proposal that could serve as a basis for secret talks in Cairo between the two sides.[47]

What had changed after Hamas's takeover was Egypt's perception of the threat Hamas posed. The way President Mubarak viewed it, Hamas's control of the Gaza Strip meant that Egypt in practice now shared a border with Iran.[48] Hamas's firing of an Iranian-made Grad rocket at an Israeli town was further proof of that. Even the Egyptian public eyed Hamas suspiciously when, after the Gaza–Egypt border was breached in January 2008, Palestinians pelted Egyptian guards with stones, and hundreds of thousands of Palestinians flooded past into Egypt, some carrying explosives and some attempting to raise Palestinian flags over Egyptian government buildings in Sinai.[49] There was a growing sense among Egyptians that their nation's sovereignty had been violated and that the Islamist regime in Gaza had become a national security danger for Egypt.

One indicator that Egypt's mediation role was sublimated to its own national and security interests was Egypt's occasional refusal to conclude a deal that was unacceptable to Egypt. In the immediate aftermath of Hamas's Gaza takeover, Israel and Hamas both appealed to Cairo to conclude the prisoner exchange deal reached prior to the outbreak of fighting in the Gaza Strip. Egypt flatly refused, sources said, because it did not want to take actions that would reverse the slippage in Hamas's popularity.[50] Mubarak explained on Egyptian state television that Egypt insisted on a period of calm before resuming negotiations with any of the parties.[51]

Egypt resumed contact with Hamas in autumn 2007 but it was no secret that Egypt was not an impartial mediator. Hamas officials, who had once been careful to praise 'fraternal Egypt' for its mediation role, began accusing it of bias against Hamas. One Hamas leader, Yunis al-Astal, said, 'Egypt is not a fair mediator. [It] mediates to pressure Hamas.'[52] Another source in Hamas told *Asharq al-Awsat* that a number of leading Hamas figures felt that 'Egypt [was] not exerting any real effort to push for concluding the deal with Israel since the achievement of such a deal would strengthen [Hamas's] position in the Gaza Strip and also out of the consideration that [Hamas] is an extension of the Muslim Brothers in Egypt.' He went on to say that Egypt was putting pressure on Hamas to accept Israel's terms for the prisoner exchange and not exerting the same pressure on Israel. Upset with Egypt's biased performance, some Hamas leaders suggested that Egypt be replaced by a European mediator, namely Germany.[53]

Egypt has also used its role as mediator to try to advance its own interests in securing its border and strengthening the hand of Mahmud Abbas. This was apparent in the way Egypt used Israel's siege on the Gaza Strip as a bargaining chip and as a means of putting pressure on Hamas during subsequent mediation between the Palestinian factions. According to Egypt's plan, the Rafah crossing, Egypt's border with the Gaza Strip, would remain closed until Hamas agreed to allow Palestinian Authority security forces (loyal to Mahmud Abbas) to return and operate the crossing.[54]

In February 2008, in response to the ongoing rocket launches, the Israeli military carried out air strikes on Hamas targets in Gaza and then on 29 February, launched a ground operation. Gaza remained blockaded and the Hamas leadership came under attack while Israeli military officials moved freely between Tel Aviv and Cairo negotiating the terms of a ceasefire. During these negotiations, both Israel and Hamas brought their numerous grievances before the Egyptian mediators. Israel insisted that any ceasefire deal include the return of Gilad Shalit and the end to all arms smuggling into Gaza. Hamas insisted that in return for a ceasefire, Israel must end its siege on Gaza and the Rafah crossing be taken out of Israel's hands and reopened. Hamas insisted that any ceasefire also include the cessation of Israel's operations in the West Bank. Egypt refused to negotiate all these issues at once. It wanted, first and foremost, a cessation of the fighting between Israel and Hamas, namely Hamas's rocket fire and Israel's military operations in the strip.[55] Ultimately, Egypt stood firm, telling both parties that the prisoners, arms smuggling, Rafah crossing, and West Bank would be dealt with separately, and Egypt succeeded in its aim. Both parties accepted the terms of a six-month *tahdi'a* (temporary truce, or calm) which went into effect on 19 June 2008.

During the months that followed, especially as the end of the six-month period drew near, the Egyptian mediators worked to try to renew the *tahdi'a*. During the second half of 2008 both Hamas and Israel made the renewal of the truce contingent on Egypt fulfilling their respective demands.

Hamas's demand in return for a ceasefire was that Egypt opens its Rafah crossing. Hamas claimed that its most important victory with regard to the *tahdi'a* was the understanding that Egypt – not Israel – would be responsible for the Rafah crossing.[56] However, the terms of the *tahdi'a* did not guarantee that the siege on the Gaza Strip would be lifted or that the Rafah crossing would be opened. Therefore when, after the ceasefire took hold the Rafah crossing remained closed, Hamas members shifted the blame for the siege onto Egypt. Hamas leader, Yunis al-Astal, told the press that the Egyptians sealed their border with Gaza even more tightly than Israel did.[57] Paradoxically, although Egypt's physical border with the Gaza Strip made Egypt a vital arbiter in the Israeli–Palestinian conflict, it also made Egypt an unwilling party to its own mediation.

Likewise, the Israelis' oft repeated demand that Egypt do more to prevent Hamas from smuggling arms via subterranean tunnels into Gaza through the Philadelphi Corridor (Egypt's border with the Gaza Strip) made any would-be achievement by the Egyptian mediators contingent on actions taken by Egypt. Egypt balked at Israel's suggestion that international monitors should be deployed along its border, viewing that as a violation of its national sovereignty. Thus, Egypt's unwillingness to take actions it viewed as compromising its national interests prevented the Egyptian mediators from securing the Israeli–Hamas ceasefire they sought in autumn 2008.

The Impact of the Egyptian Mediation

The Egyptian mediators worked day in and day out mediating Hamas–Fatah and Hamas–Israel matters and, for a disappointing year and a half, failed to achieve most of their major aims. Egypt could boast of one six-month ceasefire on the Israeli–Palestinian front and dozens of short-lived ceasefires on the inter-Palestinian front. It failed, however, to broker a power-sharing agreement between Hamas and Fatah, to conclude a prisoner swap between Israel and Hamas, to prevent Hamas from seizing power in the Gaza Strip in June 2007, to stop Hamas's renewed rocket fire, and to prevent the Gaza War in December 2008. Egypt's failures, for the most part, derived from its inability to put enough pressure on Hamas. Egypt blamed the 'interference by external parties', namely Iran and Syria, for Hamas's intractability.[58] Egyptian Foreign Minister Ahmad Abul Gheit repeatedly urged the Palestinians to make independent decisions and not to let 'others guide the Palestinian ship'.[59]

During autumn 2008 the Egyptian mediators failed to hold any sway over Hamas. First, Hamas boycotted the Egyptian-sponsored national Palestinian dialogue scheduled for November, and second, Hamas rejected Egyptian pressure to renew the *tahdi'a* with Israel. The Egyptian officials' claim that Hamas's Iranian sponsor was responsible for Egypt's failed efforts was seconded by another Gulf observer who attributed the failure of Egyptian mediation to Iran's expanding appetite for regional dominance. A Qatari analyst, Abdul Hamid al-Ansari, writing for *al-Ittihad*, says that Iran uses Hamas to torpedo Egypt's mediation efforts and thus, to 'thwart the Egyptian regional role, given that the revitalization of Egypt's regional role after a long absence … jeopardizes Iran's plans in the region'. He went on to say, 'Iran regards the Egyptian role as an obstruction of [Iran's] expansion into the Arab depth, and a force capable of weakening [Iran's] influence over its regional allies.'[60]

When Iran stepped over the line by using Hamas to challenge Egypt's traditional regional role, Hosni Mubarak went so far as to adopt a position that the Arab world perceived as anti-Palestinian and pro-United States/ Israel. Mubarak's position *vis-à-vis* the Gaza War is a prime example of that. In December 2008, Hamas flaunted its contempt for Egypt by unleashing a steady barrage of rockets on Israeli towns in defiance of Egypt's call for a renewed ceasefire. Hamas really experienced a wake-up call when, on 27 December, Israel launched 'Operation Cast Lead' and waves of Israeli jets decimated its compounds in Gaza. In a televised address, Mubarak blamed Hamas for the onslaught: 'We warned [Hamas] repeatedly that rejecting the truce would push Israel to aggression against Gaza.'[61]

Several of Egypt's actions, including its high-level consultations with Israeli Foreign Minister Tzipi Livni just prior to the war, convinced the Arab world that Egypt was backing Israel in the war. Others were that Mubarak blamed Hamas for the conflict, refused to open the Rafah crossing except to evacuate the wounded, and was relatively silent during the first phase of Israel's assault. Anti-Egyptian/pro-Palestinian demonstrations were seen across the Arab world. In Yemen, protestors stormed the Egyptian embassy, burnt the Egyptian flag and raised a Palestinian flag in its stead.[62] Al-Jazeera aired footage of carnage and bloodshed. The Muslim Brothers led demonstrations in Cairo. Israel's air campaign turned into a ground invasion and pressure mounted on Egypt to intervene to stop the shedding of Palestinian blood. Then reports surfaced that Hamas members had been invited to Cairo to discuss the possibility of a ceasefire.[63]

The potential for Egypt to serve as a useful channel commanded the attention of the Western powers. Seeing that Egypt held a common interest in achieving a ceasefire that would deprive the Iranian-backed Hamas of a victory, and seeing that Egypt had the potential to assist in preventing Hamas from rearming though the network of smuggling tunnels that connected the Gaza Strip to Egypt, the Western powers viewed Egypt's contacts with Hamas as a valuable prospect.

In particular, Egypt's potential attracted the attention of French President Nicholas Sarkozy, who was in search of a diplomatic achievement with which to enhance his position in Europe. President Sarkozy flew to Cairo for a high-profile meeting with President Mubarak and together the two announced a joint proposal for a ceasefire between Israel and Hamas.[64] President Mubarak's diplomatic efforts got the attention of US Secretary of State Condoleezza Rice, who announced that the United States had abstained from approving a UN Security Council resolution for an immediate ceasefire in the hope that President Mubarak's mediation efforts would succeed. The Egyptian initiative also got the attention of Israel and Hamas, both of which ignored the UN call for a ceasefire but met separately with Egyptian negotiators in Cairo, seeking to advance their respective demands in any would-be negotiated ceasefire.

Ultimately, the Egyptian negotiators were unable to get both sides to agree to each other's terms for a ceasefire. Egypt's proposal called for a short-term, immediate ceasefire but contained no provisions for Israel's or Hamas's additional demands. Egypt could only promise that the ceasefire would be followed by negotiations on Hamas's demand for an opening of the crossings and Israel's demand for a cessation of arms smuggling into the Gaza Strip. Israel spoke positively of Egypt's ceasefire proposal, but stopped short of endorsing it, hoping that Egypt would address the issue of the arms smuggling. Hamas said that it would study the ceasefire proposal, and then later publicly rejected it.[65] As it was, Israel declared a unilateral ceasefire that went into effect on 18 January, and a week later, Hamas announced its own ceasefire.[66]

In the aftermath of the Gaza War, Egypt's mediation efforts elided almost imperceptibly from trying to achieve a ceasefire to trying to achieve a 'lasting ceasefire'.[67] Egypt aimed to use its performance during the Gaza War to substantiate the perception that it had long held of itself – that Egypt alone was capable of mediating the Arab–Israeli conflict. This can be seen in the comments of Egyptian Foreign Minister Ahmad Abul Gheit when he said, 'The Egyptian initiative launched by President Mubarak in the presence of his French counterpart, Nicolas Sarkozy, was the only option available for reaching a ceasefire.' He went on, 'It is Egypt's power that has successfully managed the crisis … and is currently [employed] to reinforce calm.'[68] Yet, for all that Egypt basked in the glow of the spotlight, it had not achieved a crowning negotiated truce.

Conclusion

At the regional level, the Gaza War gave rise to a contest between the three Arab states historically involved as mediators in the Arab–Israeli conflict – Egypt, Qatar and Saudi Arabia. The Arab press dubbed the contest the 'war of the summits' (*harb al-qimam*). During the Gaza War, while diplomats from Western states and international institutions flocked to Cairo for consultations with the Egyptian leadership on the matter of a ceasefire, Qatari Sheikh Hamad bin Khalifa tried to steal the show by calling Arab leaders to Qatar for an emergency Arab summit to condemn Israel's offensive in Gaza. Three times the Qatari sheikh called Arab leaders to Doha to address the Gaza War and three times he was rebuffed by President Mubarak and Saudi King Abdullah. The Egyptians, who coveted their limelight and renewed regional importance and who, along with the Saudis, were unwilling to be a party to the agenda of the extremist camp (which was becoming increasingly consolidated under Iran's sponsorship) refused to attend. They said that the Gaza War could be dealt with on the sidelines of a pre-planned economic summit in Kuwait. Mainly because of Egypt and Saudi Arabia's boycott, the Qatari sheikh could not secure the required quorum for an official summit of the Arab League. Not wanting to appear irrelevant and marginalized, he convened a summit anyway. And, by inviting Hamas leader Khaled Mashal as the Palestinian representative and Iranian President Mahmoud Ahmadinejad as an observer, he ensured that his summit would get the attention of the Arab leaders who had rebuffed him.[69] Qatar's intentions were further revealed when the Qatari satellite station, al-Jazeera, aired interviews of Hamas leaders describing Egypt's inadequacies as a mediator and its complicity in the Gaza War.[70]

Qatar's efforts to upstage Egypt as the major power broker in regional conflicts ultimately failed, for in the immediate aftermath of the war Egypt remained the hub for consultations with international players who sought Cairo's expertise and vital assistance in achieving a lasting ceasefire. President Mubarak's 'ceasefire summit' held on 18 January drew the leaders of France, the United Kingdom, Turkey, Jordan, Italy, Spain, the Czech Republic, Germany and the United Nations to the Egyptian seaside resort town, Sharm el-Sheikh.[71] Mubarak opened the conference by spelling out what needed to be done to achieve a lasting ceasefire to coordinate aid and reconstruction for Gaza. President Sarkozy thanked Mubarak for his efforts and criticized the unhelpful Doha summit.[72]

Saudi Arabia reasserted its posture as supreme regional mediator and Arab coordinator in the days following President Barack Obama's swearing in ceremony, when King Abdullah and other prominent Saudi officials urged the new American president to adopt the Arab Peace Initiative as the blueprint for a peace agreement between the Israelis and Palestinians.[73]

Saudi Arabia's proclivity for regulating inter-Arab differences was also underscored in the early part of 2009. On 11 March 2009, Saudi King Abdullah hosted a mini-summit of Arab leaders that brought Syrian

President Bashar al-Assad to Riyadh for the first time in four years. The Saudi communiqué heralded the summit as a new phase in inter-Arab cooperation.[74] King Abdullah followed up with a speech at the March 2009 Arab League summit, emphasizing the need to achieve renewed Arab solidarity and coordination. He also held reconciliation meetings with the rulers of both Syria and Qatar on the sidelines of the summit. His determination to reassert the Saudis' traditional role as coordinator of inter-Arab affairs was tested when Muammar Gaddafi stood up to the microphone and unleashed a tirade of criticism at the Saudi king; however, King Abdullah held a 'reconciliation meeting' with Gaddafi within hours of the incident. King Abdullah's promotion of Arab reconciliation was cheered in certain Arab quarters, but underneath the momentary façade of inter-Arab unity, the absence of an effective inter-Arab coordinating mechanism was palpable.

Egyptian President Hosni Mubarak, still furious with Qatar's attempt to upstage Egypt's role during the Gaza War, stayed home from the March 2009 Arab League summit in Doha, Qatar. With Qatar trying to carve out a prominent regional role for itself at Egypt's expense, Mubarak was in no mood to put on a show of Arab unity. Egypt sought to preserve its revived importance to the region and sought to remind the other Arab states that without it playing a central role, they had no chance of managing regional conflicts, let alone acting as an effective regional bloc *vis-à-vis* ascendant Iran.

13

Lost Faith, Forfeited Trust: Afghan Responses to Post-9/11 International Intervention in State-Building and Insurgency

Marvin G. Weinbaum

Afghanistan has a history of foreign invaders and lengthy occupations. From the invasions of Alexander the Great through those of Islamic armies, Persian ascendance and penetration by Britain and tsarist Russia, to the current presence of international forces, the country has a history of both accommodation and resistance. For long periods Afghanistan was, for the great powers, a political, economic and cultural backwater. The most recent international involvement began in 1978 following the installation by coup of a Moscow-supported communist government in Kabul. The rural insurgency by Islamic militants prompted a Soviet invasion of Afghanistan in late December 1979 to aid a hard-pressed regime and replace a distrusted communist leader. Its ultimate aim was to thwart the emergence of a radical Islamic state whose influence could spread to the adjoining Muslim regions of the Soviet Union. Whereas earlier British and Russian incursions of the nineteenth and early twentieth centuries in Afghanistan were motivated by imperial designs, the Soviet intervention was strategically and ideologically a defensive action.

The Pakistan backed anti-communist jihad that persevered through the 1980s attracted generous external financing, above all from the United States and Saudi Arabia. A demoralized Soviet army withdrew from Afghanistan in early 1989, leaving behind a communist government that was able to retain power until spring 1992. Having taken Kabul, however, the victorious mujahideen party alliance soon dissolved in a bitter civil war over control of the national capital; little remained of international involvement aside from humanitarian assistance. Interest in Afghanistan revived with a stream of victories by a Pakistani client group, the Taliban, which appeared in 1994 and captured Kabul in October 1996. International oil and gas interests seeking to construct a pipeline from central Asia to the Indian subcontinent soon entered into negotiations. But it was the presence in Afghanistan of a group of Arab militants called al-Qaeda that drew the most attention, notably after being linked to terrorist acts against American targets in East Africa and the Persian Gulf states. Alarm over the possible contagion of Islamic extremism from Afghanistan to regional states and beyond brought wide support for UN imposed sanctions against the Taliban.

The armed intervention that began a month after 9/11 international-ized an ongoing civil war that seemed to have an end in sight. The Taliban, assisted militarily and financially by Pakistan, had reduced its adversaries in the Northern Alliance to controlling two small pockets in the country's northeast. The assassination on 9 September 2001 of the charismatic military leader of an opposition force supplied mainly by Iran and Russia appeared to seal the fate of anti-Taliban forces. A UN sanctioned, American-led attack aimed against al-Qaeda and its allied Taliban regime began what is soon to become the longest war in the United States' history.

With the attacks of 9/11, the United States adopted an offensive strategy against global terrorism that it initiated with the military campaign in Afghanistan. The international intervention was not at first about changing a regime, rebuilding a state and economy or installing a democracy, but that is what it became. The military phase of the international campaign in Afghanistan, which the USA spearheaded and which began in October 2001, was over in a matter of several weeks. Using mostly air power the USA routed the Taliban and al-Qaeda, which chose to retreat to the mountainous area adjoining Pakistan and then across the border. Only in northern areas of Afghanistan were these forces unable to escape and many were captured and killed. In the wake of the military onslaught, troops of the Northern Alliance defied inter-national requests to refrain from entering Kabul and assuming authority in the capital.

Because no prior international planning had occurred for a post-conflict Afghanistan, in early December 2001 the UN convened a conference in Bonn, Germany to which leaders from all the parties and factions that had opposed the Taliban were invited. Also present were the representatives of countries that were presumed to have a direct stake in the country's future. At the conference the disparate participants with their differing interests and visions for the country were unable to reach a consensus on establishing a political framework and timetable for achieving a self-reliant, democratic state. It took the persistence of the UN's chief representative, as well as the pressures several countries (most notably the USA, Russia, Iran and Pakistan) applied on their respective client delegates, finally to reach an agreement about selecting an interim president, undertaking to write a constitution and, subsequently, holding elections for the presidency and parliament.

The welcome accorded the international community following the ousting of the Taliban grew out of the high expectations following the virtual non-governance by the Islamic movement. International intervention succeeded in avoiding an early humanitarian crisis with the return of three million refugees, and held out promise to most Afghans of a safer and better life and a more responsive and competent government. It also followed from the fact that most Afghans have an appreciation that they lack the resources to achieve a national recovery without international assistance. Rather than being xenophobic, Afghans have historically welcomed those willing to help them, even while fiercely resisting those seen as trying to rule them or occupy them. The Soviet Union learnt this lesson the hard way.

The high expectations born of trust in the international community and central government has to a large extent been forfeited, especially in the south and east of the country. Progress in rebuilding the state, its institutions and its economy has been slow and uneven. As a consequence, a disappointing foreign presence has contributed to reigniting an insurgency that joins a regrouped Taliban together with dissident former mujahideen commanders and a reconstituted al-Qaeda. It is widely conceded that the international engagement in Afghanistan will need to be an extended one if it is to succeed. Less certain is the duration of the international community's commitment. It also remains to be seen under what conditions Afghans will continue to welcome foreign forces that have taken sides in what is a renewed civil conflict. While the application of force remains a vital component in bringing peace and reconstruction, Afghans have to be convinced that the foreign presence is not just about confronting the insurgency through arms. It will also require the support of the people who expect material improvement in their lives and a just rule from their government.

The Multiple Dimensions of Intervention

Previous multilateral and bilateral interventions in Afghanistan are revealing for what they inform us about international actors' objectives in Afghanistan and the predisposition of Afghans toward foreign intrusions. If Afghan history offers any guide about interventions in general, it would seem to suggest that unity in resisting foreign intervention is strongest in a society with a greater sense of nationhood. It would also indicate that resistance to intervention is fiercest and most sustained when the foreign forces have not only occupied territory but have also forcefully tried to impose their values and culture.

Yet, much about the post-9/11 international role in Afghanistan is distinctive in terms of motives, stakes and means compared with earlier interventions in the country, as well as those occurring elsewhere in recent years. Those in the past never sought to build a self-reliant and democratic state in Afghanistan, and the global stakes of success or failure were never as far reaching. International interventions since 2001 have been more multidimensional not only than previous ones in the country but also in comparison with other multilateral actions globally in recent decades. In addition, intervention has brought what is probably the broadest coalition of countries for the purpose of state building and national recovery since the Second World War. The intervention in Afghanistan is being watched closely for its strategies in countering international terrorism as well as its impact on the future viability of the Western alliance structure in NATO.

The post-conflict approach the United States and its partner countries have pursued towards Afghanistan has commonly been referred to as a 'light footprint' or 'nation-building light'. It involved an early transfer of political responsibility to an Afghan national leadership and differs from the policies that were initially adopted in Iraq. International agencies and non-governmental organizations were to handle national reconstruction, the revival of state institutions and humanitarian relief. A small force of US and coalition troops would be deployed to stabilize the country, with the Americans taking on the military task of dealing with the remnants of al-Qaeda and the Taliban, mostly on the frontier with Pakistan. To raise funds to support the Kabul government and the various reconstruction programmes, in January 2003 the United Nations brought together 60 countries and international agencies at a donors' meeting in Tokyo that pledged $10 billion in assistance. By their participation, they acknowledged that Afghanistan's stabilization was important for their own security. Overall, however, the amount of funds that actually reached the devastated country was small by the standards of other post-conflict situations globally.

It soon became evident that while the plans for the country's political infrastructure went ahead, the rebuilding of the country's physical infrastructure and economic base were put on a slower track. Two Loya Jirgahs, traditional assemblies of notables, were convened, first to ratify the decisions reached in Bonn and then to approve the text of a constitution. But there was little progress in ensuring the rule of law or delivering government services. Development priorities were largely put on hold in favour of security concerns, but also because of the lack of coherent and synchronized strategy based on local need assessments.

Security

After eight years of international involvement, the military intervention that initially reduced levels of physical insecurity in Afghanistan is losing ground. The number of terrorist attacks has risen steadily since 2007 with 2009 registering the sharpest increase. There was a 40 per cent increase in 2007, and 2008 was even deadlier. Wide areas of the country are affected, with the south and east most strongly contested by insurgents. The tactics used by a revived Taliban have changed with the introduction of suicide bombers and improvised explosive devices and have made the attacks more lethal. Simple criminality has also been on the rise and is sometimes difficult to distinguish from Taliban-instigated actions. Only very limited progress has been realized in an international programme designed to disarm the militias in the country responsible for continuing civil violence outside the insurgency.

Most observers agree that at the outset there should have been a larger international force to block the escape of al-Qaeda and Taliban leaders and that it was a serious error to arm and fund Afghan militias to interdict those fleeing. In addition, it is now recognized that international forces should have been deployed across more of the country after the initial military intervention. The resulting political and security vacuum allowed local and regional commanders to dig in across the country and effectively impose their largely predatory authority. These errors reflect in part the international forces' lack of understanding and planning for post-conflict situations.

The military effort in late 2009 was led by the International Security Assistance Force (ISAF), a multinational coalition of 64,500 troops that for several years have been under NATO command. There are 42 contributing countries participating in it, including all 28 NATO member countries, under the UN mandate. Under separate command from ISAF, is Operation Enduring Freedom with 38,000 Americans who, joined by small contingents from several other countries, are mainly engaged in border operations intended to pursue infiltrating insurgents near the Pakistan border. Within ISAF there are effectively two classes of forces – the British, Canadian and Dutch troops who engage the Taliban and their allies in several of the most contentious provinces in the southern part of the country, and other ISAF forces operating mainly in the north and involved essentially in peacekeeping operations. The uneven sharing of the risks and burdens reflects the various caveats set for troops created by domestic political constraints in the contributing countries.[1]

In addition, an international presence comes in the form of 26 provincial reconstruction teams (PRTs) located in provincial capitals. Begun in 2003 with just a few American teams, their number has increased, as other countries have created their own. The PRTs are mainly engaged in non-military activities, including small-scale development projects. By 2008, they are said to have carried out 7500 small-scale development projects though they receive less than 5 per cent of the assistance budget for Afghanistan.[2] Overall, the performance of PRTs is decidedly mixed. Some countries receive high marks while others are regularly criticized. Their missions are often quite different. Success appears to vary widely according to the quality and dedication of the personnel assigned. Non-governmental organizations engaged in development and humanitarian projects regularly complain that PRTs make their job more difficult and dangerous by blurring the difference between military and non-military activities. It is generally accepted that international military forces can make a contribution to development by helping to improve the country's transport and infrastructure, but ought to stay away from economic development, health, education and social rights issues.

Although for the foreseeable future, international troops will primarily continue to meet Afghanistan's security requirements, they are buying time for the country to develop an indigenous capacity for self-defence through training and equipping the Afghan National Army (ANA) and national police. The USA has taken the lead in training the ANA. After an extended period that saw heavy desertions from the army, it has risen to 92,000 and is slated to go to 130,000 or higher. Quality is a separate matter and it is acknowledged that the ANA units are of varying capability. Still, with international trainers, progress is reported and the ANA is seen as better able to take on responsibilities operating jointly with foreign troops. It is acknowledged, however, that it will be some time before the ANA can be expected to operate independently against the enemy.

The goal of eventually creating an effective 160,000-man national police from the current 84,000 is further from realization. The training programme got off to a slow start as more attention was given to building the army. Germany originally agreed to help build a police force but then limited its contribution to training higher police officials. The USA took the responsibility for broad-based training and then turned it over to private contractors. As the need for an accelerated training programme has become apparent, the US military has stepped in to assist, and several European countries have also offered police trainers. The task is difficult because police recruits are mostly illiterate and police forces are generally viewed as corrupt and incompetent. Unless a more effective locally recruited police force is established it will be difficult to achieve better governance and win the confidence of citizens who are ambivalent in their loyalties.

As in other counter-insurgency programmes, analysts accept that there is no strictly military path to success in Afghanistan. While force remains necessary in contested provinces, more emphasis is being given to having troops build relationships of trust and assistance with local populations. By connecting with social and government power structures people may become convinced that their best hope lies in aligning their loyalties with the Kabul government. Success is also predicated on transforming the environment in which the enemy operates. Through the delivery of tangible development and better district-level security, the enemy can be denied the ability to sustain an insurgency. However, broadly applied, this tactical approach demands better coordination of strategies and operations than the countries participating in the NATO-led coalition have typically been able to provide. Another problem involves the short-term deployment of troops expected to forge friendly relations in a community. A knowledge-transfer deficit arises as their replacements are forced to start virtually from scratch. Many desired objectives may be impossible to achieve without a larger deployment of international forces, especially American troops, as was recognized in revised strategies announced by the USA during 2009.

Rehabilitation and Reconstruction

For several years there were no clear goals or strategies for Afghanistan's development. Valuable time was lost because the strategies the Americans and others pursued focused on short-term stability mainly through creating alliances with local power brokers and concentrating on military means to provide security. The December 2001 conference in Bonn concentrated on the transition to a new system of government, so failed to address questions of development. Not until February 2006 did the Afghan government and international community adopt benchmarks at a London meeting that produced an Afghanistan compact, which identified three pillars of policy – security, development and governance. At the same time, there was formal acknowledgment that progress in a single area of policy required progress in the others. There emerged from the conference, which representatives from 60 countries and institutions attended, a five-year plan, the Afghan National Development Strategy (ANDS), designed to implement the compact. The Afghan government refined the plan further in April 2008 in advance of a donors' meeting in Paris in June 2008.

With ANDS the Kabul government has sought to put its own stamp on development. In exchange for sustained international support, Afghan officials have agreed to initiate reforms and institution building. Yet it is plainly evident that the government lacks the authority, legitimacy and resources with which to effectuate the Afghanistan compact and the international intervention has failed to meet its commitments. Stability and reconstruction are described as 'under-funded, under-resourced, incremental, and with little focus'.[3] Resources for reconstruction often fail to arrive in secured areas in a timely fashion, and ministries are hamstrung in being forced to comply with unreasonable procurement procedures and accounting rules.[4] Much of the criticism of the international community for its delivery of assistance focuses on weak coordination among donors and between the civilian and military efforts.

Many foreign donors agree in principle that assistance programmes should be much more 'Afghanized'. The idea is to give credit for development to the Afghan leadership rather than to the international community. It was to address some of these shortcomings that a World Bank administered reconstruction trust fund was created to coordinate donor contributions and to channel the roughly $3 billion raised by the World Bank through the government's budget. Yet, President Karzai regularly complains that the central government has little control over national policy. Kabul's own revenues are about $890 million against expenditures of $2.7 billion, leaving many of the government's basic operations externally dependent and with nothing left over for development. Overall, as one report finds, 'two-thirds of the international assistance bypasses the government and only half of the funds provided for development are disbursed in concert with the government.'[5] The 2008 report estimates that $15 billion had been spent, of which 40 per cent was repatriated to foreign consultants or otherwise does not leave the country providing the aid. Resident foreign consultants cost between $250,000 and $500,000 in yearly compensation.[6] Their employment is controversial because higher salaries are being used to attract the most qualified individuals from government-sector employment.

Inadequate as well as often wasteful and ineffective assistance is often blamed for jeopardizing Afghanistan's economic progress. In 2008 international development aid stood at $7 million a day while $100 million was spent daily on military assistance.[7] Development spending in the country during fiscal year 2009 totalled $2.3 billion. Over eight years beginning in 2002, the USA spent $11.5 billion on development. The 2008 fiscal year saw the USA expend $2 billion as against $8.6 billion for security-related programmes.[8] Between 2002 and 2008, donor countries together pledged $25 billion in non-military aid of which only $15 billion was actually disbursed. The USA provides about one-third of all development assistance to Afghanistan but had spent only $5 billion of the $10.4 billion pledged through 2008. The World Bank has delivered on only a little more than half its commitments and the EC and Germany less than two-thirds through that period.[9] Failure to deliver international aid is most often blamed on security concerns and local corruption.

The fragmentation within the international community, with its different capacities and political aims has resulted in a lack of strategic coherence particularly evident in the reconstruction sector and in implementing an opium poppy eradication programme. The UN Security Council has sought to give greater powers to the United Nations Assistance Mission in Afghanistan (UNAMA) to coordinate international development assistance. Agreed on the need for a high-profile coordinator, the UN and donor countries had sought in 2008 to appoint Paddy Ashdown, who had performed in a similar role in the Balkans. But the choice ran into objections from President Karzai who feared being upstaged and overshadowed. The UN then turned to a seasoned Norwegian diplomat Kai Eide to lead its political mission in Kabul with a mandate to increase coordination among all the international donors, and to coordinate efforts with NATO and ISAF. Eide is known to prefer to move away from a coordination approach that is operational-oriented to one that is delivery-oriented. But for him to succeed there must be greater willingness on the part of the donor community as well as the Kabul government to agree to be coordinated.

Governance and State Institutions

International state building efforts have from the outset sought to promote democratic institutions. The framework and timetable of democratization determined at Bonn concentrated on writing a constitution and holding elections for a president and parliament, goals that preoccupied the UN and donor countries. But the international community fostered institutions that Afghans poorly understood and were bound to distort. The result is a flawed constitution that, for all its progressive features, has led to governmental paralysis. By combining features of parliamentary and presidential systems, neither functions properly and the country is subject to continuous confrontation between the branches of government. Where vigorous political parties might have overcome the divisiveness between the executive and parliament, President Karzai has resisted allowing parties to contest elections.

Encouraged by the USA and others to enshrine democratic choice, the Afghan constitution provides a schedule of almost yearly national elections. The Kabul government is, however, incapable of providing the necessary security, finances and technical support for any elections. As a result, it cannot meet its constitutional obligations without continuing and massive support from the UN and USA. To make matter worse, Karzai rejected the advice of foreign electoral experts by opting for an electoral system (the single non-transferable vote) for the national assembly that virtually ensures legislative paralysis. It has resulted in electing an undisciplined body, incapable of mustering legislative majorities that can coalesce on public policies. Arguably, the international community should have resisted pushing the Afghans to adopt a Western style parliament until there had been more time for political parties to organize and public education about elections to occur. More time might have provided better conditions for consensus building among factions and more effective presidential liaison with the parliament

In concentrating on national-level institutions, the Kabul government and international actors have given far too little attention to extending the writ of the government nationwide. While some interest has been shown in enhancing the capacity of the ministries in Kabul, very little investment has gone into supporting more responsible administration at provincial and district levels, or implementing the rule of law through a trusted police force and judicial system. The most promising means to improved local governance are the community development councils (CDCs) of which there are now some 24,000. They were created under a national solidarity programme and are not directly supported by foreign aid. Where they have most succeeded, CDCs have allowed local people to participate in identifying projects and gain a sense of ownership in development activities. Increasingly, the case is made that while central authority ought to set overall development priorities, international funds are better used if they go directly to local community. Empowered CDCs, it is hoped, will give communities the incentive to resist both venial local militia commanders and the insurgents.

The international community has tried to impress on the president the need to confront the issue of corruption more seriously. The great influx of money, including the proceeds from the massive drugs trade, has fuelled corruption throughout the government and society. The international community insists that Karzai use his powers of appointment to reduce corruption and make a more vigorous attempt to bring known figures to justice. While Karzai admits to the problem, he is more concerned about not offending those governors, police chiefs and others whose loyalty he particularly values. Some call for NATO countries and others to press Karzai harder on corruption and even offer to lend military support should he decide to crack down on the most flagrantly corrupt figures, including warlords involved in the drugs trade.

Improvement in a widely distrusted and abused justice system attracts increasing attention from the international community. Afghans at every level of society suffer from both a breakdown in law and order and the means to adjudicate their grievances. Customary means alone are inadequate and the formal state-sanctioned institutions are either absent or corrupt. Criminal and anti-government elements easily exploit a broken, distrusted justice system. Italy was initially designated as the lead nation in the reform of the justice system but made little headway. In recent years, other countries have stepped in to provide for the training of judges and prosecutors, and other forms of assistance.

Transitional justice has also been on the international agenda. Human rights organizations, both inside and outside the country, have regularly raised the issue of accountability for crimes committed during previous decades, including ethnic cleansing and the torture of prisoners. Numerous high profile figures in the country have been accused of complicity or direct involvement. Yet, many of the same individuals have won seats in the parliament and receive appointments to influential government posts. Some foreign governments give protection from prosecution to notorious client warlords. Afghan officials call for patience. They cite the need for reconciliation and warn of political instability if tribunals are created anytime soon. International agencies and groups continue to discuss mechanisms for introducing justice and reconciliation but seem unwilling to press Afghan authorities on the issue.

Reconciliation of another kind is more popular among the Afghan leadership, but leaves the international community uneasy. Government officials and members of parliament have shown a preference for reducing fighting and civilian deaths through negotiations with followers of the Taliban and other anti-Kabul insurgents. Although a committee formed by the Kabul government to foster reconciliation has made little progress, there continues to be wide support for negotiations with the government's enemies. In the light of the deteriorating security across the country and growing impatience with the international community, pressure has increased for opening up a dialogue with the Taliban. Even the USA and its coalition partners seem willing to explore a political compromise. Yet, the scope and framework of any reconciliation with the Taliban and its allies is bound to be the sticking point. The government's insistence on any agreement being based on acceptance of the constitution and disarmament ensures that none of the major insurgent leaders will accept the terms. Aside from a very different vision of the purpose of the state, the insurgents reject entirely any Western presence in the country. Also, Taliban leaders are unlikely to agree to any power sharing arrangement while they feel that the insurgency is succeeding.

Drug Eradication

A more intrusive aspect of international intervention comes in programmes designed for drug eradication. The problem of poppy production and heroin trafficking was identified as early as the Bonn conference in December 2001. At that time, most of the cultivation was in three or four provinces in the south and, in the previous year, had in fact ceased altogether in the Taliban controlled areas. The successful halt to production – undertaken in a Taliban bid to gain international recognition – demonstrated what could be accomplished by the exercise of moral authority and intimidation. Following the expulsion of the Taliban and the prospect of a large-scale resumption of poppy growing, Britain was designated to take responsibility for the eradication programme. The choice of a European country reflected the fact that much of the heroin refined from the poppies ends up in Europe. Initially, the British adopted a soft strategy, approaching growers with cash payments designed to deter them from poppy cultivation. This failed miserably as farmers took the payment and also planted the illicit crops.

Over the last eight years, international attention to poppy production in Afghanistan has increased with demands that the problem be addressed aggressively through eradication. Yet the level of production has continued to grow, and now accounts for 93 per cent of the global supply of heroin. In addition to Europe, regional demand in Iran, India, and Pakistan has increased, as has the emergence of a user market inside Afghanistan itself.

Concern about poppy production is of course related to the overall breakdown in law and order and the expanding insurgency. A drugs economy that amounts to about half of the country's GDP is undermining the international community's efforts to stabilize Afghanistan. While farmers receive only meagre proceeds from their fields, drugs traffickers backed by local militias and complicit local and national officials have created a criminal network united in protecting opium poppy production. Income from the crop has also become increasingly important in sustaining the Taliban insurgency.

The means and pace of eradication is a source of controversy, often pitting the Afghan government against the USA and other donor governments, as well as revealing differences among countries under NATO command. The debate over poppy eradication is especially acute on the issue of aerial spraying, which US drug control have at times advocated as particularly effective for avoiding local political interference. Even at the highest levels of government there is deep repulsion against spraying by planes in the belief that it has a long-term detrimental effect on cultivated land and on human health. Revised counterinsurgency strategies in 2009 de-emphasize poppy eradication in favour of greater targeting of drug traffickers so as to avoid further alienating rural populations.

There are strong voices raised, moreover, against a drug policy that affects farmers and threatens to deprive them of their sole important source of income. Particular concern has been raised over the question that to enforce a policy would alienate the very poor masses whose loyalties the Kabul government desperately needs to retain. Most of the strategies advocated to prevent Afghanistan being turned into a narco-state involve alternative crops and comprehensive, integrative rural development. None are likely to succeed without sustained international assistance prompted by the global impact of Afghanistan's poppy crop.

Perceptions and Responses to Intervention

International intervention and a foreign presence in Afghanistan unavoidably confront the country's political culture. Throughout their history, Afghans have shown a determination to resist occupying forces and those who would use the country for realizing their own national interests rather than those of the Afghans. Although not peculiar to the Afghans and familiar to all tribal societies, there is a willingness to forget even deep internal division and unite against a common foreign enemy. Also, especially common in the region is a tendency to blame external forces for most national failings. All the same, without foreign assistance it is difficult to imagine Afghanistan succeeding. While its underdevelopment and deficit in human capital ensures its continuing dependency, Afghans are nevertheless unwilling to accept assistance on any terms.

Afghans are not xenophobic, as such. They have a good sense for how to distinguish between those who want to help them and those who are intent on imposing their values and rule on the country. Afghans nicely played the USA and Soviet Union against one another during the cold war. That changed in 1978 when the Afghan communists and their Soviet allies made the error of heavy handedly trying to impose what were generally considered to be alien, non-Islamic values and practices. Large numbers of Afghans turned on Moscow when it directly imposed its military might to support the communist ideologues who seized control in 1978 and remained to sustain that rule.

Any analysis of what kind of impact the international intervention and presence had on Afghanistan quickly recognizes how domestic responses have changed over the past eight years. It remains to be seen what impact these changes in attitude will have on the success of the international mission. Understanding public sentiment can help tailor international interventions and ensure that any gains that have been made are not lost.[10] Fortunately, polling and focus group data extending back over several years are available to supplement mere impressions.

The earliest and only collected evidence of where Afghan opinion stood following the 2001 intervention comes from a National Democratic Institute (NDI) report on a focus-group discussion in the Kabul area. Participants expressed gratitude that, along with the arrival of ISAF forces, peace had returned to the country. The report also found high expectations with regard to what the international community can and should do for Afghans. The bar is set high, as those participating expressed the belief that the international community would take care of the country and that the USA, in particular, was going to help rebuild it. Interestingly, however, it was already being opined in 2001 that promises made have not yet been kept.[11]

The following year NDI again measured public perceptions through interviews. Although the research does not include any enquiries directly pertaining to the international military presence in Afghanistan, it did try to assess public perception of foreign non-governmental organizations. Those the NDI consulted in 2002 expressed scepticism towards NGOs, specifically foreign ones. People were concerned about the 'elitist hiring' processes within these organizations. Presumably, this was in reference to the recruitment of well-paid foreign nationals and Afghans who had spent the years of anti-communist jihad and civil conflict in the West.[12]

By 2004, the research the Asia Foundation sponsored in Kabul offered more systematic and reliable survey data on public attitudes. Importantly, it provided valuable benchmarks of national opinion leading up to the October 2005 presidential election.

The poll found that 64 per cent of Afghans believed that their country was moving in the right direction. Only 11 per cent thought that it was on the wrong path. An overwhelming number of those who believed that Afghanistan was on the right course cited the lack of armed conflict and progress in disarming militias as the significant indicators. The major concerns among those who held the view that the country was headed in the wrong direction were the lack of reconstruction and bad governance. Only a small fraction of those with a little confidence complained that Western influence in the country was 'too great', 'possesses a danger to Islam', brings in 'too many foreigners', or that 'foreign aid causes problems'.[13]

Despite an escalation in violence in 2005, public perceptions of Afghanistan's progress continued to be positive. An ABC News opinion poll conducted in December 2005 showed that 77 per cent of Afghans thought their country was going in the right direction. Only 6 per cent thought it was on the wrong path. Asked specifically about the international intervention, 87 per cent said it was a 'good thing' that the United States 'came to the country to overthrow the Taliban', 65 per cent wanted US forces to remain in the country, saying they should leave 'only after security is restored'. But this finding must be balanced against another more disturbing one indicating that 30 per cent of Afghans agreed with the proposition that attacks on US forces in the country could be justified. The belief was most strongly held by underprivileged and socially conservative respondents. When all respondents were asked about their approval of the US work in the country, 68 per cent gave a positive grade.

However, the United Nations scored better with an 82 per cent approval rating, at a level with President Karzai who registered an impressive 83 per cent approval and his government 80 per cent.[14]

An Asia Foundation survey in 2006 recorded the first major decline in public optimism about Afghanistan's future. Only 44 per cent of those surveyed, compared with 77 per cent in 2005, said that the country was moving in the right direction: 21 per cent said it was going in the wrong direction – double the percentage recorded in 2004 and three times that of 2005. Respondents from eastern and south central provinces showed greater satisfaction with the country's progress than elsewhere. Among the satisfied, the reasons for optimism remained the same as those expressed in earlier years – good security, progress in disarming militias and peace. Of the 21 per cent surveyed who felt that the country was headed in the wrong direction, they cited 'too many foreigners' and 'danger to Islam'.[15]

A second poll World Public Opinion.org conducted in 2006 showed that Afghans rated US military forces positively overall, but the proportion with 'very favourable' opinions dropped 11 points (39 per cent to 28 per cent) from the previous year. Afghans with 'somewhat favourable' opinions remained steady at 47 per cent. But when asked in the same survey about efforts to rebuild basic infrastructure and services, a majority of Afghans express dissatisfaction. Nearly six in ten Afghans (58 per cent) describe as only fair (35 per cent) or poor (23 per cent) the progress that had been made in the reconstruction of roads, schools, hospitals and water supplies. Only 42 per cent considered the progress made to be excellent (10 per cent) or good (32 per cent).[16]

A 2007 Asia Foundation survey of the Afghan people saw a continuing decline in optimism about Afghanistan's future direction. Only 42 per cent of those polled said the country was going in the right direction, and 24 per cent said it was on the wrong track. In 2006, those who felt that the country was moving in the wrong direction cited lack of economic development as their main reason. In 2007, insecurity was the principal reason given, followed by bad government (15 per cent), unemployment (15 per cent), administrative corruption (15 per cent), corruption (13 per cent), and a bad economy (12 per cent). The explanations for optimism had also shifted. Previously, it was mostly about peace, disarming the militias and reconstruction. In 2007, 34 per cent of those who said that Afghanistan was headed in the right direction cited simply 'good security', and 19 per cent gave as their reason the reopening of schools for girls.[17]

In an ABC–BBC poll in 2007, among those who said the country was moving in the wrong direction, 24 per cent cited 'too many foreigners and foreign aid', 'Western influence too great' and 'dangers to Islam' as their reasons. By contrast, only 8 per cent of those who said that the country was on the right path attributed it to the presence of foreign aid. In the same survey of opinion, 75 per cent of those polled said that US intervention in the country to bring down the Taliban was a 'good thing'. Support for a US military presence in the country stood at 71 per cent. NATO had a lower popularity rating; 67 per cent said NATO's presence in the country was positive.

Although the Taliban was popular among only 5 per cent in the 2007 ABC–BBC opinion survey, 16 per cent of Afghans polled blamed 'Bush, US forces and America' for the increase in violence in the country. The 17 per cent who said attacks against US forces were justified reflected an increase from the 14 per cent who showed such sentiments in 2006. Yet there was a decrease from the 30 per cent who indicated sympathy for attacks against US forces in the 2005 ABC–BBC findings, perhaps as a reaction to the stepped up Taliban-instigated violence. Among the 17 per cent in 2007 who continued to sympathize with attacks on US forces, 38 per cent gave as their reason that it was because US forces were 'infidels/ foreigners', 22 per cent opposed the US military presence in the country, 11 per cent said it was in retaliation for American abuses, 16 per cent cited protection of Islam, and 9 per cent said the attacks would help protect Afghan independence.[18]

By 2008, the Asia Foundation had found that nearly as many Afghans thought that the country was going in the wrong direction (32 per cent) as found it going in the right direction (38 per cent). Insecurity was cited most often as the greatest reason for concern by 36 per cent of the respondents. This was especially pronounced by those interviewed in the country's south and the Kabul area. Economic issues accounted for many of the other concerns, including unemployment (31 per cent), high prices (22 per cent), and poor economy (17 per cent). Corruption was mentioned by 14 per cent.[19] Yet, despite the complaints, 59 per cent rated the work of the present central government as excellent or good while 42 per cent saw it as fair or poor. But these figures had dropped from 63 per cent positive in 2006 and 70 per cent in 2005. Among national institutions, the greatest confidence was expressed in the Afghan national army. At the same time there was significant concern that the army could not operate effectively without external assistance. In rating the performance of the USA, 43 per cent of respondents called it excellent or good, while 53 per cent found it fair or poor. In 2005, the comparable figures had been 55 per cent positive and 42 negative, and in 2005 it was 68 per cent positive and 30 per cent negative.[20]

A BBC/ABC survey in 2009 continued to reflect the split in public opinion on the direction the country is heading. In this poll, 40 per cent of those responding felt that Afghanistan is going in the right direction, while 38 per cent saw the country moving in the wrong direction. On government performance, 48 per cent believes that the government is doing a good job, down from 80 per cent in 2005. The Taliban continue to be perceived as the greatest threat facing the country at 58 per cent, with drug trafficking following at 13 per cent. While only 8 per cent viewed the USA as a threat, 77 per cent held that US and foreign air strikes are unacceptable because they endanger civilians. Only 16 per cent judged them acceptable as a means to defeat the Taliban. Moreover, 67 per cent say they have not felt any direct benefit from foreign aid. Although support for the presence of US forces in Afghanistan has declined in the BBC/ABC poll from 71 per cent in 2007, it remained at 63 per cent in 2009.[21]

Overall, in their assessments of international interventions Afghans are influenced as much by their perceptions, coloured by their expectations, as they are by their actual experiences. The findings cited here indicate that there is growing disappointment in the performance of the USA and its coalition partners, notably in their failure to provide security and development. Further analysis shows that the displeasure with the international forces is strongest where, predictably, the Taliban insurgency has made the greatest headway – in Afghanistan's southern and eastern provinces. In provinces more secure from the Taliban incursions, the frequent complaint is that their relative peace results in being ignored by the international aid givers.

NATO-led security forces also come in for criticism at the highest levels of government. President Karzai believes that the wide-scale arrests of Taliban supporters are responsible for discouraging Taliban from entering the government's reconciliation process. He faces continual pressure from a highly vocal if ineffectual Afghan parliament to show concern for the growing civilian casualties in the ongoing conflicts. He is willing to concede that corruption is a serious problem owing to the influx of money and governmental weakness, but rejects the suggestion that his government knowingly tolerates corruption. As already noted, Karzai is deeply dissatisfied with the share of funding that is channelled through the central government. His increasingly nationalistic tone in public, designed to suggest some independence from the United States and others was believed mostly tailored for the run-up to the August 2009 presidential election. That context, with its evidence of massive fraud on his behalf dealt a severe blow to his legitimacy. His close association in the public's mind with the international intervention that worked so much to his advantage in the 2004 election was not beneficial to his candidacy in 2009.

International Commitment

International intervention in Afghanistan had not been anticipated before 9/11. There was no advance planning or understandings among countries.

It also turned out to be a very different kind of intervention from what had been anticipated at the beginning. No one had expected a long war, though a long recovery for the state and economy were considered likely. The international community had underestimated the costs, complexity and time needed to rebuild and secure the Afghan state. In subsequent years it too frequently put its faith in individuals rather than institutions. Unlike Iraq, there was for many years a broad international consensus on the necessity of intervention. Many countries that refused to join the US military effort in Iraq felt able to demonstrate their willingness to confront global terrorism by contributing men and money to Afghanistan. Even so, they and their publics did not expect an extended commitment.

Critical to the continued overall acceptance of foreign involvement is the Afghan belief that international forces and donors are committed for the long haul. Any suggestion that they may be fatiguing or losing heart, seeking an exit strategy, raises apprehension. The growing ambivalence about where to place loyalties, especially in the Pashtun south and east, grows from the widely held conviction that the Taliban has the greater staying power. Disagreements among countries about the use of their troops and flagging public support for the mission in most European countries strengthens the belief among many people in Afghanistan that ISAF is an alliance of the unwilling. Because the USA is the leading country in terms of numbers of troops, financial assistance and political influence in Kabul, its commitment is watched most closely. A failure to resource adequately the announced counterinsurgency strategy would send a strong message.

Quite a few Afghans are convinced that, despite the current bipartisan support for military and economic assistance, Washington and the American people would lose interest in Afghanistan and the region were bin Laden to be found and the al-Qaeda network degraded. As public opinion data indicate, commitment from Afghans is also not to be taken for granted. The growing disillusionment of the public with the international role and the Kabul leadership could pose a serious obstacle to a sustained involvement. Increasingly, there are those in positions of influence who question whether the country would be better off without an international military presence. The foremost challenge facing foreign forces is to avoid being viewed as occupiers – in Afghanistan only to serve their strategic interests and at the expense of Afghanistan. Most observers and strategists have come to understand that not enough has been done to engage with and listen to the broad public. International troops will need to exercise a more discriminating use of force. Reliance on air operations has elicited the strongest adverse reactions. Even while the Karzai government seeks an American security umbrella, the leadership and public are highly reluctant to give the USA permanent military bases in the country, especially since such bases would position the USA to confront Iran militarily.

Afghanistan's small domestic revenue base and limited human capital ensures that it will remain a dependent state for the indefinite future. As it often pointed out, there is a conundrum with increased foreign commitment often seeming to result in greater dependency. International efforts may appear 'better, faster and more honest than anything the government will be able to supply'.[22] The way out is of course is for the intervention to provide for the capacity of the Afghans to grow while also demanding greater accountability. The transfer of responsibility to the Afghans for their security and reconstruction has to be an essential element in eventually reducing the international role. In the end it is the Afghans who must succeed.

It is often said that the international community is not destined to succeed in Afghanistan but neither is it destined to fail. The international community has at best had a mixed record in leading Afghanistan in what was to be its post-conflict recovery and state building. The inability to make more progress has been in no small measure a function of the size of the task after more than a generation of conflict. Errant strategies and misplaced priorities over the last eight years have made necessary tasks more difficult. Many of the approaches now showing promise would have had greater effect and been easier to implement had they come earlier in the international intervention. The international community needs a more national perspective for Afghanistan, not one centred on the capital. Assistance has also been uneven in that it is skewed toward security objectives. Development and governance have as a result lagged. Most notably, police and justice reform have been short-changed.

Other challenges confront the international community. Chances of success are dim without a regional strategy that calls for the cooperation of Afghanistan's neighbours. A common approach to Afghanistan and Pakistan is probably required, and Iran and India have to be factored in. Specifically, the insurgency cannot be overcome without removing its sanctuary in Pakistan. The ability to succeed in this civil conflict hinges as much on the earned legitimacy of the government as the size of the effort mounted by international forces. If in the end the Taliban prevails it will not be because it has greater appeal to the Afghan people but because the Kabul government and international forces have failed them.

PART V

CONCLUDING CHAPTER

14

Pious Words and Puny Deeds:
The 'International Community'
and Mass Atrocities

Rajan Menon

As the eminent Israeli historian Martin van Creveld demonstrated, the primary venue of war has shifted since the latter part of the twentieth century. When it comes to magnitude of killing, wars within states have overshadowed wars among them.[1] The horrific results – murder, pillage, rape and the uprooting of people – are ubiquitous; all one need do is open a newspaper or watch the evening news. Consider what has occurred since the mid-1970s alone in Cambodia, Iraq, Bosnia, Rwanda, the Congo, and the Sudan, where the direct and indirect effects of internal warfare have killed eight million people (five million in the Congo alone), and the truth of van Creveld's dismal thesis is apparent.

When mass atrocities occur, the invariable refrain of leaders is that the 'international community' will not stand by and witness the slaughter. But in too many cases it has done just that; or it has responded only after thousands have been killed and abused, and then, too often through half measures. Sadly, those being consumed by the carnage of civil conflict had best not become hopeful when they hear the international community express outrage. Its cavalry may never arrive, or it may reach them too late and, in all likelihood, be poorly equipped to defend them.

The (Virtual) International Community

The horrors that marked the civil conflicts that occurred since the mid-1970s raise the question of whether the term 'international community' is anything more than a cliché invoked reflexively by leaders who are at a loss for words when asked what they will do to stop a particular mass atrocity. An international community certainly exists in the material sense: states, international organizations, NGOs and multinational corporations inhabit an interconnected space through which information, goods, money and people move in volumes and speeds hitherto unimaginable.

Technological advances in transport and communications, particularly in the last decades of the twentieth century, compressed time and space and turned 'globalization' and 'global village' into household words. The degree and rapidity with which events 'there' affect life 'here', and vice versa, are demonstrated daily by the ripple effects of economic crises, the spread of diseases far beyond their points of origin, flows of refugees and drugs, and the near instantaneous transmission of news.[2]

'Community' connotes more than transactions; it suggests shared responsibility, as well as a capacity and willingness to feel at one with and assist those in need; it refers to emotional and psychological bonds and not just material ones. Despite the hopeful talk of shared values and the growing influence of norms defining acceptable conduct, there is no international community in this sense, certainly when it comes to effective collective action against mass atrocities. To assert that norms are now redefining sovereignty by forging an international consensus that sovereignty cannot shield states from responsibility for committing, or failing to avert or end, mass atrocities is easy; proving that it has occurred is another matter.[3]

Long ago Reinhold Niebuhr voiced scepticism about the capacity of a global community of connectivity to transmute into a global community of responsibility. 'A technological civilization', he observed:

> has created an international community, so interdependent as to require, even if not powerful or astute enough to achieve, ultimate social harmony. While there are halting efforts to create an international mind and conscience … modern man has progressed only a little beyond his fathers in extending his ethical attitudes beyond the group to which he is organic and which possesses symbols, vivid enough to excite his social sympathies.[4]

Niebuhr added that:

> while the rapid means of communication have increased the breadth of knowledge about world affairs among citizens of various nations, and the general advance of education has ostensibly promoted the capacity to think rationally and justly … there is nevertheless little hope of arriving at a perceptible increase of international morality through the growth of intelligence and the perfection of the means of communication.[5]

As for norms, Niebuhr's view was that universal principles reflect the underlying realities of power and that, far from restraining states or testifying to the moral progression of the international community, they enable the most powerful states to clothe their parochial interests in the appealing garb of collective and disinterested morality, while ensuring that these principle are applied selectively and at times and in ways that comport with those interests.

Influential figures now passionately dispute such assessments on the grounds that they are cynical at worst, pessimistic at best. Former United Nations Secretary General Kofi Annan, for one, insists that a global community does exist and that it amounts to more than the connections of commerce and communication. He beholds 'a shared vision of a better world', which is expressed in the UN Charter and an array of treaties, laws and conventions, and declares that 'The sceptics are wrong. The international community does exist. It has an address. It has achievements to its credit. And more and more, it is developing a conscience.'[6]

The claim that there is an international community that is unified by a conception of the common good and that it has the means to prevent the egregious violations of one of its self-proclaimed core principles (that mass murder cannot be tolerated) is an instance of the wish fathering the thought. This becomes apparent from a contrast between the features of a functional national community (by which I mean order-keeping, and not necessarily democratic, though certainly one in which the government does not employ large-scale and systematic violence against its citizenry) and those of its much-heralded international counterpart. At their best (that is, when they are democratic and stable), the former are unified by a togetherness – elusive though it may be – based on shared historical experiences, customs and a belief in a common destiny. To be sure, there is nothing static about the narratives prevalent in a national community. They change over time, are continually contested and, as a result, are transformed; and there is no shortage of humbug. The very question of who 'belongs' is rarely settled, and traditions and historical accounts supposedly intrinsic to the community's distinctiveness turn out to be invented or liberally embellished. Notwithstanding the maudlin expressions of solidarity and patriotism, the members of a national community do not feel as one because they encounter one another in ways that inhabitants of a neighbourhood or village do; they are in fact strangers to one another.[7] And while national narratives are often laden with righteous references to peace and tolerance, the creation and persistence of national communities as political units often involve violent forms of exclusion and expansion.

Still, national communities that endure create boundaries (territorial, political, psychological and cultural) that define 'us' and that distinguish between 'us' and 'them', a differentiating dichotomy critical to group solidarity, and not just in times of war. Functional national communities are ethnically, culturally and religiously pluralistic – territories governed by modern states tend towards homogeneity in only a minority of instances – but there are ties, sufficient in number and density, both instrumental and affective, to create a we-ness and to ensure that disputes are played out in a political process rather than through violence.

Nationalism can be an extraordinary violent force – one that is pitiless when challenged by the revolts of lesser nationalisms. Yet the sacrifices that people make on behalf of their nation are extraordinary. Nationalism's capacity to generate passions that trump class identity has caused Marxists much vexation. Proponents of universalism, for whom the fundamental, and higher, connection among humans is their common humanity, are no less dismayed by the resilience of what they consider a retrograde force. It is surely wrong to reify, and dangerous to deify, the nation; but to regard it as just another form of socially constructed consciousness is to be blind to its cathectic power.[8]

The 'international community', by contrast, is a fuzzier thing altogether, a crazy quilt of differences, and along every conceivable dimension – political, economic, cultural and religious. And because it is also vastly larger in size and population than its national counterpart, the sentiments of shared belonging and obligation are tenuous at best, particularly given the lack of a 'them' in relation to whom a sense of 'us' can be articulated and solidarity generated.

The difference between national communities and the international community is not a matter of emotions alone; the contrast is equally stark when it comes to governance. Functional national communities are governed by state institutions that keep order, protect citizens, bring perpetrators of violence to justice when prevention fails, enforce obligations and collect the revenue that enables the structures of the state to discharge their responsibilities to the community. Not all members benefit equally, of course, and not everything works as it should; and the state operates in ways that reflect the distribution of power among classes and groups: it is not a neutral arbitrator, its rhetoric of self-preservation nothwishstanding.

The important point given my concerns here is that parallel order-keeping, rule-enforcing, dispute-resolving mechanisms are either absent or anaemic in world politics. The closest thing there is to a set of central institutions is the United Nations and its affiliated agencies, but the very design of the UN system deprives it of the capacity to mobilize collective action effectively and reliably. The UN has no power of taxation; it depends on the voluntary, though specified, contribution of its members, and when, as happens not infrequently, they are delinquent in their dues, there is nothing much it can do except to plead and be patient. Nor does the UN have a standing army or police forces that can be used to deter or end violence in the community over which it presides. It can appeal to its members for troops, but before an international force can be assembled for peacekeeping (under Chapter VI of the UN Charter) or peace enforcement (Chapter VII), all of the permanent members of the Security Council must approve. Any one of them has the right to cast a veto to prevent the assembling of a multinational force, and they can also block lesser measures intended to punish perpetrators of mass atrocities. High-minded recommendations that the Security Council's permanent members should reach an agreement not to veto resolutions proposing action against genocide, especially when they are approved by the General Assembly by a two-thirds majority because 'a crisis poses as imminent threat of mass atrocities', will prove fruitless: the veto is an exclusive privilege, jealously held.[9]

Even when a UN peacekeeping force is created, the Security Council's 'big five' can determine how large and powerful it is and what it can and cannot do — and they do so based not on a conception of the general interest but on their national interests. Moreover, UN peacekeeping forces are often assembled from an array of countries whose military units have most likely never trained together. They also vary considerably in the quality of their training (especially for peacekeeping) and equipment, particularly because many hail from poor countries, which look to peace-keeping operations as a source of income. The commander of such a motley force is often in an unenviable position: he is expected to do a lot with little. Likewise, the UN's Department of Peacekeeping Operations has run 63 operations since 1948 with an allotment of only $54 billion and, in 2008, was overseeing 18 missions with no more than 77,804 soldiers at its disposal and on an authorized budget of $7 billion, of which $2.8 had yet to be received.[10]

International judicial structures for dealing with mass atrocities are no less feeble. Though the 1998 Rome Statute established an International Criminal Court (ICC), this institution lacks universal and enforceable jurisdiction. It also lacks a police service to track and investigate suspects and must rely on the cooperation of member states. Another weakness of the ICC is that the world's most powerful country, the United States, is not party to the Rome Statute. President Clinton signed it but did not send it to the Congress for ratification; President George W. Bush reversed the decision to sign the treaty. The United States objected to the ICC on the grounds that ratifying the Rome Treaty would expose its troops to war crimes charges and remained unmoved by the considerable efforts made to allay this concern. The United States not only stayed out of the ICC, it threatened to pull its troops from the UN peacekeeping force in Bosnia unless they received immunity from war crimes charges and also put pressure on countries that had ratified the ICC statute to sign bilateral agreements exempting US forces from prosecution. True, the United States abstained during the 2005 Security Council vote to refer the Darfur atrocities to the ICC and so enabled the referral to go forward, but it has hardly captured the moral high ground by trumpeting its commitment to human rights, approving the ICC's work to bring perpetrators of mass atrocities to justice and proclaiming the essentiality of its leadership for dealing with big global problems on the one hand, while, on the other, refusing to join the court despite determined efforts to address its objections.[11]

The ICC did issue an arrest warrant in 2009 for Sudan's president, Omar al-Bashir (who promptly responded by evicting the aid agencies serving as a lifeline to one million Darfuri refugees – and without suffering any consequences), and various Serb, Croat, Bosnian and Rwandan leaders and the former president of Liberia, Charles Taylor, have been handed over to *ad hoc* international war crimes tribunals. While these achievements are rightly lauded, it is well to remember that by the time these individuals were charged, they had participated directly or indirectly in killing thousands of people. Moreover, the ICC and the tribunals reveal the divisions that exist in the world over supranational justice even in the case of brazen crimes. Charges that they violate sovereignty and are used selectively (which many African and Middle Eastern governments voiced after Bashir's indictment) are no less common than the cheers that proclaim them as evidence that international norms against genocide are emerging. The point is not that international judicial institutions are useless, merely that they are not remotely comparable to national justice systems in bringing perpetrators of violence to book and that they are severely hampered when it comes to serving as an effective instrument against mass atrocities.

That warlords, militias and governments engaged in slaying their populations are not terribly fearful about the prospect of UN-backed military intervention or criminal prosecution is clear from the millions who have died at their hands over the past several decades. The killers have good reason to believe one or more of the following: that there will be no intervention because it will be blocked in the Security Council; that any force that is dispatched will not be very formidable; that it will be withdrawn once the human and economic costs of sustaining it mount; and that the probability of being brought to justice is remote because there are multiple means of evasion. The confidence would hardly be misplaced. Consider the two million Cambodians killed by Pol Pot's

Khmer Rouge regime; the approximately 200,000 Hutus in Burundi in 1972 and 1993; the 200,000 Kurds gassed, forcibly relocated and killed during Saddam Hussein's Anfal campaign; the tens of thousands of Bosnian Muslims slain, raped and driven from their homes by Bosnian Serbs in the first half of the 1990s; the 800,000 members of the Tutsi minority massacred, in a matter of eight weeks, by the Hutu Interahamwe and the Rwandan military; the 350,000 Darfuris who have been slain by the Janjaweed militia and its patron and partner, the Sudanese military or who have died from disease and the lack of food; and the five million killed (because of the direct and indirect effects of war) in the Congo after the proxy war broke out between the Rwandan and Congolese governments (with several other states joining the fray) in 1996.

The horrific human toll taken by the Congo conflict goes to show that the international community lacks both the will and the institutions strong enough to enforce its oft-repeated view that mass atrocities violate the values it shares. Though 6000 UN peacekeepers were eventually deployed to the Congo, they proved utterly incapable of defending the civilian population. Though the force was eventually – and none too quickly – increased to 17,000, making it the UN's largest peacekeeping operation, the ratio of troops to Congo's population was 1 to 3400. The UN troops were still unable, or in many instances simply unwilling, to protect people at risk. In November 2008, UN Secretary General Ban Ki-moon urged UN members to contribute 3000 more troops. Of the 65 governments approached, only one (Bangladesh) offered troops; one other (Belgium) offered transport aircraft.[12]

Robust institutions to prevent, stop and prosecute the perpetrators of mass atrocities are not absent because sovereign states cannot create them but because states (particularly the most powerful ones) are unwilling to countenance supranational structures that could reduce their control over decisions related to the all-important issues of making war and peace. States want collective security, but on their own terms. The result is that while there is no powerful mechanism for dealing with mass atrocities, there is no lack of haggling and temporizing when peacekeeping forces are proposed to prevent or stop atrocities. The minimum result is a delay in deployment that skews the already lopsided balance of power between victims and aggressors. Bosnian Muslims were slaughtered while the UN dithered and, to make matters worse, during the height of the Serbs' rampages, the arms embargo on Yugoslavia was retained, which put the Bosnians at a disadvantage given that the Serb forces had the direct support of the well-equipped Yugoslav army. What happened in Cambodia was far worse: no force was deployed to stop the Khmer Rouge from murdering two million people.

These failures have been criticized from opposite ends of the political spectrum. The late Jeane Kirkpatrick observed 'those who need defending are more vulnerable to the delays and ineffectiveness of a multilateral team than those who are attacking; aggressors are not required to coordinate their actions and policies with anyone.'[13] Noam Chomsky for his part charges that the United States has systematically used its peerless power and privileged position in the UN not only to block action to stop mass killings, but also even to prevent condemnations of them when it considers such steps as contrary to its interests or those of its allies or special friends.[14]

What is evident during mass atrocities is not the international community's unity and effectiveness but its inability to act, particularly when it encounters opposition from its most powerful states, precisely the ones most capable of orchestrating combined action. Let us consider some examples.[15]

Despite his oft-repeated commitment to human rights, President Carter took a hands-off position while the Khmer Rouge systematically killed more than a quarter of Cambodia's population between 1975 and 1978: he failed to call for UN action, to press American allies to condemn the Khmer Rouge, or to ask China, the Khmer Rouge's patron, to intercede. The United States had just withdrawn from Indochina after a ten-year war, and its government and citizenry were at one in their determination not to be dragged back. When the Vietnamese finally intervened in 1978 and toppled the Khmer Rouge (for reasons of their own), the United States did not view the development as the lesser of two evils, but as a dangerous extension of a Soviet-backed state's power into a neighbouring country; to Washington and China what mattered was the Khmer Rouge's value as a countervailing force.

Likewise, though the Reagan administration knew about the savagery of Saddam Hussein's Anfal campaign against the Kurds (with its mass shootings, the emptying and razing of entire villages, deportations and gassing of civilians), Washington's primary concern then was that Iraq might lose the war it was fighting (and had initiated) against Iran. The USA did not act to stop the horror or even call for others to act or even to organize a movement for sanctions against Iraq; worse, it extended credits that helped finance Saddam's grain purchases and provided him intelligence on Iranian forces. The Reagan administration even sought to dissuade members of the Congress who wanted to issue resolutions condemning the assault on the Kurds. President George H. W. Bush followed this pattern even after the Iran–Iraq war ended: his administration stressed the significance of a strong US–Iraq relationship, even though nearly 90,000 Iraqi Kurds had fled to Turkey by 1989. (It took

Saddam's invasion of Kuwait the following year to change the American attitude. When he sought to crush a Kurdish uprising and forced still more Kurds into Turkey after the Gulf war, the United States and Britain and France enforced a no-flight zone over northern Iraq and deployed troops that set up relief supply camps in Turkey and northern Iraq in what was dubbed 'Operation Provide Comfort'.)

President Bill Clinton was similarly passive during the 1994 genocide against Rwanda's Tutsi minority. Mindful of how US forces in Somalia had been mauled in 1993 and the lack of American public support for military intervention in Rwanda, his administration fell back on claims that the information about what was happening in Rwanda was incomplete and unclear and engaged in hairsplitting about whether a genocide was in fact occurring. Even measures that could have been taken short of military intervention, such as jamming Radio Milles Collines, whose broadcasts called for the extermination of the Tutsi, were not taken.

The United States has hardly been alone in viewing massacres through the lenses of national interest (though its unrivalled power and incessant statement about its commitment to human rights justifies holding it to a higher standard). Belgium withdrew its troops from the UN peacekeeping force in Rwanda (UNAMIR) and did not want other states to beef up the force (it did not really have to worry about that possibility) for fear of being seen as fleeing the scene and abandoning people to the slaughter. China and Russia used their influence in the Security Council to block the imposition of tougher sanctions on the Sudanese government as a punishment for the killing in Darfur. Also, Omar al-Bashir's government was successful in shaping the size, composition and mission of the AU–UN peacekeeping forces in Darfur in part because Beijing and Moscow had, in essence, adopted the view that humanitarian intervention to stop mass atrocities cannot trump sovereignty – a position that serves their interest in ensuring that their own acts of repression in Tibet, Xingjiang, and Chechnya are covered by that principle.

Fear of prohibitive costs in troops and treasure is not what generally prevents UN-sanctioned interventions against mass atrocities. General Roméo Dallaire, UNAMIR's commander, insists in his chilling memoirs that the genocide could have been stopped had the international community placed 'an effective military and police presence on the ground in Rwanda as soon as the Arusha Peace agreement was signed' and provided the UN force with better intelligence and logistical support and 'a budget increase of only $100 million'.[16] He adds that once the killings began, the death toll would have been far smaller had the members of the Security Council strengthened the UN force with a few thousand well-trained and well-armed soldiers: the Interahamwe had neither the arms nor the training to stand up to a modern military force. But none of the members of the Security Council wanted to do that. Rather than fill the void created by the Belgians' withdrawal, the major powers, particularly the United States, were concerned principally with avoiding involvement in an operation they feared could turn messy, that did not serve their critical national interests and that would therefore fail to win support at home. Western troops were deployed to Rwanda, but only to evacuate diplomats and other citizens, and when French military units did intervene towards the end of the conflict, they permitted Hutu forces and Radio Mille Collines to enter the zone they had secured.

Similarly, after the Sudanese government allowed an Africa Union (AU) peacekeeping force into Darfur, the organization had to plead for the fewer than 70 helicopters it needed to transport its troops to places where civilians were being attacked. The Sudanese government eventually agreed to allow a larger joint AU–UN force to be deployed to Darfur but was successful in imposing conditions that weakened and delayed it and was confident that the Chinese and the Russians would prevent the Security Council from stiffening the sanctions in response. Khartoum could be even more confident that it would not face military attacks.

States are even reluctant to take steps that fall well short of military intervention. Their response – or more accurately lack of it – to refugee crises spawned by mass atrocities is an example. Though the international community has undertaken obligations to care for refugees under the 1954 Convention Relating to the Status of Refugees, which more than 140 states have signed, UN High Commissioner for Refugees Sadako Ogata:

> faced great difficulties seeking to ensure that states lived up to the provisions of the convention, even regarding the acceptance of people in desperate flight. I sought to enlist governments and the global public for support in my efforts, insisting that borders be kept open, asking that asylum seekers' claims be fairly examined, and soliciting funds. ... The international community did not seem to exist even in the face of human tragedies. ... It is essentially a virtual community.[17]

Global Citizenship: Redefining Obligation

If the lack of an international community capable of acting against mass atrocities results in significant measure from the weakness of 'we-ness', perhaps what is needed is to change the ways in which people think about their identities, allegiances and responsibilities, so that the affection and assistance they give so readily to their families, friends, social networks, regions and national communities they give to humanity at large. Though it would seem that this is asking for a lot, there is in fact nothing fixed about the way people conceive of themselves or of their associations with others. When it comes to the collectivities to which people feel attached and for whom they are willing to make sacrifices there has been considerable variation from place to place and time to time. The modern concept of nationalism, which arose in the eighteenth century, is a relatively recent arrival; for most of history, human beings knew nothing about patriotism as we define it today; their loyalties were directed elsewhere. Seen thus, the belief that people can come to see themselves as members of an international community is, in principle, not far fetched.

Collective action against mass atrocities will become easier if individuals' conceptions of community and responsibility extend beyond their national boundaries and encompass others, regardless of who they are and where they happen to live – if we-ness becomes global. This, in simplified form, is the position of those who believe in the necessity for, and the feasibility of, 'global citizenship', which they embrace for two reasons. They believe that global interdependence is now so powerful a force that many problems – among them mass atrocities – cut across borders and cannot be addressed effectively without collective action. But they are also convinced that global citizenship is a morally superior stance in that it takes our common humanity, not our more parochial associations, as its starting point.

Perhaps the most passionate and creative advocate of global citizenship is the philosopher Martha Nussbaum, who traces its lineage to the Cynics and Stoics of ancient Greece. Though her interest in the concept – which she refers to as 'cosmopolitanism' – does not flow from a preoccupation with mass atrocities *per se*, it is fair to say that the realization of her project would vastly ease the problem of collective action aimed at dealing with them. For Nussbaum, patriotism is 'morally dangerous', and she disagrees with those such as Richard Rorty who, while abhorring its intolerant manifestations, value its inclusive forms as an antidote to the sectarian divisions that produce disunity, intolerance, even violence within countries.[18] For moral and practical (problem-solving) reasons, her preference is for 'the person whose allegiance is to the worldwide community of human beings'.[19] Debates over why 'we' should send 'our troops' and spend 'our money' to save 'them' when none of 'our' interests is at stake would be more easily concluded, with universal obligations winning out, were Nussbaum's vision to be realized. The entire us/them distinction would be rendered superfluous, the problems related to mobilizing the 'international community' would disappear and the barriers of building institutions with sufficient authority, legitimacy and resources to deploy international forces to prevent or stop mass atrocities would be surmountable.

For Nussbaum, global citizenship involves more than broadening people's intellectual horizons so that they are well informed about global problems (poverty, pollution, human rights abuses), speak different languages, travel to other countries and regard other cultures without prejudice and with wonder and open-mindedness. Such sensibilities are the bare minimum; hers is a bigger project — or so it seems initially. She is opposed to 'a morally arbitrary boundary such as a national boundary' because she is convinced that it is unjust to see someone in need of help but who lives outside the borders of one's country as less deserving of one's capacity to help than someone who lives within them.[20] Yet, her prescription ends up being essentially about empathy and sympathy and a broader education. That is because it evades the hard part: explaining how to achieve the transition from global awareness to global action. That is a critical failure because Nussbaum, like other proponents of global citizenship, sees it as a way of making the world a better place, not just a lofty sentiment. For practical outcomes that are global in scope, a change of consciousness, while essential, will not suffice; there must be institutional change as well.

Feelings of belonging are harnessed to the betterment of the national community when privileges are accompanied by duties — many of them — that require citizens to offer their energy, time and money, and even, where military service is compulsory, their lives. One cannot generally pick and choose, saying, 'I'll pay for this, but not that; I'll do this but not that,' because there are institutions with the legitimacy and capacity to force compliance. It is thus that sentiments lead to solutions. As someone committed to social justice, Nussbaum is convinced that the more widespread a global frame of reference becomes, the better the prospects for tackling tough problems, whether global pollution and poverty or genocide.[21] But when it comes to the move from inculcating universal awareness and the obligation to address concrete problems, she leaves us to assume that somehow it will work out. That implicit assumption is not justified.

Whether it is global warming or mass atrocities, then, global citizenship as a proffered solution returns us to a familiar place. In an international system dominated by sovereign states, there can be no effective and reliable collective action without institutions capable of making and enforcing laws, collecting taxes and using the resources gained thereby to frame policies and mobilize efforts to address concrete problems. Not only is a moral and intellectual commitment to global citizenship insufficient by itself, but it may also be downright dangerous in the case of mass atrocities because of the risk that it could communicate to perpetrators that the international community cannot translate its norms and moral stances ('genocide will not be tolerated') into deeds and that its bluff can therefore be called at little to no cost. Some of Nussbaum's critics contend that global citizenship is much too thin a gruel to satisfy people's cravings for identity and belonging and that it is doomed to fail as a project.[22] Perhaps so, but my interest here is in judging its usefulness for dealing with mass atrocities, and from this standpoint it has a much bigger flaw, which is that it exists in a legal institutional void and, as such, is condemned to remain an outlook, not a paradigm for action.

Is R2P the Answer?

The most recent and creative effort to surmount the obstacles that sovereignty presents to coordinated responses to mass atrocities is the 'Responsibility to Protect' (R2P) doctrine. A group of eminent people formed the International Commission on Intervention and State Sovereignty through the initiative of then Canadian foreign minister, Lloyd Axworthy, who wanted to develop an answer to a question posed after the 1994 Rwandan genocide by UN secretary general, Kofi Annan, which was roughly as follows. If intervention to protect innocents from slaughter is deemed a violation of the sanctified principle of sovereignty, what recourse is left to the international community other than to issue empty condemnations? Chaired by former Australian foreign minister (and head of the International Crisis Group) Gareth Evans and veteran Algerian diplomat Mohamed Sahnoun, the commission issued its report in December 2001.[23] There has since been a flurry of studies devoted to R2P, the most compelling and comprehensive of which is Evans's 2008 book, *The Responsibility to Protect: Ending Mass Atrocities Once and for All.*[24]

R2P rests on four interrelated premises. The first is that mass atrocities cannot be ignored because they violate basic moral precepts and have wider consequences, particularly the spread of instability and violence far beyond the scene of the crime. The second is that sovereignty is a basic and essential principle of international relations, as well as a real-life force that cannot be wished away even when the most appalling atrocities occur, and that the task lies in reconciling it with multilateral action. The third is that mass atrocities must be addressed by mobilizing the energies of the international community and that the UN is the proper institution for this purpose because it alone can represent an international consensus. Finally, R2P rests on the assumption that no state or group (whether a 'coalition of the willing' or a 'league of democracies') must be allowed to arrogate the right to act as a self-appointed entity because it would lack legitimacy and, moreover, act to serve its particular interests rather than as an instrument of the global community.

Fundamentally, then, R2P is an effort to reconcile sovereignty, which protects states from wanton interference in their internal affairs, with the proposition that sovereign governments have responsibilities to their citizens and cannot claim the right to treat them in any way they see fit and without accountability. R2P presents sovereignty and responsibility as compatible, not incommensurable. The protection of people is, in the first instance, the responsibility of their government and should not be usurped by another country or international organization; providing such protection is an obligation, not an option. The challenge R2P takes on is what to do when a government cannot or will not discharge its duty, or itself violates the rights of its citizens in ways that involve the commission of atrocities. At that point, insist R2P's proponents, the responsibility must shift to the international community. Yet, even then, armed intervention is not the doctrine's first recourse, but its last. This position reflects its recognition of the power of sovereignty and unwillingness to override it in the service of a greater good (to the extent that it can reach agreement on what that is in any given instance). R2P starts with prevention and the first step is to create early-warning mechanisms – to develop indicators of risk that are based on careful research and monitored diligently – so that measures can be taken in cooperation with the government of the country in question to avert violence. If negotiations and mediation aimed at prevention fail and the killing begins, R2P recommends additional steps such as the provision of assistance for the displaced and injured and continuing external mediation between the parties to the conflict aimed at arriving at compromises and power-sharing arrangements that restore peace. If such efforts fail, the next move is to use a range of sanctions and rewards that target those responsible for the atrocities. Only after all such measures have been exhausted and it is clear that inaction will result in continuing atrocities does multilateral military intervention emerge as an option. Then, too, it is exercised only after due deliberation in the United Nations and the authorization of the Security Council.

While it is hardheaded about the salience of sovereignty, the R2P doctrine also assumes that there is such a thing as the international community and that, for practical and moral reasons, it can and must respond to mass atrocities. Its contribution lies in offering a strategy to achieve this end in ways that do not trample the legal rights of states but that do protect people from grievous harm; in this respects it is superior to global citizenship in that it proposes a plan for bridging the chasm between values and action. In short, its supporters would agree with Kofi Annan that the international community exists, that it can agree on principles that promote the common good, and that it has both the right and the capacity to act. The endorsement of R2P by the UN at the organization's 2005 World Summit and its incorporation, albeit in qualified form, into Security Council Resolution 1674 (28 April 2006) is proof of the respect it has won and the traction it has gained. The acclamation is deserved, for R2P shows that there are numerous ways in which actions can be taken before the atrocities get to the point that debates on military intervention take place, and in key instances (Burundi after the Rwandan genocide and Kenya after the violence that followed the disputed election in 2008) the approach has proven effective.

Yet, R2P runs into some serious problems in the transition from principle to practice. The biggest one arises at the point when it becomes clear that early warning, mediation and the application of the combination of incentives and pressure on the offending parties have failed and that mass killing is imminent or already occurring. At that point R2P's follow-on remedies bump up against the claims of sovereignty because it then calls for tougher sanctions and, if they fail, armed intervention under UN aegis.

The debates about Resolution 1674 showed that, for this very reason, the members of the UN were split on R2P; not a few, including China and Russia, viewed it as an attempt to engineer an elegant run around sovereignty.[25] Furthermore, while R2P has won support from many Asian and African countries and cannot therefore easily be dismissed as another neo-colonial plot against the independence of developing countries, there remain governments that oppose it on the grounds that it will be applied to them (and then too selectively because some states have protectors and some do not) while excluding powerful states, even when their behaviour qualifies for action based on R2P.

Some who raise this objection believe that R2P threatens their sovereignty by design, others that it does so by default; but that distinction is less important than their shared suspicion of it. Thus, a principle intended to unify the international community and to develop a coordinated response to a serious problem, mass atrocities, ends up revealing the elemental divisions on this very problem. But without such consensus R2P cannot become a viable plan of action that is anywhere near as practicable as its proponents believe it to be. A thornier problem stems, ironically, from what is one of R2P's major strengths, which is to offer a plan of action aimed at gaining universal assent and legitimacy. R2P solves the posse problem only to encounter another, one that can render it inoperable, namely the Security Council veto.

In practice R2P may be able to overcome the difficulties that are bound to emerge during the creation of early-warning mechanisms, the provision of assistance for refugees, mediation, providing incentives for stopping atrocities and perhaps even the application of sanctions. However, when sanctions do not work, the massacres mount and discussions begin about authorizing intervention by a UN force, R2P's progress can still be thwarted by the opposition of one or more permanent members of the

Security Council. The dissenters could, for example, reject the claim that a particular instance of mass atrocities is in fact a serious enough threat to the peace to warrant action under Chapter VI of the UN Charter. Even without casting a veto, they could employ countless procedural tactics to prevent a force from being dispatched in time to save lives (or from arriving before thousands of people had perished) or impose restrictions on its capabilities and mandate that make it ineffectual.

What Are We Left With?

Most of the large-scale violence in the world will continue to result from atrocities within societies rather than from wars between states. The cruelties will be visited upon those least able to deter their attackers or defend themselves; worse, their governments, which have the responsibility to protect them, may frequently be the tormentors. Norms against atrocities; the UN Charter; the Universal Declaration of Human Rights; the Genocide Convention; war crimes tribunals; the ICC; NGOs documenting and publicizing human rights abuses and providing food, shelter and medicine to the victims of war; UN peacekeeping missions; peacekeeping by regional organizations like the AU and Economic Community of West African States (ECOWAS); multilateral interventions outside UN auspices *à la* Kosovo; and mediations aimed at averting civil conflicts have all – in their different ways – prevented crises from becoming far worse than they in fact were, which in some instances was still very bad indeed. Yet, based on the incidence and scale of mass killings and rape, the eviction of people from their homes, the swarms of hungry and disease-ravaged refugees, and the millions killed by mass atrocities, it is undeniable that the international community, to the extent that it exists at all, has been unable to develop either the ethical-legal consensus or the institutions with the authority and wherewithal to deal effectively with a serious and perennial problem. It has had no shortage of opportunities to do so, for there has been no shortage of mass atrocities to concentrate the mind and to spur action.

Advocates of multilateral action remain hopeful and point, for instance, to the 1999 Australian-led operation in East Timor; the 2003 ECOWAS mission in Liberia; the 2007 Security Council resolution that supplemented the pitifully small, harried and poorly-equipped 7000-man AU force in Darfur that had been deployed by mid-2005 with other troops (mostly from Africa), raising the total to 26,000; NATO's willingness to help airlift and train the AU's Darfur force from 2005 to 2007; and the Atlantic alliance's own (supposed) willingness to make peacekeeping operations beyond Europe one of its main purposes now that the cold war is over. But these successes are exceptions and moreover pale before the failures.

The AU's forces in Darfur were ill-equipped for peacekeeping operations, particularly in circumstances when war was still raging. The
enlarged AU–UN force will not remedy this problem because Sudan, with
China's support, blocked efforts to strengthen it by adding significant
numbers of non-African soldiers. Even once the force is at full strength in
Darfur (the build-up has been slow), it will be patrolling a region larger
than Spain. The lopsided force-to-space ratio, the continued fighting
between the Darfuri insurgents and Sudanese forces and the Janjaweed,
and the mission to defend refugees who remain under attack make for a
big mandate supported by meagre means.

The prospects of NATO serving as a global peacekeeper are poor.
Without direct US involvement, the alliance would not have used force in
Bosnia and Kosovo. Its non-US members, with few exceptions (Britain
and France), cannot project forces into distant war zones and sustain them
there. Despite the claim by NATO supporters that the alliance is willing
and ready to look beyond Europe, discussions on 'out-of-area' missions
generate divisions, not unity, within the alliance – and the wars in Iraq and
Afghanistan will surely worsen this problem.[26] Even if NATO were to
overcome these problems, states that are not members of the alliance and
suspect its motives will oppose its assumption of a global role.

When confronted with the worst atrocities, such as those in Cambodia
and Rwanda, the international community failed to do anything; in the
Congo what it did failed to make much difference and what will end the
conflict there is a deal between the Congolese and Rwandan governments
to rein in their proxies. The problem is not a shortage of people dedicated
to the prevention of mass atrocities or a surfeit of callousness but the
barriers to a moral and legal consensus created by an international
connectivity that is principally instrumental rather than empathic and the
obstacles to cooperative action in what remains a world in which
sovereign states – wilful, protective of their freedom of action, and
suspicious of supranationalism and binding commitments to others – rule
the roost and can negate or dilute tough collective action, even in the face
of epic cruelty. Will these conditions change so that we escape Martin van
Creveld's world? Alas, there is little reason for optimism.

Notes

Chapter 1. From Bipolar to Unipolar Order: System Structure and Conflict Resolution *Janice Gross-Stein*

1. *Human Security Brief* (2006) Vancouver: University of British Columbia.
2. Three quarters of the perpetrators of violent campaigns against civilians were also involved in ongoing state-based armed conflicts. The biggest spike in violence is in the Middle East since 2001, although a large part is accounted for by Iraq and Darfur, while there has been a steep decline in sub-Saharan Africa since the Rwandan genocide in 1994 (Jean Paul Azam and Anke Hoeffler, 'Violence against civilians in civil wars: looting or terror', *Journal of Peace Research*, vol. 39, no. 4, 2002, pp. 461–85; Stathis N. Kalyvas, *The logic of violence in civil war*, Cambridge: Cambridge University Press, 2006).
3. George Downs and Stephen John Stedman, 'Evaluating issues in peace implementation', in Stephen Stedman, Donald Rothchild and Elizabeth M. Cousens (eds) *Ending civil wars: the implementation of peace agreements*, Boulder: Lynne Reiner, 2002, pp. 50–2.
4. Michael W. Doyle and Nicholas Sambanis, *Making war and building peace: United Nations peace operations*, Princeton: Princeton University Press, 2006; Lotta Harbom, Stina Hogbladh and Peter Wallensteen, 'Armed conflict and peace agreements', *Journal of Peace Research*, vol. 43, September 2006, pp. 617–31.
5. Virginia Page Fortna, *Peace time: ceasefire agreements and the durability of peace*, Princeton: Princeton University Press, 2004; Barbara Walter, *Committing to peace: the successful settlement of civil wars*, Princeton: Princeton University Press, 2002.
6. Paul Diehl and Joseph Lepgold, *Regional conflict management*, Lanham: Rowan & Littlefield, 2003.
7. The Economic Community of West African States (ECOWAS) conducted five, the Southern African Development Community organized two, the Economic and Monetary Community of Central African States (CEMAC) led one, and the African Union (AU) organized two. Alex J. Bellamy and Paul D. Williams, 'Who's keeping the peace? Regionalization and contemporary peace operations', *International Security*, vol. 29, no. 4, Spring 2005, pp. 157–95.
8. Bellamy and Williams, 'Who's keeping the peace?', p. 167.
9. Patrick Regan and Aysegul Aydin, 'Diplomacy and other forms of intervention in civil wars', *Journal of Conflict Resolution*, vol. 50, no. 5, October 2006, pp. 736–56.
10. Edward Luttwak, 'Give War a Chance', *Foreign Affairs*, vol. 78, no. 4, July/August 1999, pp. 36–44.

11. Chester Crocker, 'A poor case for quitting', *Foreign Affairs*, vol. 79, no. 1, January/February 2000, pp. 183–6.

12. Fen Osler Hampson, Chester A. Crocker and Pamela Aall, 'If the world's getting more peaceful, why are we still in danger', *Globe and Mail*, 20 October 2005.

13. James Fearon, 'Why do some civil wars last so much longer than others', *Journal of Peace Research*, vol. 41, no. 3, 2004, pp. 275–301.

14. Francis M. Deng, 'Reconciling sovereignty with responsibility: a basis for international humanitarian action', in John W. Harbeson and Donald Rothschild, *Africa in world politics: post-cold war challenges*, Boulder: Westview, 1995, pp. 295–310; Francis M. Deng, 'Frontiers of sovereignty', *Leiden Journal of International Law*, vol. 8, no. 2, 1995, pp. 249–286; Thomas A. Weiss and David A. Korn, *Internal displacement: conceptualization and its consequences*, London: Routledge, 2006.

15. Gareth Evans and Mohamed Sahnoun, 'The responsibility to protect', *Foreign Affairs*, vol. 81, no. 6, November–December 2002, pp. 99–110; ICISS (2001) *The responsibility to protect* at http://www.iciss.ca/report-en.asp

16. ICISS, *The responsibility to protect*, pp. 15–16.

17. High-Level Panel on Threats, Challenges and Change, *A more secure world: our shared responsibility*, 2004, UN Doc.A/59/565. Available at http://www.un.org/secureworld/report.pdf

18. United Nations, *In larger freedom: towards development, security, and human rights for all: report of the secretary-general*, UN Doc A/59/2005, available at http://www.un.org/largerfreedom/contents.htm

19. See Security Council Resolution 1674, Para 4 (28 April 2006), 'reaffirm[ing] the provisions of paragraphs 138 and 139 of the 2005 World Summit Outcome Document regarding the responsibility to protect populations from genocide, war crimes, ethnic cleansing, and crimes against humanity'.

20. Carsten Stahn, 'Responsibility to protect: political rhetoric or emerging legal norm', *American Journal of International Law*, vol. 101, no. 1, January 2007, p. 109.

21. The outcome document states: 'In this context, we are prepared to take collective action, in a timely and decisive manner, through the Security Council, in accordance with the Charter, including Chapter vii, on a *case-by-case basis* and in cooperation with relevant regional organizations *as appropriate*, should peaceful means be inadequate and national authorities are manifestly failing to protect their populations from genocide, war crimes, ethnic cleansing and crimes against humanity.'

22. Thomas Friedman, *The world is flat: a brief history of the twenty-first century*, New York: Farrar, Strauss & Giroux, 2005.

23. Richard Haass, The age of nonpolarity', *Foreign Affairs*, May–June 2008.

24. Parag Khanna, *The second world: empires and influence in the new global order*, New York: Random House, 2008.

25. Fareed Zakaria, *The post-American world*, New York: W. W. Norton & Company, 2008

26. Bill Emmott, *Rivals: how the power struggle between China, India, and Japan will shape our next decade*, New York: Harcourt Brace, 2008.

27. Khanna, *The second world*.

28. Ibid.

29. T. V. Paul, 'Soft balancing in the age of US primacy', *International Security*, vol. 30, no. 1, Summer 2005, pp. 46–71; William C. Wohlforth, 'US strategy in a unipolar world', in John Ikenberry (ed.) *America unrivalled: the future of the balance of power*, Ithaca: Cornell University Press, 2002, pp. 103–4.

30. Joseph S. Nye Jr, 'Military deglobalization: long-distance military interdependence is taking new forms', *Foreign Policy*, vol. 122, January–February 2001, p. 82.

31. Paul Kennedy, *The rise and fall of great powers: economic change and military conflict from 1500 to 2000*, New York: Random House, 1987.

32. Nye, 'Military deglobalization', p. 83.

33. The incentives to proliferate exist even among the allies of a hegemonic power. As Robert M. Hathaway, *Ambiguous partnership: Britain and America, 1944–47* (New York: Columbia University Press, 1981, p. 227) explained, years later former Prime Minister Clement Atlee of Great Britain explained Britain's decision to build a bomb: 'It had become essential', he remembered. 'We had to hold up our position *vis-à-vis* the Americans. We couldn't allow ourselves to be wholly in their hands.'

34. Khanna, *The second world*.

35. Khanna, *The second world*; Mark Leonard, *What does China think?* Ottawa: Public Affairs, 2008.

36. Ian Buruma, 'After America: is the West being overtaken by the rest?' *New Yorker*, 21 April 2008, pp. 126–30.

37. Zakaria, *The post-American world*, p. 11.

Chapter 2. Same Agenda, Different Results: The UN Interventions in Cambodia and Somalia after the Cold War *Chen Kertcher*

1. Alex Bellamy, Paul Williams and Stuart Griffin, *Understanding peacekeeping*, Cambridge: Polity Press, 2004, pp. 57–92; Erwin A. Schmidl, 'The evolution of peace operations from the nineteenth century', in Erwin A. Schmidl (ed.) *Peace operations between peace and war: four studies*, London: Frank Cass, 2000, pp. 4–20; Ramesh Thakur and Albrecht Schnabel, 'Cascading generations of peacekeeping: across the Mogadishu line to Kosovo and Timor', in Ramesh Thakur and Albrecht Schnabel (eds) *United Nations peacekeeping operations: ad hoc missions, permanent engagement*, New York: United Nations University Press, 2001, pp. 3–25.

2. Willaim J. Durch, 'Introduction to anarchy: intervention in Somalia', in William J. Durch (ed.) *UN peacekeeping, American politics, and the uncivil wars of the 1990s*, New York: St Martin's Press, 1996, pp. 352–3; Paul Kennedy, *The parliament of man: the past, present, and future of the United Nations*, New York: Vintage Books, 2007, pp. 94–5; Indar Jit Rikhye, *The politics and practice of United Nations peacekeeping: past, present and future*, Clementsport, NS: Canadian Peacekeeping Press, 2000, pp. 29–32, 46–53; James A. Schear, 'Riding the tiger: the United Nations and Cambodia's struggle for peace', in William J. Durch (ed.) *UN peacekeeping, American politics, and the uncivil wars of the 1990s*,

New York: St Martin's Press, 1996, pp. 175–6; United Nations, *The Blue Helmets: a review of United Nations peace-keeping*, New York: United Nations Department of Public Information, 3rd edn, 1996, pp. 481, 315–16.

3. S/PV 3303, 4 November 1993; S/RES/880, 4 November 1993.

4. Willaim J. Durch, 'Introduction to anarchy', pp. 350–3; Trevor Findlay, *The use of force in UN peace operations*, Oxford: Oxford University Press, 2002, pp. 204–18; United Nations, *The Blue Helmets*, pp. 287–316.

5. For the academic discourse on 'peace building', see Simon Chesterman, *You the people: the UN, transitional administration and state-building*, Oxford: Oxford University Press, 2004; Roland Paris, *At war's end: building peace after civil conflict*, Cambridge: Cambridge University Press, 2004.

6. S/RES/718, 18 October 1991; S/RES/733, 23 January 1992; S/RES/814, 26 March 1993; S/23613, 19 February 1992; S/25168, 26 January 1993, annex I–IV.

7. For a detailed discussion on the phases of UN intervention in Somalia, see Chen Kertcher, *The search for peace – or for a state: UN intervention in Somalia 1992–95*, Jerusalem: Harry S. Truman Research Institute for the Advancement of Peace, 2003.

8. Marrack Goulding, *Peacemonger*, London: John Murray, 2002, pp. 339–41.

9. For detailed descriptions of the managerial and organizational problems of the operations in Cambodia, see Michael W. Doyle, *UN peacekeeping in Cambodia: UNTAC's civil mandate*, Boulder: Lynne Rienner, 1995; Trevor Findlay, *Cambodia: the legacy and lessons of UNTAC*, Oxford: Oxford University Press, 1995; Steven R. Ratner, *The new UN peacekeeping: building peace in lands of conflict after the cold war*, New York: St Martin's Press, 1995, pp. 137–208; Schear, 'Riding the tiger', pp. 135–91. For examples on Somalia, see Kenneth Allard, *Somalia operations: lessons learned*, Washington: CCRP, 1995; Walter Clarke and Jeffrey Herbst (eds) *Learning from Somalia: the lessons of armed humanitarian intervention*, Boulder: Westview, 1997; Durch, 'Introduction to anarchy', pp. 352–353; Robert B. Oakley and John I. Hirsch, *Somalia and Operation Restore Hope: reflections on peacemaking and peacekeeping*, Washington: United States Institute of Peace Press, 1995.

10. For a good general account on the long civil war in Cambodia, see David Chandler, *The tragedy of Cambodian history: politics, war, and revolution since 1945*, New Haven: Yale University Press, 1991; Marie Alexandrine Martin, *Cambodia: a shattered society*, translated by Mark W. McLeod, Berkeley: University of California Press, 1994.

11. S/23613, 19 February 1992.

12. Even in its operation in Namibia (UNTAG) between April 1989 and May 1990, its objectives were confined to supervision and not management. See Goulding, *Peacemonger*, pp. 139–75; United Nations, *The Blue Helmets*, pp. 203–29.

13. S/24090, 12 June 1992, para. 3–14; S/25154, 25 January 1993, para. 35–8; Yasushi Akashi, 'The challenges faced by UNTAC', *Japan Review of International Affairs*, Summer 1993, pp. 189–90, 196–7.

14. S/RES/840, 15 June 1993; United Nations, *The United Nations and Cambodia*, New York: UNDI, 1995, documents 90, 91, 93, 95, 96.

15. Boutros Boutros-Ghali, *Unvanquished: a US–UN saga*, New York: Random House, 1999, pp. 82–3.

16. E/CN.4/2003/114, 18 December 2002; E/CN.4/2005/116, 20 December, 2004; E/CN.4/RES/2005/77, 20 April 2005; E/CN.4/2006/110, 24 January 2006; E/CN.4/2006/110/Add.1, 8 March 2006.

17. S/23613, 19 February 1992, para. 23–51; Goulding, *Peacemonger*, pp. 245–5; Javier Pérez de Cuéllar, *Pilgrimage for peace: a secretary general's memoir*, New York: St Martin's Press, 1998, p. 461.

18. Doyle, *UN peacekeeping in Cambodia*; Findlay, *Cambodia*, pp. 59–63, 137–8.

19. The secretary general's reports show that, even when fully deployed, UNTAC had only between one to three people in the SOC government offices that UN officials considered as most important. S/24286, 14 July 1992, para. 16–18; S/24578, 21 September 1992, para. 29; S/25719, 3 May 1993, para. 57–9.

20. S/25719, 3 May 1993, para. 59.

21. S/24090, 12 June 1992, para. 3–14; Akashi, 'The challenges faced by UNTAC', pp. 189–93, 196–7; Boutros Boutros-Ghali, *Unvanquished*, pp. 34–5.

22. S/25154, 25 January 1993, para. 33–4; S/25719, 3 May 1993, para. 25; Akashi, 'The challenges faced by UNTAC', pp. 193–4.

23. Akashi, 'The challenges faced by UNTAC', pp. 192, 195.

24. S/25154, 25 January 1993, para. 56.

25. S/25154, 25 January 1993, para. 65, 72–3; Findlay, *Cambodia*, pp. 59–63.

26. S/25154, 25 January 1993, para. 57; for detailed account of failures and achievements of the supervision on civil governments, see Doyle, *UN peacekeeping*.

27. Findlay, *Cambodia*, pp. 62–3.

28. Michael W. Doyle, 'Authority and elections in Cambodia', in Michael W. Doyle, Ian Johnstone and Robert C. Orr (eds) *Keeping the peace: multidimensional UN operations in Cambodia and El Salvador*, Cambridge: Cambridge University Press, 1997, p. 153.

29. S/23613, 19 February 1992, para. 52–91.

30. S/24286, 14 July 1992, para. 1, 14; S/24578, 21 September 1992, para. 19–23; S/24800, 15 November 1992, para. 17.

31. S/25154, 25 January 1993, para. 35–8, 44–51; S/25719, 3 May 1993, para. 33–5, 39–41.

32. S/RES/792, 30 November 1992; S/25154, 25 January 1993, para. 39–42; S/25719, 3 May 1993, para. 36–8.

33. S/24578, 21 September 1992, para. 28, 34.

34. S/25154, 25 January 1993, para. 77–8.

35. S/24800, 15 November 1992, para. 11–13.; S/25719, 3 May 1993, para. 66–9.

36. S/24800, 15 November 1992, para. 19; S/25053, 5 January 1993; S/25154, 25 January 1993, para. 94–9; S/25289, 13 February 1993, para. 12–16; S/25719, 3 May 1993, para. 111–26; United Nations, *United Nations and Cambodia*, pp. 251–2.

37. S/25154, 25 January 1993, para. 94–103.

38. S/24578, 21 September 1992, para. 52–3; S/25154, 25 January 1993, para. 65–9; Sandra Whitworth, *Men, militarism, and UN peacekeeping: a gendered analysis*, Boulder: Lynne Rienner, 2004, pp. 62–3.

39. S/RES/792, 30 November 1992, para. 13; S/25154, 25 January 1993, para. 88–90; S/25289, 13 February 1993, para. 20–24; S/25719, 3 May 1993, para. 98–103. Philippe Le Billon, 'The political ecology of transition in Cambodia 1989–1999: war, peace and forest exploitation', *Development and Change*, vol. 31, 2000, pp. 785–805; Philippe Le Billon, 'Logging in muddy waters: the politics of forest exploitation in Cambodia', *Critical Asian Studies*, vol. 34, no. 4, 2002, p. 565; Sorpong Peou, 'Cambodia in 1998: from despair to hope?' *Asian Survey*, vol. 39, no. 1, 1999, p. 23.

40. Hussein M. Adam, 'A terrible beauty being born?', in William I. Zartman (ed.) *Collapsed states: the disintegration and restoration of legitimate authority*, Boulder: Lynne Rienner, 1995, pp. 69–89; Lee Cassanelli, 'Victims and vulnerable groups in southern Somalia', Ottawa, Canada, May 1995, at: http://www.cisr.gc.ca/cgi-bin; Daniel Compagnon, 'Somali armed movements, the interplay of political entrepreneurship and clan-based factions', in Christophe Clapham (ed.) *African guerrillas*, Oxford: James Currey, 1998, pp. 75–9; Kertcher, *The search for peace*, pp. 6–7; Ioan M. Lewis, 'The Ogaden and the fragility of Somali segmentary nationalism', *African Affairs*, vol. 88, no. 353, 1989, pp. 573–9; Michael Maren, *The road to hell: the ravaging effects of foreign aid and international charity*, New York: Free Press, 1997, pp. 34–6, 52–5, 106–14.

41. Jeffrey Clark, 'Debacle in Somalia', *Foreign Affairs*, vol. 72, no. 1, 1993, pp. 109–23; Steven Livingston and Todd Euchus, 'Humanitarian crises and US foreign policy: Somalia and the CNN effect reconsidered', *Political Communication*, vol. 12, no. 4, 1995, pp. 413–29; Andrew Natsios, 'Humanitarian relief intervention in Somalia: the economics of chaos', in Walter Clarke and Jeffrey Herbst (eds) *Learning from Somalia: the lessons of armed humanitarian intervention*, Boulder: Westview, 1997, pp. 77–82; Colin L. Powell and Joseph E. Persico, *My American journey*, New York: Random House, 1996, p. 550; Adam Roberts, *Humanitarian action in war: aid, protection and impartiality in a policy vacuum*, Oxford: Oxford University Press, 1996, Adelphi Paper No. 305 of International Institute for Strategic Studies, London, p. 16; James L. Woods, 'US government decision-making process during humanitarian operations in Somalia', in Walter Clarke and Jeffrey Herbst (eds) *Learning from Somalia: the lessons of armed humanitarian intervention*, Boulder: Westview, 1997, pp. 151–6.

42. S/25168, January 26, 1993, Annex I–IV.

43. On the term 'collapsed state', see William I. Zartman, 'Introduction', in William I. Zartman, *Collapsed states: the disintegration and restoration of legitimate authority*, Boulder: Lynne Rienner Publishers, 1995, pp. 1–11.

44. For the different views on the causes of the failure of the operation in Somalia, see Walter Clarke and Jeffrey Herbst, 'Somalia and the future of humanitarian intervention', in Walter Clarke and Jeffrey Herbst (eds) *Learning from Somalia: the lessons of armed humanitarian intervention*, Boulder: Westview,

1997, pp. 239–52; Durch, 'Introduction to anarchy', pp. 352–3; Oakley and Hirsch, *Somalia and Operation Restore Hope*, pp. 161–71; United Nations, *The United Nations and Somalia, 1992–96*, New York: United Nations Department of Public Information, 1996, pp. 84–7.

45. Kertcher, *The search for peace*, pp. 25–33.

46. On Boutros-Ghali's efforts during 1994 to persuade the international community to continue its support for UNOSOM II, see: S/1994/839, 18 July 1994; S/1994/898, 30 July 1994; S/1994/977, 17 August 1994. Australia, Djibouti, Kenya, New Zealand, Nigeria and Arab states supported Boutros-Ghali's stance on the need to continue the international intervention in some way. S/PV.3317, 18 November 1993; S/PV.3385, 31 May 1994; S/1994/1204, 22 October 1994; S/PV.3447, 4 November 1994.

47. Kenneth Menkhaus, *Somalia: state collapse and the threat of terrorism*, Oxford: Oxford University Press, 2004; Kenneth Menkhaus, 'The crisis in Somalia: tragedy in five acts', *African Affairs*, vol. 106, no. 424, July 2007, pp. 357–90.

48. S/1994/614, para. 2–12, Annex I, 24 May 1994; S/1994/839, para. 2, 54–9, 18 July 1994; S/1994/898, 30 July 1994; S/1994/977, para. 7–16, 17 August 1994; S/1994/1245, 3 November 1994; *Africa Research Bulletin*, November 1993, 11243; *Africa Research Bulletin*, December 1993, 11275; Abdukarim Ahmed Guleid and Jack L. Davies, 'Is it peace for Somalia?', *New African*, no. 319, May 1994, pp. 7–9; Ahmed Nur Sheikh Ali Hassan, 'Build a new Somalia', *New African*, June 1994, p. 19; Kenneth Menkhaus, 'International peacebuilding and the dynamics of local and national reconciliation in Somalia', in Walter Clarke and Jeffrey Herbst (eds) *Learning from Somalia: the lessons of armed humanitarian intervention*, Boulder: Westview, 1997, pp. 47–8.

49. *Africa Research Bulletin*, January 1991, 9715.

50. For examples of Mahdi's requests to the UN to send robust forces to Mogadishu, see United Nations, *The United Nations and Somalia*, document 1; S/23445, 20 January 1992; S/23829, 21 April 1992, para. 4, 15–22.

51. On the support that Ali Mahdi received from UN representatives, see Kertcher, *The search for peace*. For the main battles between Aidid's and Barre's forces, which established Aidid's military superiority in the centre and south, see *Africa Research Bulletin*, 10472, February 1992; *Africa Research Bulletin*, 10552–53, April 1992; *Africa Research Bulletin*, 10591, May 1992; *Africa Research Bulletin*, 11718, January 1995; Anon, 'Somalia: enemy's enemy', *Africa Confidential*, vol. 33, no. 9, 8 May 1992, p. 8; Bryan M. Booker, 'Somalia: the roots of today's conflict', *Strategy & Tactics*, no. 171, November/December 1994, pp. 53–61.

52. Bernhard Helander, Mohamed Haji Mukhtar and Ioan M. Lewis, *Building peace from below? A critical review of the district councils in the Bay and Bakool regions of southern Somalia*, in http://Arlaadinet.com, April 1995.

53. S/1994/653, 1 June 1994, para. 54–80; Drysdale, John, 'Foreign military intervention in Somalia: the root cause of the shift from UN peacekeeping to peacemaking and its consequence', in Walter Clarke and Jeffrey Herbst (eds) *Learning from Somalia: the lessons of armed humanitarian intervention*, Boulder: Westview Press, 1997, p. 131.

54. Martin R. Ganzglass, 'The restoration of the Somali justice system', in Walter Clarke and Jeffrey Herbst (eds) *Learning from Somalia: the lessons of armed humanitarian intervention*, Boulder: Westview Press, 1997, pp. 27–8; F. M. Lorenz, 'Law and anarchy in Somalia', *Parameters*, winter 1993–94, pp. 27–41; F. M. Lorenz, 'Confronting thievery in Somalia', *Military Review*, August 1994, pp. 46–55; F. M. Lorenz, 'Weapons confiscation policy during the first phases of Operation Restore Hope', *Small Wars and Insurgencies*, vol. 5, no. 3, 1994, pp. 409–25; Robert G. Patman, 'Disarming Somalia: the contrasting fortunes of United States and Australian peacekeepers during United Nations intervention, 1992–1993', *African Affairs*, vol. 96, no. 385, October 1997, pp. 519–26.

55. Drysdale, 'Foreign military intervention', p. 130–1; Terrence Lyons and Ahmed I. Samatar, *Somalia: state collapse, multilateral intervention, and strategies for political reconstruction*, Washington: Brookings Institution, 1995, p. 50; Oakley and Hirsch, *Somalia and Operation Restore Hope*, pp. 76–7; Paolo Tripodi, *The colonial legacy in Somalia: Rome and Mogadishu: from colonial administration to Operation Restore Hope*, London: Macmillan Press, 1999, p. 147.

56. S/26022, 1 July 1993; S/26317, 17 August 1993; S/26663, 28 October 1993; S/26738, 12 November 1993; S/26823, 1 December 1993, S/26824, 1 December 1993; S/1994/653, 1 June 1994; S/RES/837, 6 June 1993; S/RES/865, 22 September 1993; S/RES/878, 29 October 1993; S/RES/885, 16 November 1993; S/RES/886, 18 November 1993; S/RES/897, 4 February 1994; *Africa Research Bulletin*, July 1993, 11095–11096; *Africa Research Bulletin*, 11053–11055, June 1993; *Africa Research Bulletin*, 11095–11096, July 1993; *Africa Research Bulletin*, 11201, October 1993; Anon, 'Somalia: hope denied', *Africa Confidential*, vol. 34, no. 14, 16 July 1993, p. 8; Mark Bowden, *Black hawk down: a story of modern war*, New York: Atlantic Monthly Press, 1999; Robert Oakley, http://www.pbs.org/wgbh/pages/frontline/shows/ambush/interviews, 1998.

57. *Africa Research Bulletin*, November 1994, 11661; *Africa Research Bulletin*, January 1995, 11730; Anon, 'Somalia: Aydeed's local difficulties', *Africa Confidential*, vol. 35, no. 12, 17 June 1994, p. 7; Anon, 'Somalia: warlords restored', *Africa Confidential*, vol. 35, no. 20, 7 October 1994, pp. 1–3; Anon, 'Aydeed's dilemma', *Africa Confidential*, vol. 36, no. 1, 6 January 1995, pp. 6–7; Menkhaus, 'International peacebuilding', p. 48.

58. S/26317, para. 6–13, 15–63, Annex I and II, 17 August 1993; S/26738, 12 November, 1993, para. 34–5; Ganzglass, 'The restoration of the Somali justice system', pp. 30–3.

59. Natsios, 'Humanitarian relief intervention', pp. 77–95; John Prendergast, *The bones of our children are not yet buried: the looming spectre of famine and massive human rights abuse in Somalia*, Washington: Center of Concern, 1994.

60. An excellent account on the rationale behind the work of aid agencies in Somalia can be found in Maren, *The road to hell*. On the destabilizing effects of international aid on the political process, see Kertcher, *The search for peace*, pp. 10–11, 16–17, 26–8, 32–3.

Chapter 3.   External Mediation and Internal Ownership: The Belfast and St Andrews Agreements Compared   *Adrian Guelke*

1. Rick Wilford, 'Northern Ireland: St Andrews – the Long Good Friday Agreement', in Jonathan Bradbury (ed.) *Devolution, regionalism and regional development: the UK experience*, London: Routledge, 2008, pp. 67–8.

2. George J. Mitchell, *Making peace*, London: W. Heinemann, 1999, p. 5.

3. Eamonn O'Kane, *Britain, Ireland and Northern Ireland since 1960: the totality of relationships*, London: Routledge, 2007, p. 159.

4. Ibid., pp. 152–3.

5. This is a formula a Belgian mathematician and lawyer devised for the proportional allocation of posts. Under its terms, the first choice of ministerial portfolio goes to the party with the largest number of seats, with subsequent choices depending on the relative strength of the parties. Normally, the second choice goes to the party with the second largest number of seats, but in cases where the largest party is more than double the size of the next largest party, the formula awards the second choice to the largest party.

6. Text quoted in Michael Cox, Adrian Guelke and Fiona Stephen (eds) *A farewell to Arms? Beyond the Good Friday Agreement*, Manchester: Manchester University Press, 2006, p. 465.

7. Ibid., p. 463.

8. St Andrews Agreement, 2006, para. 9, accessed at http://www.nio.gov.uk/st_andrews_agreement.pdf

9. Kathryn Tomey, 'Peaceline plan for integrated primary', *Belfast Telegraph*, 23 May 2007.

10. Brendan O'Leary, 'The nature of the agreement', *Fordham International Law Journal*, vol. 22, no. 4, 1999.

Chapter 4   International Engagement and the Yugoslav War of Dissolution   *James Gow*

1. In this chapter I draw extensively on James Gow, *Triumph of the lack of will: international diplomacy and the Yugoslav crisis*, New York: Columbia University Press, 1997, key parts of which were adapted and expanded from James Gow, 'Nervous bunnies: the international community and the Yugoslav war of dissolution: the politics of military intervention in a time of change', in Lawrence Freedman (ed.) *Military intervention in European Conflicts*, Oxford: Blackwell for the Political Quarterly, 1994; and James Gow, *The Serbian project and its adversaries: a strategy of war crimes*, London: C. Hurst & Co., 2003.

2. See Milan Andrejevich, 'The future of Bosnia and Hercegovina: a sovereign republic or cantonisation?' *RFE/RL Report on Eastern Europe*, 5 July 1991.

3. Herbert Okun, UN special adviser and deputy-head of civilian affairs, UNPROFOR, Interview, 'Diplomacy and Deceit', Channel 4 TV, 2 August 1993, Media Transcription Service, *Bloody Bosnia*, MTS/M2578.WPS, p. 4.

4. For more extensive discussion of some of these, see Gow, 'Nervous bunnies'.

5. See, for example, Andrew Marr, 'Politicians let NATO down over Bosnia', *The Independent*, 11 September 1993.

6. See argument earlier in this chapter.

7. Manfred Werner, 'NATO's role in a changing Europe', *IISS Adelphi Paper*, no. 284, London: Brassey's for the IISS, 1994, p.98.

8. The handling of the Yugoslav crisis, following on from the Gulf conflict, offered the West a chance to confirm a partnership with Moscow that would have accorded the Russian Federation status and strengthened the positions of the reformers and Westernizers, who would thus have had something to show for their positive and friendly relations with the West. Instead, critically, over the Vance–Owen plan, the chance to lock Moscow into a collective crisis management framework was lost. Russia's initiatives were, in effect, dismissed and its willingness to back Western initiatives was taken for granted or ignored, and both resulted in a Russian retreat from open cooperation. The loss of this historic chance to cement post-cold war cooperation – one of the most important aspects of international failure – was a function of the lack of political will in Western capitals either to deal with the war in Bosnia or to seal the relationship with Russia.

9. James Gow, 'Europe and the Muslim world: European Union enlargement and the western Balkans', *Southeast European and Black Sea Studies*, vol. 7, no. 3, September 2007.

10. United Nations document B92, 23 April 2008.

11. In a qualified sense, the degree of agreement within and between a smaller number of countries prior to the US-led action over Iraq in 2003, might also be said to have generated problematic analysis and poor planning, policy or implementation, as a result.

Chapter 5 The Reactive Crisis Management of the European Union in the Western Balkans: Policy Objectives, Capabilities and Effectiveness *Stefan Wolff and Annemarie Peen Rodt*

1. This is not to deny that the EU has had two successive programmes in support of the Northern Ireland peace process since the mid-1990s and that European integration has provided institutional structures and incentives for cross-border cooperation both in Northern Ireland and in South Tyrol that have had a generally positive, albeit hardly quantifiable impact on conflict resolution in both of these cases.

2. There have been further ESDP civilian, police and military operations in the South Caucasus, Southeast Asia, Middle East and Africa, and in April 2006 the council signed a joint action establishing an EU planning team (EUPT) for a possible future EU crisis management operation in the field of rule of law (and possible other areas) in Kosovo, which has been deployed following Kosovo's unilateral declaration of independence in February 2008.

3. A. G. Kintis, 'The EU's foreign policy and the war in former Yugoslavia', in M. Holland, *Common foreign and security policy*, London: Pinter, 1997; L. Silber and A. Little, *The death of Yugoslavia*, London: Penguin Books, 1996.

4. It is estimated that between 7000 and 8000 Muslim men and boys were killed

by Serb nationalists in Srebrenica in 1995 (Silber and Little, *The death of Yugoslavia*).

5. Kintis, 'The EU's foreign policy'; N. Morris, 'Humanitarian intervention in the Balkans' in J. Welsh, *Humanitarian intervention and international relations*, Oxford: Oxford University Press, 2004; P. C. Pentland, 'The EU and southeastern Europe after Dayton', *Europe–Russia working chapters*, Ottowa: Carleton University, January, 2003. The argument here is not that the EU was responsible for these massacres, but rather that it, alongside other international organizations, failed to create conditions in which such atrocities would be impossible to commit.

6. The EU did, however, go through a learning process in the Balkans. After the Dayton agreement ended the war, the EU gradually began a more coherent and effective response to political stabilization and economic recovery in the region. The EU assumed a modest role in the first three years of the international protectorate in Bosnia-Herzegovina and contributed significantly in terms of humanitarian aid and assistance in the post-conflict reconstruction in the wider region, but it was not until after the Kosovo campaign that the EU re-emerged with a comprehensive vision for the western Balkans and a renewed claim to leadership. Today the EU, heavily engaged in crisis management is widely recognized as one of if not the most important international actor in the region (F. Cameron, 'The European Union's role in the Balkans', in B. Blitz (ed.) *War and change in the Balkans*, Cambridge: Cambridge University Press, 2006; E. Faucompret. *The dismemberment of Yugoslavia and the European Union*, Antwerp: University of Antwerp, 2001; Silber and Little, *The death of Yugoslavia*).

7. Faucompret, *The dismemberment of Yugoslavia*.

8. Marc Weller and Stefan Wolff (eds) *Institutions for the management of ethnopolitical conflicts in central and eastern Europe*, Strasbourg: Council of Europe Publishing, 2008.

9. The Petersberg declaration was the WEU's response to calls for greater burden-sharing within NATO through the elaboration of a coherent European Security and Defence Identity (ESDI) built around the WEU. In the context of the European Convention, important amendments and revisions to the Petersberg declaration were proposed by the so-called Barnier Report (European Convention, *Final Report of Working Group VIII on defense, chaired by Michael Barnier (Barnier Report)*, Brussels, 16 December 2002).

10. The Cologne summit, importantly, happened just at the end of NATO's intervention in the Kosovo crisis, which in turn visibly influenced the decision-making by heads of state and government in Cologne.

11. European Union, 'Treaty of Lisbon amending the Treaty on European Union and the Treaty establishing the European Community', *Official Journal of the European Union*, English edition, C 306, vol. 50, 17 December 2007 (available online at http://bookshop.europa.eu/eubookshop/FileCache/PUBPDF/FXAC07306ENC/FXAC07306ENC_002.pdf; accessed 3 April 2008).

12. Ibid.

13. Ibid.

14. For a somewhat different take on the capabilities problem, see U. Schneckener, *Developing and applying EU crisis management: test case Macedonia*, ECMI Working Paper no. 14, Flensburg: European Centre for Minority Issues, 2002, pp. 37–9 (http://www.ecmi.de/doc/download/working_paper_14.pdf).

15. Presidency Conclusions, European Council Meeting in Laeken, 14 and 15 December 2001, paragraph 6. SN 300/1/101 REV 1.

16. Ibid., Annex II.

17. This has also been emphasized by C. Piana, 'The EU's decision-making process in the common foreign and security policy: the case of the former Yugoslav Republic of Macedonia', *European Foreign Affairs Review*, vol. 7, no. 2, 2002, p. 211, in relation to the crisis in Macedonia: 'The creation of the post of High Representative definitely brought the visibility/continuity element that was lacking in the CFSP.'

18. C. Hill, 'The EU's capacity for conflict prevention', *European Foreign Affairs Review*, vol. 6, no. 3, 2001, p. 328.

19. European Council, Council regulation (EC) No 381/2001 of 26 February 2001 creating a rapid reaction mechanism.

20. European Commission, 'Information note: the rapid reaction mechanism supporting the European Union's policy objectives in conflict prevention and crisis management', 2002 (http://www.europa.eu.int/comm/external_relations/cfsp/doc/rrm.pdf).

21. European Union, 'Treaty of Lisbon'.

22. We do not include the most recent EU mission (EULEX Kosovo) in the following analysis.

23. European Council, *European Union Police Mission in Bosnia and Herzegovina*, official website of the council of the European Union (available online at http://www.consilium.europa.eu/cms3_fo/showPage.asp?id=585&lang=EN&mode=g; accessed 9 March 2008).

24. EUFOR was established in 1995 in Lisbon as a military force under the Petersberg tasks. Contributing nations are France, Italy, Portugal and Spain. Operational since 1998 and listed in the force catalogues of EU, NATO, OSCE and UN, it has been part of NATO operation Allied Guardian in Albania in 2000.

25. European Council, Council joint action of 12 July 2004 on the European Union military operation in Bosnia and Herzegovina, 2004/570/CFSP.

26. The operation's field commander was EUFOR military staff, but also part of the command structure of this particular operation. He reported to the EU operation commander, in this case NATO's deputy supreme allied commander for Europe. The EU military committee monitored the conduct of the operation and received reports from the operation commander as well as providing the first point of call for him in relation to the council. Even though the operation commander simultaneously had a position within the NATO command structure, he only reported to EU bodies and the chain of command remained under the EU's political control and strategic direction.

In contrast to the EU Police Mission, the EU special representative to Macedonia, Alexis Brouhns, was not part of the command chain, but acted, together with the SG/HR, as primary point of contact for Macedonian authorities and as key liaison for EU commanders in the field. This was in many ways similar to what had happened one year earlier in relation to the EU's Operation Concordia taking over from NATO's Operation Allied Harmony in Macedonia.

27. SHAPE, 'SHAPE–EU cooperation: background information', 2004, available online at http://www.nato.int/shape/issues/shape_eu/background.htm; SHAPE, 'Operation Althea', available online at http://www.nato.int/shape/issues/shape_eu/althea.htm

28. C. Hill, 'The capability–expectations gap, or conceptualising Europe's international role', *Journal of Common Market Studies*, vol. 31, no. 3, 1993, pp. 312–13.

29. Ibid., pp. 311–12.

30. G. Müller-Brandeck-Bocquet, 'The new CFSP and ESDP decision-making system of the European Union', *European Foreign Affairs Review*, vol. 7, no. 3, 2002, p. 278.

31. This is the problem of CFSP as a 'moving target'. See F. Cameron, 'The European Union's growing international role: closing the capability–expectations gap?' Paper presented at the conference on the European Union in International Affairs, National Europe Centre, Australian National University, July 2002. http://www.anu.edu.au/NEC/fraser_cameron.pdf

32. Solana, *Report on the western Balkans presented to the Lisbon European Council by the Secretary-General/High Representative together with the Commission*, Brussels, 21 March 2000, SN 2032/2/00/REV2.

33. For example, the decision to extend Operation Concordia in Macedonia was contingent on a North Atlantic Council decision to extend availability of NATO assets to the EU.

34. R. Schuwirth, 'Hitting the Helsinki headline goal', *NATO Review*, Autumn 2002, http://www.nato.int/docu/review/2002/issue3/english/art4.html

35. The two big (known) unknowns in this respect are the closure of the OHR in Bosnia and Herzegovina and the outcome, and impact, of the Kosovo final status negotiations.

36. The preference of a multilateral approach to crisis management can also be deduced from the fact that in both current crisis management operations in the western Balkans and in the brief military operation in the DRC, the European Council either did not move before the UN (DRC) or explicitly inferred the legitimacy of its operation, at least in part, from a *preceding* UN resolution. Cf. M. E. Smith, 'Diplomacy by degree: the legalisation of EU foreign policy', *Journal of Common Market Studies*, vol. 39, no. 1, 2001, p. 99.

Chapter 6. American Middle East Strategy and the Bush Legacy
Robert J. Lieber

1. See, for example, John Lewis Gaddis, *Surprise, security and the American experience*, Cambridge, MA: Harvard university Press, 2004; Robert Kagan, *Dangerous*

nation, New York: Knopf, 2006; Robert J. Lieber, *The American era: power and strategy for the 21st century*, Cambridge: Cambridge University Press, 2007.

2. This analysis of the US-Israeli relationship expands on my recent essay, Robert J. Lieber, 'Der amerikanische Freund', *Internationale Politik*, Berlin, May 2008.

3. For an earlier treatment of this relationship, see Robert J. Lieber, 'US–Israeli relations since 1948', in Robert O. Freedman (ed.) *Israel's first fifty years*, Gainesville: University Press of Florida, 2000.

4. See in particular the insightful account of this episode by Abraham Ben-Zvi, *Decade of transition: Eisenhower, Kennedy, and the origins of the American–Israel alliance*, New York: Columbia University Press, 1998.

5. Lawrence Freedman, *A choice of enemies: America confronts the Middle East*, New York: Public Affairs, 2008, argues that the Camp David agreement leading to the peace treaty was one of three watershed events in 1978–79, along with the Islamic revolution in Iran and the socialist revolution in Afghanistan, to have shaped America's Middle East role since that time.

6. The late Saadia Touval, *The peace brokers: mediators in the Arab–Israeli conflict, 1948–1979*, Princeton: Princeton University Press, 1982, made a related point, that because the USA was a 'biased intermediary' and a reliable ally of Israel, the Arabs regarded it as better able to win concessions.

7. George W. Bush, 'President Bush calls for new Palestinian leadership', Office of the Press Secretary, The White House, Washington DC, 24 June 2002, http://www.whitehouse.gov/news/releases/2002/06/20020624-3.html, accessed 9 May 2008.

8. See, for example, John F. Riley (ed.) *American public opinion and US foreign policy*, Chicago: Council on Foreign Relations, 1995, pp. 20 and 26.

9. Gallup polling data cited in Yitzhak Benhorin, 'Poll: more Americans are pro-Israeli', Ynetnews.com, 6 March 2008.

10. Jonah Newman, 'Survey: Americans see Israel as ally', *JerusalemPost.com*, 18 November 2007.

11. Poll by Public Opinion Strategies and Greenberg Quinlan Rosner Research, commissioned by the Israel Project, 31 March 2008, http://www.theisraelproject.org/site/apps/nlnet/content2.aspx?c=hsJPK0PIJpH&b=689705&ct=5155819. See also Robert Mabry, 'A six-day war: its aftermath in American public opinion', *Pew Forum on Religion and Public Life*, 30 May 2007.

12. Josef Joffe, 'A world without Israel', *Foreign Policy*, January/February 2005, pp. 36–42.

13. Douglas Feith, *War and decision*, New York: Harper Collins, 2008, who was among the policymakers involved in the run-up to and aftermath of the Iraq war, believed that strategic threat was the most important factor.

14. This discussion of the Bush second inaugural draws upon and expands on my earlier essay, Robert J. Lieber, 'Translating the Bush inaugural address', *US Foreign Policy Agenda: Electronic Journal of the US Department of State*, 24 January 2005.

15. See James Madison, *The Federalist Papers*, no. 10, 1788.

16. See Isaiah Berlin, 'Two concepts of liberty (1958)', in Isaiah Berlin, *Four essays on liberty*, Oxford: Oxford University Press, 1969; also Michael Mandelbaum, *Democracy's good name: the rise and risks of the world's most popular form of government*, New York: Public Affairs, 2008.

17. For a more comprehensive assessment of these three realities, see Lieber, *The American Era*.

18. Azar Gat, 'The return of authoritarian great powers', *Foreign Affairs*, vol. 86, no. 4, July/August 2007, pp. 59–69.

19. Robert Kagan, 'The return of history', *Los Angeles Times*, 5 August 2007.

20. Michael Ross, 'Blood barrels', *Foreign Affairs*, vol. 87, no. 3, May/June 2008, pp. 2–8.

21. Fouad Ajami, 'Bush of Arabia', *Wall Street Journal*, 8 January 2008.

Chapter 8.   The Reagan–Bush Administrations and the Middle East: Institutional and Bureaucratic Rivalries   *Robert David Johnson*

1. Robert David Johnson, *Congress and the cold war*, Cambridge: Cambridge University Press, 2005, pp. 144–241.

2. Jeane Kirkpatrick, 'Dictatorships and double standards', *Commentary*, November 1979.

3. *Washington Post*, 11 January 1981.

4. S. T. Gilbert, *Reagan and the AWACS sale to Saudi Arabia: bureaucratic politics in action*, Washington, DC: National War College, 1996.

5. *New York Times*, 24 January 1980.

6. Nicholas Laham, *Selling AWACS to Saudi Arabia: the Reagan administration and the balancing of America's competing interests in the Middle East*, Westport, CT: Praeger, 2002, pp. 1–33.

7. Ibid., pp. 34–62.

8. James A. Phillips, 'The AWACS sale: prospects for US policy', *Heritage Foundation Backgrounder*, no. 153, 16 October 1981.

9. *Wall Street Journal*, 29 October 1981.

10. *Time*, 5 October 1981.

11. *Time*, 9 November 1981.

12. *Wall Street Journal*, 29 October 1981.

13. *Time*, 9 November 1981.

14. Michael Barone and Grant Ujifusa, *The almanac of American politics 1984*, Washington, DC: National Journal, 1983, p. 411.

15. 101 *Congressional Record*, 97th Congress, 1st session, p. 25861 (28 October 1981).

16. The Nelson–Bingham amendment remained on the books for two more years, until the Supreme Court ruled its legislative veto mechanism unconstitutional *INS v. Chadha*, 462 US 919 (1983).

17. *Time*, 9 November 1981.

18. Erika Alin, *The United States and the 1958 Lebanon crisis*, Lanham, MD: University Press of America, 1994.

19. George Shultz, *Turmoil and triumph: my years as secretary of state*, New York: Charles Scribner's Sons, 1993.

20. John Kelly, 'Lebanon', *RAND Occasional Paper Series*, http:// rand.org/pubs/conf_proceedings/CF129/CF-129.chapter6.html, accessed 10 May 2008.

21. Ibid.

22. Ronald Reagan, 'Report dated September 29, 1982 from President Ronald Reagan to Hon. Thomas P. O'Neill, Jr., Speaker of the House of Representatives, consistent with section 4(a)(2) of the War Powers Resolution, relative to the use of US Forces in Lebanon', *The War Powers Resolution: Relevant Documents, Reports, Correspondence*, 103rd Congress, 2nd session, p. 78.

23. Michael Rubner, 'The Reagan administration, the 1973 War Powers Resolution, and the invasion of Grenada', *Political Science Quarterly*, vol. 100, 1985–86, pp. 627–47.

24. *New York Times*, 28 June 1983.

25. Ibid.

26. US House of Representatives, Committee on Foreign Affairs, 'Letter of September 27, 1983 to Hon. Clement J. Zablocki, Chairman, Committee on Foreign Affairs, from President Ronald Reagan', *The War Powers Resolution: Relevant Documents, Reports, Correspondence*, 103rd Congress, 2nd session, p. 83; *Washington Post*, 13 October 1983.

27. http://www.pbs.org/wgbh/amex/reagan/timeline/index_4.html, accessed 10 May 2008.

28. *New York Times*, 11 January 1987.

29. 128 *Congressional Record*, 97th Congress, 2nd session, p. 29466 (8 December 1982).

30. *Wall Street Journal*, 11 February 1985.

31. *Washington Post*, 15 April 1985.

32. *Time*, 6 May 1985.

33. Theodore Draper, *Very thin line: the Iran-contra affairs*, New York: Touchstone, 1992.

34. Charles Taylor, 'Charlie Wilson's war', *Salon*, 21 July 2003.

35. Steve Coll, *Ghost wars: the secret history of the CIA, Afghanistan, and Bin Laden, from the Soviet invasion to September 10, 2001*, New York: Penguin, 2004, pp. 19–70.

36. George Crile, *Charlie Wilson's war: the extraordinary story of how the wildest man in Congress and a rogue CIA agent changed the history of our times*, New York: Grove Press, 1997.

37. Philip Zelikow and Condoleeza Rice, *Germany unified and Europe transformed: a study in statecraft*, Cambridge: Harvard University Press, 1997.

38. Rick Atkinson, *Crusade: the untold story of the Persian Gulf war*, New York: Mariner Books, 1994, pp. 1–12.

39. National Security Directive 26, 2 October 1989, http://www.fas.org/irp/ offdocs/nsd/nsd26.pdf, accessed 10 May 2008.

40. Christian Alfonsi, *Circle in the sand: why we went back to Iraq*, New York: Doubleday, 2006, p. xx.

41. *Time*, 11 March 1991.

42.   http://www.fas.org/spp/starwars/congress/1992/h920428g.htm,   accessed 10 May 2008.

43.   Michael Gordon and Bernard Trainor, *The generals' war: the inside story of the conflict in the Gulf*, Boston: Back Bay Press, 1995, pp. 31–8.

44.   *New York Times*, 9 November 1990.

45.   *Washington Post*, 30 November 1990.

46.   *New York Times*, 21 November 1990.

47.   *Dellums v. Bush*, 752 F. Supp. 1141 (1990).

Chapter 9.   The EU and its Efforts to Resolve the Palestinian-Israeli Conflict   *Georg Simonis*

1.   Jan Zielonka, *Europe as empire: the nature of the enlarged European Union*, Oxford: Oxford University Press, 2006.

2.   Niklas Luhmann, *Legitimation durch Verfahren*, Neuwied/Berlin: Luchterhand, 1969.

3.   Fritz W. Scharpf, *Governing in Europe: effective and democratic?* Oxford: Oxford University Press, 1999.

4.   Ulrich Beck and Edgar Grande, *Das kosmopolitische Europa*, Frankfurt/M: SV Edition Zweite Moderne, 2004.

5.   Sven Biscop, *The European security strategy: a global agenda for positive power*, Aldershot: Ashgate, 2005, p. 15.

6.   New Article 8, Lisbon Treaty 12/2007.

7.   This perspective deviates from those of Markus Jachtenfuchs, 'The governance approach to European integration', *Journal of Common Market Studies*, vol. 39, no. 2, 2001, pp. 245–64; Sandra Lavenex, 'EU external governance in wider Europe', *Journal of European Public Policy*, vol. 11, no. 4, 2004, pp. 680–700; Frank Schimmelfennig and Ulrich Sedelmeier, 'Governance by conditionality: EU rule transfer to the candidate countries of central and eastern Europe', *Journal of European Public Policy*, vol. 11, no. 4, 2004, pp. 661–79; Frank Schimmelfennig and Wolfgang Wagner, 'Preface: external governance in the European Union', *Journal of European Public Policy*, vol. 11, no. 4, 2004, pp. 657–60.

8.   Article 24 of the consolidated version of the treaty on European Union, 17 December 2007.

9.   Preamble of the Barcelona Declaration; and see Sharon Pardo and Lion Zemer, *The institutional challenge of the Euro Mediterranean neighbourhood space*, CSEPS, Ben Gurion University, Beer Sheva (hsf.bgu.ac.il/europe) 2005.

10.   Rosemary Hollis, 'Europe in the Middle East', in Luise Fawcett, *International relations of the Middle East*, Oxford: Oxford University Press, 2005, pp. 307–27; Isabel Schäfer, 'Die Euro-Mediterrane Partnerschaft und der Nahostkonflikt', *Aus Politik und Zeitgeschichte*, vol. 45, 2005, pp. 22–30; Frédéric Volpi, 'Regional community building and the transformation of international relations: the case of the Euro-Mediterranean partnership', *Mediterranean Politics*, vol. 9, no. 2, 2004, p. 145–64.

11.   See http://europa.eu.int/comm/europeaid/projects/med/regional/political chapter_eu.htm

12. Patrick Laurent, 'From 'MEDA I' to 'MEDA II': What's new?' *Euromed Special Feature*, vol. 21, 3 May 2001. Patrick Laurent was then head of the Horizontal Matters Unit in the Middle-East and Southern Mediterranean directorate.

13. Miguel Angel Medina Abellán, 'The Mediterranean: the progressive construction of a common agenda', in Dieter Mahnke, Alicia Ambos and Christopher Reynolds (eds) *European foreign policy: from rhetoric to reality?* Brussels: College of Europe Studies, no.1, 2004, pp. 277–91.

14. Table 9.2 gives a general view of the characteristic features of the EMP governing structure without taking into account slight modifications between its first (1995–99) and its second (2000–05) financial regulation periods.

15. Elena Baracani, 'Pre-accession and neighbourhood: the European Union's democratic conditionality in Turkey and Morocco', in Annette Jünemann and Michèle Knodt (eds) *Externe Demokratieförderung durch die Europäische Union* (European External Democracy Promotion), Baden-Baden: Nomos, 2007, pp. 335–50; see also Dorothée Schmid, 'The use of conditionality in support of political, economic and social rights: unveiling the Euro-Mediterranean partnership's true hierarchy of objectives?' *Mediterranean Politics*, vol. 9, no. 3, 2004, pp. 396–421.

16. EUROMED, *European Neighbourhood and Partnership Instrument (ENPI), Regional Strategy Paper (2007–2013) and Regional Indicative Programme (2007–2010) for the Euro-Mediterranean Partnership*, 2007, p. 7 (www.ec.europa.eu/world/enp/pdf/country/enpi_euromed_sp.eu.pdf)

17. COM, *European Neighbourhood Policy*, Strategy Paper, Communication from the Commission of the European Communities, Brussels, 12 May 2004, COM (2004) 373 final.

18. Regulation (EC) No 1638/2006.

19. Annette Jünemann, 'Realpolitisches Nutzenkalkül oder konstruktivistischer Rollenkonflikt?' in Annette Jünemann and Michèle Knodt (eds) *Die externe Demokratieförderung durch die Europäische Union*, Baden-Baden: Nomos, 2007, pp. 295–315; Dorothée Schmid, 'Die Europäische Nachbarschaftspolitik und die euro-mediterrane Partnerschaft: das Ende einer regionalen Ambition?' in Martin Koopmann and Christian Lequesne (eds) *Die Nachbarschaftspolitik der Europäischen Union auf dem Prüfstand*, Baden-Baden: Nomos, 2006, pp. 111–28.

20. From proceedings of 9th Euro-Mediterranean meeting of Ministers of Foreign Affairs, Lisbon, Portugal, 5–6 November 2007, p. 4.

21. Council of the European Union, *Agreed conclusions of the 9th Euro-Mediterranean meeting of ministers of foreign affairs*, Lisbon: Council of the European Union, 5–6 November 2007, 14743/07 (255).

22. RSP/RIP, 2007, p. 19.

23. Almut Möller, 'The EU has to become a mature actor in its neighbourhood: the Middle East Quartet is a litmus test, *CAP News*, Centrum für angewandte Politikforschung, 19 April 2007, http://www.cap-lmu.de/aktuell/positionen/2007/eu.php. However, Roland Dannreuther, 'The Middle East: towards a substantive European role in the peace process?' in Roland Dannreuther (ed.) *European Union foreign and security policy: towards a*

neighbourhood strategy, London: Routledge, 2004, p. 161, stresses the role of the United States in forming the Quartet.

24. The United Nations secretary-general, the United States secretary of state and the foreign minister of Russia and the EU-Troika, composed of the High Representative for European foreign and security policy, the European commissioner for external relations and the European Council represented through the foreign minister of that union's country, which holds the presidency.

25. European Security Strategy (ESS), *A secure Europe in a better world: European Security Strategy approved by the European Council Brussels*, 12 December 2003, pp. 7–8 (www.consilian.europa.eu/uedocs/cmsUpload/78367.pdf).

26. The Venice declaration of 13 June 1980 established 'the right to existence and to security of all States in the region, including Israel, and justice for all the peoples, which implies the recognition of the legitimate rights of the Palestinian people'. The Essen declaration of December 1994 stated that Israel should enjoy special status in its relations with the EU on the basis of reciprocity and common interest. The Berlin declaration of 24 March 1999 introduced the notion of a viable Palestinian state. The Seville declaration of 22 June 2002 is explicit on the expected solution of the conflict: 'A settlement can be achieved through negotiation. The objective is an end to the occupation and the early establishment of a democratic, viable, peaceful and sovereign State of Palestine, on the basis of the 1967 borders, if necessary with minor adjustments agreed by the parties' (quoted by European Commission, 'The Middle East peace process, who is involved and how?' 2005, ec.europa.eu/external.relations/mepp/index.htm).

27. European Commission, 'The role of the European Union in the peace process and its future assistance to the Middle East: communication to the Council and the European Parliament, 16 January 1988, COM (970) 715 final

28. Berlin Declaration of the European Council, 24 March 1999.

29. See homepage of the European Commission (external relations): the EU and the Middle East peace process (ec.europa.eu/exernal_relations/mepp/indix.htm).

30. Action Strategy, *State-building for peace in the Middle East: an EU action strategy*, Joint paper by EU High Representative Javier Solana and EU Commissioner for External Relations Benita Ferrero-Waldner, Brussels, 2007, S. 378/07, pp. 1–2.

31. All quotations from Action Strategy, *State-building for peace*.

32. COM, *European Neighbourhood Policy*.

33. José Durao Barroso, *Shared challenges, shared futures: taking the neighourhood policy forward*, President of European Commission, European Neighbourhood Policy Conference, Brussels, 3 September 2007, p. 3 (Speech/07/502, www.ec.europa.eu/world/enp/conferences_2007_eu.htm).

34. Johannes Varwick and Jana Windwehr, 'Norwegen und Schweiz als Modellfälle für differenzierte Integration?' *Aus Politik und Zeitgeschichte*, vol. 43, 2007, pp. 15–20.

35. Barroso, *Shared challenges*, p. 3.

36. It was not possible to describe the case of Syria at length in this action plan. See European Neighbourhood and Partnership Instrument, Syrian Arab Republic, Strategy Paper 2007–2013 and National Indicative Programme 2007–2010.

37. COM, *European Neighbourhood Policy*, p. 1.

38. Ibid., p. 9.

39. COM, *Progress report Israel*, Commission staff working document accompanying the Communication from the Commission to the Council and the European Parliament 'Implementation of the European Neighbourhood Policy in 2007'. Commission of the European Communities, Brussels, 3 April 2008 SEL (2008) 394, p. 2.

40. See Barbara Lippert, 'European neighbourhood policy: many reservations – some progress – uncertain prospects', *International Policy Analysis*, Berlin: Friedrich Ebert Stiftung (FES) June 2008, p. 12.

Chapter 10. Military Intervention and Democratization: Global Order and the Radical Islamist Challenge to Lebanon   *Eyal Zisser*

1. For more see, *al-Hayat* (London), 13 September 2006; and Reuters, 12 September 2006. See also Economist Intelligence Unit, *Country report: Lebanon*, no. 4, 2006.

2. See *al-Nahar* (Beirut), 23 and 24 May 2008.

3. For more, see William Harris, *Faces of Lebanon, sects, wars, and global extensions*, Princeton: Markus Wiener Publishers, 1997. See also Eyal Zisser, *Lebanon: blood in the Cedar, from the civil war to the second Lebanon war*, Tel Aviv: Hakibbutz Hameuchad, 2009, pp. 103–7 (in Hebrew).

4. See *al-Nahar* (Beirut), 9 November 2006.

5. For more on Syrian–Lebanese relations, see Marius Deeb, *Syria's terrorist war on Lebanon and the peace process*, New York: Palgrave Macmillan, 2003; Robert G. Rabil, *Embattled neighbors: Syria, Israel and Lebanon*, Boulder, CO: Lynne Rienner Publishers, 1993.

6. For more on Hezbollah see Ahmad Nizar Hamzeh, *In the path of Hizbullah*, New York: Syracuse University Press, 2004; Judith Palmer Harik, *Hezbollah: The changing face of terrorism*, London: I.B.Tauris, 2004; Hala Jaber, *Hezbollah: born with a vengeance*, New York: Columbia University Press, 1997; Amal Saad-Ghorayeb, *Hizbu'llah: politics and religion*, London: Pluto Press, 2002.

7. See Bahman Baktiari and Augustus Richard Norton, 'Lebanon end-game', *Middle East Insight*, March–April 2000; Ahmad Nizar Hamzeh, *In the path of Hizbullah*, pp. 44–79; Eyal Zisser, 'Hizballah at a crossroads', in Bruce Maddy-Weitzman and Efraim Inbar (eds) *Religious radicalism in the greater Middle East*, London: Frank Cass, 1997, pp. 90–110.

8. See Hamzeh, *In the path of Hizbullah*, pp. 80–141; Daniel Sobelman, *New rules of the game: Israel and Hizbollah after the withdrawal from Lebanon*, Tel Aviv: Jaffee Center for Strategic Studies, 2003; Eyal Zisser, 'Hizballah and Israel: strategic threat on the northern border', *Israel Affairs*, vol. 12, no. 1, January 2006, pp. 86–106.

9. See Yoram Schweitzer, 'Divine victory and earthly failures: was the war really

a victory for Hizbollah', in Shlomo Brom and Meir Eliran (eds) *The second Lebanon war: strategic perspectives*, Tel Aviv: Institute for National Security Studies, 2007, pp. 123–34; Eyal Zisser, 'The battle for Lebanon: Lebanon and Syria in the wake of the war', in Shlomo Brom and Meir Eliran (eds) *The second Lebanon war: strategic perspectives*, 2007, pp. 135–50.

10. See Eyal Zisser, 'Lebanon: the Cedar Revolution – between continuity and Change', *Orient*, vol. 47, no. 4, 2006, pp. 460–84.

11. *Tishrin* (Damascus), 6 March 2005.

12. See *al-Nahar* (Beirut), 29 and 30 April 2005; al-'Arabiyya TV, 30 April and 1 May 2005.

13. See also Eyal Zisser, *Lebanon: blood in the cedar*, pp. 241–73.

14. See al-Manar TV, 22 September 2006.

15. See Nasrallah interview to NTV Channel, 27 August 2006. See also *al-Hayat* (London), 28 August 2006.

16. See Hamzeh, *In the path of Hizbullah*, pp. 44–79.

17. See Schweitzer, 'Divine victory and earthly failures'. See also *al-Nahar* (Beirut), 15 and 23 September 2006; al-Jazira TV, 26 September 2006.

18. See Lebanese News Agency, 5, 6 and 9 November 2006.

19. Lebanese News Agency, 6 and 7 May 2008; See al-Manar TV, 7 May 2008.

20. *Al-Nahar* (Beirut), 23, 25 and 27 May 2008.

21. See *al-Mustaqbal* (Beirut), 3 and 6 January 2007.

22. See *al-Hayat* (London), 14 and 15 April 2006.

23. See Irene L. Gendzier, *Notes from the minefield: United States intervention in Lebanon and the Middle East, 1945–1985*, New York: Columbia University Press, 1997; Anthony McDermott and Kjell Skjelsbaek (eds) *The Multinational Force in Beirut, 1982–1984*, Miami: Florida International University Press, 1991.

24. *Al-Hayat* (Beirut), 17 and 19 October 1976; Istvan Pogany, *The Arab League and peace keeping in the Lebanon*, New York: St Martin's Press, 1987; Reuven Avi Ran, *Syrian involvement in Lebanon (1975–1985)*, Tel Aviv: Ma'arachot, 1986, pp. 25–36, in Hebrew.

25. *Al-Nahar* (Beirut), 12 August 2006 and 1 March 2009; *Yedi'ot Aahronot* (Tel Aviv), 7 April 2008 and 13 February 2009.

Chapter 11. The Geopolitical Dimension of Sunni–Shi'i Sectarianism in the Middle East *Uzi Rabi and Brandon Friedman*

1. Following his public statements, 'Ubayd was dismissed from his position with the Saudi kingdom. *Washington Post*, 29 November 2006.

2. For example, Iranian-born analyst Vali Nasr's thesis regarding the rise of the Shi'a was described in his recent book, *The Shia revival*, New York: W. W. Norton and Company, 2006.

3. Interview with Hosni Mubarak, Arab satellite television channel *al-Arabiyya*, 8 April 2006.

4. Interview with king of Jordan, 'Abdallah ibn Hussein, *Washington Post*, 18 December 2004; see also *al-Hayat*, 25 March 2005.

5. *Al-Hijaz*, 15 August 2006; see also, *Ruz al-Yusuf*, 18 September 2006.

6. On this see also, Walid Tughan, 'Mustaqbal al-Arab bayna al-Sunna wal-Shi'a' ('The future of the Arabs between Sunnis and Shi'is'), *al-Masri al-Yawm*, 2 September 2006.

7. *Ruz al-Yusuf*, 18 September 2006.

8. *Al-Masri al-Yawm*, 2 September 2006.

9. See by way of illustration, *Ruz al-Yusuf*, 16 January 2007.

10. 'Al-Shi'a Yahlumun bil-Badr al-Shi'i' (The Shi'is are dreaming of a Shi'i full moon), *Ruz al-Yusuf*, 16 January 2007.

11. Ibid.

12. *Al-Sharq al-Awsat*, 2 November 2006.

13. *Al-Jazeera*, 14 February 2007, Foreign News Programme.

14. *Al-Dustur*, 22 January 2007; *al-Watan al-'Arabi*, 24 January 2007.

15. Even if there were exceptions, like Sa'id al-Sahhaf, minister of information in Saddam Hussein's regime, they do not negate the general rule. Sometimes an appointment like this served as mere lip service paid by rulers trying to make it seem as if Shi'is were also included in senior positions in the society and state.

16. *Gulf News*, 15 March 2005.

17. *Al-Watan* (Kuwait), 1 August 2008; *New York Times*, 14 February 2007. See also, *al-Sharq al-Awsat*, 18 February 2007.

18. See Kadivar's interview, 'Din, Modara va Khoshunat' (Religion, tolerance and violence), *Kiyan*, 45 (January–March 1999), pp. 6–19. Others, like Ayatollah Abu'l Qassim Kho'i argue for the establishment of an advisory council of religious law experts rather than the *velayat-e faqih*.

19. Hosni Mubarak's comments caused a wave of anger and concern among regional Shi'i communities and Iran.

20. BBC Worldwide Monitoring Service, *al-Arabiyya*, 26 January 2007.

21. *Al-Sharq al-Awsat*, 17 May 2008.

22. 'Fatah Demo Slogan: Hamas are Shi'is', Gulf 2000, 8 January 2007.

23. *Al-Jazeera*, 17 September 2005, Foreign News Programme.

24. BBC News, 22 April 2008.

25. *Al-Sharq al-Awsat*, 20 April 2008.

26. Interview with Saudi King 'Abdallah bin 'Abd al-'Aziz to the Kuwaiti *al-Siyasa*, 27 January, 2007.

27. *Al-Ahram*, 26 January 2007.

28. International Crisis Group, 'Iran in Iraq: how much influence?' *Middle East Report*, no. 38, 21 March 2005, p. 2. (hereafter: ICG).

29. Kayhan Barzegar, 'Iran and the new Iraq: security challenges and foreign problems', *Turkish Journal of International Relations*, vol. 5, no. 3 (fall 2006), p. 77.

30. ICG, 'Iran in Iraq', pp. 11, 22.

31. Kamran Taremi, 'Iranian foreign policy toward occupied Iraq, 2003–2005', *Middle East Policy*, vol. 12, no. 4 (Winter 2005), p. 28.

32. ICG, 'Iran in Iraq', p. 10.

33. Kayhan Barzegar, 'Iran, the new Iraq, and the Persian Gulf security-political architecture', *The Iranian Journal of International Affairs*, vol. 20, no. 1 (winter 2007–2008), p. 96.

34. Steven Lee Myers, *New York Times*, 22 July 2009.

35. Political sensitivities discourage publicly released census statistics, so there is no official way to verify these figures and they should be considered approximate estimates.

36. *Al-Sharq al-Awsat*, 27 January 2006.

37. US Department of State Country Report on Human Rights Practices – Kuwait, 2007, released 11 March 2008, accessed at http://www.state.gov/g/drl/rls/hrrpt/2007/100599.htm

38. Augustus Richard Norton, 'The Shi'ite threat revisited', *Current History*, December 2007, p. 439.

39. *Agence France Press*, 17 February 2008.

40. *Gulf News*, 15 March 2005.

41. Ibid.

42. *Agence France Press*, 11 July 2007.

43. 'Shaykh Abd al-Amir al-Jamri, Bahrain's leading Shi'ite cleric dies', *Associated Press*, 16 December 2006.

44. Mohammed al-Mezel, *Gulf News*, 5 October 2004.

45. *Al-Sharq al-Awsat*, 8 March 2001.

46. *Agence France Press*, 1 April 1997.

47. *Bahrain Tribune*, 26 and 28 October 2004.

48. Hasan M. Fattah, *International Herald Tribune*, 3 October 2006.

49. See, by way of illustration, *al-Hilal* (Amman), 23–29 November 2006.

50. M. A. Derhally, 'Rise of the Shi'is', *Arabian Business*, 3 September 2006.

51. *Al-Sharq al-Awsat*, 16 July 2006.

52. Shakir al-Nabulsi, 'Hal Sayasbah Lubnan al-Jumhuriyya al-Islamiyya al-Lubnaniyya' (Will Lebanon be turned into the Lebanese Islamic Republic), *al-Sharq al-Awsat*, 17 August 2006.

53. Robert F. Worth and Nada Bakri, *New York Times*, 18 May 2008.

54. BBC World Monitoring Service, 30 December 2008.

55. Accessed at: http://farsi.khamenei.ir/speech-content?id=5848

56. BBC World Monitoring Service, 28 April 2009.

57. Nicholas Blanford, 'Is the Sunni–Shiite rift mostly politics and media hype', *Christian Science Monitor*, 1 May 2008.

58. 'Umayma 'Abd al-Latif, 'The Sunni–Shi'i split: between myth and reality', *al-Ahram*, 1–7 March 2007.

59. Interview with the King of Jordan 'Abdallah ibn Hussein, *al-Sharq al-Awsat*, 23 January 2007.

60. *Iran News Agency*, 17 January 2007.

61. Abdullah al-Shayji, 'US–Iran relations worry Arabs', *Gulf News*, 10 May 2009.

62. Mark Landler, 'Syria talks signal new direction for the US', *New York Times*, 4 March 2009.

Chapter 12. Egyptian and Saudi Intervention in the Israeli–Palestinian Conflict (2006–09): Local Powers' Mediation Compared *Joseph Kostiner and Chelsi Mueller*

1. Arabic words have been cited according to the transliteration guide in the *International Journal of Middle East Studies*, a simplified system that eliminates

diacritical marks other than the 'ayn and the hamza. The only exception is proper names such as Ahmad Abul Gheit, where a particular Romanized spelling has become established in Western literature, or names of news agencies, such as *Al-Jazeera*, where a particular Romanized spelling has been established by the agency itself.

2. See for example comments by Ahmed Yusuf, adviser to Hamas leader Ismail Haniyeh, in *Guardian*, 15 January 2007.

3. Ibid; See also BBC, 22 February 2006, and the transcript of the interview with Hamas leader Khaled Mashal on 'Lateline' (Australian Broadcasting Corporation), 10 March 2006, http://www.abc.net.au/lateline/content/2006/s1589194.htm (accessed 22 April 2009).

4. See for example, *Jomhuri-ye Eslami* (Tehran), 25 November 2007, in BBC Worldwide Monitoring, 27 November 2007; *Kayhan* (Tehran), 28 November 2007, in BBC Worldwide Monitoring, 29 November 2007; and *Kayhan* (Tehran), 10 March 2009, in BBC Worldwide Monitoring, 11 March 2009.

5. See, for example, Saudi King Abdullah's interview in *Al-Seyassah* (Kuwait), 27 January 2007 (Arabic) and Egyptian Foreign Minister Ahmad Abul Gheit's interview in *Asharq al-Awsat* (London), 10 December 2006 (Arabic).

6. Egypt State Information Service, 29 January 2007.

7. *Al-Jazeera*, 15 December, 2006.

8. *The Australian*, 21 December 2006.

9. Saudi Press Agency, 28 January 2007.

10. *Haaretz*, 29 January 2007; *Al-Jazeera*, 2 February 2007.

11. *Khaleej Times*, 9 February 2007.

12. *New York Times*, 9 February 2007.

13. For a detailed analysis of the Saudi peace initiative, see Joseph Kostiner, 'Coping with regional challenges: a case study of Crown Prince Abdullah's peace initiative', in Paul Aarts and Gerd Nonneman (eds) *Saudi Arabia in the balance: political economy, society, foreign affairs*, London: Hurst & Company, 2005, pp. 352–71.

14. *Haaretz*, 12 March 2007.

15. *Haaretz*, 14 March 2007.

16. *Haaretz*, 1 March 2007.

17. *Asharq al-Awsat* (London), 26 March 2007.

18. Andrew Lee Butters, 'Can Arab leaders bring peace?' *Time*, 25 July 2007.

19. *Middle East International*, 16 May 2003, and 5 November 2003; *Gulf States Newsletter*, no. 709, 2 May 2003.

20. The text of the Mecca Agreement was printed in *Khaleej Times*, 9 February 2007.

21. Ibid.

22. Associated Press (AP), 23 June 2007; See Saudi Foreign Minister Sa'ud al-Faisal's remarks at the June 2007 summit of the Arab League in Cairo, *Al-Jazeera*, 16 June 2007.

23. *Al-Jazeera*, 29 June 2007.

24. Saudi–US Relations Information Service, 5 March 2007.

25. Scott McLeod, 'Saudis leave Rice stranded', *Time*, 30 March 2007.

26.   Martin Indyk, 'The honeymoon's over for Bush and the Saudis', *Washington Post*, 29 April 2007, p. BO5.

27.   Syrian Arab News Agency (SANA), 18 January 2009.

28.   See for example *Khaleej Times*, 22 May 2008, and Amira Howeidy, *Al-Ahram Weekly Online*, 'Doha steps in', no. 899, 29 May–4 June 2008, http://weekly.ahram.org.eg/2008/899/re6.htm (accessed 9 May, 2009).

29.   See Joseph Kostiner, 'Regulating Arab politics (part 1): the war of the summits', *Tel Aviv Notes*, The Moshe Dayan Center, 26 March 2009; and Joseph Kostiner and Bruce Maddy-Weitzman, 'Regulating Arab politics (part 2): the Doha Arab League Summit', *Tel Aviv Notes*, The Moshe Dayan Center, 7 April 2009, http://www.dayan.org/frameana.htm (accessed 22 April 2009).

30.   *World Tribune*, 11 July 2007.

31.   *Al-Ahram* (Cairo), 23 June 2007 (Arabic).

32.   *World Tribune*, 11 July 2007.

33.   *Khaleej Times*, 10 June 2006.

34.   BBC, 6 June 2006.

35.   *Boston Globe*, 26 November 2006.

36.   *Jerusalem Post*, 30 April 2007.

37.   *Haaretz*, 5 December 2006; see transcript of the interview with Egyptian Foreign Minister Ahmad Abul Gheit on *Al-Arabiya* TV (Dubai) in BBC Worldwide Monitoring, 2 October 2006.

38.   *Al-Sinnara* (Nazareth), 27 October 2006 (Arabic).

39.   Ahmad Abul Gheit, interview, *Al-Arabiya* TV (Dubai), n.d., in BBC Worldwide Monitoring, 2 October 2006.

40.   *Asharq al-Awsat* (London), 10 December 2006 (Arabic).

41.   *New York Times*, 1 January 2007; *Jerusalem Post*, 2 January 2007; *Haaretz*, 4 Janurary 2007.

42.   *Washington Post*, 2 February 2007; *Washington Post*, 6 February 2007.

43.   Associated Press (AP), 23 June 2007.

44.   *Ma'an* (Bethlehem), 7 August 2007 (Arabic).

45.   Dina Ezzat, *Al-Ahram Weekly Online*, 'Let's talk, again', no. 851, 28 June–4 July 2007, http://weekly.ahram.org.eg/2007/851/eg1.html (accessed 11 April 2009).

46.   *Al-Quds al-Arabi* (London), vol. 19, no. 5624, 30/1 June/July 2007, p. 4 (Arabic); Egypt State Information Service, 31 January 2008.

47.   *Jerusalem Post*, 3 October 2007.

48.   *Haaretz*, 27 March 2008.

49.   Ahmad Menese, 'Egyptian position on crisis of Rafah crossing and its aftermath', Emirates Center for Strategic Studies and Research, 13 February 2008, http://www.ecssr.ac.ae/CDA/en/FeaturedTopics/DisplayTopic/0,1670,771-97-33,00.html (accessed 13 May 2009).

50.   *Haaretz*, 2 August 2007; see the comments of a senior Hamas political leader, Usama al-Muzeini, on the Palestinian Information Centre website, 4 August 2007, http://www.palestine-info.co.uk (accessed 17 April 2009).

51.   *Khaleej Times*, 26 June 2007.

52.   *Asharq al-Awsat* (London), 26 September 2008 (Arabic).

53.   *Asharq al-Awsat* (London), 2 September 2008 (Arabic).

54. *Dar al-Hayat* (London), 9 March 2008 (Arabic).
55. *Dar al-Hayat* (London), 17 June 2008 (Arabic).
56. Ibid.
57. *Asharq al-Awsat* (London), 26 September 2008 (Arabic).
58. *Asharq al-Awsat* (London), 10 December 2006 (Arabic).
59. Ahmad Abul Gheit, interview, *Al-Arabiya* TV (Dubai) in BBC Worldwide Monitoring, 2 October 2006.
60. *Al-Ittihad* (Abu Dhabi), 26 November 2008 (Arabic).
61. *Los Angeles Times*, 31 December 2008.
62. *Yemen Times*, 31 December 2008.
63. See transcript of *Al-Arabiya* TV (Dubai), 2 January 2009, in BBC Worldwide Monitoring, 3 January 2009.
64. *Haaretz*, 8 January 2009.
65. George Baghdadi, 'Hamas rejects Egypt's ceasefire plan', CBS News, 8 January 2009, http://www.cbsnews.com/stories/2009/01/08/world/main 4707219.shtml (accessed 17 April 2009).
66. BBC, 18 January 2009; *Al-Hayat* (London), 26 January 2009 (Arabic).
67. Agence France-Presse (AFP), 25 January 2009.
68. Egypt State Information Service, 29 January 2009.
69. For a detailed analysis of Qatar's intervention in the Arab–Israeli conflict, see Uzi Rabi, 'Qatar's relations with Israel: challenging Arab and Gulf norms', *The Middle East Journal*, vol. 63, no. 3, 2009.
70. See transcript of the interview with Hamas leader Usama al-Muzeini, al-Jazeera, 2 January 2009, MideastWire, http://www.mideastwire.com/ downloads/The_Gaza_Crisis.pdf (accessed 20 April 2009).
71. *Ya Libnan*, 18 January 2009.
72. Edward Yeranian, 'Egypt hosts Gaza ceasefire meeting', 18 January 2009, http://www.globalsecurity.org/military/library/news/2009/01/mil-090118-voa05.htm (accessed 19 April 2009).
73. *Christian Science Monitor*, 2 February 2009; *Washington Times*, 27 April 2009.
74. *Al-Arabiya* website, 11 March 2009, http://www.alarabiya.net/articles/ 2009/03/11/68226.html (accessed 14 May 2009).

Chapter 13.   Lost Faith, Forfeited Trust: Afghan Responses to post-9/11 International Intervention in State-building and Insurgency   *Marvin G. Weinbaum*

1. See Mark Schneider's Congressional testimony of the House Committee on Foreign Affairs, 2 April 2008.
2. Center for the Study of the Presidency, *Afghanistan Study Group Report*, 30 January 2008, pp. 20–1.
3. Ali A. Jalali, former Afghan minister of interior addressing a meeting at Carnegie Endowment, 27 March 2008.
4. Zalmay Khalilzad, 'Afghanistan's new deal', *New York Times*, 20 March 2008.
5. Carletta Gall, 'Oxfam report written by Matt Waldman, the Agency Coordinating Body for Afghan Relief (ACBAR)', *New York Times*, 26 March 2008, p. A2.

6. Patrick Seale, 'An exit strategy in Afghanistan', *Gulf News*, UAE, 4 April 2008.

7. Gall, 'Oxfam report', p. A2.

8. Afghan Finance Minister Anwar ul-Haq Ahady, presentation at the US Congress, 13 April 2008.

9. Gall, 'Oxfam report', p. A2.

10. See analyses of opinion data by Rachel Ray Steele and J. Alexander Thier, *Hearts and minds: Afghan opinion on the Taliban, the government and international forces*, Washington: United States Institute of Peace, 16 August 2007, pp. 1–4.

11. National Democratic Institute of International Affairs, 'Afghan perspectives on democracy: a report on focus groups in the Kabul area on the eve of the emergency Loya Jirga', May 2002, p. 38 http://www.accessdemocracy.org/library/1411_af_report_052802.pdf

12. National Democratic Institute of International Affairs, 'A society in transition: focus group discussions in Afghanistan', December 2003, p. 436 http://www.accessdemocracy.org/library/1677_af_focusgroups_120103.pdf

13. Asia Foundation, Kabul, Afghan Media Resource Centre, 'Democracy in Afghanistan', 13 July 2004, p. 435H http://www.asiafoundation.org/pdf/afghan_voter-ed04.pdf

14. ABC News Poll, 'Life in Afghanistan', 7 December 2005, p. 431H, http://abcnews.go.com/images/Politics/998a1Afghanistan.pdf

15. Asia Foundation, Kabul, 'A survey of the Afghan people, 2006', http://www.asiafoundation.org/pdf/AG-survey06.pdf

16. Stephen Weber, Steven Kull, Clay Ramsay, Evan Lewis and Mary Speck, 'Afghan public opinion amidst rising violence', a World Public Opinion Organization Poll, 14 December 2006. D3 Systems and Afghan Center for Social and Opinion Research in Kabul http://www.worldpublicopinion.org/pipa/pdf/dec06/Afghanistan_Dec06_rpt.pdf

17. Asia Foundation, Kabul, 'A survey of the Afghan people', 2007, p. 426H http://www.asiafoundation.org/pdf/AG-survey07.pdf

18. BBC–ABC–ARD, Public Opinion Poll, 3 December 2007, p. 424H http://news.bbc.co.uk/2/shared/bsp/hi/pdfs/03_12_07_afghanpoll2007.pdf

19. Asia Foundation, Kabul, 'A survey of the Afghan people', pp. 5–6, 8. http://asiafoundation.org/resources/pdfs/Afghanistan2008.pdf

20. Ibid. Tables, p. 7.

21. http://news.bbc.co.uk/2/hi/south_asia/7872353.stm

22. Richard Holbrooke, *Washington Post*, 3 March 2008, p. A19.

Chapter 14. Pious Words, Puny Deeds: The 'International Community' and Mass Atrocities *Rajan Menon*

1. Martin van Creveld, *The transformation of war*, New York: Free Press, 1991.

2. A plethora of books demonstrate this reality, though they differ dramatically on its causes and consequences. See, for example, John Micklethwait and Adrian Wooldridge, *A future perfect*, New York: Crown Books, 2000.

3. On the supposed consensus on redefining sovereignty, see the report of the Genocide Prevention Task Force, organized by the United States Holocaust

Museum, the American Academy of Diplomacy, and the United States Institute for Peace and co-chaired by former Secretary of State Madeleine K. Albright and former US Senator and Secretary of Defense William S. Cohen, *Preventing genocide: a blueprint for US policymakers*, Washington: Inter Press Service, pp. 101–4. A substantial scholarly literature is dedicated to highlighting the shift in, and power of, norms on sovereignty and human rights. See, for example, Martha Finnemore and Kathryn Sikkink, 'International norm dynamics and political change', *International Studies Quarterly*, vol. 17, Autumn 1998, pp. 887–912; Thomas Risse, Stephen Ropp and Kathryn Sikkink (eds) *The power of human rights: international norms and domestic change*, Cambridge: Cambridge University Press, 1999.

4. Reinhold Niebuhr, *Moral man and immoral society*, New York: Charles Scribner's Sons, 1932, p. 49. See also, Reinhold Niebuhr, *The children of light and the children of darkness*, New York: Charles Scribner's Sons, 1944, Chapter 5, 'The World Community'.

5. Niebuhr, *Moral Man*, p. 85.

6. Kofi Annan, 'Problems without passports', *Foreign Policy*, September–October 2002, pp. 30–1. This issue of the magazine contains a segment with different perspectives on the question: 'What is an International Community?'

7. See Benedict Anderson, *Imagined communities: reflections on the origin and spread of nationalism*, revised edition, London: Verso, 2006; and Eric Hobsbawm and Terence Ranger (eds) *The invention of tradition*, Cambridge: Cambridge University Press, 1992.

8. On this point, see, in particular, Walker Connor, *Ethnonationalism: the quest for understanding*, Princeton: Princeton University Press, 1994; and Anthony Smith, *Nations and nationalism in a global era*, Cambridge, UK: Polity Press, 1995.

9. See Genocide Prevention Task Force, *Preventing genocide*, pp. 106–7.

10. United Nations, *UN peacekeeping operations: background note*, 31 January 2008, available at: http://www.un.org/Depts/dpko/dpko/bnote.htm

11. The statute was adopted in 1998 and entered force in 2002. As of January 2009, 108 states had ratified the treaty and another 40 had signed but had yet to ratify it.

12. Anon, 'UN struggles to find new peacekeepers for Congo', Reuters, 3 February 2009, available at: http://www.reuters.com/article/worldNews/idUSTRE5126L820090203; Anon, 'UN accused of failing to protect Congolese', msnbc.com, 9 February 2009, available at: http://www.msnbc.msn.com/id/29264533/

13. Jeane J. Kirkpatrick, 'The shackles of consensus', *Foreign Policy*, September/October 2002, p. 37.

14. Noam Chomsky, 'The Crimes of 'Intcom'', *Foreign Policy*, no. 132, September/October 2002, pp. 34–5.

15. I rely here on the detailed analysis of various cases of mass atrocities in Samantha Power, *A problem from hell: America and the age of genocide*, New York: Basic Books, 2002.

16. Roméo Dallaire, *Shake hands with the devil: the failure of humanity in Rwanda*, New York: Carol & Graff Publishers, 2003, p. 514.

17. Sadako Ogata, 'Guilty parties', *Foreign Policy*, no. 132, September/October 2002, p. 40.

18. Martha C. Nussbaum, 'Patriotism and cosmopolitanism', in Joshua Cohen (ed.) *For love of country: debating the limits of patriotism*, Boston: Beacon Press, 1996, p. 4. For further elaboration and attempts to show that cosmopolitanism is fully compatible with more immediate attachments, see Kwame Anthony Appiah, *The ethics of identity*, Princeton: Princeton University Press, 2005, especially Chapter 6 on 'Rooted Cosmopolitanism'; Kwame Anthony Appiah, *Cosmopolitanism: ethics in a world of strangers*, New York: W. W. Norton and Company, 2006; Nigel Dower, *Global citizenship: a critical introduction*, London: Routledge, 2002; Hans Schattle, *Practices of global citizenship*, Lanham, MD: Rowman & Littlefield Publishers, 2007.

19. Nussbaum, 'Patriotism', p. 4.

20. Ibid., p. 14.

21. Ibid., p. 12.

22. See for example, Benjamin J. Barber, 'Constitutional faith', in Joshua Cohen (ed.) *For love of country: debating the limits of patriotism*, Boston: Beacon Press, 1996, pp. 30–7.

23. ICISS (International Commission on Intervention and State Sovereignty) (2001) *The responsibility to protect*, available at: http://www.iciss.ca/report2-en.asp

24. Gareth Evans, *The responsibility to protect: ending mass atrocities once and for all*, Washington, DC: Brookings Institution Press, 2008. The United States Holocaust Museum's Genocide Prevention Task Force adopts many of the ideas associated with R2P, but focuses on developing an American comprehensive strategy to stop genocide. See Genocide Prevention Task Force, *Preventing genocide*.

25. See the summary of China's position on R2P during the Security Council debate following the adoption of Resolution 1674, at http://www.google.com/search?client=firefox-a&rls=org.mozilla%3Aen-US%3Aofficial&channel=s&hl=en&q=r2p+2006+security+council&btnG=Google+Search. Also see Yuri Fedotov, 'Russian ambassador challenges R2P principle', *Guardian*, 18 July 2008, http://www.ir2p.org/2008/07/18/russian-ambassador-challenges-r2p-principle/

26. See Rajan Menon, *The end of alliances*, New York: Oxford University Press, 2007, Chapter 3.

References

ABC News Poll, 'Life in Afghanistan', 7 December 2005, http://abcnews.go.com/ images/Politics/998a1Afghanistan.pdf

Abdukarim Ahmed Guleid and Jack L. Davies (1994) 'Is it peace for Somalia?' *New African*, no. 319, May, pp. 7–9

Action Strategy (2007) *State-building for peace in the Middle East: an EU action strategy*, Joint paper by EU High Representative Javier Solana and EU Commissioner for External Relations Benita Ferrero-Waldner, Brussels, S. 378/07

Adam, Hussein M. (1995) 'A terrible beauty being born?', in William I. Zartman (ed.) *Collapsed states: the disintegration and restoration of legitimate authority*, Boulder: Lynne Rienner, pp. 69–89

Ajami, Fouad (2008) 'Bush of Arabia', *Wall Street Journal*, 8 January

Akashi, Yasushi (1993) 'The challenges faced by UNTAC', *Japan Review of International Affairs*, Summer, pp. 189–97

Alfonsi, Christian (2006) *Circle in the sand: why we went back to Iraq*, New York: Doubleday

Alin, Erika (1994) *The United States and the 1958 Lebanon crisis*, Lanham, MD: University Press of America

Allard, Kenneth (1995) *Somalia operations: lessons learned*, Washington: CCRP

Anderson, Benedict (2006) *Imagined communities: reflections on the origin and spread of nationalism*, revised edition, London: Verso

Andrejevich, Milan (1991) 'The future of Bosnia and Hercegovina: a sovereign republic or cantonisation?' *RFE/RL Report on Eastern Europe*, 5 July

Annan, Kofi (2002) 'Problems without passports', *Foreign Policy*, September–October, pp. 30–1

Anon (1992) 'Somalia: enemy's enemy', *Africa Confidential*, vol. 33, no. 9, 8 May, p. 8

Anon (1993) 'Somalia: hope denied', *Africa Confidential*, vol. 34, no. 14, 16 July, p. 8

Anon (1994) 'Somalia: Aydeed's local difficulties', *Africa Confidential*, vol. 35, no. 12, 17 June, p. 7

Anon (1994) 'Somalia: warlords restored', *Africa Confidential*, vol. 35, no. 20, 7 October, pp. 1–3

Anon (1995) 'Aydeed's dilemma', *Africa Confidential*, vol. 36, no. 1, 6 January, pp. 6–7

Anon (2009) Anon, 'UN struggles to find new peacekeepers for Congo', Reuters, 3 February, available at: http://www.reuters.com/article/worldNews/idUSTRE5126L820090203

Anon (2009) 'UN accused of failing to protect Congolese', msnbc.com, 9 February, available at: http://www.msnbc.msn.com/id/29264533/

Appiah, Kwame Anthony (2005) *The ethics of identity*, Princeton: Princeton University Press

Appiah, Kwame Anthony (2006) *Cosmopolitanism: ethics in a world of strangers*, New York: Norton & Company

Asia Foundation, Kabul, Afghan Media Resource Centre (2004) 'Democracy in Afghanistan', 13 July, http://www.asiafoundation.org/pdf/afghan_voter-ed04.pdf

Asia Foundation, Kabul, Afghan Media Resource Centre (2006) 'A survey of the Afghan people, 2006', http://www.asiafoundation.org/pdf/AG-survey06.pdf

Asia Foundation, Kabul, Afghan Media Resource Centre (2007) 'A survey of the Afghan people', p. 426H http://www.asiafoundation.org/pdf/AG-survey07.pdf

Asia Foundation, Kabul, Afghan Media Resource Centre (2008) 'A survey of the Afghan people', pp. 5–6, 8. http://asiafoundation.org/resources/pdfs/Afghanistan2008.pdf

Atkinson, Rick (1994) *Crusade: the untold story of the Persian Gulf war*, New York: Mariner Books

Azam, Jean Paul and Anke Hoeffler (2002) 'Violence against civilians in civil wars: looting or terror', *Journal of Peace Research*, vol. 39, no. 4, pp. 461–85

Baktiari, Bahman and Augustus Richard Norton (2000) 'Lebanon endgame', *Middle East Insight*, March–April

Baracani, Elena (2007) 'Pre-accession and neighbourhood: the European Union's democratic conditionality in Turkey and Morocco', in Annette Jünemann and Michèle Knodt (eds) *Externe Demokratieförderung durch die Europäische Union* (European External Democracy Promotion), Baden-Baden: Nomos, pp. 335–50

Barber, Benjamin J. (1996) 'Constitutional faith', in Joshua Cohen (ed.) *For love of country: debating the limits of patriotism*, Boston: Beacon Press, pp. 30–7

Barone, Michael and Grant Ujifusa (1983) *The almanac of American politics 1984*, Washington, DC: National Journal

Barroso, José Durao (2007) *Shared challenges, shared futures: taking the neighbourhood policy forward*, President of European Commission, European Neighbourhood Policy Conference, Brussels, 3 September (speech /07/502, www.ec.europa.eu/world/enp/conferences_2007_eu. htm)

Barzegar, Kayhan (2006) 'Iran and the new Iraq: security challenges and foreign problems', *Turkish Journal of International Relations*, vol. 5, no. 3 (fall)

Barzegar, Kayhan (2007–2008) 'Iran, the new Iraq, and the Persian Gulf security-political architecture', *The Iranian Journal of International Affairs*, vol. 20, no. 1 (winter)

BBC–ABC–ARD (2007) Public Opinion Poll, 3 December, p. 424H http://news.bbc.co.uk/2/shared/bsp/hi/pdfs/03_12_07_afghanpoll2007. pdf

Beck, Ulrich and Edgar Grande (2004) *Das kosmopolitische Europa*, Frankfurt/M: SV Edition Zweite Moderne

Bellamy, Alex J. and Paul D. Williams (2005) 'Who's keeping the peace? Regionalization and contemporary peace operations', *International Security*, vol. 29, no. 4, Spring, pp. 157–95

Bellamy, Alex, Paul Williams and Stuart Griffin (2004) *Understanding peacekeeping*, Cambridge: Polity Press

Benhorin, Yitzhak (2008) 'Poll: more Americans are pro-Israeli', Ynetnews.com, 6 March

Ben-Zvi, Abraham (1998) *Decade of transition: Eisenhower, Kennedy, and the origins of the American–Israel alliance*, New York: Columbia University Press

Berlin, Isaiah (1969) 'Two concepts of liberty (1958)' in Isaiah Berlin, *Four essays on liberty*, Oxford: Oxford University Press

Biscop, Sven (2005) *The European security strategy: a global agenda for positive power*, Aldershot: Ashgate

Blanford, Nicholas (2008) 'Is the Sunni–Shiite rift mostly politics and media hype', *Christian Science Monitor*, 1 May

Booker, Bryan M. (1994) 'Somalia: the roots of today's conflict', *Strategy & Tactics*, no. 171, November/December, pp. 53–61

Boutros-Ghali, Boutros (1999) *Unvanquished: a US–UN saga*, New York: Random House

Bowden, Mark (1999) *Black hawk down: a story of modern war*, New York: Atlantic Monthly Press

Buruma, Ian (2008) 'After America: is the West being overtaken by the rest?' *New Yorker*, 21 April, pp. 126–30

Bush, George W. (2002) 'President Bush calls for new Palestinian leadership', Office of the Press Secretary, The White House, Washington DC, 24 June, http://www.whitehouse.gov/news/releases/2002/06/20020624-3.html, accessed 9 May 2008

Butters, Andrew Lee (2007) 'Can Arab leaders bring peace?' *Time*, 25 July 2007

Cameron, F. (2002) 'The European Union's growing international role: closing the capability–expectations gap?' Paper presented at the conference on the European Union in International Affairs, National Europe Centre, Australian National University, July. http://www.anu.edu.au/NEC/fraser_cameron.pdf

Cameron, F. (2006) 'The European Union's role in the Balkans', in B. Blitz (ed.) *War and change in the Balkans*, Cambridge: Cambridge University Press

Cassanelli, Lee (1995) 'Victims and vulnerable groups in southern Somalia', Ottawa, Canada, May, at: http://www.cisr.gc.ca/cgi-bin

Center for the Study of the Presidency (2008) *Afghanistan Study Group Report*, 30 January

Chandler, David (1991) *The tragedy of Cambodian history: politics, war, and revolution since 1945*, New Haven: Yale University Press

Chesterman, Simon (2004) *You the people: the UN, transitional administration and state-building*, Oxford: Oxford University Press

Chomsky, Noam (2002) 'The crimes of "Intcom"', *Foreign Policy*, no. 132, September, pp. 34–5

Clark, Jeffrey (1993) 'Debacle in Somalia', *Foreign Affairs*, vol. 72, no. 1, pp. 109–23

Clarke, Walter and Jeffrey Herbst (1997) 'Somalia and the future of humanitarian intervention', in Walter Clarke and Jeffrey Herbst (eds) *Learning from Somalia: the lessons of armed humanitarian intervention*, Boulder: Westview, pp. 239–52

Clarke, Walter and Jeffrey Herbst (eds) (1997) *Learning from Somalia: the lessons of armed humanitarian intervention*, Boulder: Westview

Coll, Steve (2004) *Ghost wars: the secret history of the CIA, Afghanistan, and Bin Laden, from the Soviet invasion to September 10, 2001*, New York: Penguin

COM (2004) *European Neighbourhood Policy*, Strategy Paper, Communication from the Commission of the European Communities, Brussels, 12 May 2004, COM (2004) 373 final

COM (2008) *Progress report Israel*, Commission staff working document accompanying the Communication from the Commission to the Council and the European Parliament 'Implementation of the

European Neighbourhood Policy in 2007'. Commission of the European Communities, Brussels, 3 April 2008 SEL (2008) 394

Compagnon, Daniel (1998) 'Somali armed movements, the interplay of political entrepreneurship and clan-based factions', in Christopher Clapham (ed.) *African guerrillas*, Oxford: James Currey, pp. 75–9

Connor, Walker (1994) *Ethnonationalism: the quest for understanding*, Princeton: Princeton University Press

Council of the European Union, *Agreed conclusions of the 9th Euro-Mediterranean meeting of ministers of foreign affairs*, Lisbon: Council of the European Union, 5–6 November 2007, 14743/07 (255)

Cox, Michael, Adrian Guelke and Fiona Stephen (eds) (2006) *A farewell to Arms? Beyond the Good Friday Agreement*, Manchester: Manchester University Press

Crile, George (1997) *Charlie Wilson's war: the extraordinary story of how the wildest man in Congress and a rogue CIA agent changed the history of our times*, New York: Grove Press

Crocker, Chester (2000) 'A poor case for quitting', *Foreign Affairs*, vol. 79, no. 1, January/February, pp. 183–6

Dallaire, Roméo (2003) *Shake hands with the devil: the failure of humanity in Rwanda*, New York: Carol & Graff Publishers

Dannreuther, Roland (2004) 'The Middle East: towards a substantive European role in the peace process?' in Roland Dannreuther (ed.) *European Union foreign and security policy: towards a neighbourhood strategy*, London: Routledge, p. 151–69

Deeb, Marius (2003) *Syria's terrorist war on Lebanon and the peace process*, New York: Palgrave Macmillan

Deng, Francis M. (1995) 'Reconciling sovereignty with responsibility: a basis for international humanitarian action', in John W. Harbeson and Donald Rothschild, *Africa in world politics: post-cold war challenges*, Boulder: Westview, pp. 295–310

Deng, Francis M. (1995) 'Frontiers of sovereignty', *Leiden Journal of International Law*, vol. 8, no. 2, pp. 249–286

Derhally, M. A. (2006) 'Rise of the Shi'is', *Arabian Business*, 3 September

Diehl, Paul and Joseph Lepgold (eds) (2003) *Regional conflict management*, Lanham: Rowan & Littlefield

Dower, Nigel (2002) *Global citizenship: a critical introduction*, London: Routledge

Downs, George and Stephen John Stedmen (2002) 'Evaluating issues in peace implementation', in Stephen Stedman, Donald Rothchild and

Elizabeth M. Cousens (eds) *Ending civil wars: the implementation of peace agreements*, Boulder: Lynne Reiner, pp. 50–2

Doyle, Michael W. (1995) *UN peacekeeping in Cambodia: UNTAC's civil mandate*, Boulder: Lynne Rienner

Doyle, Michael W. (1997) 'Authority and elections in Cambodia', in Michael W. Doyle, Ian Johnstone and Robert C. Orr (eds) *Keeping the peace: multidimensional UN operations in Cambodia and El Salvador*, Cambridge: Cambridge University Press

Doyle, Michael W. and Nicholas Sambanis (2006) *Making war and building peace: United Nations peace operations*, Princeton: Princeton University Press

Draper, Theodore (1992) *Very thin line: the Iran-contra affairs*, New York: Touchstone

Drysdale, John (1997) 'Foreign military intervention in Somalia: the root cause of the shift from UN peacekeeping to peacemaking and its consequence', in Walter Clarke and Jeffrey Herbst (eds) *Learning from Somalia: the lessons of armed humanitarian intervention*, Boulder: Westview Press

Durch, Willaim J. (1996) 'Introduction to anarchy: intervention in Somalia', in William J. Durch (ed.) *UN peacekeeping, American politics, and the uncivil wars of the 1990s*, New York: St Martin's Press, pp. 350–3

Economist Intelligence Unit (2006) *Country report: Lebanon*, no. 4

Emmott, Bill (2008) *Rivals: how the power struggle between China, India, and Japan will shape our next decade*, New York: Harcourt Brace

European Commission (1988) 'The role of the European Union in the peace process and its future assistance to the Middle East: communication to the Council and the European Parliament, 16 January, COM (970) 715 final

European Commission (2002) 'Information note: the rapid reaction mechanism supporting the European Union's policy objectives in conflict prevention and crisis management', http://www.europa.eu.int /comm/external_relations/ cfsp/ doc/rrm.pdf

European Commission (2005) 'The Middle East peace process, who is involved and how?' ec.europa.eu/external.relations/mepp/index.htm

European Convention (2002) *Final Report of Working Group VIII on defense, chaired by Michael Barnier (Barnier Report)*, Brussels, 16 December

European Council (2001) Council regulation (EC) No 381/2001 of 26 February creating a rapid reaction mechanism

European Council (2004) Council Joint Action of 12 July 2004 on the

European Union military operation in Bosnia and Herzegovina, 2004/570/CFSP

European Council (2008) *European Union Police Mission in Bosnia and Herzegovina*, official website of the council of the European Union (available online at http://www.consilium.europa.eu/cms3_fo/show Page.asp?id=585& lang =EN&mode=g; accessed 9 March 2008)

European Neighbourhood and Partnership Instrument (2007) Syrian Arab Republic, Strategy Paper 2007–2013 and National Indicative Programme 2007–2010

European Security Strategy (ESS), *A secure Europe in a better world: European Security Strategy approved by the European Council Brussels*, 12 December 2003, pp. 7–8 (www.consilian.europa.eu/uedocs/cmsUpload/78367. pdf)

European Union (2007) 'Treaty of Lisbon amending the Treaty on European Union and the Treaty establishing the European Community', *Official Journal of the European Union*, English edition, C 306, vol. 50, 17 December (available online at http://bookshop. europa.eu/eubookshop/FileCache/PUBPDF/FXAC07306ENC/FXA C07306ENC_002.pdf; accessed 3 April 2008)

Evans, Gareth (2008) *The responsibility to protect: ending mass atrocities once and for all*, Washington, DC: Brookings Institution Press

Evans, Gareth and Mohamed Sahnoun (2002) 'The responsibility to protect', *Foreign Affairs*, vol. 81, no. 6, November–December, pp. 99–110

Faucompret, E. (2001) *The dismemberment of Yugoslavia and the European Union*, Antwerp: University of Antwerp

Fearon, James (2004) 'Why do some civil wars last so much longer than others,' *Journal of Peace Research*, vol. 41, no. 3, pp. 275–301

Fedotov, Yuri (2008) 'Russian ambassador challenges R2P principle', *Guardian*, 18 July, http://www.ir2p.org/2008/07/18/russian-ambassador-challenges-r2p-principle/

Feith, Douglas (2008) *War and decision*, New York: Harper Collins

Findlay, Trevor (1995) *Cambodia: the legacy and lessons of UNTAC*, Oxford: Oxford University Press

Findlay, Trevor (2002) *The use of force in UN peace operations*, Oxford: Oxford University Press

Finnemore, Martha and Kathryn Sikkink (1998) 'International norm dynamics and political change', *International Studies Quarterly*, vol. 17, Autumn, pp. 887–912

Fortna, Virginia Page (2004) *Peace time: ceasefire agreements and the durability of peace*, Princeton: Princeton University Press

Freedman, Lawrence (2008) *A choice of enemies: America confronts the Middle East*, New York: Public Affairs

Friedman, Thomas (2005) *The world is flat: a brief history of the twenty-first century*, New York: Farrar, Strauss & Giroux

Gaddis, John Lewis (2004) *Surprise, security and the American experience*, Cambridge, MA: Harvard University Press

Gall, Carletta (2008) 'Oxfam report written by Matt Waldman, the Agency Coordinating Body for Afghan Relief (ACBAR)', *New York Times*, 26 March, p. A2

Ganzglass, Martin R. (1997) 'The restoration of the Somali justice system', in Walter Clarke and Jeffrey Herbst (eds) *Learning from Somalia: the lessons of armed humanitarian intervention*, Boulder: Westview Press, pp. 27–8

Gat, Azar (2007) 'The return of authoritarian great powers', *Foreign Affairs*, vol. 86, no. 4, July/August, pp. 59–69

Gendzier, Irene L. (1997) *Notes from the minefield: United States intervention in Lebanon and the Middle East, 1945–1985*, New York: Columbia University Press

Genocide Prevention Task Force (2008) *Preventing genocide: a blueprint for US policymakers*, Washington: Inter Press Service

Gilbert, S. T. (1996) *Reagan and the AWACS sale to Saudi Arabia: bureaucratic politics in action*, Washington, DC: National War College

Gordon, Michael and Bernard Trainor (1995) *The generals' war: the inside story of the conflict in the Gulf*, Boston: Back Bay Press

Goulding, Marrack (2002) *Peacemonger*, London: John Murray

Gow, James (1994) 'Nervous bunnies: the international community and the Yugoslav war of dissolution: the politics of military intervention in a time of change', in Lawrence Freedman (ed.) *Military intervention in European Conflicts*, Oxford: Blackwell for the Political Quarterly

Gow, James (1997) *Triumph of the lack of will: international diplomacy and the Yugoslav crisis*, New York: Columbia University Press

Gow, James (2003) *The Serbian project and its adversaries: a strategy of war crimes*, London: C. Hurst & Co.

Gow, James (2007) 'Europe and the Muslim world: European Union enlargement and the western Balkans', *Southeast European and Black Sea Studies*, vol. 7, no. 3, September

Haass, Richard (2008) 'The age of nonpolarity', *Foreign Affairs*, May–June

Hampson, Fen Osler, Chester A. Crocker and Pamela Aall (2005) 'If the world's getting more peaceful, why are we still in danger', *Globe and Mail*, 20 October

Hamzeh, Ahmad Nizar (2004) *In the path of Hizbullah*, New York: Syracuse University Press

Harbom, Lotta, Stina Hogbladh and Peter Wallensteen (2006) 'Armed conflict and peace agreements', *Journal of Peace Research*, vol. 43, September, pp. 617–31

Harik, Judith Palmer (2004) *Hezbollah: the changing face of terrorism*, London: I.B.Tauris

Harris, William (1997) *Faces of Lebanon, sects, wars, and global extensions*, Princeton: Markus Wiener Publishers

Hassan, Ahmed Nur Sheikh Ali (1994) 'Build a new Somalia', *New African*, June

Hathaway, Robert M. (1981) *Ambiguous partnership: Britain and America, 1944–47*, New York: Columbia University Press

Helander, Bernhard, Mohamed Haji Mukhtar and Ioan M. Lewis (1995) *Building peace from below? A critical review of the district councils in the Bay and Bakool regions of southern Somalia*, in http://Arlaadinet.com, April

High-Level Panel on Threats, Challenges and Change (2004) *A more secure world: our shared responsibility*, UN Doc.A/59/565. Available at http://www.un.org/secureworld/report.pdf

Hill, C. (1993) 'The capability–expectations gap, or conceptualising Europe's international role', *Journal of Common Market Studies*, vol. 31, no. 3, pp. 305–28.

Hill, C. (2001) 'The EU's capacity for conflict prevention', *European Foreign Affairs Review*, vol. 6, no. 3, pp. 315–33

Hollis, Rosemary (2005) 'Europe in the Middle East', in Luise Fawcett, *International relations of the Middle East*, Oxford: Oxford University Press, pp. 307–27

Hobsbawm, Eric and Terence Ranger (eds) *The invention of tradition*, Cambridge: Cambridge University Press, 1992

Howeidy, Amira (2008) *Al-Ahram Weekly Online*, 'Doha steps in', Iss. 899, 29 May–4 June, http://weekly.ahram.org.eg/2008/899/re6.htm (accessed 9 May 2009)

Human Security Brief (2006) Vancouver: University of British Columbia

ICG (International Crisis Group) (2005) 'Iran in Iraq: how much influence?' *Middle East Report*, no. 38, 21 March

ICISS (International Commission on Intervention and State Sovereignty) (2001) *The responsibility to protect* at http://www.iciss.ca/report-en.asp

Indyk, Martin (2007) 'The honeymoon's over for Bush and the Saudis', *Washington Post*, 29 April, p. BO5

Jaber, Hala (1997) *Hezbollah: born with a vengeance*, New York: Columbia University Press

Jachtenfuchs, Markus (2001) 'The governance approach to European integration', *Journal of Common Market Studies*, vol. 39, no. 2, pp. 245–64

Joffe, Josef (2005) 'A world without Israel', *Foreign Policy*, January/February, pp. 36–42

Johnson, Robert David (2005) *Congress and the cold war*, Cambridge: Cambridge University Press

Jünemann, Annette (2007) 'Realpolitisches Nutzenkalkül oder konstruktivistischer Rollenkonflikt?' in Annette Jünemann and Michèle Knodt (eds) *Die externe Demokratieförderung durch die Europäische Union*, Baden-Baden: Nomos, pp. 295–315

Kagan, Robert (2006) *Dangerous nation*, New York: Knopf

Kagan, Robert (2007) 'The return of history', *Los Angeles Times*, 5 August

Kalyvas, Stathis N. (2006) *The logic of violence in civil war*, Cambridge: Cambridge University Press

Kelly, John (2008) 'Lebanon', *RAND Occasional Paper Series*, http://rand.org/pubs/conf_proceedings/CF129/CF-129.chapter6.html, accessed 10 May

Kennedy, Paul (1987) *The rise and fall of great powers: economic change and military conflict from 1500 to 2000*, New York: Random House

Kennedy, Paul (2007) *The parliament of man: the past, present, and future of the United Nations*, New York: Vintage Books

Kertcher, Chen (2003) *The search for peace – or for a state: UN intervention in Somalia 1992–95*, Jerusalem: Harry S. Truman Research Institute for the Advancement of Peace

Khalilzad, Zalmay (2008) 'Afghanistan's new deal', *New York Times*, 20 March

Khanna, Parag (2008) *The second world: empires and influence in the new global order*, New York: Random House

Kintis, A. G. (1997) 'The EU's foreign policy and the war in former Yugoslavia', in M. Holland, *Common foreign and security policy*, London: Pinter

Kirkpatrick, Jeane (1979) 'Dictatorships and double standards', *Commentary*, November

Kirkpatrick, Jeane (2002) 'The shackles of consensus', *Foreign Policy*, no. 132, September/October

Kostiner, Joseph (2005) 'Coping with regional challenges: a case study of Crown Prince Abdullah's peace initiative', in Paul Aarts and Gerd

Nonneman (eds) *Saudi Arabia in the balance: political economy, society, foreign affairs*, London: Hurst & Company, pp. 352–71

Kostiner, Joseph (2009) 'Regulating Arab politics (part 1): the war of the summits', *Tel Aviv Notes*, The Moshe Dayan Center, 26 March

Kostiner, Joseph and Bruce Maddy-Weitzman (2009) 'Regulating Arab politics (part 2): the Doha Arab League summit', *Tel Aviv Notes*, The Moshe Dayan Center, 7 April, http://www.dayan.org/frameana.htm (accessed 22 April 2009)

Laham, Nicholas (2002) *Selling AWACS to Saudi Arabia: the Reagan administration and the balancing of America's competing interests in the Middle East*, Westport, CT: Praeger

Landler, Mark (2009) 'Syria talks signal new direction for the US', *New York Times*, 4 March

al-Latif, 'Umayma 'Abd (2007) 'The Sunni–Shi'i split: between myth and reality', *al-Ahram*, 1–7 March

Laurent, Patrick (2001) 'From "MEDA I" to "MEDA II": What's new?' *Euromed Special Feature*, vol. 21, 3 May

Lavenex, Sandra (2004) 'EU external governance in wider Europe', *Journal of European Public Policy*, vol. 11, no. 4, pp. 680–700

Le Billon, Philippe (2000) 'The political ecology of transition in Cambodia 1989–1999: war, peace and forest exploitation', *Development and Change*, vol. 31, pp. 785–805

Le Billon, Philippe (2002) 'Logging in muddy waters: the politics of forest exploitation in Cambodia', *Critical Asian Studies*, vol. 34, no. 4, pp. 563–83

Leonard, Mark (2008) *What does China think?* Ottawa: Public Affairs

Lewis, Ioan M. (1989) 'The Ogaden and the fragility of Somali segmentary nationalism', *African Affairs*, vol. 88, no. 353, pp. 573–9

Lieber, Robert J. (2000) 'US–Israeli relations since 1948', in Robert O. Freedman (ed.) *Israel's first fifty years*, Gainesville: University Press of Florida

Lieber, Robert J. (2005) 'Translating the Bush inaugural address', *US Foreign Policy Agenda: Electronic Journal of the US Department of State*, 24 January

Lieber, Robert J. (2007) *The American era: power and strategy for the 21st century*, Cambridge: Cambridge University Press

Lieber, Robert J. (2008) 'Der amerikanische Freund', *Internationale Politik*, Berlin, May

Lippert, Barbara (2008) 'European neighbourhood policy: many reservations – some progress – uncertain prospects', *International Policy*

Analysis, Berlin: Friedrich Ebert Stiftung (FES) June (http://library.fes. de/pdf-files/id/ipa/05426.pdf)

Livingston, Steven and Todd Euchus (1995) 'Humanitarian crises and US foreign policy: Somalia and the CNN effect reconsidered', *Political Communication*, vol. 12, no. 4, pp. 413–29

Lorenz, F. M. (1993–94) 'Law and anarchy in Somalia', *Parameters*, winter, pp. 27–41

Lorenz, F. M. (1994) 'Confronting thievery in Somalia', *Military Review*, August, pp. 46–55

Lorenz, F. M. (1994) 'Weapons confiscation policy during the first phases of Operation Restore Hope', *Small Wars and Insurgencies*, vol. 5, no. 3, pp. 409–25

Luhmann, Niklas (1969) *Legitimation durch Verfahren*, Neuwied/Berlin: Luchterhand

Luttwak, Edward (1999) 'Give War a Chance', *Foreign Affairs*, vol. 78, no. 4, July/August, pp. 36–44

Lyons, Terrence and Ahmed I. Samatar (1995) *Somalia: state collapse, multilateral intervention, and strategies for political reconstruction*, Washington: Brookings Institution

Mabry, Robert (2007) 'A six-day war: its aftermath in American public opinion', *Pew Forum on Religion and Public Life*, 30 May

McDermott, Anthony and Kjell Skjelsbaek (eds) (1991) *The Multinational Force in Beirut, 1982–1984*, Miami: Florida International University Press

McLeod, Scott (2007) 'Saudis leave Rice stranded', *Time*, 30 March

Madison, James (1788) *The Federalist Papers*, no. 10

Mandelbaum, Michael (2008) *Democracy's good name: the rise and risks of the world's most popular form of government*, New York: Public Affairs

Maren, Michael (1997) *The road to hell: the ravaging effects of foreign aid and international charity*, New York: Free Press

Marr, Andrew (1993) 'Politicians let NATO down over Bosnia', *The Independent*, 11 September

Martin, Marie Alexandrine (1994) *Cambodia: a shattered society*, translated by Mark W. McLeod, Berkeley: University of California Press

Medina Abellán, Miguel Angel (2004) 'The Mediterranean: the progressive construction of a common agenda', in Dieter Mahnke, Alicia Ambos and Christopher Reynolds (eds) *European foreign policy: from rhetoric to reality?* Brussels: College of Europe Studies, no.1, pp. 277–91

Menese, Ahmad (2008) 'Egyptian position on crisis of Rafah crossing and its aftermath', Emirates Center for Strategic Studies and Research, 13

February, http://www.ecssr.ac.ae/CDA/en/FeaturedTopics/Display Topic/0,1670,771-97-33,00.html (accessed 13 May 2009)

Menkhaus, Kenneth (1997) 'International peacebuilding and the dynamics of local and national reconciliation in Somalia', in Walter Clarke and Jeffrey Herbst (eds) *Learning from Somalia: the lessons of armed humanitarian intervention*, Boulder: Westview Press, 1997, pp. 42–63

Menkhaus, Kenneth (2004) *Somalia: state collapse and the threat of terrorism*, Oxford: Oxford University Press

Menkhaus, Kenneth (2007) 'The crisis in Somalia: tragedy in five acts', *African Affairs*, vol. 106, no. 424, July, pp. 357–90

Menon, Rajan (2007) *The end of alliances*, New York: Oxford University Press

Micklethwait, John and Adrian Wooldridge (2000) *A future perfect*, New York: Crown Books

Mitchell, George J. (1999) *Making peace*, London: W. Heinemann

Möller, Almut (2007) 'The EU has to become a mature actor in its neighbourhood: the Middle East Quartet is a litmus test, *CAP News*, Centrum für angewandte Politikforschung, 19 April, http://www.cap-lmu.de/aktuell/ positionen/2007/eu.php

Morris, N. (2004) 'Humanitarian intervention in the Balkans' in J. Welsh, *Humanitarian intervention and international relations*, Oxford: Oxford University Press

Müller-Brandeck-Bocquet, G. (2002) 'The new CFSP and ESDP decision-making system of the European Union', *European Foreign Affairs Review*, vol. 7, no. 3, pp. 257–82

al-Nabulsi, Shakir (2006) 'Hal Sayasbah Lubnan al-Jumhuriyya al-Islamiyya al-Lubnaniyya' (Will Lebanon be turned into the Lebanese Islamic Republic), *al-Sharq al-Awsat*, 17 August

Nasr, Vali (2006) *The Shia revival*, New York: W. W. Norton and Company

National Democratic Institute of International Affairs (2002) 'Afghan perspectives on democracy: a report on focus groups in the Kabul area on the eve of the emergency Loya Jirga', May http://www. accessdemocracy.org/ library/1411_af_report_052802.pdf

National Democratic Institute of International Affairs (2003) 'A society in transition: focus group discussions in Afghanistan', December, http:// www.accessdemocracy.org/library/1677_af_focus groups_120103.pdf

Natsios, Andrew (1997) 'Humanitarian relief intervention in Somalia: the economics of chaos', in Walter Clarke and Jeffrey Herbst (eds) *Learning from Somalia: the lessons of armed humanitarian intervention*, Boulder: Westview, pp. 77–95 .

Newman, Jonah (2007) 'Survey: Americans see Israel as ally', *JerusalemPost.com*, 18 November

Niebuhr, Reinhold (1932) *Moral man and immoral society*, New York: Charles Scribner's Sons

Niebuhr, Reinhold (1944) *The children of light and the children of darkness*, New York: Charles Scribner's Sons

Norton, Augustus Richard (2007) 'The Shi'ite threat revisited', *Current History*, December

Nussbaum, Martha C. (1996) 'Patriotism and cosmopolitanism', in Joshua Cohen (ed.) *For love of country: debating the limits of patriotism*, Boston: Beacon Press, pp. 3–17

Nye, Joseph S. Jr (2001) 'Military deglobalization: long-distance military interdependence is taking new forms', *Foreign Policy*, vol. 122, January–February, pp. 82–3

O'Kane, Eamonn (2007) *Britain, Ireland and Northern Ireland since 1960: the totality of relationships*, London: Routledge

O'Leary, Brendan (1999) 'The nature of the agreement', *Fordham International Law Journal*, vol. 22, no. 4

Oakley, Robert B. and John I. Hirsch (1995) *Somalia and Operation Restore Hope: reflections on peacemaking and peacekeeping*, Washington: United States Institute of Peace Press

Ogata, Sadako (2002) 'Guilty parties', *Foreign Policy*, no. 132, September/October, p. 40

Okun, Herbert (1993) UN special adviser and deputy-head of civilian affairs, UNPROFOR, Interview, 'Diplomacy and Deceit', Channel 4 TV, 2 August, Media Transcription Service, *Bloody Bosnia*, MTS/M2578.WPS

Pardo, Sharon and Lion Zemer (2005) *The institutional challenge of the Euro Mediterranean neighbourhood space*, CSEPS, Ben Gurion University, Beer Sheva (hsf.bgu.ac.il/europe)

Paris, Roland (2004) *At war's end: building peace after civil conflict*, Cambridge: Cambridge University Press

Patman, Robert G. (1997) 'Disarming Somalia: the contrasting fortunes of United States and Australian peacekeepers during United Nations intervention, 1992–1993', *African Affairs*, vol. 96, no. 385, October, pp. 519–26

Paul, T. V. (2005) 'Soft balancing in the age of US primacy', *International Security*, vol. 30, no. 1, Summer, pp. 46–71

Pentland, P. C. (2003) 'The EU and southeastern Europe after Dayton', *Europe–Russia working chapters*, Ottowa: Carleton University, January

Pérez de Cuéllar, Javier (1998) *Pilgrimage for peace: a secretary general's memoir*, New York: St Martin's Press

Phillips, James A. (1981) 'The AWACS sale: prospects for US policy', *Heritage Foundation Backgrounder*, no. 153, 16 October

Piana, C. (2002) 'The EU's decision-making process in the common foreign and security policy: the case of the former Yugoslav Republic of Macedonia', *European Foreign Affairs Review*, vol. 7, no. 2, pp. 209–26

Pogany, Istvan (1987) *The Arab League and peace keeping in the Lebanon*, New York: St Martin's Press

Powell, Colin L. and Joseph E. Persico (1996) *My American journey*, New York: Random House

Power, Samantha (2002) *A problem from hell: America and the age of genocide*, New York: Basic Books

Prendergast, John (1994) *The bones of our children are not yet buried: the looming spectre of famine and massive human rights abuse in Somalia*, Washington: Center of Concern

Presidency Conclusions, European Council Meeting in Laeken, 14 and 15 December 2001. SN 300/1/101 REV 1

Rabi, Uzi (2009) 'Qatar's relations with Israel: challenging Arab and Gulf norms', *The Middle East Journal*, vol. 63, no. 3

Rabil, Robert G. (1993) *Embattled neighbors: Syria, Israel and Lebanon*, Boulder, CO: Lynne Rienner Publishers

Ran, Reuven Avi (1986) *Syrian involvement in Lebanon (1975–1985)*, Tel Aviv: Ma'arachot, in Hebrew

Ratner, Steven R. (1995) *The new UN peacekeeping: building peace in lands of conflict after the cold war*, New York: St Martin's Press

Reagan, Ronald (1982) 'Report dated September 29, 1982 from President Ronald Reagan to Hon. Thomas P. O'Neill, Jr., Speaker of the House of Representatives, consistent with section 4(a)(2) of the War Powers Resolution, relative to the use of US Forces in Lebanon', *The War Powers Resolution: Relevant Documents, Reports, Correspondence*, 103rd Congress, 2nd session

Regan, Patrick and Aysegul Aydin (2006) 'Diplomacy and other forms of intervention in civil wars', *Journal of Conflict Resolution*, vol. 50, no. 5, October, pp. 736–56

Rikhye, Indar Jit (2000) *The politics and practice of United Nations peacekeeping: past, present and future*, Clementsport, NS: Canadian Peacekeeping Press

Riley (ed.) John F. (1995) *American public opinion and US foreign policy*, Chicago: Council on Foreign Relations

Risse, Thomas, Stephen Ropp and Kathryn Sikkink (eds) (1999) *The power of human rights: international norms and domestic change*, Cambridge: Cambridge University Press

Roberts, Adam (1996) *Humanitarian action in war: aid, protection and impartiality in a policy vacuum*, Oxford: Oxford University Press, Adelphi Paper No. 305 of International Institute for Strategic Studies, London, p. 16

Ross, Michael (2008) 'Blood barrels', *Foreign Affairs*, vol. 87, no. 3, May/June, pp. 2–8

Rubner, Michael (1985–86) 'The Reagan administration, the 1973 War Powers Resolution, and the invasion of Grenada', *Political Science Quarterly*, vol. 100, pp. 627–47

Saad-Ghorayeb, Amal (2002) *Hizbu'llah: politics and religion*, London: Pluto Press

St Andrews Agreement (2006) accessed at http://www.nio.gov.uk/st_andrews_agreement.pdf

Schäfer, Isabel (2005) 'Die Euro-Mediterrane Partnerschaft und der Nahostkonflikt', *Aus Politik und Zeitgeschichte*, vol. 45, pp. 22–30

Scharpf, Fritz W. (1999) *Governing in Europe: effective and democratic?* Oxford: Oxford University Press

Schattle, Hans (2007) *Practices of global citizenship*, Lanham, MD: Rowman & Littlefield Publishers

Schear, James A. 'Riding the tiger: the United Nations and Cambodia's struggle for peace', in William J. Durch (ed.) *UN peacekeeping, American politics, and the uncivil wars of the 1990s*, New York: St Martin's Press, 1996, pp. 135–91

Schimmelfennig, Frank and Ulrich Sedelmeier (2004) 'Governance by conditionality: EU rule transfer to the candidate countries of central and eastern Europe', *Journal of European Public Policy*, vol. 11, no. 4, pp. 661–79

Schimmelfennig, Frank and Wolfgang Wagner (2004) 'Preface: external governance in the European Union', *Journal of European Public Policy*, vol. 11, no. 4, pp. 657–60

Schmid, Dorothée (2004) 'The use of conditionality in support of political, economic and social rights: unveiling the Euro-Mediterranean partnership's true hierarchy of objectives?' *Mediterranean Politics*, vol. 9, no. 3, pp. 396–421

Schmid, Dorothée (2006) 'Die Europäische Nachbarschaftspolitik und die euro-mediterrane Partnerschaft: das Ende einer regionalen Ambition?'

in Martin Koopmann and Christian Lequesne (eds) *Die Nachbarschaftspolitik der Europäischen Union auf dem Prüfstand*, Baden-Baden: Nomos, pp. 111–28

Schmidl, Erwin A. (2000) 'The evolution of peace operations from the nineteenth century', in Erwin A. Schmidl (ed.) *Peace operations between peace and war: four studies*, London: Frank Cass, pp. 4–20

Schneckener, U. (2002) *Developing and applying EU crisis management: test case Macedonia*, ECMI Working Paper no. 14, Flensburg: European Centre for Minority Issues, http://www.ecmi.de/doc/download/working_paper_14.pdf

Shultz, George (1993) *Turmoil and triumph: my years as secretary of state*, New York: Charles Scribner's Sons

Schuwirth, R. (2002) 'Hitting the Helsinki headline goal', *NATO Review*, Autumn, http://www.nato.int/docu/review/2002/issue3/english/art4.html

Schweitzer, Yoram (2007) 'Divine victory and earthly failures: was the war really a victory for Hizbollah', in Shlomo Brom and Meir Eliran (eds) *The second Lebanon war: strategic perspectives*, Tel Aviv: Institute for National Security Studies, pp. 123–34

Seale, Patrick (2008) 'An exit strategy in Afghanistan', *Gulf News*, UAE, 4 April

SHAPE (2004) 'SHAPE–EU cooperation: background information', available online at http://www.nato.int/shape/issues/shape_eu/background.htm

SHAPE (2004) 'Operation Althea', available online at http://www.nato.int/shape/issues/shape_eu/althea.htm

al-Shayji, Abdullah (2009) 'US–Iran relations worry Arabs', *Gulf News*, 10 May

Silber, L. and A. Little (1996) *The death of Yugoslavia*, London: Penguin

Smith, Anthony (1995) *Nations and nationalism in a global era*, Cambridge, UK: Polity Press

Smith, M. E. (2001) 'Diplomacy by degree: the legalisation of EU foreign policy', *Journal of Common Market Studies*, vol. 39, no. 1, pp. 79–104

Sobelman, Daniel (2003) *New rules of the game: Israel and Hizbollah after the withdrawal from Lebanon*, Tel Aviv: Jaffee Center for Strategic Studies

Solana, J. (2000) *Report on the western Balkans presented to the Lisbon European Council by the Secretary-General/High Representative together with the Commission*, Brussels, 21 March, SN 2032/2/00/REV2

Sorpong Peou (1999) 'Cambodia in 1998: from despair to hope?' *Asian*

Survey, vol. 39, no. 1, pp. 20–6

Stahn, Carsten (2007) 'Responsibility to protect: political rhetoric or emerging legal norm', *American Journal of International Law*, vol. 101, no. 1, January, pp. 99–120

Steele, Rachel Ray and J. Alexander Thier (2007) *Hearts and minds: Afghan opinion on the Taliban, the government and international forces*, Washington: United States Institute of Peace, 16 August

Taremi, Kamran (2005) 'Iranian foreign policy toward occupied Iraq, 2003–2005', *Middle East Policy*, vol. 12, no. 4 (winter)

Taylor, Charles (2003) 'Charlie Wilson's war', *Salon*, 21 July

Thakur, Ramesh and Albrecht Schnabel (2001) 'Cascading generations of peacekeeping: across the Mogadishu line to Kosovo and Timor', in Ramesh Thakur and Albrecht Schnabel (eds) *United Nations peacekeeping operations: ad hoc missions, permanent engagement*, New York: United Nations University Press, pp. 3–25

Tomey, Kathryn (2007) 'Peaceline plan for integrated primary', *Belfast Telegraph*, 23 May

Touval, Saadia (1982) *The peace brokers: mediators in the Arab–Israeli conflict, 1948–1979*, Princeton: Princeton University Press

Tripodi, Paolo (1999) *The colonial legacy in Somalia: Rome and Mogadishu: from colonial administration to Operation Restore Hope*, London: Macmillan Press

Tughan, Walid (2006) 'Mustaqbal al-Arab bayna al-Sunna wal-Shi'a' ('The future of the Arabs between Sunnis and Shi'is'), *al-Masri al-Yawm*, 2 September

United Nations (1995) *The United Nations and Cambodia*, New York: UNDI

United Nations (1996) *The United Nations and Somalia, 1992–96*, New York: United Nations Department of Public Information

United Nations (1996) *The Blue Helmets: a review of United Nations peace-keeping*, New York: United Nations Department of Public Information, 3rd edn

United Nations (2005) *In larger freedom: towards development, security, and human rights for all: report of the secretary-general*, UN Doc A/59/2005, available at http://www.un.org/largerfreedom/contents.htm

United Nations (2008) *UN peacekeeping operations: background note*, 31 January, available at: http://www.un.org/Depts/dpko/dpko/bnote. htm

US House of Representatives, Committee on Foreign Affairs, 'Letter of September 27, 1983 to Hon. Clement J. Zablocki, Chairman, Committee on Foreign Affairs, from President Ronald Reagan,' *The War Powers Resolution: Relevant Documents, Reports, Correspondence*, 103rd Congress, 2nd session

van Creveld, Martin (1991) *The transformation of war*, New York: Free Press

Varwick, Johannes and Jana Windwehr (2007) 'Norwegen und Schweiz als Modellfälle für differenzierte Integration?' *Aus Politik und Zeitgeschichte*, vol. 43, pp. 15–20

Volpi, Frédéric (2004) 'Regional community building and the transformation of international relations: the case of the Euro-Mediterranean partnership', *Mediterranean Politics*, vol. 9, no. 2, p. 145–64

Walter, Barbara (2002) *Committing to peace: the successful settlement of civil wars*, Princeton: Princeton University Press

Weber, Stephen, Steven Kull, Clay Ramsay, Evan Lewis and Mary Speck (2006) 'Afghan public opinion amidst rising violence', a World Public Opinion Organization Poll, 14 December. D3 Systems and Afghan Center for Social and Opinion Research in Kabul http://www.worldpublicopinion.org/ pipa/pdf/dec06/Afghanistan_Dec06_rpt.pdf

Weiss, Thomas A. and David A. Korn (2006) *Internal displacement: conceptualization and its consequences*, London: Routledge

Weller, Marc and Stefan Wolff (eds) (2008) *Institutions for the management of ethnopolitical conflicts in central and eastern Europe*, Strasbourg: Council of Europe Publishing

Werner, Manfred (1994) 'NATO's role in a changing Europe', *IISS Adelphi Paper*, no. 284, London: Brassey's for the IISS

Wilford, Rick (2008) 'Northern Ireland: St Andrews – the Long Good Friday Agreement', in Jonathan Bradbury (ed.) *Devolution, regionalism and regional development: the UK experience*, Routledge: London

Whitworth, Sandra (2004) *Men, militarism, and UN peacekeeping: a gendered analysis*, Boulder: Lynne Rienner

Wohlforth, William C. (2002) 'US strategy in a unipolar world', in John Ikenberry (ed.) *America unrivalled: the future of the balance of power*, Ithaca: Cornell University Press, pp. 103–4

Woods, James L. (1997) 'US government decision-making process during humanitarian operations in Somalia', in Walter Clarke and Jeffrey Herbst (eds) *Learning from Somalia: the lessons of armed humanitarian intervention*, Boulder: Westview, pp. 151–6

Yeranian, Edward (2009) 'Egypt hosts Gaza ceasefire meeting', 18 January, http://www.globalsecurity.org/military/library/news/2009/01/mil-090118-voa05.htm (accessed 19 April 2009)

Zakaria, Fareed (2008) *The post-American world*, New York: W. W. Norton

& Company

Zartman, William I. (1995) 'Introduction', in William I. Zartman, *Collapsed states: the disintegration and restoration of legitimate authority*, Boulder: Lynne Rienner Publishers, pp. 1–11

Zelikow, Philip and Condoleeza Rice, *Germany unified and Europe transformed: a study in statecraft*, Cambridge: Harvard University Press, 1997

Zielonka, Jan (2006) *Europe as empire: the nature of the enlarged European Union*, Oxford: Oxford University Press

Zisser, Eyal (1997) 'Hizballah at a crossroads', in Bruce Maddy-Weitzman and Efraim Inbar (eds) *Religious radicalism in the greater Middle East*, London: Frank Cass, pp. 90–110

Zisser, Eyal (2006) 'Hizballah and Israel: strategic threat on the northern border', *Israel Affairs*, vol. 12, no. 1, January, pp. 86–106

Zisser, Eyal (2006) 'Lebanon: the Cedar Revolution – between continuity and Change', *Orient*, vol. 47, no. 4, pp. 460–84

Zisser, Eyal (2007) 'The battle for Lebanon: Lebanon and Syria in the wake of the war', in Shlomo Brom and Meir Eliran (eds) *The second Lebanon war: strategic perspectives*, pp. 135–50

Zisser, Eyal (2009) *Lebanon: blood in the Cedar, from the civil war to the second Lebanon war*, Tel Aviv: Hakibbutz Hameuchad (published in Hebrew)

Notes on Contributors

Jean-Pierre Filiu is Professor at the Paris Institute of Political Studies (Sciences Po). His *Apocalypse in Islam* (University of California Press, 2010) was awarded the main prize at the French History Convention.

Brandon Friedman is a doctoral student in the Department of Middle Eastern and African History and junior research fellow at the Center for Iranian Studies, Tel Aviv University.

James Gow holds the chair of the International Peace and Security Programme at King's College London. He is the author of *The Serbian Project and Its Adversaries: A Strategy of War Crimes* (McGill-Queen's University Press, 2003).

Janice Gross Stein is Belzberg Professor of Conflict Management and Director of the Munk Centre for International Studies at the University of Toronto. Among her recent publications is *The Unexpected War: Canada in Kandahar* (Penguin, 2008).

Adrian Guelke is Professor of Comparative Politics in the School of Politics, International Studies and Philosophy at Queen's University, Belfast. He is the author of *The New Age of Terrorism* (I.B.Tauris, 2009).

Robert David Johnson is Professor of History at Brooklyn College and the CUNY Graduate Center. His most recent book is *All the Way with LBJ: The 1964 Presidential Election* (Cambridge University Press, 2009).

Chen Kertcher is a doctoral student in the School of History, Tel Aviv University, and a junior research fellow at the S. Daniel Abraham Center for International and Regional Studies. He is the author of *The Search for Peace – Or for a State: UN Intervention in Somalia 1992–95* (Truman Center, 2003).

Joseph Kostiner is Professor in the Department of Middle Eastern and African History at Tel Aviv University. He is the author of *From Chieftaincy to Monarchical State: The Making of Saudi Arabia 1916–1936* (Oxford University Press, 1993).

Robert J. Lieber is Professor of Government and International Affairs at Georgetown University. His most recent book is, *The American Era: Power and Strategy for the 21st Century* (Cambridge University Press, 2007).

Rajan Menon is Monroe J. Rathbone Professor and Chairman of the Department of International Relations at Lehigh University, Bethlehem, Pennsylvania. He will join the City College of New York as the Spitzer Professor of Political Science in 2010. Most recently he authored *The End of Alliances* (Oxford University Press, 2007).

Chelsi Mueller is a doctoral student in the Department of Middle Eastern and African History and junior research fellow at the Center for Iranian Studies, Tel Aviv University.

Annemarie Peen Rodt is a post-doctoral researcher at the Centre for Ethno-Political Studies at the University of Exeter. She completed her doctoral degree at the Centre for International Crisis Management and Conflict Resolution at the University of Nottingham.

Georg Simonis is Professor in the Faculty of Cultural and Social Sciences at the Institute of Political Science, FernUniversität in Hagen, Germany. His edited volume, *External Governance of the EU* (VS Verlag) is forth-coming.

Marvin G. Weinbaum is Professor Emeritus at the University of Illinois, a former US State Department intelligence and research analyst, and currently scholar-in-residence at the Middle East Institute in Washington. Recently he edited the volume *South Asia Approaches the Millennium: Reexamining National Security with Chetan Kumar* (Westview Press, 1995).

Stefan Wolff is Professor of Political Science and Director of the Centre for International Crisis Management and Conflict Resolution at the University of Nottingham. He has widely published on ethnic conflict and its management, including *Ethnic Conflict: A Global Perspective* (Oxford University Press 2006).

Eyal Zisser is Professor in the Department of Middle Eastern and African History and Director of the Moshe Dayan Center for Middle Eastern and African Studies at Tel Aviv University. He is the author of *Commanding Syria: Bashar al-Asad and the First Years in Power* (I.B.Tauris, 2005).

Index